F. M. (Francis Marion) McAdams

Every-Day Soldier Life

Or a History of the One Hundred and Thirteenth Ohio Volunteer Infantry

F. M. (Francis Marion) McAdams

Every-Day Soldier Life
Or a History of the One Hundred and Thirteenth Ohio Volunteer Infantry

ISBN/EAN: 9783337133610

Printed in Europe, USA, Canada, Australia, Japan

Cover: Foto ©ninafisch / pixelio.de

More available books at **www.hansebooks.com**

OR

A HISTORY

OF THE

One Hundred and Thirteenth Ohio Volunteer Infantry.

BY

F. M. McADAMS, RICHWOOD, OHIO,

SERGEANT OF CO. E.

COLUMBUS, O.
CHAS. M. COTT & CO., BOOK PRINTERS.
1884.

NOTE.

At the Eighth Annual Reunion of the 113th O. V. I. held at Columbus, O., August 11th, 1881, the plan of a regimental history was discussed. It was determined to have a history written and published, and the author was assigned to that duty. The labor has been one of no small magnitude, and I now present it to my comrades and the public with the hope that when its defects and merits are duly estimated, there will be a balance in my favor.

THANKS.

The data from which this work is compiled consists mainly of the author's record of every-day affairs taken on the spot. But to my messmate, ISAAC GREEN, Company E; P. H. WHITEHEAD, Company B; LOYAL H CLOUSE, Company F, and Captain GEORGE McCREA, for notes and records of value, I desire to make public acknowledgment.

JOHN P. SLEMMONS, Clerk in the office of the Adjutant General of Ohio, deserves our thanks for many courtesies extended to Miss MAMIE A. WHITE, who so ably performed her duties in copying the original Muster-Out Rolls and other papers.

F. M. McADAMS.

RICHWOOD, OHIO, 1884.

PREFACE.

There are yet living hundreds of brave men who served in the One Hundred and Thirteenth Ohio Volunteer Infantry, who share with the writer a desire to have their names and deeds preserved in history. This humble effort has been undertaken more as a labor of love than of pecuniary profit, and if these pages shall rescue from the oblivion that usually attends the rank and file of armies, their names and their heroism, and be the means of perpetuating to future generations that proud place in the annals of the army to which my comrades are entitled, I shall feel amply rewarded for my labors.

This is not a history of the war; not a review of campaigns and sieges, but a record of duties, deeds and trials of the man who bore the musket and made victory for the country and fame for his commander. And, if it is found to be a work in which the common soldier is the hero, the apology offered is merely an explanation that the material on hand was of that kind which dealt principally with the enlisted men.

I have found it a source of constantly increasing regret, that in the beginning of my career as a soldier, I did not foresee the demand for these pages, and that I would be chosen to compile the same for publication. In that case I might have made greater and more diligent efforts to collect and preserve facts and make a record of incidents which are now forever lost. It need not seem strange to my comrade readers, if in this record of three long years of service in camp and field, there should occur many omissions of important and interesting events. It would have required more than human skill to have kept a faithful, faultless account of all incidents, accidents and adventures occurring in all parts of a command in which more than a thousand men were the actors. My aim has been to present such general incidents of every-day soldier life as have escaped the pen of the more competent historian, and such as will prove of most interest to men with whom I shared the life of a common soldier, leaving to others the weightier matters of the great civil war.

From Camp Chase, 1862, to Tod Barracks, 1865, by way of the mountains, the rivers and the sea, there lies a multitude of daring deeds by daring men worthy of a place in history.

It is hoped that this record will be a source of gratification to many a parent, sister, brother or child of those of our number who went forth with us but who returned not to tell the story of their services; while to those of us who shared in it and still live, it will serve to keep in memory the duties, names and services of ourselves and our comrades till we shall be commanded to "fall in" to cross the great pontoon which spans the dark river, separating us from the land of rest and eternal peace; and at the last grand roll call may we all answer—"here." F. M. M.

EVERY-DAY SOLDIER LIFE,

OR

A HISTORY OF THE ONE HUNDRED AND THIRTEENTH OHIO VOLUNTEER INFANTRY.

AUGUST, 1862.

15. Enlisted at Urbana, Ohio, for three years, or during the war. Joseph Swisher and Harrison Walburn enlisted at the same time. We returned to our homes, and began to put our affairs in condition to be off for Camp Chase in a few days.

28. Boarded a train at Urbana, bound for Columbus. On the train I met for the first time those who are to share with me the uncertain life that lies before us. They are from the farms and workshops of the western part of Champaign county. A few are men of mature age, many are youthful, and all seem in good spirits and anxious for adventure. I can see on the cheeks of more than one of them the effects of their first battle, that of tearing themselves from home and its endearments to choose the life of a soldier.

In two hours our train lands us at Columbus. Disembarking, we made a half successful effort to form in two ranks. It was not done gracefully. Some of the men, recognizing no authority in those who were attempting to form us into column, took up a line of march of their own; the more tractable ones under command of John F. Riker, then moved up High street to the Capitol grounds, where we rested for a time. At 5 P. M. we started for Camp Chase, a distance of four miles, which place we reached without incident.

Several companies of recruits intended for the regiment are already here; on inquiry I learn that they came from Madison, Licking and Franklin counties.

Our arrival at dark made it difficult to procure comfortable quarters. Without tents, and with only a blanket and heaven's canopy for a covering, and a split stick of wood for a pillow, I spent one weary hour after another in an unsuccessful effort to sleep. Would have had better success had it not been for a number of our men who devoted the greater part of the night to noisy revelry.

From " Reminiscences of the Camp and Field," written by me several years later, I quote:

" Night was spreading her dark mantle over earth when we reached camp, weary, hungry, dusty, thirsty, footsore and not a little out of tune besides. The experiences of the first day and night in the service I recall with peculiar feelings. We had changed the life of a civilian for that of a soldier; had given up the domestic endearments of home life, and had already marked a day in a new era. * * * A proper regard for the truth compels me to say that this was not a shady, secluded grove, with fountains of living waters and falling cataracts; on the contrary, it is a farm of several hundred acres, flat, unshaded and nearly destitute of grass. Here and there are numerous buildings in which are the several offices of the camp, besides others which are used as store houses for clothing, commissary supplies, ordnance, &c."

29. Morning came, and we spend the day looking about, strolling over the camp, killing time and making acquaintances in our own and other companies. When night came, we gathered into little groups and discussed the various events of the day. With new blankets and better accommodations we spent the night comfortably.

The Ohio State Journal speaks of the arrival of our company as follows:

"Captain Riker, of Champaign county, arrived here last evening with ninety men. This is the oldest looking company we have seen. We noticed several gray-haired men. This is all right, and there is more of deliberate valor and bravery to be expected from men of riper years. The company joins the 113th regiment."

30. We made the acquaintance of Dr. J. R. Black, who, I learn, is to be our surgeon. He is from Newark. We were critically examined by him, and all accepted but one lad, Joseph Loudenback, who takes it philosophically, and starts for home.

This evening, when all was hushed in the stillness that succeeds "taps," the voice of song accompanied by a guitar, broke the silence. The matchless sweetness of the singer's voice, the deftness with which he touched his instrument, together with the strange surroundings, made the effect irresistible, as he sang—

> "Don't stop a moment to think, John,
>   Our country calls, then go;
> Don't fear for me nor the children, John,
>   I'll care for them, you know.
> Leave the corn upon the stalk, John,
>   The fruit upon the tree,
> And all our little cares, John,
>   Yes, leave them all to me.
>
> CHORUS—"Then take your gun and go,
>   Yes, take your gun and go,
>   For Ruth can drive the oxen, John,
>   And I can use the hoe.
>
> "I've heard my grandsire tell, John,
>   He fought at Bunker Hill,
> He counted all his life and wealth
>   His country's off'ring still;
> Would I shame that brave old blood, John,
>   That flowed on Monmouth Plain?
> No; take your gun and go, John,
>   Though I ne'er see you again.
>
> "The army's short of blankets, John,
>   Then take this heavy pair—
> I spun and wove them when a girl
>   And worked them with much care;
> A rose in every corner, John,
>   And here's my name, you see;
> On the cold ground they'll warmer feel,
>   Because they're made by me.
>
> "And now, good-bye to you, John,
>   I can not say *farewell;*
> We'll hope and pray for the best, John,
>   His goodness none can tell—
> May His arm be round about you, John,
>   To guard you night and day.
> Be our beloved country's shield
>   Till war shall pass away."

One of our men, named Baldwin, sickened of his bargain and chopped off his fingers. This was an act of shameful cowardice, and if he lives to have grandchildren, they will share in his shame for this act.

The affair was made a source of amusement, for J. L. Edmiston, the wag of the company, mounted a stump and delivered a sermon from the text, Matt. v, 30, "And if thy right hand offend thee, cut it off, and cast it from thee."

SEPTEMBER, 1862.

1-5. We have been taking lessons in squad drilling, putting our quarters in better condition, and in other ways occupying the weary hours.

6. One of our tents caught fire last night and burned up. The man with soda water and ginger bread had a brisk trade with us across the guard line. Think he came out loser. Soldiers are full of tricks.

8. Have been taking a lesson in doing guard duty—two hours on and four off. There is some novelty in it, which I suppose will wear off. Loss of sleep goes hard with me. Pacing back and forth on a beat for two hours is a monotonous duty, and gives opportunity for reflection.

9. Nearly one-third of the men are absent on short furlough. Others are absent without leave; but they return after a time, and all goes well. Green and I go beyond the lines and spend part of the day in the shady wood. In the evening we have our first battalion drill. It was not much of a success, but we can do better next time. A few of our men have seen service in the three month's regiments, and have had valuable experience.

11. Harry Walburn and I missed roll call this morning, and were threatened with punishment. The 95th is camped to the west of us. They have been to the front, received their initiation, and are now full of experience. A heavy rain fell, accompanied by wind, prostrating many of our tents. A newsman came into camp to-day and sold some papers dated several days ago. His next visit will be one of interest. He will do his family a service by taking a policy on his life.

12. A squad of good-looking prisoners are brought in and placed in the prison east of our camp, giving us our first sight of rebels.

14. This is the Sabbath. Sergeant McCrea took a number of us to the Scioto river, and as cleanliness is akin to godliness, we did the next best thing to worshiping by washing. Captain H. Z. Adams preached in camp this evening. I make the acquaintance of Avery and Rose, of Company D. The Licking county men are men of intelligence. Drill exercises occupy most of our time. We expect our clothing soon. Many of the boys are writing to their friends.

17. We are having a drill before breakfast, and are looking for one at midnight, soon. When we get better acquainted with our duties we shall probably perform them more cheerfully.

18. Our clothing was issued to us to-day: One pair pants, one pair bootees, two pair drawers, two pair socks, one blouse, two shirts. Clothing and feeding a great army must be a heavy expense to our government.

21. This is the Sabbath. Boys of Company D, accompanied by some ladies of Licking county, make us a call, and spend an hour pleasantly. A lady in camp is like a shade in the desert. If we had more *shade* of this kind it would seem more pleasant.

22. The washerwoman presents her bill of five cents. These extravagances must be stopped—I must do my own housework.

23. Drew one hundred and twenty-two pounds of bread this morning for our company. Overcoats were issued to us. With these cool nights an overcoat will not be a bad thing to sleep with.

25. Captain David Taylor's company receive a number of visitors to-day. A good dinner, a flag presentation, speeches and music, and some lady visitors, all in that company, make us a little envious. When will our good time come? Dress parade in the evening; these new clothes *do* look well.

28. Sunday has come again. A few of us take to the woods. Some write to friends. Others manage to go to the city, and on their return are noisy and quarrelsome.

29. We received to-day our arms—the Enfield rifle. They are rusty and in bad order. Would like to trade mine for a milk cow or a hand organ. Swisher returned from home, bringing some delicacies for our palates. Nothing tastes better than the good things which *mother* sends us.

Cartridge boxes and waist belts were issued to us to-day. We begin to look like soldiers. I can shoulder arms as well as a full grown man.

OCTOBER, 1862.

1. We have grown weary of the monotonous duties of camp and are anxious for adventure. We would be better pleased if we were in Dixie.

5. I have been ill for a day or two. The nights are cool. Many visitors come into camp, bringing some delicacy for friends. These are always shared by all in the mess until they are gone. A friend with feed is a friend indeed, according to a new version.

7. This has been a day for clearing up and putting things to rights. Brooms, shovels and other implements are in demand.

15. The dull duties of camp continue from day to day, but we are becoming more soldierly every day. Our desire to leave Camp Chase grows stronger every day. Men who have gone home on a self-made furlough have returned and are faring sumptuously in the guard house. The following is our regimental organization:

Colonel, James A. Wilcox; Lieutenant Colonel, John G. Mitchell; Major, Darius B. Warner; Adjutant, Chas. C. Cox.

25. Our stay at Camp Chase ends to-day, and we are marching to Columbus. At 4 P. M. we board a train of cars and are soon running toward Zanesville, where we arrive late in the night. We remain in the cars till morning, and at daylight march to our new camp some distance from the city. It had been snowing through the night, and snow lay on the ground the depth of three inches. We had prepared a day's rations before striking tents yesterday morning, but that was gone hours before we left the train. Arriving in camp without breakfast is a serious joke. Some swine, which had strayed into camp, fell victims to the hungry appetites of the boys. Don't know who is to pay for the hogs, but the butchers went to the guard house with heroic stoicism.

Camp Zanesville is on Licking Creek and we are camped two hundred yards from the bank. The situation is a pleasant one; the scenery is delightful; the grand old hills lift their summits skyward and the silvery Licking winds through the valley like a thread of silver. Think I will like it here; hope the pie-women will sell better pies than those we have been eating at our former camp.

A much better feeling exists among the enlisted men than formerly; the transition from citizen to soldier progresses satisfactorily, and the men who chafed and rebelled at the rigorous duties and careful discipline of a month ago, submit to the same now with a cheerfulness which augurs future good. Colonel Wilcox has been untiring in his efforts to fit us for service, and in some cases his motives have been misunderstood and much ill feeling, bordering on insubordination, has, at times, shown itself. Now that it is apparent that the commanding officer has been doing all that could be done to prepare us to enter the field, clothed, equipped, and properly disciplined, those who busied themselves in keeping alive a feeling of disobedience, have grown less and less sour, and cheerful obedience on the part of the greater numbers gives much encouragement. Our quarters here are wooden buildings, large, comfortable and well ventilated. The water is plentiful and of good quality.

NOVEMBER, 1862.

1. We are much pleased with our new camp, and have made many agreeable acquaintances in city and country. Nearly every day small squads of men are passed out for a trip into the country, and on their return they give favorable accounts of the manner in which they have been treated by the citizens. To-day I made a trip of a few miles out among the hills, accompanied by Captain Bowersock. We found plenty of chestnuts, and at the house of a Mr. Burlingame we had a good dinner. We shall not soon forget the kindness of the people in the vicinity of camp.

3. A party who went to the city last night on a trip for pleasure failed to respond to the roll-call this morning, and it is believed they fell into the hands of the patrol force and are now in the city jail. A strong guard is stationed in the city day and night, with orders to arrest and imprison all enlisted men found on the street after nine o'clock in the evening. The order is vigorously enforced.

4. Five men were placed in the dungeon to-day for refusing to muster; they say they will rot there before they will muster.

5. The men who went to prison to rot yesterday were mustered to-day and say they feel better. The guard house is an uncomfortable place to stay.

6. I spent to-day as provost guard in the city, making our headquarters at the city jail. At night after my first two hours' duty I retired to one of the cells in the jail and lay down to rest. Some one, coming into the jail soon after, shut the cell door and made me a prisoner for the remainder of the night. I am not used to being jailed.

7. I was liberated at eight o'clock, and our party, being relieved by another, returned to camp.

9. Sunday. The Sabbath brings its duties as do other days. General inspection took place in the morning, and our arms and accoutrements had to be put in order. Captain Riker took command of a squad of men and marched to the country for recreation. Some of us got a good supper with a countryman, north of camp.

10. At ten o'clock this morning a fire broke out in one of the wooden buildings occupied as quarters. The regiment was drilling at the west end of camp, and before we could reach the scene of the fire it was beyond control. The main part of camp was destroyed, including guns, accoutrements, and the personal effects of many of the men. The cause of the fire cannot be ascertained, but the drafted men, who occupy a part of the camp, are charged with it.

15. We have been rebuilding our quarters and are again pretty well re-established. The losses sustained by the enlisted men of several of the companies prove to be great. Many a pack of cards, several violins and some other outfits of amusement will have to be replaced. At squad drill this afternoon Lieutenant Colonel Mitchell, in giving me some instructions in warding off a blow aimed at the head, told me to *strike* at him. I obeyed literally, bringing my Enfield down with force, while he placed his rifle in position to arrest the blow. Instead of the gun barrel, his finger received the blow, and he retired to quarters for repairs. I regretted this very much, as I ought to have *motioned* instead of *striking*. Mrs. Mitchell, being in camp, gave the damaged finger of her husband proper attention. A woman is a handy piece of furniture, even in camp.

17. The weather is cool and bracing. We have completed our new quarters, and, as the tools we have been using will be needed when we go elsewhere, they were carefully stowed away where the most diligent search will not bring them to light. This theft is charged to Company A, but they aver that no member of that company was ever caught stealing. The tools will turn up in due time.

25. One day has succeeded another and the monotony of camp life begins to be somewhat oppressive, but we have at length become so soldierly that the restraints and discipline of this kind of a life do not vex us as formerly. Have made the acquaintance of Captain Munson; the Captain is more social than military in his make-up, and is a matchless story teller. His yarns are always pointed and witty. We came here with only seven companies; the eighth company is being recruited and will be commanded by Captain Sullivant, who is a very young man.

27. This is Thanksgiving Day. Nearly the entire command went to Zanesville. A few worshipped at the churches, others feasted with acquaintances, others filled up with liquid hilarity. The conduct of the average soldier on the march returning to camp in the evening, was decidedly untactical, but then he was patriotic and seemed to wish that the Governor would make a thanksgiving day of every Thursday. Colonel Wilcox is much pleased at our good behavior and says he feels proud of us.

DECEMBER, 1862.

1. The measles prevail in camp, and a dozen or more have been sent to the hospital with that disease. Of these one or two are having the disease in a dangerous form, but are being well cared for by the surgeon, assisted by an efficient corps of nurses. Doctors Black and Harlow are men of acknowledged medical skill.

13. Have been enjoying a ten-day furlough at home, and returning to camp this evening I find all in good shape. Those who had the measles have nearly all recovered.

14. While on duty as guard to-day I made the acquaintance of Corporal Mason, Captain Nichols and Captain Wells. These are men of intelligence and good social qualities.

15. We saw the last of Camp Zanesville this morning. We have spent fifty days here, some of them very pleasant ones. We marched to Zanesville early in the forenoon, and after some time spent in loading an immense amount of baggage, we took the cars for Camp Dennison, passing through Newark, Columbus, West Jefferson, London, South Charleston, Xenia, and Loveland, reaching our destination late in the evening. We are quartered in building No. 27.

While at Camp Zanesville Company H was recruited and added to the seven companies composing the command. Our object in coming to Camp Dennison is to add another company, (I) making nine companies in all.

The regiment remained at Camp Dennison thirteen days, during which time no important event occurred. The time was spent in perfecting the men in a knowledge of company and battalion drills and such other duties as pertain to camp life. This camp seemed to be much less attractive than either of our former ones, and when the order to leave was received there was general rejoicing. The ninth company, which was added to us during our stay at this camp, was recruited for another regiment, the 109th perhaps, but as that organization was never completed, the men were consolidated with the 113th.

Company I is composed principally of Germans, and was recruited in the vicinity of Dayton.

28. Sunday. Early this morning orders were received to move. We were placed on a train and a brief run of little over an hour found us in Cincinnati, destined for Louisville, Ky. The people of Cincinnati greeted our arrival with some demonstrations of patriotism, for, though it was Sunday, there was some shouting, throwing of hats and waving of handkerchiefs.

Disembarking from the cars we marched to the river, boarded the steamer "Superior," and were soon moving down stream. We suffered not a little discomfort by our crowded condition on the boat, and the common soldier noticed that the commissioned officers fared better than himself. The sixty staterooms of the boat were occupied principally by the officers, and I presume they paid extra for them. Night came on but quite a number of the soldiers kept awake nearly all night, compelling those who would have slept to share their wakefulness. I tried to sleep on the upper deck, but I found it like sleeping on the back of a huge turtle, and at ten o'clock I went below and tried it with somewhat better success. At 2 A. M. Captain Taylor woke me and told me of a good place in the engine room, to which I went and for the remainder of the night slept well.

29. We reached Louisville at daylight. At 8 A. M. we left the boat, and marching through the city to the western suburbs, the regiment stacked arms on a vacant lot to the right of the pike, but being without tents we suffered considerably from the piercing wind. Tents were furnished late in the day. A trio of strolling musicians, father and two daughters, visited our camp, furnished some good music, took up a fat collection and departed.

31. Lieutenant Bowersock, Sergeant McCrea, privates Gardner, Rock, Fudge and Hallan, arrive in camp from home, bringing for several of us many a token of good-will from mother, sister and *wife*.

JANUARY, 1863.

1. At ten o'clock last night the camp was alarmed by a hurried command to fall in line and stand ready to march. Much confusion ensued, but coolness at length followed, and we were standing to arms when the city clock struck the midnight hour, announcing the death of the old year and the birth of the new. We were at length sent to quarters with instructions to hold ourselves in readiness to move at short notice. I think the affair was created to train us to put on our breeches and other harness in the night. It was a success.

This is a fine day. We had general inspection at 10 A. M.

4. This camp is called "Camp Laura" in compliment to the wife of our Lieutenant Colonel. Don't know that Mrs. Mitchell will be pleased or displeased at this intended civility. Women are so curious.

An order was received this afternoon to get ready to march immediately. We obeyed, but the order was countermanded, and after the requisite amount of raw profanity was indulged in, the men returned to quarters. Soldiers "as they run" are not excessively pious. The arrival of a mail from Ohio adds to make the sunshine of the day more genial and bright.

5. This is Monday. I know this by knowing that yesterday was a busy day. We blacked our bootees, washed, scrubbed, cleaned house, and if the weather had been fine we would have gone visiting We bade farewell to "Camp Laura" at 8.15 this morning, and at 9.40 our train moved out of the city toward Nashville, a southerly direction. Our destination is "Big Run Trestle" or Muldraugh's Hill. Crossed Salt River at Shepherdsville, and halting at Colesburg the horses of the regiment were unloaded, after which the train moved on two miles further to our destination. During the unloading of the animals I found a chance to get a good meal at a house near the track, and while eating it the train moved on without me. I am fond of my feed. Coming up to the command I found the site of our future camp had been chosen, and camping preparations were going on. James L. Edmiston had cared for my effects during my absence, but he was a little disappointed that I had not brought him something to eat. The rest of the day was spent in completing our camp and in assisting Quartermaster Scarritt to unload supplies of various kinds. While a number of soldiers were thus engaged one of them lost his hold on a barrel of sugar and it rolled down a steep hill, bursting as it went. Scarritt indulged in a few expletives; the rest of us indulged in the sugar.

6. Previous to our coming here the place was held by a regiment of Illinois troops. These were captured a few days ago by John Morgan's command, who, after burning two large trestles of the railroad track, moved on and left the place unoccupied. A force of mechanics will be put to work at once repairing the road, and our business is to see that they are not molested. This road is an important link in the great chain of supplies that must sustain our armies further south.

The country hereabouts is wild, rocky, and rough to a degree that is indescribable, and suggests the idea that the Great Architect finished his work here by the consolidation of scraps and fragments. The people seem to be the poorest of the poor, rude and illiterate. We have a better idea now of the meaning of the term, "poor white trash," than ever before.

9. A part of the regiment was sent to-day to the upper trestle,

where they will camp and remain. Last evening we had dress parade,—the first since leaving Camp Dennison. We call this "Camp Lucy." It may be that Colonel Wilcox has a grudge against some Buckeye Lucy and wants to avenge himself in this way. This is in Hardin County, thirty-six miles southwest of Louisville.

10. Major Warner returned from Louisville, bringing a mail, the first we have had for several days.

11. It has been raining for several days and the gorges of these hills are on a high.

12. Captain Taylor with twenty-five men was sent out to strengthen our pickets, there being rumors of an attack by the enemy.

15. Snow began to fall last night and has continued all day and now is about thirty inches deep. As the soldiers wade about doing picket and other out-of-camp duties the snow runs into the pockets of the shortest of them. Several hogs, which took refuge in a log house in the valley, met a fate somewhat similar though more fatal than befell the man who journeyed between Jerusalem and Jericho. Swine cannot be too cautious in coming into a camp like this. This deep snow may possibly have provoked this deed of blood and tenderloins.

Last night I stood picket in a dark gloomy section of country a mile from camp. James S. Ports of Company D was one of my partners. Before night came on we cut an old dry stub of a tree, set fire to it and burned it to coals; this melted the snow and dried the ground. Spreading our bedding on the warm, dry ground, we slept comfortably, otherwise we must have suffered. Years ago while camping in northern Ohio, I had learned this of my father, who is a practical hunter. A squad was sent out some distance to-day for a load of straw. They report that they saw a—*school house*. Now, what use would a school-house be in this land, I would like to know?

18. A member of Company I froze to death last night.

20. Continued exposure in this inclement weather has resulted in much sickness, and during the past few days two deaths have occurred in Company A, namely, James S. Harvey and George T. Reno. Their homes are at London, Ohio.

22. A squad of half a dozen men visited Colesburg last night, bent on adventure. Finding the door of a freight car ajar, one of them entered to explore, while the others awaited orders on the outside. The car contained sutler's supplies, destined for Nashville and the front. A barrel of luscious apples and a monster cheese escaped from the car, and were carried by the hungry outsiders to a safe distance from the track, and in the direction of camp. Here a halt was ordered, the head of the barrel was knocked in and the cheese was cut into pieces suitable to be handled. Each of the party then took off his drawers, and by tying the ankles in a knot prepared them to receive the booty. The apples and cheese were then distributed and the party, groaning under their load, trudged toward camp. The supplies were secreted among the rocks in the vicinity of camp, and—well, there are tales that must not be told out of school.

We were first camped in the valley and near the creek, but some days ago we climbed to the summit of the ridge on the north and pitched our tents overlooking the valley. Some earth-works of a simple character constructed of dirt and gum logs have been built under the management of Colonel Wilcox, but the disposition of the men to shirk duty under various pretenses makes the working force very weak. A soldier will dare, do and suffer, but will not work. Nearly every able-bodied man in camp, including some of the officers, has been acquiring a geographical knowledge of the country by scouting by day and planning new adventures by night, but if there is a suspicion that he is to be on duty to-morrow, he answers the sick call, and by some strategy gets excused.

Now and then the missionary spirit shows itself. Corporal S., who is my messmate, and somewhat accustomed to deeds of piety at home, has an appointment to preach at a cabin in the country next Sabbath. If we move before then there will be a mutual disappointment; the natives will miss hearing a good sermon, and the Corporal will miss a good country dinner.

Captain Taylor's company (B) went out to Rolling Fork to do duty for a few days. They relieved part of the 50th O. V. I.

24. Milt. Doak and Edmiston conspired to rob a woman of her last rooster, to-day, and proceeded in this manner: Milt. entered the cabin in feigned agony over a pair of frozen ears; the heart of the old lady was touched, and her sympathy went out toward the suffering boy. Edmiston, finding her attention taken up, as he desired it should be, scouted on the premises, and finding a solitary rooster on the corner of the house, carried it off triumphantly. Doak thawed out presently and started in pursuit, followed by the irate woman, who had now seen the trick. The boys were not overtaken. The fowl made a savory mess, for I shared in eating it, on the promise that an account of the affair should never go into print. I have kept my promise.

26. Work on our defenses progresses slowly, partly because of bad weather, and partly because of too weak a force. Some of our men have spent the day rabbit hunting, but found no game. They brought in a fine lot of "Kentucky twist." Tobacco will be tobacco before the war ends.

27. Orders were received this forenoon to prepare to move, an order that all seemed willing to obey, and the work of preparation began at once. We had an immense amount of baggage of various kinds, and its preparation for shipment occupied several hours, so that dark was upon us before we left Colesburg, bound for Louisville. Our train was overloaded and made little progress, so that the entire night was consumed in the trip of thirty-six miles.

28. We disembarked at daybreak, and by noon had our tents pitched and awaiting orders. At 3 P. M. we marched to Portland, three miles below the city, where we boarded the steamer St. Patrick, occupying all her capacity and crowding us quite uncomfortably.

First Lieutenant Samuel A. Hughes resigned, as has also Captain H. Z. Adams, Company G.

30. We continue to remain anchored at the wharf. Several men deserted to-day. Hardly a company but lost some men in this way. Here we received pay to December 31st, 1862. Most of the men needed their pay badly. Lying at this wharf is a large fleet of steamers loaded with soldiers.

FEBRUARY, 1863.

1. This is Sunday. At 4:20 P. M. our boat left the wharf and proceeded down the Ohio. Being a fast boat we make good time, and before night set in we had passed a number of other boats going down, all crowded with men in blue, all going we knew not where.

2. About noon we reached Evansville, Indiana, where we remained an hour, then pursuing our downward way arrived at Smithland, the mouth of the Cumberland river. Here we took on a quantity of coal. Black hats were issued to us. A lottery was one of the incidents of the trip, and it came near resulting in some vacancies among the commissioned officers.

3. We left Smithland at 11 A. M., and steered up the Cumberland, having Nashville for our destination. The weather being agreeably fine, the men sought the sunshine, and resting on the guards of the boat, admired the scenery of the country through which we traveled.

The St. Patrick passed a number of boats on the way, and the bantering and cheering of the men from one boat to the other was very exciting.

After night set in, comrades Avery, Rose and Cressey, of Company D, and Asa Kite and myself, made the banks of the Cumberland echo with the voice of song. Those D boys run to music like ducks to water. At eight o'clock a light in the river ahead of us created a sensation. It drifted nearer and nearer to our boat, and at length floated past, proving to be a burning barge which had been loaded with hay and other army supplies, and which had been fired and set afloat to destroy our fleet of boats.

4. We find our boat anchored on the north bank at a place called Donelsonville, which is on the opposite shore. A battle occurred here yesterday, the Confederates being defeated and driven from the field, leaving their dead and wounded. A number of boats besides our own are anchored here, all loaded with troops. The names of these boats are: James Thompson, Crescent City, St. Patrick, Lady Franklin, Victress, Victor No. 2, Horizon, Wild Cat, St. Cloud, Liberty No. 2, Jacob Strader, Thomas Pattin, Allen Collier, Silver Lake, Clara Poe, Champion, James Johnston, Bostonia, Nashville, Robert R. Hamilton, Duke, Express, Leslie Combs, B. C. Levi, Diamond, Odd Fellow, Venango, John H. Groesbeck, Cottage, Charley Miller and Hornet, besides six gunboats. Squads of our men have rowed over to the battlefield to satisfy their desire to see how it looks. Fifteen of us in a yawl made the attempt to cross, but a passing steamer came near running over our little craft, and to save ourselves we drifted toward the north shore and against a loaded barge, upon which we jumped and were saved from what seemed to me a watery grave.

During the afternoon the regiment left the steamer and spent two hours on land, drilling, during which time the boat was scrubbed and cleaned up, after which we again went on board. At five o'clock this evening a brisk snow fell.

During the past day or two we made the acquaintance of Mr. Grayback. He is a lively, ticklish creature, and as a multiplier has no equal.

5. Companies E and G are on duty to-day, occupying the upper deck. The snow is several inches deep, and continues falling. Dover and Donaldsonville are on opposite sides of the river, where our fleet is at anchor. The St. Patrick is at the Dover side. Now the Odd Fellow is being lashed to us on the right side, 11:15 A. M. We

are now steaming up the Cumberland; the boats are moving two abreast, and the sight is one of the grandest the eye ever beheld. The pilots of the several boats are protected by a shield made of heavy boiler iron. The following commands are represented in this fleet: Seventy-eighth Ill. V. I., One Hundred and Twenty-fifth O. V. I., Ninety-second O. V. I., Thirty-sixth O. V. I., One Hundred and Twenty-fourth O. V. I., Eighty-ninth O. V. I., Eleventh O. V. I., Ninety-eighth O. V. I., One Hundred and Twenty-first O. V. I., Ninth Ill. Battery, Seventh O V. I., Eighty-second O. V. I., Third Ky. Battery, and the One Hundred and Thirteenth O. V. I.

Asa Kite and I found and occupied a nook behind the wheel-house of the boat when we first went aboard. We have traveled with comfort with plenty of room and fresh air. The men in other parts of the boat have suffered on account of their crowded condition.

7. We have been moving steadily up stream without accident or notable incident. We passed Clarksville in the night, besides towns and villages, the names of which I could not learn. At five o'clock this afternoon the city of Nashville appeared in view, and our journey down the Ohio and up the Cumberland is at an end.

8. By a little figuring we ascertain that this is Sunday, but we are not to go ashore until to-morrow. This is a disappointment. We have been huddled together without conveniences for cooking, eating or sleeping since the twenty-eighth of last month, and much sickness and suffering has ensued. I predict that when our term of service ends it can be said that our stay at Muldraugh's Hill and our trip on the St. Patrick resulted in more deaths than our severest battle. If I had had my own way we would have marched across the State of Kentucky from Muldrough, and it would have been a trip of pleasure compared to what our imprisonment on the St. Patrick has been. But then we would have missed getting these black hats. A member of Company F, figuring for a discharge, shot off a finger. He ought to be yoked with Baldwin of Company E.

9. Leaving the boat at nine o'clock this morning the regiment marched through the city of Nashville and camped four miles to the south, on the right hand of the pike. The location is a good one and the surrounding country presents a good appearance, but shows many signs of the ravages of hostile armies.

10. It rained during last night and rendered us very uncomfortable. R. Gardner and George Conard, of Mess 3, are sick. I found a sutler of another regiment and bought a mutton ham for a dollar, a pound of cheese for fifty cents, and a pound of butter for forty

cents. Corporal Gillispie, of Company D, died at Nashville to-day. The 78th Ill. V. I. camped east of us.

11. This is washday with us. It has not been washday till now since we left Portland. Washday is a melancholy day for—graybacks; they are apt to get soap in their eyes.

12. Struck tents at sunrise and moved in a southerly direction, reaching Franklin, distance fourteen miles, late in the afternoon. Passed fine houses and well-improved farms on the way. Many of our men fell out of the march in the first five miles. Many articles of clothing and other heavy baggage were abandoned by the weary ones who lacked the muscle to carry all they had packed. Being in fine bodily health I stood the march well, and was with a few of my company who halted and stacked arms at the end of the march. Our forces vacated this post early this morning. A scouting party of rebel cavalry had dashed in during the day but fled at our approach. General Gilbert, who has command of our forces, directed a few shots after them upon our arrival, and I presume he scared them some. Our force consists of the 113th, 121st, 98th, 125th Ohio, and the 78th Illinois regiments of infantry, besides a battery. Franklin is on the railroad leading from Nashville to Decatur, Alabama. Our exhausted comrades kept arriving till after dark, and I think they all came in safely at last.

13. Our regiment, taking ten teams, went to the northwest of camp for forage. We took five loads of corn from each of two planters, three miles out. Saw numbers of slaves; this is nearly the first we have seen of the peculiar institution. There is nothing attractive in it for me.

14. Rain. Moved camp half a mile eastward. Have a bad eye, but many a man in camp is worse off. Asa Kite and I went to a farm house near camp and procured some clover hay for our bed. Took Edmiston to the hospital after dark. Last night the crowing of a cock was heard some distance from camp, and to-night an expedition has gone out to reconnoiter and bring in the offender. Have not tasted chicken since we left Muldraugh's Hill. S. E. Bailey scouted into the country recently for something to eat. He came to the house of a Tennesseean and asked him what he could sell a soldier. The man brought out a sack of dried apples and offered to sell them. Bailey showed a silver watch and told the citizen that he would trade him that for the apples, but that he must have some money to boot. The citizen offered Bailey $50 and the apples for his watch. The offer was at length accepted, the youth expecting to receive "secesh" money in the trade. What was his surprise when the old fellow counted out the greenbacks and handed them to Bailey, telling him that Lincoln money was of no value to him. The old watch was worth about eight dollars.

15. The Sabbath has come again, and with it a knapsack drill before daylight. It will take considerable piety for the rest of the day to make a good average, on account of the spontaneous profanity of the morning drill. After breakfast we have inspection, then the camp is to be swept and our quarters properly arranged. Visited Edmiston in the camp hospital.

16. From 5:30 to 6:30 A. M. is occupied in drilling. This compels early rising and gives an appetite for breakfast. We have plenty to eat and enough to do to keep our blood in good circulation.

17. Company E went on duty as outside pickets. The day was rather agreeable, but it rained almost uninterruptedly during the night. Stationed on the post next to me was Doak. In the silent midnight hour he fancied he heard the measured step of some one approaching him. I heard the click of the hammer of his musket and his command to halt. The command was repeated, and then the report of his musket sounded through the woods. In the silence which followed the same measured step was again heard. His fancy had pictured an approaching foe, but it was only the large drops of rain falling from the tree above his head to the leaves on the ground near his feet.

20. John A. Wygant, Company C, died last night. The regiment prepared another camping ground a short distance west, and occupied it in the afternoon. Albert Hodge died at Nashville. This is the first death in Company B.

22. Had company inspection, and judging by the amount of extra work going on it must be Sunday. It is Washington's birthday. Lieutenant Colonel Mitchell read an order of General Rosecrans touching the anniversary. A salute was fired at sunset. Washington was a greater man than General Gilbert.

23. Weather is cool and the ground freezes some of nights. The regiment went foraging north of camp, and at the farm of one Carter procured more than forty loads of corn. Carter is an officer in the C. S. A. On our way to camp I scouted under a hint from Lieutenant Bowersock, and brought in three hams and some onions. Have enjoyed the trip very much.

25. The Pioneer Brigade was organized to-day. Two men were detailed from each company (eighteen in all) and reported for that

purpose. A destructive raid was made on the sutler. A sutler is a necessary nuisance.

28. We were called to arms between one and two o'clock this morning, and stood to arms nearly an hour, it having been reported that our pickets had been fired upon. The bugle at last sounded us to quarters.

MARCH, 1863.

2. The regiment went foraging again to-day. We loaded some of our wagons with corn belonging to a man whose son is in the rebel army. I took advantage of being a guard at the house, and possessed myself of a quantity of onions and turnips. I am opposed to vandalism, but I am fond of vegetables. Further on we relieved Blake Crothers of a large lot of corn, and most of the other provisions with which his ample buildings were stocked. We got ninety-six wagon loads in all. Dever Kauffman, of Company F, died this morning.

3. The Pioneers went to the country and worked at making *fascines*. Bought a Tennessee turkey to-day for a two-dollar bill, Michigan money.

4. A brisk snow fell this morning. A skirmish with the enemy took place south of Franklin. The report of artillery could be heard in camp.

5. The noise of a battle in the direction of Springhill was heard during the forenoon. At 2 P. M. we marched in that direction. Crossing the Harpeth, we marched through the village of Franklin and two miles beyond, where we halted for two hours. The troops who had been engaged during the day, having been overpowered by Van Dorn's army, came back in full retreat, having suffered a heavy loss. Colonel Coburn, I think, had command of the defeated forces. Great indignation is expressed because our force was not sent to his assistance.

A large number of troops are now camped here. Corporals H. H. Walburn and Wm. H. Protsman, both of Company E, died to-day at Nashville.

7. Breakfasted on beef soup, crackers and coffee. Rain fell nearly all last night.

9. We marched in the direction of Springhill. Camped for the night in a pasture a mile south of town. Our advance skirmished with the enemy during the day with uncertain results. Slept without tents.

10. At three o'clock this morning a heavy rain fell. We got up and shirked as best we could till after daybreak, when it partially cleared up. We marched at 11 A. M., leaving our dinners cooking in the pot. After going five miles we camped in the woods on the left. Rain fell nearly all the afternoon, and at intervals through the night.

11. We remained in camp. Our troops took what they wanted and more than we needed from citizens in the vicinity. I went to the house of Washington Miller and bought a bushel of dried apples for $1.50, confederate money.

This man has two sons in the rebel army. The soldiers broke open his meat house and carried off his meat, valued at $500. While I was looking on, I heard him tell his colored chattels to go and help themselves to what meat they could get, or they would starve. We stayed where we had spent the previous night.

12. We returned to Franklin, eighteen miles, by 4 P. M. Some of the men gave out and many suffered with sore feet.

14. Some of the men received by express boxes of delicacies and articles of comfort and convenience from home. Home is a better place than this.

15. The Sabbath. Visited some friends in the hospital and wrote for some who are too ill to write.

17. Captain William C. Peck, of Company C, and Captain Nathan Strauss, Company I, have resigned.

18. A prayer meeting is held of an evening near the spring; the exercises are full of interest. It takes one's thoughts home, and recalls the peaceful scenes of long ago.

20. This place, is being strongly fortified, and for that purpose heavy details for fatigue duty are being daily made. The pioneers are busy making and hauling *fascines* and *gabions* which are placed in the walls of the works in course of construction.

22. Saw a prominent field officer in the seclusion of the brush of a fallen tree, busy on a *hunt* this forenoon. Graybacks are no respecter of persons, and are equally disrespectful to officer and soldier. In this they differ from the Government we are serving.

25. A rebel force raided our rear near Brentwood, in the direction of Nashville, to-day, and destroyed the railroad for some distance. This will check our supply of mail and bread. We were called into line late in the evening, expecting to march toward Nashville, but did not.

28. Am not well. The train arrived from Nashville at 4 P. M., bringing the first mail for nearly a week. Its arrival was greeted with deafening cheers. John Southard and I scouted south of camp, found and dug some potatoes, but they had been too badly frozen to be good.

30. The 113th went on picket beyond the town and across the Harpeth.

APRIL, 1863.

1. Companies F and E were inspected by Captain Stacy. The pioneers have been permanently detached from their respective companies and regiments, and to-day took up quarters west of the railroad at an old building.

5. The regiment received two month's pay to-day. Twenty-six dollars is quite a pile if one can keep beyond the reach of the sutler.

10. The monotony of camp life was broken to-day by a daring attack of the enemy's cavalry and a battery of artillery. He dashed into town on the gallop, shouting and firing on a small force of our men on that side of the river. These stood their ground and unhorsed a fair share of all who came within range. It was all over, and the attacking party had fled in a few minutes, leaving evidences of his defeat behind him in the shape of his dead and wounded, and several fine horses. My friend Hanawalt, of Company G, is sick in the field hospital.

11. Arthur Wharton, Company B, died in the regimental hospital to-day. His body was sent to the home of his family at Hebron, Licking county, Ohio.

13. The following special order has been issued by General Rosecrans:

HEADQUARTERS DEPARTMENT OF THE CUMBERLAND, }
MURFREESBORO, TENN., *April* 10, 1863. }

SPECIAL FIELD ORDERS }
No. 97 }

IX. The following named enlisted men of the 113th Ohio Volunteers, are hereby detailed to proceed to Columbus, Ohio, and report to the Adjutant General of the State for authority to recruit a tenth company for their regiment.

They will report semi-weekly by letter to these Headquarters their whereabouts, and the number of men they have recruited. The Quartermaster

Department will furnish the detail necessary transportation to Columbus and return, with such recruits as they may obtain.

    Sergeant GEORGE MCCREA, Company "E."
    Sergeant M. D. L. PARR, Company "F."
    Corporal WILLIAM ARMSTRONG, Company "A."
      By command of
        MAJOR GENERAL ROSECRANS
H. THRALL, *Captain and Assistant Adjutant General.*

14. James L. Edmiston and J. F. Barger, having been discharged, start home. Jim has a soul as big as all outdoors, but he lacked the body to make a soldier. He has been a warm and faithful friend of mine from our first acquaintance.

15. Have been made wagon master of the Pioneer Brigade, and will enter at once upon my duties. I learn that there will be plenty of work in it. This will keep me separated from my command to some extent.

20. It is now eight months since the regiment entered Camp Chase. In that time each soldier has made many acquaintances in his regiment. We have discovered that the character and standing of a man as a citizen at home is no certain criterion by which to measure him as a soldier. The man who, as a citizen, was the recognized bully of his neighborhood, and who was always ripe and ready for a fight with his neighbors, is the first to falter and shrink from duty, and to show the white feather when danger threatens; while the modest, timid, bashful man, becomes the trusty, fearless soldier, who would suffer rather than desert his post or disobey an order. The reckless dare-devil improves in his morals, while the conduct of his more professing comrade becomes greatly modified. In some instances the man of giant proportions and strength becomes a prey to disease, grows weak and helpless, and finally finds his way to the hospital, or is a constant attendant at the surgeon's call, while the spindling boy of sixteen has rounded into hardy manhood, and seems to thrive on duty, danger and exposure. Thus it seems that no human foresight could determine who would or who would not render valuable service to the country.

Up to this time nine officers have resigned their commissions and retired from the service. I would follow their example, but the Governor of Ohio would probably decline to accept it, knowing that he could not fill my place as readily as that of a captain or a lieutenant.

I learn that in Ohio the supply of would-be commissioned officers exceeds the demand, while a likely soldier, suitable for the front rank, is valued at the price of a good horse.

25. The work of fortifying goes on; besides a fort on the north bank of the Harpeth, defenses are being constructed on Roper's Knob, an eminence a mile to the northeast.

29. Went beyond the lines in company with six muleteers; captured and brought in four mules; paid twenty-five cents for a dozen eggs for Lieutenant Charles Sinnet.

30. This day was set apart as a day of fasting and prayer, but I am compelled to say it was not much observed. Colonel Wilcox has resigned and returned home. He has few equals as an officer, and his retirement at this time in our history will be seriously felt by our regiment. We had been a long while learning to understand him, but now that we have learned to know him better, we value him more. No one questions his motives in leaving the service, and our best wishes follow him in his retirement.

MAY, 1863.

1. Our cavalry engaged the enemy at daylight some distance to the south. General Gilbert went out at two o'clock in the morning with a number of regiments, but returned before noon, having killed seven of the enemy and captured forty-three prisoners.

2. Sunday. Went out with a company of teamsters toward Nashville to hunt mules and recreate. We captured two mules and had a quarrel amongst ourselves about the ownership of a chicken. Got a good dinner.

5. Have had a number of teams at work hauling lumber for the construction of quarters. We procured the lumber from a seminary in the southern suburbs of town.

Captain Avery, of General Gilbert's staff, caused the arrest of our party for taking the lumber without his permission. After giving us some advice, which we failed to appreciate, he dismissed us.

6. The 113th crossed the Harpeth, and camped south of town. The contrabands at our camp had an old-fashioned dance, and we acted the part of admiring spectators. While in Franklin to-day, I plucked a full-blown rose, and will send it home to my wife.

8. Sergeant M. Hays, John Scureman and Fred Steirs, Company B, having been left at the hospital at Nashville, joined their company to-day.

9. The command recrossed the Harpeth, and occupied the camp from which they moved on the 6th.

10. Attended preaching at Franklin, and listened to the first sermon for five months, and was so much interested that I forgot the text and the name of the preacher.

11. The 33d Indiana has an excellent band, and they discourse splendid music of an evening. One of the few things I would rather hear than a brass band is a dinner bell. That reminds me that we get plenty to eat here, but forage for the animals is scarce.

17. Went beyond the pickets in company with James A. Baker; dined with a farmer east of camp. John F. Riker, Captain of Company E, has resigned, and started home to-day. Dr. Harlow has also resigned.

20. Lieutenant W. R. Hanawalt has been assigned to duty in the Pioneer Brigade. He is a fast friend of mine.

27. The regiment received one month's pay. Thirteen dollars would not start a respectable faro bank.

28. M.G. Doak and I dined with Mrs. McGavock east of camp. We were treated very hospitably. Buttermilk is a good thing for a stomach that has been regaled with army feed for so long.

29. The Paymaster is here again and disbursed the promises of the United States to the extent of $26 to each enlisted man. The officers get more, but then they have to work for theirs. Having plenty of cash, I went to Franklin and bought two pounds of dried apples for forty cents, preparatory to a swell. Have now been paid $157.50 since enlistment.

30. Went to the Widow McGavock's, and got some pie plant, sweet milk and strawberries. I am favorably impressed with her and shall be her friend while these supplies last.

There are indications of a movement of Rosecrans' army, and we are expecting an order to move at any time. This will be good news, for we have grown weary of our stay here. The troops have done an immense amount of fortifying here, and those who come after us will have little to do but enjoy the benefits of our labor.

31. Rode into the country with Doak and Brigham, of the 113th, and Millet, of the 78th Illinois. Millet and I captured a fine young mare, and proposed making her a present to one of our officers. As we drew near to camp the cavalry outposts put us under arrest, and escorted us before Captain Avery, A. A. G. on the staff of General Gilbert. The Captain was much incensed at us, but listened to our

plea, and finally sent us to our command, and that was the end of it. We will let the officers steal their own horses.

JUNE, 1863.

1. Orders have been received to be ready to move to-morrow.

2. We marched at 8:30 A. M. Traveled seven miles, and our route struck the Wilson pike in the direction of Triune, which place we reached late in the afternoon. Camped on a high ridge on the right of the pike. The roads are soft and part of the train failed to get into camp to-night.

One of our wagons upset in the creek, creating some sulphuric profanity and wetting the equipage badly. We are fourteen miles from Franklin.

5. Took charge of the train of the regiment. Triune is twenty-three miles from Nashville.

10. Have just returned from a trip to Nashville for supplies. We brought an immense quantity of grain, pork, flour, clothing, and other army supplies. Quartermaster Swisher issued clothing this evening. Assistant Surgeon T. C. Tipton has resigned and goes home. Captain David Taylor, Jr., has also resigned.

11. Our camp was attacked by the enemy at 10 A. M., and for two hours things went lively. The enemy then withdrew, leaving a number of prisoners in our hands.

15. Things move quietly in camp, but there are indications that our stay here will be brief. The teamsters of the regimental train hired a colored cook to-day. His name is "Dad." He claims to be a preacher, but if he can preach no better than he can cook the cause will certainly suffer. We shall hold Dad as a probationer for a while and see what outcome there is in him.

16. The regiment shifted its position to one further south and more in the shade. The country is overgrown with plenty of rich clover, but I have not seen a single stack of hay in Tennessee. The times are not favorable to hay making. Lieutenant Hamilton has arrived from Ohio and is on duty as regimental adjutant.

22. Five of our teams joined a large supply train and went to Nashville for flour and other supplies. I accompanied them. We reached Nashville at 1 P. M. It is very dusty. I visited some of our sick at Hospital No. 9.

23. Our forces moved in the direction of Murfreesboro.

25. Our train reached Murfreesboro this afternoon. We have had a bad road and a serious time. I find Lieutenant Swisher, A. Q. M., Doak, and a number of convalescents stopping here. The regiment, with the main army, has gone on toward Shelbyville. Still it rains.

26. The train which brought flour from Nashville was unloaded here, and, after reloading with commissary supplies, again moved, going to the front. Quartermaster Swisher and I went to Murfreesboro and got a good dinner at a hotel. Such meals as we ate would soon bring a hotel to bankruptcy.

28. Sunday. Colonel Mitchell is in Murfreesboro and is suffering with something like varioloid. Some prisoners were brought in from the front to-day.

29. We are preparing to join the regiment. The regimental wagon and the portable bakery, both having been abandoned between here and Triune, were brought in to-day. It rains.

30. Left Murfreesboro at 7 A. M., joining the regiment at Shelbyville at sundown.

On my way, and when within six miles of Shelbyville, I stopped at a house for dinner. The lady told me that I was now in the house where Vallandigham first stopped after being put through the lines of our army, the house at that time being General Bragg's Headquarters. The great Val. tarried here until a carriage could be sent from Shelbyville to convey him thither. As he approached the town, the road was thronged by rebel troops, who called on him for a speech. One of General Bragg's staff officers, who had been a fellow congressman with Val., spoke to the soldiers, excusing the martyr (?) from speaking, and saying that the peculiar circumstances under which their distinguished visitor was placed made silence the better policy. The soldiers then asked that they might get sight of him, and Mr. Vallandigham, to gratify them, stood on the carriage steps. It has rained every day for a week, and the men have suffered much discomfort in consequence.

For a record of events since the regiment left Triune, I make the following extracts from the diary of Comrade Isaac Green:

"*June 25*. We received marching orders on the morning of the 23d, and since then we have been marching through dust, rain and mud in unlimited quantities. Our march was in a southeasterly direction for a distance of twelve miles. Camped in a cornfield, where we find plenty of company, the forces at Triune having marched by different routes and centered here. Yesterday the bugle call to fall in sounded directly after dinner, and in the midst of a heavy rain and plenty of mud, we moved in the direction of Shelbyville.

"The 113th was on duty as train guards, and as a consequence, we made progress slowly; but it was fully as tiresome as steady marching, for the roads had been so used up by the forces which had passed that our animals could move their loads with difficulty. Night came on, and still we trudged on through rain, darkness and mud, five miles further, where we came to our camp. The closing act of the trip was to wade into a mud hole and assist in lifting an ambulance in which Colonel Mitchell was riding. It was now past midnight, and it was next to impossible, under the circumstances, to find comfortable shelter for the rest of the night. I spread my blanket on the ground and stretched my weary limbs thereon; but a torrent of rain soon roused me, and, seeking a friendly tree, I propped myself against it in a half comfortable way, and, throwing my blanket over my head, I half slept the weary time away. At four o'clock this morning we were roused up and again trudged on in a soaking rain. We at length reached the pike, where we halted and constructed shelters of rails. It ceased raining about noon.

"The sun is sinking in the west; we are in line anticipating an attack. A large cavalry force and some artillery are feeling for the enemy in our front. Every few seconds I can hear the boom of cannon in our front at no great distance.

"*June 26.* We have not moved ahead to-day, as many expected. We have been sheltering ourselves from the rainy torrent by putting rails and blankets up in shape to turn the water. Last night a mounted soldier rode into camp at one o'clock, and shouted, 'Fall out, fall out.' We were soon out, but the regimental commander soon sent us to our bunks again. At three o'clock we were again called out, but after standing to arms a short time we again lay down to rest.

"*June 30.* We are now at Shelbyville. On the 27th, last Saturday, we received marching orders to move toward this place, a distance of seven miles. Our force of cavalry drove the enemy in our front the whole distance, and at such a rate as to prevent our infantry from getting a shot at them.

"It is said that the cavalry and artillery drove them out of the town before seven o'clock. They brought back three cannons and more than five hundred prisoners.

"On the 28th, Sunday, a force was sent back to where we had our camp the day before, reaching there before sundown. The next day we thought we would certainly go back to Murfreesboro, but instead of doing so, we marched toward Shelbyville again; we marched about eleven miles through a hard rain, and then camped. This morning we moved on four miles further, and are now in sight of the town.

"From here to Murfreesboro is twenty-seven miles, and from here to our camp of yesterday morning is eighteen miles. Can any one wonder that I and others have sore feet?

"We have been eight days on the way from Triune; it has rained every day and every night but two.

"General Granger has issued an order against pillaging from citizens in this vicinity, as the people of this part of the State are regarded as loyal to the Federal Government. We are now in the Reserve Corps.

"On the second morning from Triune we were ordered to lay aside all our baggage, and to carry nothing but a blanket, haversack, gun and equipments. Tents and knapsacks were left at Murfreesboro, and we are spoiling to see them coming up, for we are much in need of our little all which our knapsacks contain. I need a clean shirt badly; the one I have on has been on duty for these many days.

"*July 2.* Our knapsacks and tents came to hand to-day. I find mine in good condition, and am agreeably surprised. We occupy quarters in the town.

"The citizens greeted our coming with unmistakable signs of real joy. The stars and stripes wave from many dwellings and other places. One lady, who held in her hand a small flag, said that she had carried it in her pocket for months to keep the rebels from finding it.

"As the rebels left town upon our approach, they were compelled to cross the Duck on a bridge above town. It is reported that many were crowded off the bridge and drowned. Four bodies were found this forenoon lodged against a sand-bar some distance below the bridge. Yesterday the body of a rebel lieutenant was found near the bridge below town. A navy revolver, some letters, and thirty cents in silver were in the pockets of his clothing.

"That the bridge above town was not burned is evidence that the rebels were driven out in a hurry, and lacked time to apply the torch.

"No rain for two days. What are we coming to?"

JULY, 1863.

1. Shelbyville is the county seat of Bedford county. It has been a place of some wealth and beauty. It is on the right bank of Duck River. The people claim to be loyal, and they may be; some undoubtedly are.

4. This is the Nation's birthday, and I suppose that in our native State of Ohio the people are making noisy demonstrations of their patriotism, which is all well. Just now I would feel better, and have more respect for the eagle of America, if the skippers in our meat were not so numerous.

The day was observed to some extent, and a Mr. Cooper, a citizen of this town, who has suffered much for the cause of the Union, made an address of ability.

When our troops advanced on this town last Saturday, the force of rebels, commanded by Colonel Leadbetter, made a hasty retreat, going southward, and crossing the Duck on the bridge near town. In their haste many were crowded off the bridge, and some drowned. The body of one of these was found to-day in the river below a dam opposite the town. It had been constantly in an eddy and under the fall of the water from the dam for several days, and was a shocking sight. A grave was made on the bank for its reception. Some men then approached it on a raft, and, tying a string of bark to one limb, towed it ashore. Placing a broad board in the water under the body, it was lifted out and carried to the grave. The board was then turned so that it rolled in. Hardly a more shocking sight can be thought of. The men, in their haste to finish their task, neglected to remove the bark from its fastening on the leg. I mentioned this to one of the soldiers, and he reminded me that this was as it should be, and that the devil could use that as a means of securing his own. Soldiers are apt to make very heartless remarks.

Many of the fathers and sons of the families of Shelbyville were compelled to fly from their homes several months ago when the rebels occupied the town and country. These are now returning, and the greetings of friends, long separated by the cruel fate of war, are frequent and joyous.

5. Captain Levi T. Nichols is acting Provost Marshal. To-day he sent me with a coffin three miles into the country towards Murfreesboro to bury a citizen. The hearse was a heavy army wagon, drawn by four large mules, and driven by Henry Leaf, of Company B. When we arrived in the neighborhood where the man had died, we learned that he was already buried. We returned to camp, and now have a coffin on our hands.

6. Some contrabands revealed the whereabouts of a secreted box to one of our pickets to-day. The box belonged to a rebel captain, and was secreted in a stable not far from the post. Carpenter and Green fished it out of its hiding place. It contained knives and forks, a pan, canteen, coffee pot, wooden bucket, fifty pounds sugar and several photographs.

7. Doak, Brigham and I went blackberrying. This is a great country for berries, but cream is scarce.

8. A detachment of soldiers and a train of seventeen wagons went into the country for grain and forage. We went seven miles to the southeast, and loaded our wagons with corn, procuring it of Mrs.

Campbell and Mr. Dean. Took supper with Mrs. Kizer, and halted for the night close to a village.

9. Our party returned to camp, bringing in many fruits of the trip. It is reported in camp that General Grant celebrated the Fourth in the capture of Vicksburg.

12. Went blackberrying again to day, and got a quantity of berries. We think of bringing in a cow next; berries are much better with cream. The Chaplain of the 121st O. V. I., preached at the Presbyterian Church.

13. Lieutenants Swisher and Toland gave a supper in their quarters this evening. Captain Bowersock, Captain Messmore and Lieutenant Bostwick were among the guests. I never remember of seeing stewed berries make men feel their oats as these men did. Leaf has been sleeping in that coffin since our trip mentioned on the 5th.

14. We moved from town to day, and went into camp on the bank of Duck River, nearly a mile from the village. We have a nice location.

16. The weather is fine, with an occasional shower. The men swim every day in the river. The contrabands of our camp had a huge dance this evening. I have noticed that a darkey never gets too old, nor too badly crippled to dance. Dad, our cook, has an engagement to preach in the wagon yard next Sunday. The companies drill an hour and a half each day.

17. Wrote to Mrs. McAdams to day, reminding her that this is her birthday, and that she is growing old. A year ago to-day I was at home; where I will be a year hence, who can tell? Went with two teams to the country and got two loads of grass.

19. Went foraging to-day to the premises of Mr. Davis, three miles west of town. Rol. Reed and I got a good dinner at a farm house. Loaded our teams with grass and oats.

22. A detachment of troops under Lieutenant Colonel Pierce, 98th O. V. I., with thirty-nine wagons, went on a foraging expedition to the farm of one Dwiggins, five miles south of camp. We found a field of oats, and securing two reaping machines and a number of cradles, we proceeded to cut, bind and load the crop. Dwiggins raises good oats, but I presume he will not thank us for our gratuitous labor, nor for leaving his reaper in the field where we finished. Returned to camp after dark.

Green complains that some one has stolen his plate and that he will have to take his meals from a wooden bucket.

23. Forty-three teams and a detachment of the 121st Ohio, in

command of Lieutenant Colonel H. B. Banning, made a trip to the Dwiggins farm to-day. Sergeant Blotter and I dined with Mrs. Nease.

25. The 113th, commanded by Lieutenant Colonel Warner, went to Dwiggins' farm with thirty teams, and loaded them with feed for the animals. Adjutant Hamilton, A. J. Powell and I took dinner with Mrs. Rollins, wife of Dwiggins' overseer.

26. Sunday. The brigade was reviewed by General Whittaker. Reed and I swam the river and went blackberrying. A foraging party took twenty-one wagons five miles south of camp and secured eighteen loads of oats, corn and hay, the property of a rebel who had gone off with Bragg

Companies are being enlisted and organized for service in the Union army A corporal of the 98th O. V. I. was punished with the buck and gag for lack of diligence while on picket.

29. A large party of foragers with forty-five teams visited Mr. Dwiggins' farm to-day and completed the work of taking all he had. There is a bright side to this for Dwiggins, but I fear he will not be able to see it.

AUGUST, 1863.

1. The weather is excessively warm, and the several company commanders are erecting shady arbors in front of their quarters, using for that purpose the cedar that grows abundantly here. A prayer meeting was held last night in the grove; these meetings are of recent origin, and at first were attended only by a very few; now the attendance is greatly increased, and the interest has also increased.

4. The troops were reviewed by General Rosecrans. The Paymaster paid us two months wages, and now we are puzzled to know what to do with the money. Mail from the North arrives as promptly as if nothing of a hostile character was disturbing the land.

5. Took my old white horse to the river and gave him a lesson in swimming; he swims like a duck, and appears pleased with the exercise. General Rosecrans told us yesterday that we got too much fried meat, and said he thought he would have to take us over the mountains to fatten us up.

6. To-day is Thanksgiving day, and was appointed by the President. No particular attention was given to it, which was not as it should be. Perhaps General Rosecrans does not believe in praying as much as in fighting. He is said to be an ardent catholic.

7. Leaf went foraging, leaving Reed and Dunlap to do camp work. Lieutenant Swisher and I rode to town and spent some time pleasantly. Sergeant J. W. Ingrim, who has been absent at hospital, joined the regiment to-day. He is greatly improved in health.

9. General Whittaker reviewed the troops to-day, and there was pomp and parade in profusion. I attended on horse back, and was very weary before it was over. There would be fewer reviews if the generals and other subordinate officers had to foot it as the enlisted men do. Eight men have been taken from each infantry regiment to serve in a battery. The evening prayer meetings increase in interest. General Baird has been succeeded by General Whittaker as brigade commander.

12. The 113th and 98th Ohio, marched from Shelbyville to Wartrace, arriving at Wartrace at one o'clock in the afternoon. This is in Bedford county on the Nashville and Chattanooga R. R., and fifty-five miles from Nashville. It is a small village or station, and the object in our coming here will appear in the future.

14. It is the season for ripe peaches in this climate, and the neighboring citizens are bringing in the luscious fruit and exchanging for other necessaries, such as coffee, salt and soap. A blooming lass comes in now and then, mounted on a mule, carrying a sack of string beans, a jug of buttermilk and some other tempting edibles. I am almost astonished at the supply of, and the demand for buttermilk. A number of regiments which had been occupying this post, moved towards the front as we came in.

15. The weather is excessively dry and warm. A part of the regiment is on duty several miles from camp, guarding some convalescent animals. There is said to be several hundred of these broken down brutes. The troops performing this duty are having a protracted picnic, and are enjoying it immensely. Several sheep which attempted to hook the boys, have been made to take the oath of allegiance to the camp kettle and the frying pan.

20. John Creath and I rode some distance into the country to the southeast, looking up some forage for our stock. We stopped at the house of a citizen and ingratiated ourselves into his favor sufficiently to induce him to ask us to stay to dinner. Being weak at our stomachs, we could not decline. This was near the village of Fairfield. We returned to camp early in the afternoon. Company E has returned from guarding the camp of convalescent animals.

21. Started in company with George A. Graves of Company D, to Shelbyville on a train. After proceeding a few miles our engine gave

out so as to be unable to proceed with the whole train, and the two rear cars were left on the track; Graves and I remained with these cars, expecting the engine would return from Shelbyville and take this part of the train also. We remained here till night came on and then went to the house of a Mr. Phillips, where we stayed all night. A careful inspection of arms and accoutrements took place. Company I left early this morning to guard a bridge in the direction of Tullahoma.

22. Returning to the train, we were run back to Wartrace by an engine from that direction. We again started for Shelbyville where we arrived in due time. Stopped at Fowler's boarding house for the night.

23. Our object in coming here is to repair a wheel of the portable bakery belonging to Colonel Mitchell and Lieutenant Colonel Warner, and though it is Sunday, we are at work in a shop which some man has vacated.

24. Have been sick for a day or two, unable to work, and so I left Graves to complete the work, and I returned to Wartrace on the noon train. The railroad connecting these places is only a branch, twelve miles long, and is badly out of repair and poorly equipped. Slept with Brigham in the commissary department. The nights are very cool, and a woolen blanket is essential to comfort.

28. I returned to Wartrace to-day from a trip with a supply train to Murfreesboro, via Shelbyville. On my way between this and S., having four teams and empty wagons with me, I loaded the wagons with green corn in the field of J. H. Roane, giving Mr. R. a receipt for the same.

29. Several days ago a train jumped the track two miles from this station toward Nashville, and a vast quantity of sacked corn was unloaded and abandoned. To-day I hauled one thousand and twenty-nine sacks of it to our camp. Lieutenant Swisher will go to Shelbyville to-morrow for cattle. That means that we are to have beef. Our rations are generally good and plentiful, but we do not hesitate to visit corn fields, orchards, vegetable patches and the like, for variety. We have not lost our appetites for honey and other delicacies.

30. Lieutenant Swisher has returned with his drove. It consists of six head of cattle and three sheep. The cattle are assorted sizes, and their condition is such that we will kill them at once to keep them from dying a natural death. The sheep are a rare variety, but as the wool has peeled off of them, we shall not be troubled to shear them. The cars which are in use on this road are made at Dayton, Ohio.

SEPTEMBER, 1863.

1. Loak and I took the train this morning, and went south as far as Anderson, distance forty-eight miles, to visit some friends of the 2d O. V. I. We reached our destination late in the evening, and were cordially received by the boys of the Second.

2. The Second marched early this morning, terminating our pleasant visit. Our return to Wartrace was without incident of note. Both of us complain of being ill.

Wm. J. Minton, Co. D, died in camp this morning. I was sent to Shelbyville for a coffin, but failing to find one, I returned late at night.

4. The Chaplain of the 98th O. V. I. held services over the remains of Comrade Minton; the discourse was one of rare ability.

5. Charles Swazey, of the 98th O. V. I., went with me to the country, taking four teams for forage. We were not successful, and returned to camp empty. Chatfield and I planned to make a trip of the same kind in the direction of Flat Creek, but the plan was cut short by an order to prepare to march. A good part of the night was spent in preparations for moving.

6. We marched from Wartrace at nine o'clock in the direction of Tullahoma, which place we reached in the evening, distant seventeen miles. A wagon of the regimental train gave down within four miles of Tullahoma, and we proceeded without it. After night came on I returned for the wagon, and with proper assistance brought it to camp. This took me nearly all night, and I was fatigued beyond description. Company B, which has been on guard duty at Normandy for five days past, joined the regiment this evening.

7. The column resumed the march at eight o'clock, reaching Decherd at sundown. Before the train moved, Colonel Warner ordered the baggage with which it was loaded to be overhauled, and all cumbrous and useless stuff to be abandoned. It turned out that the Colonel's baggage needed overhauling worse than any other, but all shared a similar fate. The order was impartially enforced, and the plunder left on the ground was surprising in quantity and variety.

From Tullahoma to Decherd is sixteen miles. The march was without unusual incident. A wheel of Leaf's wagon gave out after proceeding four miles, delaying the train several hours. Crossed Elk River six miles from Decherd. The weather is very dry and the road dusty.

8. The regiment marched early, passing through Cowan, a small

town at the foot of the mountain. Here Colonel Mitchell joined the regiment, having been absent sick at hospital since the latter part of June. The ascent of the mountain began at eight o'clock, and, after a hard day's march, the regiment having reached the summit, descended to the valley below and camped. The train made the ascent with great difficulty and with many mishaps. The near hind wheel of Leaf's wagon broke down half a mile up the mountain side. I returned to the valley, procured two wheels of a pontoon train, and after much vexatious delay reached the disabled wagon. The train failed to reach camp, but halted on the mountain's summit and spent the night. The duties of the day had been very laborious to me, and I realized that the position of Wagon Master was one of great responsibility and labor. During the afternoon the front wheel of Sam Hoover's wagon gave out, and this caused some delay. It was a lucky thing for us that I got *two* front wheels in the valley yesterday instead of *one*.

The portable bakery, which was in charge of a poor horse and two colored servants, Dad and Henry, was abandoned on the mountain.

9. The regiment moved southward at 7 A. M.; reached and crossed the line into Alabama at noon. Marched fifteen miles and went into camp. Dry and dusty. The whole army seems to be moving in the direction of Chattanooga. The train descended the mountain and reached the valley during the forenoon. Two of our wagons became disabled in the valley, causing delay and annoyance. We passed the little town of Anderson during the evening. Henry Leaf's near hind wheel gave way, and Henry used some profane expletives.

10. At daylight we again marched southward, reached Stevenson, Alabama, about eight o'clock, and, after a march of fifteen miles, went into camp at Bridgeport, on the right bank of the Tennessee River. The men complain of the dust and sore feet. They have plenty to eat and are in good spirits. The regimental train came up to the regiment late in the evening.

11. Remained camped, and the troops enjoyed and appreciated the needed rest. Some are repairing the wagons, some are shoeing the mules, swimming in the river, writing letters, or sleeping in their shelter tents. One lad is torturing music from a violin. This is more an exhibition of muscle than of skill.

12. The brigade crossed the Tennessee at 5 P. M., and camped on the left bank. The river is spanned by pontoon boats, the rebels

having burned the bridges some time ago. We are thirty-one miles from Chattanooga.

Swisher's horse died last night. The train crossed the river long after dark, and it required great care to keep the animals from crowding off into the water. The men belonging with the train were up nearly all night. Some of the baggage was unloaded, and four of the wagons were sent back to Bridgeport for forage.

13. Sunday. We marched at daylight, passed through the corner of the State of Georgia, (we are told) and, after a march of fourteen miles, went into camp in the mountain (Raccoon?) During the day we passed a long wagon train, with which were five hundred prisoners from Bragg's army. Our train moved with great difficulty, and did not come up with the command. A barrel of mean whisky had been loaded too handy to the end gate of the wagon, and several of the train men, including Dad, the cook, got shot.

14. The column moved about midnight, halting at sunrise to take breakfast. Crossed Lookout Mountain, with Chattanooga in sight on our left, and camped in the valley five miles nearly south of Chattanooga, and in Walker county, Georgia. Company E is put on picket. The men are short of food, and everything like meat is being sacrificed. The country is almost destitute of anything eatable, and destitution is the fate of the people.

The route from Cowan to this place has led us over mountains, valleys, gorges, ravines, rocks and jungles. No description can do justice to the scenery we have seen, especially as we rounded the side of old Lookout and beheld the valley, the city and the river at our feet. What an imposing sight it would have been to view our column of blue-coated heroes, the long line of artillery, the miles of wagon train, the detachments of cavalry, and all the attendants of a great army, as it wound around the mountain, above the clouds, and then descended into the valley beyond.

15. Colonel John G. Mitchell takes command of the brigade. Quartermaster Swisher went to Chattanooga and stored some desks, boxes and other plunder. Brigham and I rode out toward the foot of Lookout, and procured some apples.

17. The brigade and two additional regiments moved out early, and marched in a southerly direction. A detachment of cavalry and six pieces of artillery accompanied us. About four o'clock in the afternoon three of the advance regiments deployed as skirmishers, and, advancing, were met by a force of the enemy, who showed some resistance, and then fell back beyond the little town of Ringgold.

The other regiments were put in line on and under cover of a hill, those on top of the hill moving in the direction of town, and at the same time two pieces of our artillery opened fire upon the enemy for a time. After a time the enemy threw a few shots, but made no other show of fight. The object of a reconnoissance having been accomplished, we retired in the direction of our former camp, near Rossville. After marching six miles we halted for the night. We were weary, and lying down, we were soon in dreamland. About ten o'clock we were awakened by a shower of shot and shell, the enemy reminding us that we had neglected to put out our fires. There was a scramble for traps of all kinds, and the fires were soon extinguished. We shifted to a new position, and spent the rest of the night resting on our arms.

18. The command returned to the camp from which we moved yesterday morning. A quantity of whisky was issued to the men. In the evening we were ordered to march to guard a position a few miles south. We reached our post of duty at ten o'clock, made the necessary disposition of the force, (two brigades) and slept without fires, though it was disagreeably cold. A strong force of the enemy was within a mile of us, but we were unmolested. We are near Reed's Bridge.

19. We breakfasted without water, and then returned to our former camp by one o'clock in the afternoon. We found the wagons loaded, and all things packed as if some movement of importance was on the program. We drew rations, and while the beef boiled we made other plans looking towards active work. At five o'clock, the 2d and 3d brigades moved out three miles to a position near a church (McAfee). Heavy fighting has been going on at times during the day, but we do not know the results. We rested in our position during the night, suffering much from cold.

CHICKAMAUGA.

The following account of the battle of September 20th, 1863, is not a history of that bloody event, but only the record of a man who stood in the ranks and bore his share of the trials of the day. The account may be defective, and in some respects erroneous, but it is preferred to any other for the reason that it treats of the minor details which have been overlooked by the more pretending historian.

"*September 20.* This morning our brigade advanced half a mile in line of battle. . . . . . We are hurried off in the direction of heavy cannonading. Upon reaching the Lafayette Road we formed in line, and one of our batteries fired several rounds at some rebels in the distance. We advanced in line on the left of the road nearly a mile. We then turned by the right flank and filed left into the road, and hurried on in the direction of heavy firing in front. Another brigade was to the right of the road, and in a few minutes we were all together, covering a considerable space, and in full view of the enemy, who, seeing our position, began shelling us. The first shot struck near my feet, the next burst over our heads. One of our batteries then engaged that of the enemy, enabling us to move out, dodging shells as we went. In this movement we came very nearly running into a strong force of the enemy, and were going further to the left than we designed to go.

"Our column then turned to the right, double-quicked into a field, part of which was in corn, and there rested for a short time.

"Company F had been on picket, and now joined their place in the line. They brought two prisoners and report that they had killed four others. All remained quiet for half an hour. To our right was a thick woods, where the musketry firing began at one o'clock. We moved into the edge of the timber and halted. The firing increased to a tremendous roar and lasted several minutes. Just at this time a number of our regiments charged the enemy with a terrible yell, driving them back some distance, and then the order was reversed to some extent, and the roar of musketry increased. Our brigade moved in that direction in quick time. Now General Whittaker came down the hill and told us to go in on the double-quick, which we did. When we reached the crest of the hill, we were four or five deep, and for a brief time the utmost confusion reigned, resulting from the falling back of the 86th Illinois, through our ranks. There was a shower of bullets flying in our midst all the while, a small tree keeping one from spoiling my hide. Presently the right of our line seemed to give way, and an order was given to fall back slowly, keeping up the fire as we went. William Carpenter of my company was shot through the lungs but walked part of the way down the hill. At the foot of the hill we rallied and re-formed, determined to have the hill top in our possession. In this we succeeded, and for nearly half an hour it was comparatively quiet in our front. For a time we lay on our faces under cover of the hill. Then the contest was resumed with increased vigor. We advanced and fell back by turns until sundown, when our ammunition becoming exhausted, we were compelled to quit the field and leave many of our dead and wounded in the hands of our enemy. I confess my inability to describe a battle, and I feel that no pen can do it justice.

"I cannot say that I was much excited or frightened, although my comrades fell dead and wounded on either hand. The air was thick with smoke, and the trees seemed to bend and reel before the storm of lead and iron.

"The enemy had plenty of artillery, and he trained his guns upon us with fatal accuracy. Under all this we stood as sheep before the slaughter, only yielding when ammunition was out. Our regiment's loss is: killed, 27; wounded, 98; missing, 66. We fell back to our camp in the morning, pretty well fagged out. When we left the field our Company, (E) numbered only eight men."

21. Our forces have fallen back, and are fortifying on Mission Ridge to impede the march of the enemy, and check him so that the shattered army can be rallied and placed in a position of defense. It is not possible to state the extent of yesterday's disaster. Our trains were sent during the afternoon of yesterday and last night towards Chattanooga. Our regimental train reached the city at four o'clock, having been four hours in driving as many miles. The road is crowded with trains and troops, all disputing for the right of way. The regiment is on the Ridge doing its part to hold the enemy at bay. Fighting continues to some extent, but no general engagement has taken place to-day. It is probable that the enemy paid so dearly for his victory of yesterday, as to be unable to follow up his advantage. We hope so.

Last night Companies E and F held the skirmish picket line for some time after the main force retired, then they fell back too, and in the afterpart of the night stacked arms with the other companies in a grove in the northern part of the city.

The wounded are being sent to Stevenson and other points in our rear.

22. The regiment is lying still to-day. We can hear the roar of cannon in the direction of Rossville. Many reports of the enemy's movements are afloat. Moved our train across the river and parked on the bottom, half a mile from the river.

23. We are lying in double column at half distance. Last night at ten o'clock a brisk fire occurred at the front, and we were out in line ready for action. Quiet ensued and we again slept. Late this afternoon our brigade and others crossed the river and camped on a high woody hill, called Stringer's Ridge, overlooking the river and the besieged city. We are a rusty looking army of men, having had no leisure to put ourselves and our equipments in order since we left Wartrace. No rain has fallen this month, and the dust is deep and stifling. Several who were reckoned among the killed or missing of the battle on the 20th, have come in, and now our loss falls below our first estimate. One of the curiosities of the engagement is Chatfield's blanket, containing forty-nine bullet holes.

24. We begin to be on short rations for the men. Our animals are being fed by our own efforts in gathering grass and fodder along the river. The men get a limited supply of hard bread, meat, coffee and sugar. There is no real suffering, but the outlook for plenty to eat is not good.

26. Very little seems to be transpiring between the two armies, each seems to be watching the movements of the other.

Went down the river on a foraging trip, securing some fodder and a few ears of corn. Returned to camp with a good appetite.

27. Sunday. Quartermaster Swisher went foraging with several teams, and did not return. I spent the day liesurely. Brigham, Rannebarger and I sang a good deal in the evening. Rol. Reed and I suffered the loss of our knapsacks by having them stolen from our tent.

28. Swisher returned to-day from his foraging trip. He had been out northeast fifteen miles, and found some corn, an article we are much in need of.

29. Took a number of teams, including two of our regimental train, and went up the river twenty miles for corn. We found a large field of good corn near the bank of the river. We began loading, but night came on, and we stopped work and slept under the wagons till morning.

30. Finished our loads and then set out on our return to camp. We came in late and it was raining briskly. After a big supper I slept well, except that the tent blew down in the night and disturbed our rest for a time.

OCTOBER, 1863.

2. We have had a big rain, converting the dust into soft mud, but it is a change which gives variety. Dr. Wilson, of the 1st Ohio Infantry, has been transferred to our regiment as Surgeon. To-day I crossed the river to the camp of that regiment and hauled the Surgeon's effects over to our camp. The new Surgeon is a sturdy bachelor.

The regiment left camp at seven this morning for Sequatchie Valley, a train of three hundred wagons having been destroyed by the enemy. Of this trip Comrade Green writes as follows:

"Marched until after midnight, and camped on the top of a high mountain, commanding a view of many miles, and above other mountains surrounding it. The fog below us at sunrise looked like a vast lake. It was the grandest sight I ever witnessed.

"The rebels have possession of the road by which we marched to Chattanooga last month. This makes it necessary to haul our supplies by a wagon route on the right bank of the river, which makes the trip fifteen miles further.

"The train which was destroyed yesterday was insufficiently guarded, and the rebels, finding this out in some way, crossed the river at Cotton Ford, fell upon the train, shot the mules, burned the wagons, and then recrossed to the south side of the river in safety. The train was loaded with commissary supplies on the way to our hungry army. This stroke at our stomachs will be felt many days hence. I have had but two-thirds of a cracker since five o'clock yesterday, and we must return to Chattanooga before we get more. An ear of corn in my haversack must do for my supper. I certainly think that if old Job had been a soldier he would have used cuss words.

"4. Sunday. The *reveille* sounded at two o'clock. We breakfasted on parched corn, ascended to the top of the mountain, and moved toward Chattanooga. At 10 A. M. we countermarched, and, returning to the valley, camped on the same site where we spent last night. Just before descending the mountain, two daring fellows of the 3d Ohio, being in an orchard at some distance from their command, were dashed down upon by two rebels, who ordered them to surrender. Grabbing a stone apiece, they told the "Johnnies" that they were not used to surrendering, and that they must ground their weapons and surrender. Strange as it may seem, the rebels complied, and were marched into camp by their unarmed captors."

5. The troops who were sent to Sequatchie Valley came in this evening. Though they had a hard trip of it and had very little to eat, they speak of the experience of the scout in glowing terms of praise.

At the front quiet reigns in a great measure. The pickets of the two armies are growing quite intimate, sitting about on logs and discussing the events of the great battle. Sometimes they exchange tobacco for coffee and make other little trades of mutual benefit. They are anxious about the result of the approaching election in Ohio. From our position, by the aid of a field-glass, a signal flag can be seen waiving to and fro on Lookout. It is in the hands of a rebel who is signaling to the Confederate Commander, what he sees in the valley below him. Looking down into our camp from his perch above the clouds, he can see every movement, and almost count the guns in our fortifications. At 11 A. M. the enemy opened on us from their batteries on the point of Lookout, and during the day, till sunset, they paid us their cast-iron compliments in a very unneighborly way. A shell entered the door of a dog tent near which two soldiers of the 18th Ohio were standing, and buried itself in the ground. One of them said gruffly, "There, see what you get by leaving your door open." Lieutenant Swisher left yesterday for Stevenson, having in charge eleven thousand horses.

7. I started with a train of twenty-one teams to Stevenson, Alabama, for supplies. Taking the down river road, we crossed the mountain, descended into the valley, camping sixteen miles from Chattanooga and twenty-eight miles from Stevenson. The train is in charge of Lieutenant John J. Mercer, 78th Illinois.

8. Passed through Jasper, a small town twelve miles from Bridgeport, reaching Stevenson at dusk.

11. Am still at Stevenson. Lieutenant George McCrea passed through here to-day on his way to the regiment. He has been on recruiting service in Ohio since the regiment was at Franklin. I am glad to see him and he is glad to be on the way to join his comrades.

13. Our train left Stevenson yesterday morning and drove twenty miles on its return to the front. We are loaded with supplies for man and beast. I write in a sutler tent at the base of the mountain while the train drags its slow length along up the ascent. A large supply train is in our front and the steep and slippery mountain road makes our progress tedious. This is election day in Ohio. How I would love to be in camp that I might vote for John Brough for Governor. It is raining copiously. This is my birthday. I was added to the population of Ohio twenty-five years ago. The vote in Company B was: for Brough, 27; Vallandigham, 7.

15. Moved on. One of our loads upset on the side of a declivity near a stream, which is now on a high from recent rain. We cannot cross. Hunted chestnuts, butchered a bullock, dried our clothes and waited for the water to subside.

16. The stream having fallen sufficiently, we crossed and proceeded on our way. Began descending the mountain in the afternoon. One wagon upset, another came uncoupled, but all ended in our reaching the valley, where we parked four miles from camp. I rode on in, for I was homesick and wanted a letter from my wife. McCrea got in in time to vote on the thirteenth. I can give but little of the election news in camp. Polls were open by companies, and the voting lasted from 10 A. M. to 5 P. M. In Company E, R. H. Seely, D. H. Chatfield and J. H. Girard were chosen judges; A. M. Grafton and Isaac Green, clerks. Owing to the absence of many of the men on various duties beyond camp, only twenty-three votes were cast: Brough, 16; Vallandigham, 7. No other company of the

regiment cast as heavy a vote for the peace-on-any-terms candidate.

Some of the men are down near the river, west of camp, procuring brick to make a chimney for Colonel Mitchell.

The enemy built rafts of logs up the river a day or two ago, and floated them down to break our pontoons. The trick was discovered in time to tow the rafts to shore before they accomplished the design.

17. The impression prevails that we may stay on Stringer some time yet, and the men are busy building huts and dug-outs in which to live. Axes, wedges and froes are in demand to make these chestnut trees into logs, puncheons and clapboards for building purposes. With rude tools and ruder materials we are putting up houses that will be very comfortable, but not very ornamental.

18. Sunday. Some are giving the day a proper observance by ceasing to work on their houses, but many others are falling trees, carrying logs, making boards, etc. A soldier sees very little of God's day of rest.

From our camp we get a fine view of the river, the city, and of our main army in their camps south of Chattanooga. We can see the glimmer of their camp fires at night, and during the day the untiring motion of the rebel signal post on Lookout's side goes on. Our batteries sometimes toss shell and solid shot at the feet and over the head of the brave "Jonny" who handles the signal flag, but he stands at his post with a daring devotion equal to the boy who stood on the burning deck. Grit is a thing to be admired, even in a rebel.

Of a clear day we can see the camp of Bragg's army on Mission Ridge and stretching westward to the base of Lookout. Such a thing as two great armies lying side by side in plain sight of each other, each unable to attack the other, is a strange feature of the war.

21. Several men of the company have been out on an independent scout for something to eat. They found a young cow tied near the house of her owner, and in trying to take possession of her they were set upon by two fierce dogs, which disputed their right to the cow. But the cow was led to the picket line by a rope. She was then knocked in the head with a hatchet, and her carcass was soon boiling in the kettles. The boys must have beef.

22. Lieutenant Swisher and I start with an empty train to Bridgeport, going the river road. Ascended the mountain with great difficulty by doubling teams in places. Camped five miles from the mountain summit.

23. Moved ahead in a heavy rain. Just before we began the descent we met General Grant and his attendants on their way to Chattanooga. Built a fire in a stable, and, while waiting to descend to the valley, we dried our clothes. Reached the valley and halted for the night. Went to a house and paid fifty cents for some corn bread.

24. After driving a few miles several of our teams became exhausted, and we halted in consequence. Rol. Reed and I proceeded ahead with his team several miles, halting close to the Soldiers' Home, and near the house of Mr. Kelly. Lieutenant Swisher and A. J. Powell, who had been in advance looking for corn, returned, and I accompanied them back to the exhausted train. Here we drew two barrels of flour, a box of meat and a bag of coffee of Lieutenant Drake, who was on his way to Chattanooga with a train loaded with supplies.

Returned with Swisher to where we had left Reed. Then, accepting Kelly's hospitality, we spent the night in his house, *sleeping on a feather bed!*

25. Sunday. Reed and I drove ahead with his team. Gathered some corn in a field by the roadside, and while feeding some to my horse he bit off the end of my finger on my left hand. Tied up the finger with the back of Reed's vest, crossed Sequatchie Creek on a pontoon, took a hasty dinner at Jasper, drove on beyond Battle Creek, and spent the night before a fire in the open air.

26. At Bridgeport. Arrived here at 10 A. M. Drew corn for the mules on the requisition of Captain Pollock. Half rations is the order for the animals now, but by doubling the number of mules in my train I drew plenty of corn. This is the first square feed they have had in a long time.

28. At Stevenson. Came here on a railroad train from Bridgeport this morning. Troops of the Twelfth Corps are coming in and passing on to the front. Hooker's men wear better clothes than we do. Saw General Hooker yesterday for the first time. He was in the act of emptying the contents of a long bottle down his throat. Spent the night with J. S. McAfee, of the Second Ohio. Joe was a pupil of my first school.

29. Returned to Bridgeport on a train with the 66th Ohio.

NOVEMBER, 1863.

3. Started at 2 P. M. yesterday on our return to Chattanooga. We are camped at Jasper for the night. Several of the 113th, who have

been sick at hospitals at Nashville and other points, are of our party, on their way to the regiment. Sergeant Horton read Alice Seymour to us during the evening before we slept.

4. Being overloaded, we unloaded several tents and chests by the roadside, erected a tent, and left the whole in charge of James Hurrigan, Company F, and Sergeant Cloud, Company A. Moved on and met Lieutenant Scarritt on his way to Nashville. Took the obscure road leading to Kelley's Ferry, and halted some distance from the ferry. Spent the night in a sweet potato patch.

5. Drove on to the ferry, but found no means of crossing. Proceeded up the river, and, late in the afternoon, one of our wagons upset over a fence into a garden close to the river bank. Pitched a wall tent and stayed here all night.

6. Resumed our trip, following an almost extinct road along the river bank. Our weary train reached a point four miles from camp at dark, and there halted for the night. Being mounted, I rode into camp, finding nine of my wife's letters awaiting my arrival.

We now have a Chaplain. Rev. Joseph Morris has been transferred to the 113th from some other field of labor. His first sermon, preached last Sunday, is favorably spoken of. He has made a good impression on the men thus far. We have had a sutler at times, but at this time there seems to be a vacancy in that department.

7. Our brigade has been reorganized. Colonel Mitchell is again in command of the 113th, and General John Beatty succeeds him in command of the brigade.

The new organization is as follows: 113th O. V. I., Colonel John G. Mitchell; 121st O. V. I., Colonel H. B. Banning; 108th O. V. I., Lieutenant Colonel Carlo Piepho; 98th O. V. I., Major James M. Shane; 3d O. V. I., Captain Leroy S. Bell; 78th Ills. V. I., Colonel Van Vleck; 34th Ills. V. I., Colonel Van Tassell.

Short rations prevail to an extent that is very distressing. The men gather up and eat the scattered corn where the mules eat their scanty fare. They hover around the commissary department and pick up every crumb that falls from the bread boxes. They scout to the country and appropriate to their own use all they can find that is eatable. The animals fare much worse than the men. Hundreds of these have starved to death, and their carcasses can now be counted by scores on the river bottom and elsewhere.

But a better day seems at hand; two steamers are now plying between here and Bridgeport, and our wagon trains are daily bringing in food for the hungry. The men appear to bear their hardships with cheerfulness, and their faith in the good time coming, seems unshaken.

Now that Rosecrans has been displaced, and his command placed in other hands, the soldiers are inquiring into the causes that brought it about. They conclude that the old hero has been doing too well, and that the Administration does not want a man in command who does all that can be done to end the war. The adoring soldier points to the time when Rosecrans took command of his army, and to the long list of successful actions and campaigns which drove the defiant enemy from his stronghold in Kentucky, to his late position beyond the line of Tennessee. Having shared in the crimson glory of his brilliant record, they are now willing to share in his unjust humiliation.

9. Started with two teams for Bridgeport, and am now halted for the night at South Side Coal Mines. The recent engagements on Lookout Mountain have opened a new and better way to Bridgeport. We now cross the river near camp, and travel the road by which we first marched to Chattanooga. One of my teams, driven by Ben. Anderson, gave out early in the day, and I sent him back to camp. The remaining one is driven by J. E. Buzzard. Slept on a feed trough before a fire, suffering with cold. One of the mules, Bogus by name, made his final kick; that is, he died, during the night.

10. Reached Bridgeport at 2 P. M.

13. At Stevenson. Came here from Bridgeport this morning on business for Lieutenant L. S. Windle of the 113th. Expect to return to-night.

14. At Stevenson. Came here from Bridgeport on the cars last night. Quartermaster Scarritt is here, and thinks I had best not start for the front till to-morrow. Bought a $7.00 hat and made plans for starting early.

15. Sunday. Pulled out early, going towards Battle Creek, but learning that a pontoon crossing the creek had been taken up, we returned to Bridgeport, crossed the Tennessee and reached Shellmound before dark, giving me an opportunity to explore the celebrated Nickiejack Cave. This is eight miles from Bridgeport.

17. Our train reached Whiteside yesterday evening, and to-day we landed in camp with better loads and with much less difficulty than by the former route. Several letters await me.

"Lookout Mountain resembles a straw rick in appearance, a huge straw rick, mind you, beginning about nine miles southwest of Chattanooga, running up by a gradual slope to within two miles of the city, where it assumes nearly a perpendicular stop, overhanging the town, almost, at the height of thirty-four hundred feet. On the highest point an immense rock hangs out as if to threaten destruction to everything in the valley below. On this overhanging rock the enemy have siege guns planted. These guns are daily belching their displeasure at our camps south of the city, or at the troops of Hooker, westward.

"Brown's Ferry is the name of a crossing of the river three miles below the city, where we have a pontoon, and where we have been for some time constructing a landing for our boats which ply between here and Bridgeport. On account of the rebels holding Lookout Mountain, our boats cannot yet run up to the city, and are compelled to discharge their loads at Brown's Ferry. The river is so low now that no boats have been up since Sunday, but they are said to be running up as far as 'Kelley's Ferry,' six miles below here." [G.]

"Rations were issued to-day at the following rate: two-thirds bread, whole rations of coffee, half of sugar. If we could get beans or hominy now and then, neither would be thrown away as we used to do when full rations of various articles were issued." [G.]

18. "To-day we had issued to us some articles furnished by the Christian Commission. These consisted of needles, pins, thread, pens, handkerchiefs, snatch bags, combs, &c., &c. We have often needed such things, but this is the first time we have ever received them, which is a strange fact. Some of these articles are accompanied by patriotic letters addressed to the soldier by the donor. Being almost entirely out of money, and having no means of procuring supplies of this kind, the soldiers' expressions of appreciation of these kind tokens are abundant and genuine. After dinner Spotty and I took some coffee and went to the country to barter for some corn bread. Two miles from camp we found a house inhabited by a number of women. They were lean, lank and shabbily clad and exhibited little signs of intelligence. We bolted into the house, the inmates telling us to take seats. There were only two unoccupied seats; Spotty made for the better one, leaving one for me which had very little bottom, and which kept going down, down, down, as I put my weight upon it. Modesty, coupled with the forbidding appearance of things in the house, kept us from making known the object of our visit. The women were addicted to tobacco and a number of children shared in the general squalor of the household. It is now after night and my bunk mates are abed. The pen in which we live deserves a description. It is built of logs which cost us no little labor, for we cut them at the foot of the hill and carried them to the summit of the ridge. It is six logs high, the gable being 'boarded' with pine branches woven together so as to turn the rain to some extent. The roof consists of our shelter tents stretched tightly in the shape of a roof. The door and chimney are in the northeast end, the latter being constructed of sticks and mud, and is a success. The furniture consists of a stool, bench, table, cupboard and bedstead. The bench is built on four legs driven into the ground, and is immovable. Our cupboard is a cracker box suspended by a rope from a nail in the wall. The bedstead is built on four forks, supporting a platform of small poles, upon which is spread our bedding materials. These consist of leaves, brush and blankets. We have two plates, two spoons, two knives and a long-necked bottle.

"We were inspected to-day by General Beatty, our new brigade commander. The General makes a good impression on the rank and file of his command. Ours is now the 2d Brigade, 2d Division, 14th A. C." [G.]

22. Sunday. This afternoon we received four months' pay. I have now been paid by the Government, as follows: At Zanesville, $47; Portland, $58.50; Franklin, $52; Shelbyville, $26; Chattanooga, $52.05; total, $265.55. This includes $77 bounty. We are allowed $42 worth of clothing a year. We are on the eve of some important movement, and our brigade has been ordered to be ready to move at any time. Howard's command, the Eleventh Corps, has crossed the pontoon next to the city, and is taking position to the south. A number of officers and enlisted men crossed the river to Chattanooga for the purpose of sending money to their homes. By some means not yet explained, Sergeant Lafayette Parr, Company F, was drowned. His body was not recovered.

23. We were up at three o'clock making preparations for the day's work. The noise of rebel trains can be heard beyond the Ridge, and the rebels seem to have an intimation of an attack. An artillery and infantry engagement took place during the afternoon, and lasted till dusk. As night came on, Mission Ridge was lighted up with the flash of the guns of the enemy, and their prolonged roar echoed through the valleys. We expect to take a hand in the game to-morrow. We are still on Stringer's Ridge.

24. Our division moved at 4 A. M., going up the river to Caldwell's, near the mouth of Chickamauga Creek. Here a pontoon spanned the Tennessee, but there were many troops in our front, and we did not cross till nearly 2 P. M. The division took a position nearly half way from the river to Mission Ridge, stacked arms, and listened to the preliminary music of an approaching great conflict.

25. Much more has transpired to-day than I can hope to write. We took up a position half a mile closer to the Ridge, where we lay all day, while the terrible conflict, which had been pending for days, went on. At four o'clock in the afternoon the noise of the conflict indicated to us that the enemy had been driven from his stronghold on Mission Ridge, and that the day had been a Chickamauga to our enemies. We rested on our arms awaiting orders. Night came on,

Late in the afternoon I went with Brigham with a load of rations, and issued to the men as they lay at the base of the Ridge. From my position on Stringer I viewed the events of the day; saw the blue-coated lines as they marched in solid phalanx to meet the enemy; saw the smoke of the guns of Bragg's veterans, as they sent a deadly welcome to their advancing foe; saw the invincible columns of the Union as they ascended the side of the Ridge, and heard the shouts of victory as the Confederates fell back in full retreat. Oh for a pen or tongue that could depict it.

26. The Division moved at one o'clock this morning, crossed the Chickamauga and gave pursuit to the retreating army. The First Brigade of the Division was in the advance, the second next. At Chickamauga station, at day light, we came in sight of the rear of their army, and our brigades formed in line to attack them, but they retreated and we halted for breakfast. Vast quantities of stores were burning at the depot, including a pile of corn meal the size of a hay stack. During the afternoon the order of pursuit was changed and the second brigade took the head of the column, driving the enemy's rear guard until night came on, when, as we neared Graysville, a brigade of the enemy, under command of General Manny, made a stand and for some time disputed our advance. The contest lasted about an hour, after which the enemy withdrew. During the forenoon I loaded some rations for the officers of the regiment, and in the company of George W. Brigham, started to reach the command, and not finding them where we had left them yesterday, we started on after them, passed Chickamauga station, and at night camped in a deserted rebel camp. Brigham returned to our camp on Stringer.

27. The second brigade moved in the advance, reached Igou's Valley, near Ringgold, Georgia, and camped. The team which I had loaded with rations for the officers made such slow progress behind so many trains and batteries, that I had the driver turn it to one side and halt. We then unhitched the mules, and packing the load upon the mules we pressed on, leaving the road and taking to the woods and fields on either side. In this manner we reached the regiment and issued our load to the hungry officers, many of whom will never know at what sacrifice it was accomplished. Started to return to Stringer, but meeting Brigham on his way to the regiment with rations, I turned back with him, and after driving ahead till long after dark, we halted and slept in a meeting house, called " Hurricane Church."

28. At 2 A. M. Brigham and I moved ahead with our supplies,

reaching the camp of the 113th before daylight, and before they had
risen from sleep. Issued to the men and started to return to Stringer.

MARCH TO KNOXVILLE.

The author, being assigned to duty which pertained to the bringing
of supplies from Bridgeport and Stevenson, did not accompany the
regiment on the Knoxville campaign. The following account of it is
furnished by Comrade Isaac Green :

28. The division remained camped in Igou's Valley during the forenoon, a heavy rain falling. At noon we marched in an easterly direction, going four miles, then halted for orders.

29. Sunday. We marched in the direction of Knoxville, made a distance of twenty-four miles and camped near Cleveland, Tennessee.

30. Marched fifteen miles and camped a mile from Charlestown.

DECEMBER, 1863.

1. Waited part of the day for supplies, and when they arrived they consisted of middlings, of which we made batter and baked into cakes. Passed through Charlestown, marched twelve miles and camped.

2. We continue to move in the direction of Knoxville. Passed through Mount Verb during the afternoon. Distance traveled, twenty miles.

3. Marched fifteen miles and camped at Sweetwater River, four miles from Loudon.

4. Marched at daylight, passing through Loudon at 7 A. M., and hurried forward up the river seven miles to a place where we are planning to cross.

5. We remain at a halt to-day. We have been marching through a well improved country, and the inhabitants give evidence of loyalty to the Union by many expressions of joy upon our approach. Now and then the flag of our country is to be seen floating from a staff in a door yard, and the people crowd to the road and watch our column with open-mouthed wonder. Several of the men stopped at a house recently and asked the proprietor for something to eat. He stoutly averred that he had nothing, but the Yankees opened the cupboard, and appropriated milk, potatoes and molasses in abundance.

6. Sunday. Crossed the river and passed through Morgantown on the opposite side. Here we were met by a courier bearing the news that Longstreet had been repulsed at Knoxville, and that further effort to reach and assist our forces there would be unnecessary. Our camp is in Monroe county, bordering on the line of North Carolina. A citizen

joined himself to Company H yesterday, and asserts his intention of becoming a member of the 113th.   [Kimbro?]

7. Started at 9 A. M., and marched seventeen miles in the direction of Chattanooga. Passed through Madisonville at 2 P. M. This is a neat little village of sixty or seventy houses. Our custom has been to rest five minutes every hour during the day, and half an hour at dinner; but to-day we have been cut short of rest almost entirely. We have a pot of mush boiling for supper, and I am too hungry to wait for it to get well done. Who wouldn't be a soldier?

8. Marched at daylight, made twenty miles, and camped a mile and a half from Columbus, Polk county. During the day a family passed us on their way to the North. The lady divided a churn full of salt among us soldiers, an act of real kindness on her part. A Ray, Company E, then stole a piece of meat from her wagon, and made off with his booty. This coming to the knowledge of the Provost Marshal, Ray was tied to a tree till the brigade passed. He was afterwards tied to an artillery carriage and labeled with the word "THIEF," and marched six miles in that condition. Served him right.

9. We remained camped while a bridge is being put across the Hiawasse at this point. A bridge was burned by the rebels last week here, and must be replaced. Company E went on picket.

15. The several days of our stay in this one place have made us anxious to be on the move. We started at an early hour, and, marching a northeasterly course, crossed the Chestna River, instead of the Hiawasse, as we had expected. Then, taking a southwesterly course, we crossed the Hessefon about noon, marched eight miles further, and camped, having made twenty-two miles in all.

16. Have marched twenty-one miles to-day, and are now in camp at McDonald's Gap, a miserable place in a mountain range. Reached here long after dark in a heavy rain. It was no trifle to build a fire and prepare our suppers in such a rain as this. And now, at a late hour, I make this record. How? Well, I throw my gum blanket over my head, making a shelter for my writing materials, leaving a space for the camp fire to shine in on my paper. Often I write in this manner the events of the day.

17. We have marched thirteen miles to-day, and are now camped on the Chickamauga, six miles from Chattanooga, and on a hill. It is distressingly cold. I shudder to think how we are to spend the night, for we are shivering with cold and aching with pain.

18. Marched at noon, and reached Chattanooga at 4 P. M. The pontoon is broken, and we cannot cross to-night to our camp. I spent the night with my only brother at the camp of the 94th O.V.I.

19. The troops crossed at daylight, and occupied the old camp on Stringer's Ridge, from which they moved on the twenty-fourth of last month. The men are ragged and jaded, many of them being without shoes. It is like getting home to be again in our shanties, and to know that we are to have a rest. [G.]

20. Three months ago to-day the great conflict took place at Chickamauga. Many of our wounded have returned to duty, and a great change has taken place in affairs hereabouts. The myriads of rebel tents that dotted the country south of here are pitched many miles further south; Bragg no longer makes his morning salutes from Lookout.

"While on the Knoxville march I saw but two country churches, one a log and the other a frame. Saw one school house and heard of another. Judging by what I saw of the citizens they know very little concerning the uses to which school houses are put. Many of the women use tobacco, and few of them are handsome, according to my ideas of beauty.

"One day I stopped at a house with a view of getting something to eat. One of the women began talking to me of hard living, bushwhacking, &c. She held in her arms a small child, which she kissed frequently, while the juice of tobacco ran down over her chin in a manner which destroyed my appetite. Fearing she might grow familiar, and want to kiss me, I left the house. I next stopped at a house occupied by an old lady who was so ignorant she could not tell me which was east or west, nor how far it was a mile ahead." [G.]

Sergeant Halliday has been appointed to the position of Quartermaster Sergeant.

25. We spent our Christmas a year ago in Camp Dennison. That was as dull as this. Our thoughts take a retrospect of years gone by, when this anniversary brought together our friends, and when feasting and festivity were on the program. We have no turkeys and pot-pies; no claret and champagne to cheer us on the occasion. But we must be content with hard bread and fat meat. After this cruel war is over we will make up for the deficiencies of to-day. Who can tell what the coming year has in store for us, or where we will be this date next year?

Two of our regimental teams have been turned over to the brigade train, and we are now on the eve of vacating this camp.

26. The brigade moved across the river into Chattanooga, thence in a southeasterly direction, beyond Mission Ridge, and camped near a church sometimes called McAfee's Chapel. This is in Catusa County, Ga. It has rained much during the day, and the surroundings do not impress us favorably with the new camp. We are to go into permanent quarters here for the winter. On our way hither we saw many things to remind us of the Confederate army—villages of log huts, graves of the fallen, clothing, redoubts and miles of riflepits.

27. Sunday. As soon as it was light the men began active preparations to construct quarters. Axes and hatchets were kept busy in cutting trees and preparing building materials. Though the rain fell in uncomfortable profusion, the work went on uninterrupted. I returned to Stringer's Ridge with the teams to bring forward some materials which we could not haul yesterday. Spent the night in Brigham's quarters with A. Ranneberger, Rollin Reed and Isaac Slocum.

28. Left the Ridge with Ranneberger's two-horse wagon, crossed the Tennessee in a swing boat, and returned to the regiment. The work of building quarters progresses rapidly. Slept with Lieutenant Scarritt and F. M. Riegel in the quartermaster's tent.

29. Spent part of the day at the house of Mrs. Mitchell, out in the country. Returning to camp, I found an order relieving me from duty as wagon master, and instructing me to report to my company for duty. I have been detached since June 5th, and have seen enough hard work in that time to make this a welcome order.

31. The 113th marched and relieved the 75th Indiana Infantry, at a bridge crossing Chickamauga Creek, five miles in an easterly course from our camp. Companies E and G went on duty at once. The other companies put up temporary quarters. It turned very cold during the afternoon and evening.

Isaac Green, M. Huddleston, Wm. C. Brinnon, John Wilson, James O. Kite and I were posted near the house of Mrs. Simpson, and at a vacant blacksmith shop, in which we have a big fire. The old structure is well ventilated, and if cool air and plenty of it, is a good thing, we are fortunate.

JANUARY, 1864.

1. This is the coldest day we have ever felt in the service. It is with difficulty that we keep from suffering. I occupied a place in Mrs. Simpson's house while writing a letter to Mrs. McAdams. Mrs. Simpson's family consists of the mother, three unmarried daughters, a married daughter, a colored woman and several children. They are open rebels, but their treatment of us has been rather courteous than otherwise. The male head of the family is supposed to be with Bragg's army.

A year ago to-day we were at Louisville, Kentucky, and had seen very little of hard service. We think now we are pretty well broken in, for the year 1863 has given us a taste of about all that pertains to the life of a soldier.

The retrospect of the past year shows that steady progress has been made toward putting down the rebellion, and it can safely be predicted that another year will close its eyes in death.

2. The cold is not so intense. We still hold our position at the bridge, and our post of duty at the blacksmith shop is not an unpleasant one. The single men at the post have joined pleasure with duty, and guarding and sparking goes on, first at the shop, then at the house.

Green procured an oven of Mrs. S., and has been baking our flour into buscuits during the day. He is a good baker as well as a good soldier. The mail came out this evening. The Simpsons all ate with one knife to-day, for some of our thieving soldiers stole their knives and forks. This was reported to our regimental commander, and a guard was placed at the house to protect the inmates from loss and insult. These women deserve better treatment than they have received.

3. Sunday. The weather moderates.

"I was on guard from 9 to 11 A. M., and had more fun than at a goose picking. Our ambulance driver has no feed for his horses, and Major Sullivant ordered that some bran in the cellar of Mrs. Simpson's house be appropriated for the animals. The driver, instead of proceeding to take the bran, went into the smoke house for salt. One of the girls, seeing this, fastened him in as a prisoner of her powerful strategy. She then released him, advising him to ask for what he wanted in the future. He then expressed his intention of taking the bran, but the girl intercepted him at the cellar door, braced herself against it, and defied him to go in. The driver called to me for assistance. This placed me in an awkward predicament, but, after exhausting my art of persuasion on her, I took hold of her pouting form and boosted her away by main strength. It was something of a hug-scuffle, and a source of mutual enjoyment. We thought our victory complete, but judge of our surprise when Miss S. stepped into the cellar, fastened the door from the inside, leaving the driver and me on the outside. To hoist the door off its hinges was the next thing to do. This we did, and the girl bounded out of the cellar into the house, denouncing us as thieves of the lower type. We got the bran." [G.]

6. Shallow Ford is the name of the point where we have been on duty for several days past. We were relieved this morning by the 85th Illinois Infantry, and returned to our camp near Rossville. It has been raining for several days. Although Mrs. Simpson and her

daughters are out-and-out rebels, we evidently made a good impression upon them, for they admitted that the men of the 113th treated them better than the soldiers who were on duty there before us. Green thinks that he and the girl he imprisoned in the cellar parted on good terms.

From "The Citizen Soldier," by General John Beatty, I make the following extracts:

"My quarters are in the State of Tennessee, those of my troops in Georgia. Just a moment ago I asked Wilson the day of the week, and he astonished me by saying it was Sunday. It is the first time I ever passed a Sabbath from daylight to dark without knowing it. . . .

"I am quartered in a log hut. A blanket over the doorway excludes the damp air and the cold blasts. There are no windows, but this is fortunate, for if there were, they, like the door, would need covering, and blankets are scarce. The fireplace, however, is grand, and would be creditable to a castle.

"The forest in which we are camped was, in former times, a rendezvous for the blacklegs, thieves, murderers, and outlaws generally, of the two states, Tennessee and Georgia. An old inhabitant informs me he has seen hundreds of these persecuted and proscribed gentry encamped about this spring. When an officer of Tennessee came with a writ to arrest them, they would step a few yards into the State of Georgia and laugh at him. So, when Georgia sought to lay its official clutches on an offending Georgian, the latter would walk over into Tennessee and argue the case across the line. It was a very convenient spot for law-breakers. To reach across this imaginary line and draw a man from Tennessee, would be kidnapping, an insult to a sovereign state; and in a states rights country such a procedure could not be tolerated. Requisitions from the governors of Georgia and Tennessee might, of course, be procured, but this would take time, and in this time the offender could walk leisurely into Alabama or North Carolina, neither of which states is very far away. In fact, the presence of a large number of these desperadoes, in this locality, at all seasons of the year, has prevented its settlement by good men, and, in consequence, there are thousands of acres on which there has scarcely been a field cleared or a tree cut. . . . .

"What a country for the romancer! Here is the dense wilderness, the Tennessee and Chickamauga, the precipitous Lookout with his foothills, spurs, coves and waterfalls. Here are cozy little valleys from which the world, with its noise, bustle, confusions and cares, is excluded. Here have congregated the bloody villians and sneaking thieves; the plumed knights, dashing horsemen, and stubborn infantry. Here are the two great battlefields of Chickamauga and Mission Ridge. Here neighbors have divided and families separated to fight on questions of national policy. Here, in short, everything is supplied to the poet but the invention to construct the plot of his tale, and the genius to breathe life into his characters. . . ."

"Some benevolent gentleman should suggest a sanitary fair for the benefit of the disabled horses and mules of the Federal army. There is no suffering so intense as theirs. They are driven with whip and spur on half and quarter food, until they drop from exhaustion, and then abandoned to die in the mud hole where they fall. At Parker's Gap, on our return from Tennessee, I saw a poor, white horse, that had been rolled down the hill to get it out of the road. It had lodged against a tree, feet uppermost; to get up the hill was impossible, and to roll down certain destruction. So the poor brute lay there, looking pitiful enough, his big frame trembling with fright, his great eyes looking anxiously, imploringly for help. A man can give vent to his sufferings, he can ask for assistance, he can find some relief in crying, praying, or cursing; but for the poor exhausted and abandoned beast there is no help, no relief, no hope.

"To-day we picked up on the battlefield of Chickamauga the skull of a man who had been shot in the head. It was smooth, white, and glossy. A little over three months ago this skull was full of life, hope, and ambition. He who carried it into battle had, doubtless, mother, sisters, friends, whose happiness was, to some extent, dependent upon him. They mourn for him now, unless, possibly, they hope still to hear that he is safe and well. Vain hope. Sun, rain, and crows have united in the work of stripping the flesh from his bones, and while the greater part of these lay whitening where they fell, the skull has been rolling about the field, the sport of the winds. This is war, and amid such scenes we are supposed to think of the amount of our salary, and of what the newspapers may say of us."

7. Lieutenant Swisher started home on a furlough.

8. Half an inch of snow fell last night. Flour has been issued to us of late instead of bread. We can make batter cakes and biscuits that will pass inspection, and delight the inner man, but baking light bread is one of the lost arts.

9. Our quarters are now completed, and a description of the one in which I am quartered ought to be recorded :

It is ten by fourteen in its dimensions, seven feet high, and covered with our own make of clapboards. The door end stands to the west and the door opens outward. The chimney is also in the west end. The east gable has a six-light window, filled with glass eight by ten. Our bunks extend from the window toward the fire, leaving a space to the right for the table, which is a homely affair. Four three-legged stools fill the place of chairs, and are real handy things to have around. We have christened our house "Metropolitan Hall," the name being in large letters over the door outside. The dedication took place in due form, several invited guests being present, all of whom, together with the proprietors, took the oath several times. All we lacked in the ceremonies was a brass band and something more to eat.

Notwithstanding our comfortable quarters we do not sleep warm of nights. We get up in the night and warm by the fire, and then return to our bunks to sleep.

Stratton and I went to the country, and procured two haversacks full of unbolted flour and two candles, for which we paid seventy-five cents. After our return to camp we baked some biscuits, and ate breakfast, dinner and supper all in one meal. We have struck upon a plan of keeping a feed store on a small scale. Some of our comrades wanted to buy some bread, and we sold them all we could spare, and the money thus realized will be invested in supplies again.

10. Sunday. Chaplain Morris distributed some reading matter among the men, our mess receiving "The Religious Telescope."

11. The 10th Illinois Infantry, camped near us, started home on veteran furlough. Stratton and I went to their camp and bought some culinary outfit. We then went into the country, and paid a Miss Conner $3 for six dozen biscuits. Paid Mrs. Lomineck $1 for ten candles. Returned to camp and ate three suppers. Sergeants Souder and Flowers made us an evening visit, and the Hall rang with the voice of song. A rumor has been in circulation to the effect that our feed store business had failed, and to deny the statement we posted on the outside of the shanty door the following:

NOTICE.

" *This firm, which was recently reported as having failed, has recovered from its embarrassment, and is now doing a cash business. All claims against us will now be promptly cashed.*
METROPOLITAN HALL."

14. Procured a pass for Green and myself. Went out to a mill on Chickamauga Creek, where we tried to buy breadstuff for our feed store. Failing in this, we retraced our steps till we came to Mrs. Mitchell's, where we bought one hundred and twenty-four biscuits for $5. Returning to camp, we sold out in a few minutes, making a profit of $9.60. The cars run to Chattanooga to-day, the first time since our army has been in possession of the city.

15. Went on picket one and a half miles south of camp, taking the place of Sergeant H. C. Scott. Lieutenant McCrea had charge of the post. We had a good fire at the reserve post, and our stay of twenty-four hours was rather pleasant than otherwise. Dress parade has again been introduced. Think we had dress parade at Wartrace last, before this.

We now have company drill from 10 to 11:30 A. M.; battalion drill from 2:30 to 4 P. M. A regimental guard has been put on, and altogether we have time to cut a little wood and cook our rations between duties.

When I get command of this department things will be different. I will see that every enlisted man has a brigadier general to cook and wash for him.

18. The pickets were on the alert last night more than usual, and an extra company was sent out to strengthen the line, but nothing was seen of the looked for enemy.

Seely has been out in the country for supplies. He brings twenty-four dozen biscuits, for which he paid $12. The Metropolitan mess has now a cash basis of $30.

One hundred and seventy rebel deserters reported to General Beatty to-day at his headquarters in camp. They are tired and want to go home. I wish they would all do that, don't you?

Took Seely's place on picket to-day, the post being under command of Captain A. L. Messmore. Captain M. is from Fayette county, O. and is a fine looking and good officer. I slept with him, and listened to his experience in Kansas.

20. Green is on picket again. Seems to me he does more duty than any man in the camp. Seely and I went out to Mrs. Mitchell's to replenish our stock of provisions. Paid $4 for sixty-six biscuits, and $6 for a ream of paper.

21. The unarmed men of the 113th were marched to Chattanooga, six miles, and received their arms and equipments. I accompanied the party and drew a Springfield rifle for myself. Bought $4.20 worth of ink.

22. The 113th has only nine companies in the service. For some months past a number of men have been recruiting for the tenth company, and to-day a number of the new men arrived in camp, and were quartered temporarily with the other companies. Of these, Booker R. Durnell and John W. Walker, were made welcome at the " Hall."

25. Came off of picket at 9:30 A. M. Found an express box in camp from home. It contained a great coat, an army blanket, a pair of boots, a lot of stationery, dried peaches, dried apples, green apples, canned peaches, two pair socks, apple butter and fifteen postage stamps. Now we will live like brigadiers while these supplies last.

27. Camp life has grown monotonous, but drill duties give it some variety. We are expecting to march soon, and are holding ourselves in readiness. We gave a supper at the Hall this evening. Our guests were Captain John Bowersock, Lieutenant George McCrea, Milton G. Doak, John Snyder, John H. Walker, Booker R. Durnell, R. H. Seely, Milton L. Stratton, Isaac Green and myself. Didn't we have a lively time? Distributed the mess fund, each receiving $5.82.

28. The Brigade marched early this morning in the direction of Ringgold. Took dinner near Chickamauga Creek, one and a half miles from Ringgold. Rested forty-five minutes, marched a mile down stream, crossed a bridge, passed through the town, and halted for the night half a mile south of town. Green, Stratton and I slept on a brush heap.

29. Breakfasted early, and at daybreak we about-faced, and returned to our Rossville camp at 2 P. M. The object of our trip was to ascertain the position and strength of the enemy south of Ringgold.

31. Lieutenant Swisher, who has been home on furlough, joined the regiment to-day. Deserters from the rebel army are coming in daily, in squads and singly. They give a doleful account of the situation in rebeldom.

FEBRUARY, 1864.

3. Started to Jasper, Tenn., in company with John Cloud, Company A, to bring forward to the regiment some goods which I left there several months ago. These were four mess chests, a wall tent and a hospital tent fly. Procuring a pass of General Beatty, we reached Chattanooga the same evening, spending the night with friends in the camp of the Second Ohio.

4. Crossing the Tennessee on the swing ferry, we proceeded down right bank to Kelley's Landing, and spent the night at the house of one David McNab. The boys of the Third Ohio camped near the landing were having a dance at this house the same evening. And such a dance!

5. Cloud remained at the house of McNab, while the son, Alex., accompanied me with a team to Jasper. Reaching our destination,

we loaded the baggage and started on our return. Reaching the house of a Mr. Starling, a brother-in-law of McNab, we spent the night.

6. Reached Kelley's Landing at 3 P. M., and placed our goods in a house on the bank of the Tennessee. Spent the night with McNab. He is a clever Union man, and has suffered much at rebel hands.

7. Ferried our baggage to the opposite side, pitched our tent on the sand near the river, and, procuring transportation papers of Captain L. S. Bell, of the Third Ohio, we waited for a boat.

8. At 9 P. M. last night the steamer Chattanooga touched at the landing, on her way up, and, hurrying our goods on board, we were soon moving on.

Daylight found us but a short distance above the landing, and during the day we passed two places in the river which were difficult to navigate. At one of these a rope was thrown ashore, one end of which was carried up stream and fastened to a tree; the other end was fastened to a capsail on the bow of the boat. Then by means of lever power, the boat is wound up the stream. At the other, the more difficult of the two, there are constructed on shore above the *suck*, two windlasses or crabs, by means of which the boat was pulled through. She ran so near the bank on one side that I could have stepped off very easily.

Reaching Chattanooga at 3 P. M. we stored our goods and proceeded to camp to find that the 113th had moved yesterday to Tyner, a distance of ten miles in an easterly direction. We find in the old camp a few men of the regiment who were left behind in charge of some things which could not be taken along with the troops when they marched.

10. All the men set out to join the command at Tyner. Riegel and I rode ahead and halted at the house of Mrs. Simpson, at Shallow Ford. They seemed pleased to see us. Reached our regiment at 3 P. M. Tyner is nine miles from Chattanooga, and is a small station on the East Tennessee and Georgia railroad.

I find Green at work putting the finishing touches on a rail pen which is to be our quarters. Peter Baker, who was wounded at Chickamauga, and who returned to duty since I left on the third, is in the pen with the mumps. The situation is not inviting by any means, but is a little better than nothing. Tyner is in Hamilton county.

11. The men are busy at their quarters. We raised ours higher and finished the chimney, but it is not as comfortable as Metropolitan

Hall. We have to stand to arms of a morning one hour before daylight. This is a plan of discipline, but not a means of grace.

Captain Nichols, Sergeant Grafton, E; William Brunk, H; H. B. Briley, G; and P. H. Whitehead, B; started to Ohio on special duty.

15. Somebody raided the sutler last night, and Sergeant Barber, of Company K and I, made an unsuccessful search for a clue to the thief. Have been in the service eighteen months, and to-day I start on the second half of my three years.

16. Picketed northeast of camp, the post being in charge of Lieutenant McCrea, of the 113th, and a lieutenant of the 78th Illinois. We suffered from cold, notwithstanding we burned all the rails within our reach. Troops are marching in great numbers in the direction of Knoxville. John H. Johnson, Henry McAlexander and James O. Kite were on duty with me.

General John Beatty has resigned his commission, and will return to civil life. His farewell address is as follows:

> "HEADQUARTERS 2d BRIGADE, 2d DIVISION, 14th ARMY CORPS, *February* 9, 1863.
>
> "I desire to announce to you that nearly one month ago I tendered the resignation of my position in the army, and to-day have received official notice of its acceptance. I am, therefore, no longer your commander. In separating from the brigade with which I have been connected for the past four months, I desire to offer my sincere thanks to the officers and men for the numerous manifestations of kindness to myself, and for that soldierly conduct which has rendered my associations with them most agreeable. It is hardly necessary to refer to the reasons that have induced me to return to civil life. It may be proper, however, to say that I entered the army in April, 1861, have been through the working part of three years, and, in resigning my position, entertain, undiminished, that faith and confidence in the final triumph of the Union cause with which I first entered the army.
>
> "Lieutenant Colonel Carter Van Vleck, 78th Illinois Volunteers, assumes command. My acquaintance with his character as a soldier and a man satisfies me that I shall leave the management of the brigade in competent and faithful hands, and that you will have no cause to regret the change. Trusting the time will soon come when you can be permitted to return to your homes, and enjoy in peace the rewards to which your great sacrifices and your gallant conduct entitle you, I bid you farewell. JOHN BEATTY,
> *Brigadier General.*"

This announcement creates universal regret throughout the entire brigade. The General is held in great esteem by officers and men, and no one questions the motives that prompt him to retire to civil life.

17. Rockwell H. Seely, my messmate, received his discharge from the service to-day, and will soon be homeward bound. The grounds for his discharge are general debility and the total loss of his voice. The regiment received new shelter tents. The weather is disagreeably cold and a high wind prevails.

23. The division marched from Tyner at 5:15 P. M. going southerly. We packed all our effects and have an understanding that we are not to return. My load consisted of two woolen blankets, one rubber blanket, one great coat, one rubber coat, one pair trousers, one shirt, one pair drawers, two pairs socks, one piece of tent, haversack full of rations, gun and equipments. I was overloaded and will march lighter another time. Reached Ringgold, fourteen miles distant, at midnight. Halted in the suburbs of town and rested till morning. Company K, being unarmed, remained in camp.

24. Reveille sounded long before daylight, and preparing and eating a hasty breakfast, we awaited orders. Moved at 8 A. M. and took up a position in Thoroughfare Gap, a mile south of Ringgold. Here we formed in line near a bridge which crosses the Chickamauga. Some fighting can be heard in the direction of Tunnel Hill, eight miles further south. Lieutenant Colonel D. B. Warner, who has been absent for some time, joined the regiment.

25. Our brigade marched back to Ringgold and halted in the suburbs. The men demolished fences and outbuildings to procure lumber for temporary quarters. When the war is over the owners of the property thus despoiled will have plenty of leisure to rebuild it again. We leave a black mark wherever we go nowadays. Colonel Mitchell, who has been home on leave of absence, joined the regiment to-day. James O. Kite and I visited a widow in town, and bought a $10 bill C. S. money for $1 in Lincoln money. The husband of this woman was killed at Fort Donelson. Our forces engaged the enemy near Dalton, fifteen miles from here. Some of our wounded are being sent back this far. Company E went on picket north of town.

26. Major Sullivant surprised our picket post by riding up to us, unannounced, finding some of us asleep and without equipments on. He seemed displeased at it. Company B, Lieutenant John W. Kile, relieved us, and our company joined the regiment. Lieutenant Chas. Sinnet, 4th Battalion, Pioneer Brigade, is here. This is Catoosa County.

27. The command remained quiet at Ringgold. Our troops who have been to the front at Dalton, are now returning. Lieutenant Colonel Warner takes command of the regiment.

28. Sunday. At 9:30 A. M. we took up our line of march toward Chattanooga. Halted three miles from Ringgold and spent the night in the woods. A fire broke out in the dry leaves in camp and a lively time ensued.

29. Marched at 2:10 P. M., reaching our old camp at Rossville late in the afternoon. Our quarters here, from which we moved on the 7th inst., are still standing. Men of the regiment, who did not march with us from Tyner, came here two days ago and had some things prepared for us upon our arrival. Corporal Baker, who is to take Seely's place in the mess, having recovered of the mumps, has the hall warm and cozy. He had a warm welcome and a good supper for us. It rains.

TENTING ON THE OLD CAMP GROUND.

We're tenting to-night on the old camp ground,
  Give us a song to cheer
Our weary hearts, a song of home
And friends we love so dear!

CHORUS.

Many are the hearts that are weary to-night,
  Wishing for the war to cease;
Many are the hearts looking for the right,
  To see the dawn of peace;
Tenting to-night, tenting to-night,
  Tenting on the old camp ground.

We've been tenting, to-night, on the old camp ground,
  Thinking of the days gone by;
Of the loved ones at home, that gave us the hand,
And the tear that said, Good-bye!—*Chorus.*

We are tired of war on the old camp ground:
  Many are dead and gone,
Of the brave and true, who've left their homes;
  Others have been wounded long.—*Chorus.*

We've been fighting to-day on the old camp ground;
  Many are lying near—
Some are dead, and some are dying—
  Many are in tears!—

CHORUS.

Many are the hearts that are weary to-night,
  Wishing for the war to cease,
Many are the hearts looking for the right,
  To see the dawn of peace:
Dying to-night, dying to-night,
  Dying on the old camp ground.

MARCH, 1864.

1. The Paymaster paid us $26 each to-day. What to do with such a pile of money is a grave question. Recruits are coming in for the different companies. They have good clothes, large knapsacks and unsatiable appetites. This is a bad place for a man who has too much appetite.

5. A rumor prevails in camp that a force of the enemy is at Lee & Gordon's Mills, south of here. We have prepared two day's rations, and expect to go out to see them to-morrow. Green has been sick, but is at his meals again.

6. Sunday. We were in line before day; then stacked arms and ate breakfast. Instead of marching we had general inspection, occupying two hours or more. Later in the day a copy of "The Christian Banner" fell into my hands. In it I find the following:

LEAVE ME AND SAVE THE FLAG.

"Captain J. M. Wells was slain in the battle of the 20th of September, in North Georgia. He was a Christian gentleman and a noble patriot, as well as a brave soldier. His funeral was preached in Wesley (M. E.) Church, Columbus, Ohio, by his pastor, Rev. Joseph M. Trimble.

"In the sermon reference was made to his company bearing the flag of the regiment. When Captain Wells was shot, Sergeant W. P. Souder led him out of the ranks and seated him at the foot of a tree, giving him water once or twice. The Captain urged the Sergeant to leave him and protect the flag. On returning to look after his wounded captain, he found him looking at a daguerreotype picture of his wife and babes. This picture, with his watch and sword, he delivered to his friend, requesting him to send them with his body to his family, telling them he died as a Christian and a soldier. The narration prompted from an officer present the following lines:

> ' Leave me and save the glorious flag!
>   We'll conquer or we'll die,
> And in our God we'll put our trust,—
>   The God who rules on high;
> And he'll protect the good old flag
>   That's floating to the weather.
> The glorious flag—the stars and stripes—
>   Shall wave and wave forever.
>
> ' Leave me to die, ye noble boys;
>   Defend your country's cause;
> Maintain the Union of the States.
>   The Constitution. Laws.

> Protect the flag, our country's flag;
> Still float it to the weather.
> The glorious flag—the stars and stripes—
> Shall wave and wave forever.
>
> 'Farewell, my wife and prattling babes;
> It's hard with you to part;
> I feel my life-blood flowing fast;
> Death's chill is on my heart.
> But leave me, boys, and raise the flag,
> Still floating to the weather.
> The glorious flag—the stars and stripes—
> Oh! may it float forever.' "   L. V. B.
>
> *Columbus, O., Nov. 1, 1863.*

8. Captain John Bowersock started home on a twenty-day furlough. The picket was re-enforced last night in anticipation of an attack. Peach trees are in bloom. Sam Bishop will start home to-morrow.

13. Sunday. Major Sullivant inspected the regiment to-day. An agent of the Christian Commission preached a good sermon for us. Now and then we get a taste of Sunday. We now have five hundred and sixty-three enlisted men.

15. Bought fifty candles of a member of a Michigan battery, paying $3.25 for them. Had general inspection by Captain David F. Roatch, 98th O. V. I.

The arrival of our regimental band this evening created a sensation in camp. The band is organized as follows:

Leader, Edward Schellhorn; Second Leader, Clark W. Cottrell; First B Flat, Henry Pfoutch; Second B Flat, Thomas E. Shepherd; First E Flat Alto, Nicholas Shimmel; Second E Flat Alto, Jeremiah Bair; Third E Flat Alto, Raper Ellsworth; First Baritone, John Wolf; Second Baritone, Henry Sillbach; B Bass, John M. Hemphill; First Contra Bass, Daniel R. Taylor; Second Contra Bass, Martin Leonard; Bass Drum, Joseph H. Newcomb; Snare Drum, Joseph Low; Cymbals, Richard Schellhorn.

16. Captain A. L. Shepherd, First Lieutenant William H. Baxter, and Sergeant Monroe Elliott, Company K, arrived in camp and reported for duty. Each of these men has seen service in the 66th O. V. I.

Sanitary supplies were distributed to us to-day by lot. Green held a winning ticket, and drew the articles named below:

A gilt-edged Testament, two tracts, four sheets of paper, five envelopes, one pencil, skein of thread, paper of tea, piece of court-plaster, piece of soap, paper of pepper, paper of cloves, package of loaf sugar, ball of yarn, fine comb, pin cushion, a dozen pins, four needles and a postage stamp. These were accompanied by a letter, which is here appended:

EAST HAMPTON, *October* 28, 1863.

Dear Soldier.—Although you are a stranger to me, I thought I would write you a short letter to send with the comfort bag I have been making for you. I hope these things I have put in it will add a little to your comfort. If they do, I shall be very glad I made it. A gentleman who belongs to the Christian Commission came and spoke to us about the soldiers, and wanted our Sabbath School to make some comfort bags and send to them. So our class of eight little girls have made over thirty. We hope they will do some good.

I have some dear friends in the army, and feel an interest in all the soldiers, and I often pray for them. Do *you* love Jesus, and do you love to pray to him? I hope you do, for *I* love him, and he is the best friend I have. I hope you love to read about his life, and that you will read my Testament which I send you, and that you will try to live as he wants you to. I hope God will spare your life and bring you to your home again; but if he sees best to have you die, far away from home and friends, I hope Jesus will be with you then, and hope we may meet in heaven. I wish you would answer my little letter, if you can find time to do so, and tell me something about yourself. I send an envelope, directed right. And now a kind good-bye. From your little friend,

ANNA.

22. Snow has been falling during the night and is now ten inches deep. The following shows how it is done on picket:

HEADQUARTERS 2d BRIGADE, 2d DIVISION, 14th ARMY CORPS,
CAMP NEAR ROSSVILLE, GA., *March* 8, 1863.

CIRCULAR—
All guards will fall in at the approach of officers. Grand guards will present arms to general officers, to colonels commanding brigades, to the officer of the day and to their regimental commander, *once a day*, should he visit the pickets.

Outposts will stand to arms and salute no person. At the approach of officers, sentinels will face to the front and stand at *attention* without saluting. They will not sit down, but will walk their beats constantly during their two hours of duty. Outposts will not sleep, but will be on the alert during their four hours off duty. Sergeants will examine passes at roads; passes recognized only at roads.

This circular will be read to the men by the commanding officers of the grand guard every morning before posting the pickets. All disobedience of orders will be reported at once, and the offender promptly punished.

The commanding officer of the grand guard, on being relieved, will transmit this circular to his successor. In case of a march, or pickets being permanently relieved, it will be handed to the inspector. By order of

COLONEL JOHN G. MITCHELL.

23. To-day a spirited battle took place in camp; not a bloody affray with the roar of cannon and the clash of musketry as an accompaniment; not a struggle in mortal combat in which the shouts of the victor and the groans of the vanquished added interest to the scene; but one in which friend vied with friend in strategy and skill. The snow being in good packing condition probably suggested the idea to some of the men that a snowball battle would be a source of grand fun. The preliminaries were soon arranged. The 98th O. V. I. and 78th Illinois arrayed on one side, and on the other the 121st O. V. I. and the 113th O. V. I. Positions were taken, the strength of the opposing forces was carefully ascertained by reconnoitering parties, which played their several parts with tactical precision. At length the main body became engaged and the charging and retreating by turns went on at an interesting rate. The war was carried to Germany, for the 108th O. V. I. finally shared in the contest, and in the end each party proclaimed his side victorious. All ended well and the occasion will long be remembered because of the solid fun it furnished. If nations could only settle their difficulties by snowballing battles, or by pounding one another over the head with pillows, war would be stripped of most of its horrors.

27. The men make occasional trips to Lookout Mountain, climb its rugged sides to its summit, view the splendid scenery, talk poetry, drink from the gushing fountains on its sides, and then return to camp with an appetite which destroys the peace of the mess. These romantic rambles ought to be made when we are drawing full rations.

31. The Second Division, commanded by General Jeff. C. Davis, was reviewed by General Geo H. Thomas, accompanied by General Palmer. Each of the several commanders was accompanied by his respective staff officers, and there was parade and pomp in profusion. Those who were mounted enjoyed the review very much, but the footmen indulged in some profane expletives, which led me to think they would enjoy full rations much better than a review which kept them on the jump for four hours. Schellhorn's band came in for its share of the glory of the occasion. What a grand thing is music when you are short of milk! The bass drum is minus one head.

APRIL, 1864.

1. The recruits are being initiated into the delights of picket duty. A number of deserters, belonging to our own command, are kept under guard near Division Headquarters. One of them got away by some trick last night, but was retaken in trying to crawl through the picket line. Truly the way of the transgressor is hard, even in Georgia.

2. Major Sullivant made to Adjutant General Cowen the following historic report of the 113th:

HEADQUARTERS 113th O. V. I.,
CAMP NEAR ROSSVILLE, GA., April 2, 1864.

ADJUTANT GENERAL COWEN:

Sir—Accompanying you will find the complete muster rolls of this regiment, in compliance with Gov. Brough's order of February 19th.

The organization of this regiment was commenced in August, 1862, at Camp Chase. It proceeded slowly, however, for some time, and in October we were ordered to Camp Zanesville to fill up our ranks. We remained there until December 14th, when we were ordered to Camp Dennison, numbering at that time thirty-two commissioned officers and seven hundred and twenty-one enlisted men. The 109th O. V. I. was then consolidated with the 113th, giving us an additional company. On the 28th of December we were transferred to Louisville, Ky., numbering thirty-five commissioned officers and eight hundred and fifty-seven enlisted men. On the 5th of January, 1863, we removed by rail to Muldraugh Hill, Ky., where we remained guarding the railroad bridge until the 27th of January, when we moved back to Louisville and embarked on the steamer St. Patrick, for Nashville. Owing to the crowded condition of the boat, the voyage was very unpleasant, and the health of the regiment suffered to such an extent that it has even now scarcely recovered from its effects. Nashville was reached February 8th, whence we soon proceeded to Franklin, Tenn., and on the 13th of February went into camp. We remained there several months, occasionally exchanging the quiet of camp life for a scout or a long march in anticipation of meeting the enemy.

When Earl Van Dorn made so determined an attack upon our forces at that place, the regiment was ordered to Triune, on the 2d of June, 1863, and on the 24th of that month, in company with the entire Army of the Cumberland, we took up our line of march toward Rebeldom, and participated in the trying scenes of the successful "Tullahoma Campaign." Our brigade formed a portion of the right wing of the army, and, although it was not our fortune to become actively engaged, we endured with all necessary fortitude the exposures and severities of the march, and entered Shelbyville on the 1st of July, and viewed the waving of Union banners and shouts of welcome from the noble population of that celebrated Union town. We encamped at that place, and remained until August 11th, when we were ordered to Wartrace to guard the Nashville & Chattanooga railroad. Thence we commenced marching on the 5th of September toward Chattanooga, and participated in the severe hardships of the Chickamauga Campaign, marching day and night for three weeks over rough mountain roads and across numerous streams, and making frequent reconnoissances toward the enemy's position. Finally, on the afternoon of Sunday, September 20th, in company with two brigades of our corps (the reserve corps), we were precipitated upon the hosts of the enemy, who were advancing in a vast army to overwhelm our left and destroy the army. Public opinion, as well as official reports, give to the force of which we formed a part, the credit of having that day saved the army from a terrible disaster.

We took into action an aggregate of four hundred and ten officers and men. Our loss was: Killed—officers, 4; men, 19; wounded officers, 2; men, 103; missing men, 19.

After the battle the regiment retired with the army to Chattanooga, and there remained during the siege by Bragg's army. What the Army of the Cumberland suffered during that time for want of food and clothing is now a matter of history, and unnecessary for the annalist of a single regiment to dilate upon. In the battle of Mission Ridge, November 23d, our division, (we having been transferred to the 2d Brigade, 2d Division, 14th Army Corps,) was held in reserve under General Sherman, and after the battle led in pursuit of the enemy, with whose rear guard we had a sharp contest, on the afternoon of the 26th, near Chickamauga Station.

After the rebels were driven below Dalton, Sherman's column was ordered by General Grant to march to the relief of Burnside, whom the latest reports represented as besieged by Longstreet, with only a small supply of provisions on hand. Burnside reported that he could only hold out until the 3d of December. This gave our forces about four days to reach him, but the necessity was urgent, and the troops willingly undertook the forced marches necessary to succor the army at Knoxville, although in clothing they were entirely unprepared for such a journey, and had started from Chattanooga with only two day's rations. The weather was extremely cold, and large numbers of the men were barefooted, and, as we were forced to depend upon the country through which we marched for provisions, the privations and sufferings of the men were probably unexampled in the history of this war. Upon our arrival at the little Tennessee, within twenty miles of Knoxville, news was received that Longstreet had retreated. We were therefore directed to retrace our steps, and finally reached our old camps at Chattanooga on the 20th of December, having been constantly on the move for four weeks. On the 2d of January, 1864, we were transferred to the camp we now occupy, where we have since remained, with the exception of an occasional fortnight's absence guarding some railroad station in the vicinity, or taking part in a reconnoissance toward the enemy's position at Dalton.

The tenth company (K), having been recruited under authority of the Governor, was completed about the 1st of March, and at that time the regiment numbered: Commissioned officers, twenty-six; enlisted men, seven hundred and five. The regiment is in excellent health and condition, and ready to do good service to the country in the approaching campaigns.

Very respectfully, your obedient servant,

L. STARLING SULLIVANT,

Major Commanding 113th *Ohio Volunteers.*

4. Green was on picket in the rain last night. He says: "It was so dark I could not keep my beat, and the rain fell in torrents. I leaned against a tree and took it like an ox. Oh! didn't I love my country about then?"

Captain Bowersock returned from his furlough yesterday. Captain Benjamin, Company B, came in also. The latter was wounded at Chickamauga, and this is the first we have seen of him since that day. We are glad to see them both.

5. Have been on regimental guard, Lieutenant Baxter being officer of the guard. Two men of Company C were drunk and noisy. Lieutenant B. and I tied them both to trees, with a bayonet in the mouth of each. They remained tied till the effects of the whisky abated and they became quiet. This created not a little excitement in camp, and resistance was threatened, but none offered.

6. One of the men who created the trouble yesterday was again tied up. This time he was placed on his back with his feet tied on either side of a big stump, where he remained till the *spirits* left him. These men are recruits and have not yet had their breaking-in.

7. John Craig and John G. Ganson reached the regiment to-day and will be assigned to Company E. Lieutenant Colonel Warner, who has been for some time past in command of the Third Ohio, has returned to the regiment and will be in command. M. L. Stratton and Isaac Green visited the battlefield of Chickamauga to-day, and this evening have much to say of what they saw. The quarters of Company K were partially destroyed by fire.

9. Henry Dewitt and I went to Chattanooga on some business. Sent $30 to Mrs. A. Cleveland for Lieutenant Geo. H. Lippincott.

11. D. H. Chatfield, who has been on recruiting service in Ohio since October, joined his company to-day. He left a corporal, but returns a second lieutenant. The duties of the day closed with dress parade, prayer meeting and a dance.

15. The chaplain, assisted by a number of the soldiers, has erected a bower church by planting a lot of pine bushes in a square, about 25 by 25 feet. A brush roof is constructed over the whole, which gives it a verdant, cozy appearance. Meetings of considerable interest are being held here of evenings. Half a mile southeast of us stands McAfee's Chapel, a former place of worship. This building is now full of army stores, consisting of bread, meat, coffee, salt, candles, kraut, vinegar, and whisky. Captain Orr has charge of these supplies.

16. Captain Chas. P. Garman and Lieutenants Crouse and Dun-

can returned to duty to-day, having been at home on furlough for some time.

17. Robert Doak of the Sixty-sixth, Bennett and Hunter of the Second—all Champaign county boys—visited friends in our regiment. The Second is at Graysville.

26. The time drags heavily. During the past ten days the monotony of duties has been almost distressing. However, we are that much nearer the end of the war, and that much nearer our respective destinies. General Davis, our division commander, has issued an order prohibiting enlisted men from wearing boots in our future movements. Fortunately for me I sold to Lieutenant Kile my $8 boots some days ago, but Green has an expensive pair on hands (feet), which he says will not be thrown away to comply with the order of anybody. Many of the men have boots that have cost high prices, and to be compelled to abandon them and wear shoes will be next to an outrage. I notice that General Davis wears boots. The weather for some time past has been warm and spring-like, and the men insist on drilling without their blouses. Of course this was not granted. Lieutenant Colonel Warner has ordered that all lights be extinguished in our quarters immediately after *taps*, and that no men be allowed to roam through camp at late hours. All persons using profane and obscene language, or who are found creating disturbance in camp, are to be reported to their company commanders. This is as it should be, but some of the men complain loudly of it.

Springtime is upon us, but there has been no plowing done in all this country, nor will there be. The farmers are nearly all from home; those who are at home have no teams nor seed. The citizens have been getting their living of our government for months. When the army goes forward from here their case will be pitiable.

The evening meetings at the lower church continue and the interest increases. Chaplain Morris is untiring in his zeal to fit the men for a better life. Twenty-two men rose to their feet, in one of the meetings, expressing a desire to lead new lives.

30. The end of our stay at Rossville approaches. We are instructed to send home or abandon all surplus baggage, and a large number of boxes and packages are now at headquarters to be shipped to the North. Officers are allowed only a change of clothing, and the men will not be permitted to carry heavy knapsacks.

This afternoon I went to Chattanooga to express some goods belonging to men of Company E. We were mustered for pay.

MAY, 1864.

1. Sunday. Every preparation is being completed for moving, and it is understood that this is our last day in camp at Rossville. We came here the day after Christmas, and though our stay in this camp has been mainly comfortable, it has, of late, been very monotonous, and the troops have become restless and want to be doing something. The prospect of entering upon a campaign against the enemy, and of penetrating further and further into his country, has a fascination in it for the soldiers, and they are in fine spirits to-day. Chaplain Morris preached morning and evening, and the exercises were well attended and full of interest.

2. The Second Division filed out of camp at half past eight this morning, heading southeasterly. I confess to a feeling of regret in leaving "Metropolitan Hall." I may never again sleep under its rude but friendly roof, nor hear the echo of music within its walls. I must exchange its comforts for the rude life that awaits us on the tented field. The 113th had two hundred and fifty-eight files of men this morning, and her total strength is six hundred and seven men. The day has been cool and pleasant, with a shower in the forenoon. We reached Ringgold at 3 P. M. and pitched tents near the Chickamauga, nearly a mile from the town. During the evening many of us visited and explored a cave in the vicinity of camp. We learn that our entire corps is here.

3. Yesterday and the day before was spent quietly resting in our camp, where we halted on the 2d. The men cut down large chestnut trees, and peeling the bark from the logs in great strips, spread it on a platform of poles for a bed, leaving the raw or flesh side of the bark up. The owner of this forest will not need to cut down any rail timber for some time.

The Division moved at 6 o'clock A. M., passing through Ringgold and beyond Thoroughfare Gap, filed into line, stacked arms and rested. Here, seated on my knapsack, I wrote a letter to my wife. The circumstances were so peculiar that the dimness that seemed to obscure the lines on my paper could not be attributed to age, for I am not yet twenty-six. During the day we received mail, and my share was a letter containing the picture of my wife and our boy. These must go with me to the end. The Fourth, Fourteenth, Twentieth, and Twenty-third corps are now here. Our advance has confronted the enemy during the day, and the booming cannon has echoed over hill, ridge and valley.

6. Major I. S. Sullivant joined us to-day. All were glad to see him. He has been absent for some time on furlough. No leaves of absence are being granted now; men are needed in their places in the ranks or elsewhere. We do not move till to-morrow.

7. The whole column move toward Tunnel Hill. Our advance and the enemy keep up a lively contest in which musketry and artillery rattle and roar by turns. The enemy gave way and fell back in order. Our brigade took a position within a mile of the town, our line running east and west. Later in the day we passed to the right of town and camped one and a half miles to the east, where we spent a quiet night.

8. Sunday. Remained camped during the forenoon, during which time Chaplain Morris preached a short discourse. We are watching the contest between the two lines of skirmishers at the entrance to the gap, which is called Buzzard's Roost.

At 2 P. M. the Brigade formed and took a position at the entrance of the gap. Our line is parallel with the railroad and facing east. Our purpose is to drive a force of the enemy from the ridge in our front. A line of skirmishers, Companies I and H (commanded by Captain Durant and Captain Watson), of the 113th, was deployed in our front. The skirmish line commanded by Colonel H. B. Banning, 121st O. V. I., moved promptly, and the Brigade, commanded by Colonel John G. Mitchell, followed in line of battle at a proper distance. For several hundred yards our way lay through a tangled mass of underbrush, through which we moved with great difficulty. Crossing a creek near the base of the ridge we began the ascent. Up, up, up we go, each moment expecting to receive the fire of the foe. But the crest of the ridge is reached without a shot, for the enemy had fled at our approach and taken a position on a ridge running parallel with this one, and from which they began firing at us, the shots whistling about our heads in a manner not to be relished. As we moved along the top of the ridge, one of our men, William McManus, Company I, was shot and fell down dead within a few feet of me. This is our first loss in the campaign. Our chaplain took charge of the body, and the column descended to the valley and halted an hour in an open field. We then countermarched, crossed the point of the ridge before mentioned, and, ascending a ridge to the east, stacked arms and halted for the night. Half the men of each company returned to the camp from which we moved early in the afternoon, to bring forward the knapsacks and baggage which had been left behind. I went on this duty, bringing baggage belonging to Green and myself. We were all very tired, and the rebels were kind enough to let us rest well during the night.

9. Two guns of Battery C, 1st Illinois Artillery, were dragged up and placed in position on the ridge. These kept up a heavy fire on the enemy's position south of the railroad, on the side of a huge hill. At dusk the skirmish firing in our front became very earnest, and an additional company (E) was sent forward to strengthen our line. The men took their position and for an hour lay on their faces, while the bullets spattered on the gravel and among the rocks of the ridge. Later in the night rations were issued to us, and by the time this was attended to it was past midnight.

10. Three additional guns were put in position during last night on this ridge, and to-day they have been pounding away at the rebels in front, right and left. The infantry withdrew from the crest of the hill and sheltered themselves behind it. Here they dug little excavations in the hillside so that they might rest secure, without the risk of rolling down the hill. Company G are on the skirmish line.

11. The incidents of to-day have been much the same as yesterday. A battery of the enemy got the range of our guns late in the afternoon, and for a time their fire grazed the hill, passed over our heads and exploded in the valley below. In the evening our brigade withdrew into the valley, where we spent the night comfortably.

12. Marched in the direction of Tunnel Hill at sunrise. After going two and a half miles in this direction, we took a road leading in a more southerly course, and through a country very little improved. At dark we halted and took supper in a cornfield, then resuming the march, we continued till after midnight. Our way during the night lay through a narrow pass or gap, with high and precipitous rocks and cliffs on either hand. I am told that this defile is called Snake Creek Gap. This is a flank movement on the enemy. I like it better than fighting their front. John Ganson was sick to-day, and has been in an ambulance part of the time. Have marched twenty-two miles.

13. Marched soon after daylight, going nearly east. Halted at 8 A. M., stacked arms in a valley. Knapsacks were unslung, piled, and left in charge of a guard. Tents and blankets were packed and slung, and then the command rested. We are now on the enemy's right flank. He holds a strong position at Resaca, near this, and on the Western & Atlantic railway, fifty-two miles from Chattanooga, in Gordon county, Georgia. Every preparation being made indicates a battle.

At 3 P. M. we marched toward Resaca. We can hear the contest as we approach. Our brigade shifted from one position to another during the evening, but our regiment did not become engaged. Parts of the brigade sustained some loss. We spent the night in a woods on the right of a road that appears to run north and south.

14. Our position was changed frequently during the forenoon. A brisk engagement took place east of us at 1 P. M., and we moved in that direction, formed a line in the edge of a cornfield, moved across the field in line of battle, and rested in a ravine at the east edge of the field. Then moving by the left flank, we formed a new line three hundred yards to the north, in a thick wood, immediately west (?) of the enemy's fortifications. We again shifted position nearly a quarter of a mile, and again lay down. Chaplain Morris passed along the line exhorting the men to trust in God, do their duty, and all would be well. The Chaplain has the grit. Then, moving by the left flank, we lay down at the base of a ridge, which protected us from a terrific fire of the enemy. The 108th Ohio, and 34th Illinois, were more exposed, and suffered some loss. The 45th O. V. I. took a position near us. They had lost heavily during the day. Night coming on, we retired to the edge of the cornfield, where we had formed in line first in the afternoon.

15. Sunday. Before breakfast our regiment took a new position, one and a half miles to the southeast, on a ridge, overlooking a valley, and in sight of the enemy's position at Resaca. We occupied works which had been constructed last night. The main body of the regiment sheltered itself behind the crest of the hill, occupying the pits by companies, in relief, three hours at a time. After dark, when all was quiet, a spirited colloquy took place between the blue and the gray. The rebel shouted: "Say, Yank, where is Hooker?" and the reply was: "You will hear from Joe soon enough." "Says Johnnie, have you any corn bread? Want to trade for coffee?" The rebels boasted how they intended to whip us to-morrow. Their many taunts met as many cutting replies. Then both sides would loose temper, and exchange shots.

At midnight a very heavy firing opened to our left, and the regiment crowded into the rifle-pits, ready for an attack.

16. The promised whipping is indefinitely postponed. Johnnie is gone from our front this morning, and we are glad. Early in the forenoon we returned to the valley where we left our knapsacks on Friday last. Taking these again, we were soon moving rapidly southward. Passed fine farms, good houses and other evidences of improvement. The ladies on our way are tastily dressed and appear to be cultivated. Our march lasted till after dark, and we have moved rapidly nearly all day.

Some are inquiring to know if General Davis' horse has given out, and if we are halted on that account. Have marched about twenty miles. We are eighteen miles from Rome, which is our destination.

17. Marched early, and at noon halted for dinner, four miles from Rome. Rested an hour, and moved ahead. Within two miles of the town our advance began to exchange shots with the enemy's outposts, and the musketry grew fierce and fiercer as we neared the town. Our forces took position in line on either side of the Somerville road. The 34th Illinois Volunteers (Veterans) was sent forward with instructions to bring on an engagement, and then retire so as to bring the rebels within reach of our line. The order was executed, but the wily foe did not follow when the 34th fell back. The 22d Indiana Infantry shared in the attack, and both regiments suffered losses. The enemy fell back, crossed the river into Rome, and burned the bridge behind them. Our troops remained in line and threw up a line of rifle pits the entire length of the line, before morning.

18. It is thought that the enemy has left Rome, and that we will soon cross and occupy the town. The brigade went into camp near a number of fine residences near where the fight occurred yesterday. A fatigue party buried some of the rebel dead left on the field, and citizens report that they carried off a great many as they fell back.

Roses are in bloom; I sent one in a letter to my wife to-day.

A line of rifle pits run through the door yard of one of these fine mansions, and the fence has disappeared. We are teaching these people to take a joke. Rome had a population of about three thousand, but at present many of the able-bodied men are absent in the Confederate army.

19. Part of the division crossed the river and occupied the town, the enemy having left the town for good. A great quantity of tobacco, captured in Rome, was distributed among the men to-day. Thank you, I don't use the weed. Companies K, C, G and E went on picket at dark.

23. Our stay here has lengthened out beyond our expectations, and we have had a very pleasant visit among the Romans. Sorry we have to move before their garden stuff gets fit for use. This evening the second brigade crossed the Oostalauna into Rome, filed right, crossed the Etowah on a pontoon below the site of the bridge des-

troyed by the retreating rebels, and went into camp a mile further on. The Oostalauna and Etowah rivers unite here, forming the Coosa. Rome is the county seat of Floyd county, and has been a good business place.

Isaac L. Gray, Jacob Fudge and Daniel R. Baker, Company E, deserted to-day. They will be able *to steal* their way to Ohio.

24. Our division moved in the direction of Van Wert, and after a brisk march of eighteen miles, formed a junction with the troops of the fifteenth and sixteenth corps. Our route shows little of the ravages of war. Camped in a peach orchard.

25. Moved ahead, leaving Van Wert to our right. Took dinner in a cornfield and again moved in a southerly course. At 3 P. M. a heavy firing was heard several miles ahead of our column, and in consequence we quickened our pace, some times going at double quick. A heavy rain set in at dark, but we pressed forward in the darkness. Went into camp late in the night, wet, hungry and tired. We now learn that Hooker had an engagement with the enemy, causing the firing mentioned.

26. Dried clothes and tents. Marched three miles to the east, and rested two hours. We then left-faced, and with left in front, went back two miles, took a road bearing left and passed through Dallas, the county seat of Paulding county, Ga. We received a large mail and drew three day's rations, late at night.

27. We seem to be near the main line of the enemy. At 8 A.M. our brigade marched a mile northeast, halted and stacked arms. Ate an early dinner and then shifted position to a hill half a mile to the southeast. We are hid by the trees and thick underbrush. Heavy firing goes on at all points of the line. Company C went on the skirmish line during the night.

28. We held our position till evening; then moving northwardly one and a half miles, we formed a line in the edge of the woods, with an open field in our front Our line runs north and south. During the night we made our position secure by constructing works of rails and dirt. Heavy cannonading goes on, day and night, but we are becoming accustomed to it, and sleep well.

29. Sunday. The 113th picketed on the left of the 14th A. C., two and a half miles from our works. Company E rested in the shade, in reserve during the day, but went on the front line at night. We divided to four posts, with a corporal and six men to each. Anthony Shimel, John W. Taylor, John Wilson. John Wank, Daniel

8

Walker, Joseph Warner and myself were on a post together, and we tried to enjoy the situation.

Several times during the night the pickets of the enemy opened up on us with heavy firing and deafening yells, but neither of them had any fatal effect. When all was quiet they seemed to want information, and would shout at us such questions as these: "Say, Yank, do you want some tobacco?" "Yank, don't you wish you was a union?" "Where's Hooker?" We answered as courteously as the case required.

30. The 121st O. V. I. relieved us at 8 A. M., and we returned to our former position and spent the day resting, washing, sleeping, etc. I have been reading "Beyond the Lines, or a Yankee Prisoner Loose in Dixie." The weather is very warm.

31. The 34th Illinois is skirmishing in our front to-day. The enemy have been annoying our part of the line by an almost continual fire from a battery on the summit of a very high hill in our front. We took shelter in trenches, then took to the woods in the rear and each man sought a place of safety. After an hour we returned to the trenches and remained unmolested till evening. One of our musicians had his horn broken by a fragment of shell.

JUNE, 1864.

1. At midnight, last night, the 113th vacated her works, and moving two miles to the left, stopped in an old field grown up with small pines. Remained till past noon to-day. Then moving to the left, we passed a part of the line occupied by the 20th A. C., and took supper in a hollow. At dusk we occupied a part of the line a mile further to the left, relieving the 100th O. V. I., and the 112th Illinois Regiments, of the Twenty-third Corps. Slept in line with arms and accoutrements on. Company H took the skirmish line. Our line and that of the enemy are within rifle range of each other, and that brings the skirmishers almost face to face. There is no harmony between the two sets of skirmishers, and they are kept hid from each other continually. Some of our skirmish pits fill with water, and the occupants must keep the water tossed out or stay out themselves, exposed to the shots of the enraged foe.

3. Still holding our position in the rain and mud. The balls of the enemy whiz over our heads too closely for safety and comfort.

Last night and the night before we fell in and stood in line in our works, expecting the enemy was moving upon us, but they came not. It rains.

4. Our brigade was relieved soon after daylight. Moved to the rear in a heavy rain, prepared and ate breakfast, then moved to the left four miles. Took dinner, drew rations, put up our shelter tents, and stayed for the night. It rains.

5. Drew fresh beef, put it on the fire to cook, but moved before it was half done. Marched a mile to the northeast. Here the right wing of the regiment went into position, and the five left Companies, H, E, K, G and B, went on the skirmish line, relieving troops of the 145th New York Infantry. All is quiet in our front, and we are told that the rebels have vacated this part of the line.

6. The pickets were called from post and formed on Company K, near a frame house. Here are seven rebel deserters who had come in and surrendered to Captain Shepherd's company. They are dirty, poorly clad, ignorant and forbidding in their appearance. After an hour waiting, the five right Companies, A, F, D, I and C, with the brigade, came along, and we moved, all together, several miles to the right, went into line in the edge of a woods near a cornfield. Here we constructed the customary rail barricade, got supper, took a wash, and then slept for the night quietly away.

7. We are resting where we halted yesterday. This is two miles from Ackworth, and thirty-five miles from Atlanta. The country hereabouts is very little improved, a large per cent. of the whole country being a dense forest.

10. Yesterday and the day before we rested quietly in the shade. At 8 A. M. to-day we moved eastward, and after a march of six miles or less, halted in a peach orchard. Here we spent an hour waiting for the wagon trains of the 15th A. C. to pass. During the afternoon we traveled seven miles, a tremendous rain pouring upon us. I am ill, and have marched with great difficulty. Was very glad when the order was given to stack arms.

11. We are now confronting the rebel army, and the usual roar of musketry goes on. Countermarched some distance during the forenoon, put up tents, let it rain and took dinner. In the evening we moved on a mile and closed by divisions, *en masse*, within half a mile of the railroad, near Big Shanty, a station about twenty-seven miles from Atlanta.

12. Sunday. There seemed to be a little respect paid to the day.

The skirmishers were not as noisy as yesterday. Another torrent of rain fell. A high, ugly hill a mile or more in our front is the stronghold of the enemy. A somewhat flat and open scope of country lies between us and the rebel lines.

13. Rain again to-day. Six prisoners were taken by the pickets of our brigade.

14. About noon we took arms, and, preceded by a heavy skirmish line, the brigade moved in line of battle in the direction of the line of the enemy, about a mile, the enemy falling back as we pressed forward. We halted on the north edge of a large, open field, where we put up works.

15. At ten o'clock A. M. I went with other men to get beef. During our absence a fierce artillery fight took place on McPherson's right and to our left, east of the railroad. Our lines advanced and held the ground. Our pickets gained the further side of the field and put up the necessary protection. When we advanced during the engagement many of the rebel pickets ran toward our lines with white flags floating from their arms in token of surrender. It was a clear case of desertion. Our men cheered them heartily. While this was going on the excitement caused our men to place themselves in conspicuous positions to witness what went on, thus making themselves targets for the rebel sharpshooters. A shot, which must have been fired from a distance of half a mile, struck James Steward, Comany E, 34th Illinois, and Cyrus G. Platt, commanding Company G, 113th O. V. I., wounding both fatally. The ball passed through Steward's head and lodged in Platt's. He lived till four o'clock this afternoon. Few men hold such a place in my esteem as this man who has just laid down his life for his country. I became acquainted with him early in our term of service, and that acquaintance has grown riper and sweeter as trials and dangers thickened. A few minutes before he fell he passed and addressed me pleasantly, and as he passed on, Sergeant Stratton remarked that Lieutenant Platt was among the worthy men of our regiment. His death casts a gloom over the whole regiment. Late at night we stood to arms in expectation of an assault by the enemy, but he failed to come.

16. My health improves. We have had a day or two without rain. Heavy skirmishing goes on right and left. In our front it is more quiet. I have drawn a pair of new shoes. Have been trying to patch a gap in my pants but gave it up. I was not intended for a tailor. Rebel deserters report the death of Lieutenant General Polk, of the

C. S. A. We improved our works to some extent, and now, if Johnnie wants to come, we are ready.

17. I learn to-day that the mountain to the southeast is called Kenesaw. We have held ourselves in readiness to move all day. A brisk fight took place on our left and in the front of the 16th A. C. Rain. A rebel signal on the mountain is kept in motion almost continually, day and night. The enemy made a feint in our front at ten o'clock last night, causing us the trouble of getting ready to welcome him, but he halted too far away to suit us. James Anderson, Company C, was wounded in the neck to-day.

18. Rained nearly all day. This evening our line was advanced nearly five hundred yards, and established on the further edge of the cornfield. The enemy seemed not to observe us and offered no resistance.

19. Sunday. During the day our line was advanced closer to the mountain, the rebels having given way. But he holds a strong position yet on the mountain. Company E went on the skirmish line at the base of the mountain. We were not to fire unless the enemy advanced, consequently we had rather an agreeable time. Late in the afternoon our artillery engaged the enemy and they exchanged compliments over the heads of us skirmishers in a very discourteous manner, many of our own shells falling nearer our skirmish line than the enemy.

20. Part of the line of skirmishers was relieved at 3 A. M., leaving sixteen of Company E still on duty. I was among this number, and I preferred this duty rather than to return to the main line. There is something fascinating about this thing of crouching behind a pile of rocks and being fired at by the foe; it is a game at which two can play, with equal chances of winning.

The artillery practice was resumed early in the forenoon, and continued at intervals during the day, both sides firing over our heads. Many of our shells fell short, and endangered our own skirmishers. In one case rather a strange thing happened: Two skirmishers of the 108th Ohio, on our left, were lying on their faces, side by side, with their feet toward our battery. A shell from one of our guns struck between them, burying itself in the earth. Neither of the men were injured, but one of them had his pants leg torn open from the foot to the waist.

At night Captain Shepherd's company came to our relief, and we joined the line, half a mile in the rear.

21. Considerable rain fell. We are in line, half a mile west of Kenesaw's base. Comparative quiet reigns. I procured the consent of Lieutenant Colonel Warren to use a log stable which stood on our right, to construct better defences in our front. We soon had the logs in position, and by ten o'clock at night we had a complete work constructed.

22. Early in the day the enemy began shelling us from the summit of Kenesaw, and he made a full day's work of it. Our batteries and sharp shooters put in their work diligently, but there was no let up to him. We can see the gunner as he rams the charge home, then comes a puff of smoke, and in two or three seconds the shots come shrieking through the air, sometimes striking in the timber in our rear, sometimes plowing up the dirt in our front, and bounding over our heads and landing a thousand feet behind us. About dinner time we were driven into our pits, leaving our dinners on the fire. We remained sheltered till our dinners were over-cooked. The boys were so mad at this, that they omitted to return thanks at their meals.

Near midnight, while Dr. Wilson was dressing the wounds of one of the men, the light of the candle he was using attracted the attention of the rebel gunner on the mountain, and a shot was fired which was well aimed. It carried off a leg apiece for Esau Rice and Albert Fields, of our regiment, who were assisting the surgeon in his duties. How shall I ever forget the shrieks of these men? The day and night have been full of terror to us all. During the night we packed up, and for a time expected to move out.

23. Our batteries and skirmishers made it lively for the enemy all day, with little reply from that side till late in the evening. Some of the left companies strengthened their works during the night. We rested unusually well.

24. This has been rather a quiet day. Some of us have not had our clothes off to sleep for many days. A little quiet and rest just now would be appreciated. The rebel guns on the mountain seem to have dissappeared.

25. We learn that yesterday was a day of fasting and prayer with the rebels. If we had known it sooner we would not have disturbed them in their devotions as we did. This statement explains their silence during the day. They have my permission to fast and pray continually. But the prayer of the wicked is an abomination.

They have been shelling us furiously again to-day. There are ten or twelve guns on a side and they fire by volleys. A man may dodge *one* shot, but when they come by the dozen it confuses him. The weather is warm and clear. At dusk we are under orders to move.

26. Sunday. At 1:30 A.M. we retired to the rear quitely, marched first in the direction of Big Shanty, then filing left, we moved toward the right of our line about four miles. Halted and spent the day. I visited the 66th O. V. I. and took dinner with Coffee, Hendrix, Parker and Doak. I am needing sleep; have been rising too early and too often of late.

27. The day dawned bright and pleasant. There is an air of sober business on the faces of our officers; coming events are casting their shadows before. Early in the morning we piled our knapsacks and surplus baggage, and made other necessary plans for an attack. Knots of staff, field and company officers can be seen in earnest consultation, and I can overhear the officers and men telling each other what they wish to have done in case the worst happens. The enemy is strongly intrenched in our front, and it gradually dawns upon us in the ranks, that we are to carry his works by assault. The troops of Thomas and McPherson are to charge at two different points—McPherson at Little Kenesaw, and Thomas a mile further south. We learn, also, that the charge is to be led by the two brigades of McCook and Mitchell.

KENESAW.

The brigade formed in line of battle on an elevation, with a ravine in our front at a distance of two hundred yards. After a halt of twenty minutes, during which time the 34th Illinois V. V. Infantry were deployed as skirmishers, we fixed bayonets and moved briskly down the slope, passed over our reserve lines, which lay in trenches near the ravine, clambered through the little rivulet at the bottom of the ravine, and began the ascent of a gentle slope, at the top of which the enemy lay waiting our approach. As we left the ravine, our line, which thus far had been moving in splendid order, began to falter by reason of the obstructions which impeded our advance. Saplings and underbrush had been cut and cross-lapped in a manner that made it impossible to keep in line, or to advance singly, with any rapidity. Those who managed to struggle through and move on, received a welcome of death from the foe, for they had now opened upon our ragged line a murderous fire. Parts of our line reached within a few feet of their works; many of our men crowded up to the works only to be shot down; a few climbed upon their works and were made prisoners. But the greater number, sheltered behind trees and rocks, began firing at the enemy. This continued some minutes—minutes that seemed ages. It now seemed plain that the plan of attack had failed, and that further effort to take the works would be madness.

An order was given to fall back, and one by one, each man caring for himself, the men retreated to the rear, leaving the dead and wounded where they fell. I fell back from one tree to another, at each of which I tried to find safety. Reaching a ditch, which had been used as a picket station, I crouched into it, and rested for a time, the bullets and shells of the enemy flying thick and noisy over my head. At length, John E. Davis, Company K, came along, wounded, and I took him toward the rear. Then coming across Cyrus Parmer, Company E, who was wounded in the leg, I gave Davis in charge of H. L. Hobart, Company D, and with Parmer on my back, I carried him some distance, then with the help of three of the others, we placed him on a blanket, and carried him to a place in the rear, where our wounded were being collected. Then returning toward the line, I assisted others to carry off William Jenkins. Later in the day a fragment of the several companies rallied into line and began the erection of works fronting the enemy, and fifty yards from the ravine I have mentioned.

Night came on, and we began to plan to bring off our wounded. Many had remained on the field till nightfall, and now returned unharmed. These had taken shelter behind logs and rocks, from which they could not escape except at the risk of being killed or wounded. Others lay uncared for and exposed to a continual fire all the afternoon. Late in the night, when we thought it possible to go onto the field with any degree of safety, a party of four, Wm. Cisco, George Carroll, Leonard Keitzleman and myself, took a blanket and proceeded cautiously forward in the direction of a point where several of our men had fallen. We halted and listened. The groans of a wounded man were heard in a left oblique direction. We spoke cautiously, and an answer came promptly. We groped our way to the sufferer, and found him to be Sergeant Henry C. Scott, of my own company. Placing him on our blanket with great difficulty, we carried him back to our works in safety. He was mortally wounded, and expressed his thankfulness for our effort to bring him off. Still later, I went again on the field with Isaac Green,

Jonathan Merica, Andrew Heller and John Wilson. We found and brought off Corporal Peter Baker. His wounds were serious, but we hoped they would not prove fatal. Similar efforts were made by the men in other companies, and in this manner nearly all our wounded were rescued. The following list of the killed or mortally wounded is very nearly accurate:

A—Everett W. Jackson, Louis H. Kennedy.

F—Lieutenant E. Crouse, Sergeant Lyman Lincoln.

C.—Titus Chamberlain, John Martin, Hiram Wilcox.

H.—John W. Carter, Freeman Dulen, Michael O'Connell, Andrew J. Rhoades, Eugene H. Palin, Elisha Stetler.

E.—Captain John Bowersock, Sergeant H. C. Scott, Jacob Hees.

K.—Corporal Ezra Allen, Stephen V. Barr, William Coppin, Hiram Hancock, Levi Romine, Joseph Wilkinson, Lemuel P. Jones, Booker R. Durnell.

G.—Sergeant Joseph Parker, Levi Griffin.

B.—Amos D. Leady.

Several who are reported missing are doubtless among the killed. Our total loss in killed, wounded and missing is one hundred and fifty-three. We are not humiliated in our failure to carry the works of the enemy; all was done that brave men could do. But for the obstructions which impeded our advance we must have succeeded. Hundreds, yea thousands of incidents occurred that could add interest to this account. Otho W. Loofborrow of Company G, fell into the hands of the enemy, but after dark he gave them the slip and came bounding into our lines. Lieutenant Colonel Warner was shot in the right arm; it will require amputation. Lieutenant McCrea was overcome with heat, and for a while was in a dangerous condition. George Nichols got cornered on the field, and did not get away till night came on. W. P. Souder, Company C, was wounded in the left leg and remained on the field till late in the afternoon, when he was carried off by his comrades.

M. Quad in the Cincinnati Enquirer speaks of this from a rebel standpoint, and says:

HOWARD'S ATTACK.

" From where Howard's men formed in columns of assault to the first Confederate works is not more than six hundred yards. The Federal troops could not be seen on account of the thickets, but they could be plainy heard, and the men behind the breast works were ready and waiting. There was a sharp artillery fire along this front for twenty minutes before the Confederate pickets were driven in, but it did not result in the loss of a single life. I talked with several Confederates who were at the front, and each one told the same story. Tons upon tons of solid shot and shell were hurled at the mountain side, but struck the trees and rocks, and resulted in nothing further than demoralizing some of the men who had not been under fire before. One who traverses the sides of Kenesaw to-day will find where the pines were split and the rocks shattered by this artillery fire, but the men down behind the works were as safe as the women of Marietta in their homes.

STRIKING THE ABATIS.

All along the front against which Howard was to advance the Confederate works were protected by abatis. An abatis is a death-trap to add to the horrors of war. In some cases it is a slashing. Trees are fallen criss-cross, the smaller branches trimmed out, and he who approaches must have the activity of a panther to wriggle through and climb over. An abatis of this sort can not be passed by a hunter left free to make his way, without a detention of from ten to fifteen minutes. What, then, must such an obstruction be to a column of assault, the men loaded down with accoutrements, and a murderous fire being poured into their faces at a range of a hundred feet? In other cases the abatis is formed of sharpened sticks and rails and limbs, one end made fast in the earth just in front of the works, the other sharpened and pointed to such an angle as would strike a man's breast. To reach the works behind, the assaulters must pass this obstruction or tear it away, and they must work under the deadly aim of the men defending the works. It was only in rare instances during the war that an abatis was carried.

Howard's column advanced with great enthusiasm, driving in the Confederate skirmishers and picket all along the front, but when they dashed at the real Confederate line they found an abatis in their front. Then, for ten minutes, war became slaughter. The bluecoats would not retreat—they could not advance.

We knew they were coming and we were ready. I had sixty rounds of cartridges, and I had them in a heap on the ground beside me. On my part of the line we had a log on the crest of the breastworks. This was raised about four inches, and our guns were thrust between the log and the earth. This not only protected our heads, but gave us a dead rest and a sure aim. One of the heads of an assaulting column struck the abatis just opposite me. Some of the men threw down their guns and began to tear at the limbs, while others opened fire. You can judge what sort of a place it was when I tell you that I fired seventeen shots as cooly as a hunter would fire at a squirrel, and I hit a man every time. There was a boy fifteen years old alongside of me with a shot gun, and I believe he killed and wounded twenty men. I was glad to see the column retreat. It looked too much like cold blooded murder to kneel there and take dead aim on a man so near that you could see the color of his eyes and hair.

BEATEN BACK.

Howard's troops were beaten back, but they only retreated to break into groups and keep up the fight from behind trees. It would have been better to have fallen back to the lines. Their fire inflicted no damage, and the Confederates were given a chance to pick off many gallant officers.

The bravest man would not have lost prestige by a speedy retreat, but the Federals stayed there. Along the Confederate breastwork is a fringe of trees. It was there that day. The Federals did not get between this fringe and the works except in a few instances. Their fire, therefore, must have been shooting at random in the direction of the Confederates. In nine cases out of ten the Confederates could not see their target, but fired into the woods. On a front of eighty rods, by about the same depth, I saw tens of thousands of scars of that conflict. Trees were so riddled by musket balls that, where still living, they present the strangest and most grotesque appearance. One tree, about the size of a man's body, was girdled excepting a space three inches in width. Others, struck by shot or shell at a point six feet above the ground, were split open to the first limb, perhaps twenty feet above the ground. There is one standing there and growing thriftily, through which a solid shot passed and left a hole in which a man may thrust his arm until his hand appears on the other side of the tree. Logan might have deemed it bravery to hold men in position when they were losing ten to one, but it was not. No man is so reckless that he does not demand a fair show for his life. The Federals loaded and fired and held their lines, but to advance further was impossible. When seven out of every ten officers in the various commands had fallen, and some of the regiments had lost a third of their number, the order was given to fall back out of range of the musketry, and to take advantage of the lay of the ground to hold much of the ground gained.

PALMER'S ATTACK.

Palmer was further down the line opposite Hardee's Corps. Under cover of the woods he quietly massed for the assault, and when the signal came his men made a gallant rush. Hardee, too, had a strong skirmish line in his front, and before this was driven in, the men behind the breastworks were prepared for the storm. The abatis was not so strong in front of Hardee, but it was strong enough to stop the advance. A winrow of small trees not larger than a man's leg, cut so that the tops fall outward, will check and hold a column of assault until it is decimated. The trees on this front were smaller, and in some places the Federals crept through them and were killed within fifty feet of the Confederate muskets.

In front of two Companies of Wright's Brigade, of Chetham's Division, and not over two hundred feet away, was a knoll perhaps a hundred feet wide on the crest. This knoll was mostly clear of trees, and the Federals, in surging from right to left and back, were in plain view as they crossed it. The slaughter right there was something awful. Seventy or eighty muskets and a piece of artillery using grape had a dead fire on the knoll, and after the repulse, some of the Confederates crept forward and were horrified at the sight. The dead were so thick that they lay piled upon each other, and streams of blood could be traced for ten feet. Men had been hit by three or four bullets, and there was hardly a body which did not present a ghastly sight. In 1869 a Confederate ex-soldier from Kentucky found imbedded in the bark of a tree two hundred feet behind this knoll a Federal soldier's belt plate. The explosion of a shell must have torn him to fragments and sent that plate to the spot where it was found.

REPULSE.

The longer Palmer remained, the hotter grew the fire, and, like Logan and Howard, he at length sounded the retreat. He had done all that a commander could do, and soldiers never stood up to their work with more pluck, but it was asking them to accomplish the impossible. Bullets and shot and shell followed the retreating lines far into the woods, and scores of men were killed after having passed through the dangers of the actual assault without a scratch."

28. We are busy at work on our defences. The enemy continue to shell us, and the fight between the pickets rages furiously. John H. Johnson and I went to Brigade Headquarters and got some krout for Chatfield, and some whisky for the company. Late this evening a truce was agreed upon, and our dead were properly buried. The stench of the battlefield begins to be very offensive.

The body of Captain Bowersock was brought off and buried in the rear of his company. Two solid shot were placed in the grave. Sergeant Scott died to-day, and was buried in a coffin at Big Shanty, by Lieutenant Swisher.

29. Another truce prevailed to-day from 9 A. M. to 1 P. M., and our men finished burying our dead comrades. Soon as the truce ended, the combatants resumed the work of death. Went back to the place from which we moved on Monday, and assisted Lieutenant McCrea prepare a "Muster Roll" for his company. Made an inventory of the personal effects of Captain Bowersock.

30. A brisk fight took place before daylight in our front and to our left. It lasted about fifteen minutes, resulting in the killing of one man of the 98th O. V. I. The woods in the vicinity of our line was illuminated by the light of exploding shells. Heavy skirmish firing goes on continually between the opposing lines. Trees in our front have been chipped by bullets in a manner that is astonishing.

JULY, 1864.

1. We still confront the rebels at Kenesaw, and the rebels still confront us. We had another attack at midnight last night, resulting in a heavy loss of ammunition and some swearing. A soldier hates to have his rest broken.

3. Sunday. We find no enemy in our front this morning. Kenesaw is no longer his, but ours. He slid out last night, and we will soon be in pursuit. After breakfast we went forward and spent some time on the battle field of the 27th inst. It presented evidences of a great struggle. At 8 A. M. we started in pursuit of Johnson's army, in the direction of Marietta, reaching that place in two hours, having moved at a very slow rate. Remained nearthe town till noon, and then proceeding four miles further, we seem to be nearing the rebel rear. Many rebel deserters have come into our lines to-day. Our troops are in good spirits. Camped in a thick woods. Marietta is the county seat of Cobb county, and is twenty miles from Atlanta.

4. We are celebrating the birthday of the Nation by firing an occasional salute on the works of the foe in our front. Company E was on the skirmish line all day, and it was very interesting. A year ago we were at Shelbyville, Tenn., and on that day Vicksburg was taken by General Grant. Where will we be July 4th, 1865.

5. The enemy vacated his position last night and we were in full pursuit before seven o'clock. We pressed his rear all day and the rattle of musketry and roar of artillery was continuous. Many prisoners and deserters fell into our hands. The 113th occupied a line of incomplete works which the 121st had vacated. John Bricker, Company K, was killed this evening. We are nearing the Chattahoochee river and our camp is a short distance from Vining, eleven miles from Atlanta.

10. Sunday. We have been in front of the rebels since the 5th, but nothing of especial moment has taken place. Johnson's army fell back across the Chattahoochee last night, destroying the bridge after he crossed. We seem to be in undisputed possession of this side of the river. In company with Bailey, Company K, Low, Company B, and J. O. Kite, Company E, I made a tour of inspection of the works just vacated by the rebels. It is very strange that they build such strong works and then vacate them without an effort to resist our approach.

12. Company E relieved the pickets of the 34th Illinois Vol-

unteers, east of the C. & A. railroad, and in the evening the 94th O.
V. I. took our places. We get a mail.

17. Sunday. A pontoon bridge is being completed across the
Chattahoochee this morning. The river is one hundred and fifty
yards wide at this point. About noon we crossed to the south side,
advanced some distance from the river, driving the rebel skirmishers
before us. Later in the evening we advanced a mile, by the right of
companies to the front. We threw up a line of works. This is my
wife's birthday; we have been married three years, and she is
twenty-one.

18. Part of the brigade went to the front, but at noon returned
without any particular adventure. During the afternoon we again
went to the front, threw up some works and spent the night.

19. We held our position till evening, and moved out to Nancy's
Creek, (Peachtree.) About sunset the Third Brigade became engaged, and for a time we were exposed to the enemy's fire. Levi
Thomas, Company G, and John Weber, Company A, were killed, and
two other men of the 113th were wounded. Companies I, E and K
carried the logs of an old house, standing near the stream, and constructed a bridge, finishing it at midnight. While we were thus
engaged, my attention was attracted to a body floating in the stream.
I dragged it out, and beheld the body of a beardless youth, who had
been shot through the body, and had fallen into the creek unobserved
by his comrades. No one will ever tell that boy's mother the story
of her son's death.

20. At three o'clock this morning we crossed the stream and threw
up a line of rifle pits in a cornfield, where we remained all day and
all night.

21. The rebels left our front last night, and before breakfast the
113th moved to the front to reconnoiter. At the distance of a mile
we began to erect works, but left them unfinished, and returned to
our rifle pits in the cornfield. After dinner, the regiment again went
out and picketed to the southeast. Companies D, I, K, G and B,
went on the outposts, the other five companies were in reserve.
There has been hard fighting on our left, but we know little of the
particulars.

22. At 10 A. M. the regiment returned to its former position in the
cornfield, and at noon the whole brigade moved with the division in
the direction of Atlanta, the rebels having again fallen back. The
division halted on several hills within four miles of Atlanta. Here

we fortified and sent out a skirmish line. We are confronting the enemy again.

23. Spent the day fortifying. Our batteries are shelling the city of Atlanta.

24. Sunday. Am not well. I am in good spirits, however, and if I had swallowed Dr. Wilson's prescription instead of putting it in my vest pocket, I might be in better health.

26. Was on picket to-day, the line being commanded by Captain Otway Watson. We had an agreeable time, and were exposed to very little danger.

28. The brigade made a reconnoisance to the southwest, returning late at night. Spent the night a mile from our works. The men are much scattered, and but few are with their companies at the halt. There has been some hard fighting to-day, of which we learn no particulars.

29. Instead of returning to our own works, we occupied a partially completed line which had been constructed by other troops. This is near the place where the battle raged yesterday, and a number of us visited the field during the day. The dead of both sides remain unburied, and the scene presents some pictures that are shocking, even to a soldier.

30. At noon our brigade moved to the right and threw up a line of works a mile from our position of last night. The weather is oppressively warm.

31. Our brigade scouted several miles in the direction of the left of the enemy, and then returned to our position of the morning in a tremendous rain. We had left our baggage in our line, and as a consequence we got very wet, and we remained wet all night.

AUGUST, 1864.

1. Quiet reigns to-day. The rebel lines at this point are not as close to ours as usual. This may explain why it is so quiet. My wife's letter of June 27th is at hand, containing $5. It has been a long time coming.

2. Companies H, E, K, G, and B, went on the skirmish line in front of our brigade, and with the troops of the 15th A. C. in front of us. This is a strange position indeed. The woods are a dense mass of brush.

4. Yesterday was a quiet day with no incident or movement worth recording. This morning, long before day, orders were given to be ready to move, but we spent the forenoon resting in line. After dinner the whole division moved to the right three miles, leaving knapsacks and baggage behind. Here we fortified in a thick woods. This day was set apart by the President as a day of fasting and prayer, but things hereabouts went on after the usual plan, eating all we had and praying for more.

5. During the forenoon we advanced a mile further south, halted and constructed a line of works under a heavy artillery fire. Half the men returned and brought up our knapsacks. Two men were wounded this evening. Remained in our works during the night.

6. The command constructed and occupied another line of defense two hundred yards in advance. The enemy's artillery have range of us and his shelling has annoyed us sorely. Johnson, Company I, had a leg shot off by a shell, and a man in Company B was wounded. It has been a day of great peril.

7. Sunday. Quiet remained at the front till three in the afternoon, when it was ascertained that the enemy in our front had given way. We moved our line to the front at once, driving in or capturing the pickets who made a strong effort to hold us in check. Our line halted at their vacated picket line, and while the foe raked us with shot and shell we threw up rifle-pits and sheltered ourselves behind them. While we advanced across a clear field to take up a position here, the enemy had plain view of our line and from a battery to our left front he sent in the solid shot in a manner that made my hair stand on end. Captain Jones, who commanded the 113th at the time, shouted: "Steady, men, guide right—steady, men, guide right," and the men kept their places like grains of corn on the cob. While we were busy at our defenses, Sergeant Cyrus T. Ward, Company E, was wounded in the hip. A few minutes later a shell carred off the head of Anthony Shimmel of the same company. By desperately hard work we had our defenses in good shape when night came on. The enemy seems to know that he has a good range of our works, and he keeps reminding us of it every few minutes. After dark, P. T. Bowman and I carried the body of Shimmel to the rear, dug a grave and gave it burial. On a tree near the grave we cut his name, company, and regiment. Shimmel was a German and a brave soldier.

8. An occasional shot is given and received from either side by the artillery. The skirmishers seem to be earning their $13 a month, judging by their continuous firing.

Late in the evening the regimental bugler, Uriah A. McComb was shot and killed while putting up a tent for regimental headquarters. Judson Swisher caught him as he fell and ministered to him in his dying moments.

9. The smell from a dead horse in front of us is almost as unbearable as the enemy's artillery. Henry S. Gingery, Company B, was badly wounded this afternoon. Major Sullivant is now sick and in the rear, leaving the regiment under command of Captain Jones.

10. It has been raining for several days past. We work wet, eat wet, and sleep wet. Found time to-day to write a letter or two. The enemy's guns annoy us as usual, and the thing is getting a little old.

11. The day is warm and clear. Several men were wounded on the skirmish line to-day, among them Jacob Huben, Company K, who gets a bad shot in the leg.

12. Before day we moved back to the line of works from which we moved Sunday. Remained here till sunup, when we moved a mile to the right, relieving troops of the 23d A. C. We are now behind strong works and in a good shade. The men complain of short rations.

14. Sunday. This is called Willis' Mills, but why it is so named I cannot tell. The Chaplain of the 98th O. V. I. preached to the brigade to-day. An occasional bullet whizzed over the audience, suggesting that carnal and spiritual things occupy disputed ground. Companies A, K and G are in front of the brigade, skirmishing. Andrew Heller, Company E, died in Division hospital yesterday.

15. The line in our front is very quiet. The 78th Illinois Volunteers hold the skirmish line. They are first-class soldiers. We have known them a long while. Two deserters came into our lines. Two years ago to-day I enlisted. Am glad of it now. I might have waited and joined a regiment composed of ordinary men. The officers and men of the 113th are composed of superior material.

18. Our line is very quiet, if I except the firing by the pickets of both lines. We can hear heavy fighting toward Atlanta, but learn no particulars.

19. Companies C, D, E and H occupy the skirmish line. The First and Third Brigades moved out of the line, leaving the Second to occupy the space which has been held by the entire division.

One of Company B was wounded. In the evening we can hear the music of the enemy's bands very plainly.

21. Mike Huddleston and I went to the rear to-day and gathered elderberries. On our return we saw six rebel deserters coming in under guard. We have no mail for a day or two, and we learn of a raid in our rear near Dalton. John Craig foraged some corn to-day. My messmate, John Ganson, has the colic. That is a bad thing to sleep with.

25. Lieutenant McCrea is not well, and has been back at the tent of Quartermaster Swisher. To-day I went to see him, and assisted him with some accounts pertaining to the company. We made a Clothing Receipt Roll for July and August. Letters from Ohio reach us in five days from their date.

26. For a day or two nothing has happened on this part of the line out of the usual course of daily duty. A strong picket line is maintained close to the enemy's pickets. The two lines often agree not to fire on each other during the day and night; but the next day a new detail comes on, and hostilities again open. An order to move has been issued, and we are harnessed and ready.

27. At 3:30 A. M. we retired from the line at Willis' Mills, and, moving out two miles, halted in an orchard near a farm house and cotton mill. Several good looking women, and a negro with six toes attracted our attention. Late in the evening a light defense was thrown up in our front. The rebels exchanged a few shots with our rear.

28. Sunday. The division moved at the dawn of day, and for several miles we marched briskly. Halted at 7 A. M., stacked arms and rested. At 9 A. M. we moved southward, passed the 4th A. C., and again halted. The 121st was deployed and drove the rebels from a woody hill on our left flank. At 2:30 P. M. we reached the railroad leading westerly from Atlanta. Companies K, G, H and E stood picket in front of the brigade. We had no dinner.

29. The division did not move. We understand this movement to be to flank the enemy out of Atlanta. We know nothing of the details of the plan, but are doing our share in the movement with the utmost confidence of its success. What transpires within a day or two from this will make good reading for our descendants. The companies of the 113th which went on picket yesterday were relieved at 5:30 P. M. We have had plenty of meat and sweet potatoes, but it came near getting us into trouble. We ate two big suppers and enjoyed a splendid spell of nightmare.

30. *Reveille* sounded early. At seven we marched, going south by

southeast. At 11 A. M. we halted for dinner. Company E was placed on the left of the moving column as flankers. The line moved on four miles further, where it halted for the night. We traveled fourteen miles to-day, mostly southeasterly. Many of the men fell out during the afternoon, and reached the regiment long after we stacked arms. A mail was distributed.

31. Before daylight orders came to be ready to move at once. We did not march, but remained halted till noon, during which time our artillery shelled a wagon train of the enemy in the distance. Our men are living high on the products of the land. Chickens, hogs, cattle, sheep, geese, turkeys, corn, flour, meal, potatoes and everything eatable is brought in by the quantity. Soldiers have consciences, but they make very little use of them.

At 11:30 A. M. our brigade *left faced*, and moving left in front, reached a sorghum field at the distance of a mile. Rested an hour. Moved again in an easterly direction, and after going three miles, we halted near a house, at which General Baird had his headquarters. A guard was on duty vainly trying to prevent the soldiers from pillaging the premises. It was no use. They had everything their own way. A lady was exchanging greenbacks for Confederate money, giving six dollars in greenbacks for fifteen dollars of the worthless promises of the waning Confederacy. I felt sorry for her and for myself. I wished that I had my knapsack full of cheap money, and that she had an inexhaustible supply of greenbacks. I would have stayed with her.

Half a mile beyond this our brigade filed left, and formed a line running nearly north and south.

Bolt, Cisco and Craig, who were after beef when the regiment moved at noon, now came up, bringing no beef, but plenty sweet potatoes which they foraged on the way. They reported that they had received the beef but had abandoned it. Then a majority of the company resolved itself into a cursing committee, and the sulphur was ignited. Cisco stood to the front, while Bolt and Craig were held in reserve. The attacking party was repulsed.

At 8 P. M. Captain Jones, the regimental commander, came along the line and told us we would remain here and throw up works. A big fire was built in our rear, and by its light we cut trees and put the logs in position for our protection. We slept at eleven at night. Our column is nearing the Macon & Western railroad, and we are now more than twenty miles from Atlanta. We have been in close proximity to the enemy at times during this afternoon, but we have exchanged only an occasional shot with him.

BATTLE OF JONESBORO, GEORGIA.

SEPTEMBER, 1864.

1. At 11 A. M. our forces moved out from the works we had occupied last night, and heading southward, moved slowly in the direction of Jonesboro. At 2:30 P. M. our column passed that of the 17th A. C., and having crossed a small creek, we filed left from the road on which we had been marching, and were moving easterly, when a shot from a battery a thousand yards southeast of us, revealed to us the position of the enemy's line. The battery was in the edge of the woods, concealed from our view. The first shot was succeeded by others in quick succession, and our column, being in an open field, and in plain view, made an attractive mark. Their first shots passed above our heads, but others that followed struck the earth in front of us, or bursted dangerously near.

The 113th formed in line facing the battery, and then left faced and moved to the northeast in an effort to get beyond the range of their fire. We were still in plain view of the rebels' guns, and he was dropping his shells along our line in a fatal manner. One struck in Company I, killing George Kelsey and wounding others. Some of our men sought shelter in a brushy swamp on our left, and those who remained obeyed an order of Captain Jones, to lie down in a gully, which had been washed out by high waters. By this time our artillery was in position, and a few well directed shots from them silenced the rebel guns, and permitted us to rally and move on.

We ascended a hill to a position near a hewed log house, where we halted and stacked arms. Here the brigade was sheltered by a woods in our front. The staffs of the division and brigade commanders reconnoitered the ground in our front, and laid plans for the immediate future. After more than an hour, we took arms and marched left in front into a cornfield, in the direction of the lines of the enemy. Here the command, "by company into line," brought us into line of battle, and descending the slope we reached a ravine running from right to left, and situated more than three hundred yards from the enemy's line. Here a halt was ordered. Our position was a good one, being hidden from our foes by an intervening hill, covered with corn.

Three companies of the 98th O. V. I., commanded by Captain Roatch, went forward to skirmish, and the other companies of that regiment constructed rifle pits in front of us, near the crest of the hill. The rear ranks of the 121st Ohio, and 34th Illinois, constructed rifle pits in our rear, on the slope we had descended. While this work went on, the 113th rested in line at the bottom of the ravine. When these pits were completed, an attacking column was formed.

All being in readiness, the signal was given, and the attacking column dashed forward, crowding the road to victory as to a feast of fat things; at the same time the second line moved from the ravine and dropped into the line of rifle-pits before mentioned. In a moment more a deafening shout at the rebel line told the story of triumph, and the second line moved at a double quick to the support of the first. As the second line moved up it was met by a body of rebel prisoners who were being double quicked to our rear for safe keeping. We were now at the rebel works. Here lay the cast off equipments and the arms of many prisoners, and here stood the guns of Govan's Battery which had *very* recently changed owners. It was the same one that had terrorized us early in the afternoon, but now, that the muzzles were pointed the opposite directon, it looked harmless. Here lay the dead and the dying, the one having crossed the great pontoon, the other calling for mercy from that unfailing source opened on Mount Calvary. To say that he was not heard would be to limit God's power to save.

As the 113th struck the works of the enemy a rebel field officer confronted Captain Jones and said: "Where shall I go?" Seizing him by the collar of his coat, and giving him a vigorous jerk, Captain Jones said, "go to the rear, and that —— quick."

It was now five o'clock; the enemy had either fallen back or had surrendered when the assault was made. The works of the foe were strong and properly constructed, but no *abatis* or other materials impeded our approach, consequently our men dashed into their very pits before halting to fire a shot.

Quickly re-forming our line, we occupied a position nearly a quarter of a mile to the rear of the works we had taken. We again shifted to the southeast a short distance, and finally, crossing a hollow, ascended to the crest of a hill, and relieved the 121st Ohio, which was confronting a fragment of a brigade of rebels in a cornfield. Having no defenses for our protection, we kept partly hid behind the crest of the hill for a time. We would assume a crouching position while loading our guns, then rising to our feet we would fire, and then drop to the ground again. Having procured tools, we began digging pits in the usual manner for protection, a part of the line keeping up the fire. It was very dark, long before we began our works, and our aim was guided by the flash of the guns of the enemy, and his aim was guided by ours in like manner.

The firing grew less and less active as the night lengthened, and finally only an occasional flash could be seen in our front. Toward midnight a call was made for a man from each company to stand as *videts* at some distance in front of the line, the object being to watch the movements of the rebels and prevent a surprise. I volunteered, and took my position at a large tree nearly a hundred feet in front of our line. A naughty rebel found out my hiding place, and wasted several shots at me. He grew tired, and finally departed without saying good night.

My attention was attracted by the groans of a wounded man some distance from me. I groped my way toward where he lay, listened, and again moved cautiously forward. In this way, I at length found the unfortunate sufferer. His name was Albert Fonnest, of Company C, 78th Illinois. He was wounded through the body below the ribs, and his life blood was fast flowing away. I went back to our line, reported the fact to Captain Shepherd, of the 113th, and he sent a messenger to the 78th, to inform the man's comrades of his dying condition. I returned to my post at the tree. Half an hour later, four men of the 78th Illinois came out near me, looking for their wounded comrade. I led them forward to the place where he lay, spoke to him, shook him, felt his pulse, and found that he was dead. They carried him off the field, and I returned to my company, having been relieved by James O. Kite. I lay down and slept the sweet sleep which is the fruit of hours of toil and exposure. It seemed that more had transpired since noon than I would ever be able to tell.

2. Early this morning we ascertained that no enemy confronted us, and the extent of our victory of yesterday began to be made known. We find that we have possession of the Atlanta & Macon railroad, and our enemies are in full retreat.

The campaign began on the second of May, and is now ended. Four months of marching, toiling and fighting. Hardly a day in all that time that our ears have not heard the cannon's roar or the crack of musketry.

The town of Jonesboro is only a short distance—half a mile from our line, and in company with Ganson and Kite, I made a trip of inspection to the village. Upon our return we found the command ready to move. The Second Division marched to the suburbs of town and halted. While we rested, General Jeff. C. Davis and staff rode up. The General was cheered by his men. He spoke a few words, expressing his admiration of our conduct yesterday. At noon we crossed the railroad and took dinner. Later in the day we erected a line of works near the town and running north and south. Our troops are at work destroying the railroad, and after dark the course of the track can be traced by the fires burning the ties and heating the rails.

3. A tremendous rain washed us out at daylight, making *reveille* unnecessary. At 10 A. M. the brigade began to tear up and destroy the railroad. At noon we returned to our works. Late in the evening we resumed the work of destruction, but after a few minutes we were ordered to quit. I was much pleased at this, for destroying railroad track is too much like work to suit me. We can hear heavy fighting in the direction of Lovejoy Station.

In the evening Captain Watson read to the 113th the following orders:

HEADQUARTERS MILITARY DIVISION OF THE MISSISSIPPI,
IN THE FIELD NEAR LOVEJOY STATION, GA., *September* 3. 1864.
SPECIAL FIELD ORDERS,
No. 2.

The General commanding announces with great pleasure that he has official information that our troops under Major General Slocum, occupied Atlanta yesterday at eleven o'clock A. M., the enemy having evacuated the night before, destroying vast magazines and stores, and blowing up, among other things, eighty car loads of ammunition, which accounts for the sound heard by us on the night of the first instant. Our present task is, therefore, well done. and all work of destruction on the railroad will cease.

By order of
MAJOR GENERAL W. T. SHERMAN,
[OFFICIAL.]   L. M. DAYTON, *Aide-de-Camp*.
T. WISEMAN, *Captain and A. A. G.*

HEADQUARTERS 2d DIVISION, 14th ARMY CORPS,
JONESBORO, GA., *September* 3. 1864.

The General commanding takes great satisfaction in transmitting the above order to his command, and avails himself of the opportunity of expressing his admiration of the conduct of his Division on the 1st instant, in the glorious and successful charge on the enemy's works. The General is proud of his command, and congratulates officers, non-commissioned officers and privates upon the near ending of a long, arduous and gloriously successful campaign.

By order of

BRIGADIER GENERAL JAS. D. MORGAN.

[OFFICIAL.]   T. WISEMAN, *Captain and A. A. G.*

JAS. S. WILSON, *Captain and A. A. G.*

These orders with their facts and congratulations fall pleasantly upon the ears of all the troops, and I predict that the stories of the campaign will be told, and these orders will be read by the men of this army to their descendants for generations.

4. Sunday. We are holding ourselves in readiness to move. John Ganson and I went to Jonesboro and witnessed the unloading of several hundred wounded rebels of Stevenson's Division. These men had been wounded in a charge on the 15th A. C. on the 31st ult. Many of them had lost an arm or a leg, and I saw one who had both legs off close to the body. Nearly all of them suffered without complaint, and were evidently a different class of soldiers from those we have been picking up as deserters, of late. We talked with one of them, Captain Rogers, 34th Georgia. He was wounded in the bowels, but said he hoped to recover and be able to again enter the service. He said that they *must* succeed, it could not be otherwise. He had entered the service with a company of one hundred and twenty-five men, and since then a number of recruits had been added, but now Captain Rogers and three others are all that are left. His home was at Trenton, eighteen miles from Chattanooga.

6. We remained camped during the day yesterday. The men improved the occasion to wash their clothing, and write letters to their friends in Ohio, telling of the fall of Atlanta, and of the noble part each man had taken in bringing it about.

We expected to move at daylight, but at 7 A. M. we fell in, changed front to rear, and re-pitched our camp on the same site.

At noon the call of " strike tents " sounded, and the whole division was soon moving toward Atlanta. At the end of two hours, marching in a zigzag manner, we halted and stacked arms near the hewed log house where we formed in line to charge on the 1st instant. Here I made a map of the country, and the position of the lines of the opposing forces. Near this house are the graves of a number of the 98th O. V. I. who were killed on Thursday last. Among these is the grave of Adjutant John H. Reeves, with whom I had some acquaintance. The 98th lost about forty in killed and wounded. Their men built a rude fence around the graves of their dead comrades in the evening. A heavy rain fell this afternoon. The rebels dashed into Jonesboro after we retired, and I learn that several hundred of them were made prisoners.

7. At 7 A. M. we resumed the march toward Atlanta. Reaching the Jonesboro & Atlanta road, we halted while other parts of the column took the advance. After a march of ten miles we camped at Rough and Ready, a small village on the railroad, eleven miles from Atlanta. Had a mail distributed to us, the second mail since we lay at Willis' Mills. Spent the night quietly.

8. We had an early breakfast, but did not move till eleven o'clock. Moved out to the road, halted two hours, and then moved in the direction of Atlanta, leaving the East Point railroad to our left. When within three miles of Atlanta a halt was ordered, and the brigade formed in close column, fronting toward the railroad. General James D. Morgan, our division commander, then mounted a stump in our midst, secured our attention, and read special congratulatory orders from General Grant and President Lincoln, touching the taking of Atlanta. As the General concluded reading, he remarked that we should never cheer ourselves, and that he was opposed to noise except when it was made in order. He then proposed three cheers for our *cause*, three for General Sherman, and three for "the old warhorse, General George H. Thomas."

When General Morgan had finished and left the stump, Colonel John G. Mitchell, commanding the Second Brigade, proposed three cheers for our old and our new division commanders, meaning Generals Davis and Morgan.

We again took arms, marched three-fourths of a mile, filed left, and went into camp near the Macon & Western railroad, and near a suburb of the city of Atlanta, called Whitehall.

Many of our men who have been wounded during the campaign just ended, joined us this evening in camp. Lieutenant George H. Lippincott, Company K, and Sergeant Stratton, Company E, are of this number. They are looking smooth and glossy, and have evidently enjoyed their vacation. The Sergeant Major reports the casualties of the campaign, from May 2d to September 2d, 1864, as follows: Commissioned officers killed, 4; commissioned officers wounded, 7; enlisted men killed, 31; enlisted men wounded, 132;

enlisted men missing, 7; total, 181. This is more than twenty-nine per cent. of the whole number who started with the regiment from Rossville. The per cent. of killed of the officers is greater than among the men, while the per cent. of wounded is much less than of the men. All the missing are enlisted men.

The distances on the railroad from Chattanooga, along which we have campaigned for four months, are as follows:

Chattanooga, 0; Chickamauga, 8 miles; Ringgold, 21; Tunnel Hill, 29; Dalton, 36; Tilton, 45; Resaca, 52; Calhoun, 58; Adairsville, 67; Kingston, 77; Cass, 84; Cartersville, 89; Allatoona, 96; Acworth, 101; Marietta, 116; Vining, 125; Atlanta, 136.

10. The 113th went on picket duty a mile to the south of camp, leaving enough men in camp to take care of it, and some of the officers and men to work on company papers. Now that we are at the end of a long campaign, there are many papers to make out and many statements to be forwarded to the various departments of the Government. This requires much careful work. I began on a muster roll for May and June, remaining in camp for that purpose. Our supply of mail is very meagre, for it is reported that General Wheeler's cavalry is back in Tennessee raiding on our line of transportation. This is very unkind, and we may have to go up and see him about it.

11. Sunday. The 113th came in from their picket duty. The men complain of the red-tapeism of the picket line. We have been so long unused to falling in at the approach of a general officer and other regulation requirements, that we take them up again reluctantly, and sometimes swear about it.

Passes are being issued to a limited number of the men to visit the city. I am too busy just now to take my turn. Business before pleasure. A mail was received.

12. Those who visit the city find many interesting things about which to talk and write. Green and Stratton have been in the city to-day. Green says:

"We stopped at a house of two mulatto families named Badger. We find them cultivated and polite in their manners, and we received marked courtesies at their hands. The men are dentists, and stand high in their profession, use good language, and seem to be in good circumstances. We visited the site of the rolling mill which the rebels burned before leaving the city. Near this we saw five wrecked locomotives and many cars, which had been loaded with ammunition, and which had been destroyed by the enemy. Before reaching camp we stopped at the house of a Methodist preacher, where we fed on corn bread, wheat bread, sweet potatoes, and other substantial delicacies. The reverend sinner spoke his Southern sympathies freely, and was packing up to leave the city and share in the *expulsion* in conformity with the order of General Sherman.

"A great many citizens are leaving Atlanta, some going north, but the great majority going southward. They are furnished transportation by our army as far south as Rough and Ready. I noticed one fine looking young woman in an ambulance headed south, crying piteously, and I thought she did look enchanting in her tears. I concluded that there was one handsome lady in Dixie." [G.]

13. Hats, drawers and socks were issued to the regiment to-day. Trains of cars have passed loaded with citizens and household goods, destined for Rough and Ready. The men are preparing for company inspection, which comes to-morrow. A pugilistic affair took place between two men of Company K. The smaller man came out second best.

15. The nights begin to be quite cool, and a blanket is more a thing of comfort and value than heretofore. Another long train loaded with citizens and their goods left the city to-day, passing our camp, for Rough and Ready. Solomon Bradford, a one year recruit, joined Company E to-day. He is a native of Alabama, and looks to be as stout as an ox. Fred Pence, who deserted at Camp Chase two years ago, joined Company E to-day.

25. The past ten days have been remarkable for their dullness and lack of interest. Each day has had its little duties of roll calling, guard mounting, policing, scrubbing, washing, writing and eating. Company officers have been busy with rolls, statements and reports—the accumulation of months on the front line. The 113th is on picket a mile south of camp. We come on duty of this kind about once in fifteen days, which is rather light duty.

Yesterday our mess completed a new shanty. Sergeant Flowers came to see us in the evening, and we made the occasion memorable by a vocal concert. John G. Ganson, John H. Johnson and Joseph Girard have been made corporals. This may seem only a trifling thing to some, but when a man gets an appointment like this at the end of two years of service, and at the close of a long and eventful campaign, it means more than a commission in the organization of a regiment. A trifling soldier may get such a place when he enters the service, but not afterwards. The nights grow colder, and we hope to get more blankets soon.

Lieutenant Chatfield and I took a walk in the direction of Atlanta after a busy day on his papers.

27. Inspection, which was to take place yesterday, came off to-day. I had planned to go to the city, but did not go. Made discharge papers for William Huffman, Company E. Green has turned carpenter, and is working at Brigadier Headquarters.

28. Stratton and I spent the day in the city, visiting many places of interest and dining with friends of Company I, 66th O. V. V. I. Returning to camp, we find the regiment with tents struck and the whole division ready to move. Finally all returned to quarters and spent the night. We have been here twenty days, and would prefer going away to staying longer. A day or two ago Captain Jones issued to me a warrant, as follows:

TO ALL WHO SHALL SEE THESE PRESENTS, GREETING:

Know ye, *That reposing special trust and confidence in the patriotism, valor, fidelity and abilities of Corporal Francis M. McAdams, I do hereby appoint him Sergeant in Company E, of the 113th Regiment of Ohio Infantry Volunteers, in the service of the United States, to rank as such from the first day of September, one thousand eight hundred and sixty-four. He is, therefore, carefully and diligently to discharge the duty of Sergeant by doing and performing all manner of things thereunto belonging.*

And I do strictly charge and require all non-commissioned officers and soldiers under his command to be obedient to his orders as Sergeant. And he is to observe and follow such orders and directions from time to time as he shall receive from me, or the future commanding officer of the regiment, or other superior officers and non-commissioned officers set over him, according to the rules and discipline of war.

This Warrant to continue in force during the pleasure of the commanding officer of the regiment for the time being.

Given under my hand at the headquarters of the regiment at Whitehall, Ga., this twenty-sixth day of September, in the year of our Lord one thousand eight hundred and sixty-four.

TOLAND JONES,

By the Commanding Officer,   *Captain Commanding the Regiment.*
    JAMES R. LADD,
A. G. O., No. 103.   *Adjutant of the Regiment.*

29. We remain in camp, with all packed and ready for orders. At 5 P. M. a tran of box cars ran down to our camp from Atlanta. Into and upon this we climbed, and at dusk, with bands playing and colors flying, we ran back to Atlanta. An hour later we were moving northward in the direction of Chattanooga. Many of us had not been on a train for nearly two years, and the novelty of riding and sleeping on top of a box car did not wear off immediately. By the time the majority had fallen asleep a brisk rain set in, and comfortable rest was at an end. Our train had a heavy load and moved slowly. Daylight found us halted at Allatoona, forty miles from Atlanta and ninety-six miles from Chattanooga.

30. We moved on at a slow rate, and at 5 P. M. reached Chattanooga. In half an hour our train was on its way north, on the Nashville and Chattanooga railroad.

OCTOBER, 1864.

1. During last night we ran from Chattanooga northward, and this morning we awoke to find our train halted at Stevenson, Alabama, a distance of thirty-eight miles from Chattanooga.

At 11 A. M. our train switched on to the Memphis and Charleston railroad, and moved toward Huntsville, which we understand is our destination at present. We passed through a splendid country, and enjoyed the ride very much. During the day we passed Bellefonte, Larkinsville, Woodville, Paint Rock and Brownsboro, and, reaching Huntsville at 8:30 P. M., the brigade took shelter in a car house.

Huntsville, the county seat of Madison county, is a fine place and situated in a splendid country. It is distant from Stevenson fifty-eight miles, and two hundred and twelve miles from Memphis.

A rebel force under Forest appeared before the town two days ago, and demanded its surrender. General R. S. Granger, being in command, refused, and a fight ensued, resulting in the defeat of Forest. The approach of our division gave him a plea to withdraw. So, now, we are here, with no rebels to make it interesting.

2. Sunday. The division went into camp south of the city, near a large spring. At 3 P. M. we again boarded the train, and moved toward Decatur. After a run of four miles, the train stopped and remained till morning, a heavy rain falling during the night. I spent the night on an open car, on which was a piece of artillery and some corn in the husk. There was neither comfort nor sleep for me.

3. This morning our train moved ahead, and at 11 A. M. reached a point where the track was destroyed, three miles from Athens. Here the troops disembarked and marched forward to Athens, reaching that place early in the afternoon, and going into temporary camp. Athens is the county seat of Limestone county, Alabama, and a fine place, though it has suffered much by both armies.

It has rained to-day, and the air is chilly and disagreeable. I spent the night in the upper story of a frame stable, and fared well. We find seven hundred and fifty cavalry doing duty here.

4. The division marched from Athens early in the morning. Took dinner in a cornfield on the left of the road, ten miles from Athens. At 4 P. M. we reached Elk River, at Benford's Ferry, two and a half miles from the Tennessee River. The troops stripped off their clothes, tied them in bundles, and, placing the bundles on the muzzles of their guns, waded the river, which at this ford was about three and a half feet deep. It was rare sport and a grand sight, but, in the absence of a special artist, a sketch was not preserved. Four miles further on the division went into camp near a small village called Rogersville. A tremendous rain fell as we were camping, and we slept wet. Received a mail. We have marched eighteen miles.

5. We moved ahead, passing through the dirty little town of Rogersville. The roads are deep with mud, sand and water, and the men are suffering with sore feet. It is reported that several men died yesterday from over-exertion. This is hardly probable. We hear of these things, but seldom see them. Took dinner thirteen miles from Florence, and, marching six miles further, went into temporary camp near the mouth of Shoal Creek and on the right bank of the Tennessee River. I have a pair of sore feet. Built a rail bed and slept well.

6. Eight companies of the 98th O. V. I. went forward on a reconnoissance toward Florence. The First and Third Brigades are beyond Shoal Creek; the Second remains on the left bank. Companies E and K of the 113th, and two companies of the 98th, went on a foraging trip, taking two teams. They found great quantities of meat, potatoes, peaches, apples and chickens. This is a fine country, and there is plenty for man and beast.

7. Kite, Girard, Snyder and I went down to the bank of the Tennessee, at the mouth of Shoal Creek, where I wrote to my wife. Returning to camp at noon, we found the command ready to move. We reached Florence, and camped a mile east of town. We find this to

be a neat place, the county seat of Lauderdale county, Alabama. The country is well improved, and everything is more inviting than any place we have seen since we were in Middle Tennessee.

8. To-day our brigade marched through the principal streets of Florence, with music sounding and banners flying. Of course we attracted the attention of the citizens, consisting of women and negroes. Some of the women are good looking, but the greater number are of the razor-blade or elm-peeler pattern, long as rails and sour looking. I went with Captains Orr and Swisher to Foundry Mills, four miles north of Florence, taking five wagons with us loaded with corn to be ground into meal. Took supper with a Mr. Sport, an employe of the Mills. Swisher and I spent the night with the family named Gresham.

9. Sunday. Captain Swisher and I arose very early, and, leaving the house without disturbing the family, we rode back to camp, leaving the teams and a squad of men at the Mills to finish grinding the corn. After our return to camp, we took thirteen teams into the country and brought in a full supply of corn. Late in the evening I returned to Foundry Mills, and brought in the men and teams we had left there, reaching camp late in the night. There was a frost this morning, the first of the season.

10. The division moved early toward Athens, on the same road by which we reached Florence last week. Took dinner fourteen miles from Florence. The roads are good and the marching very agreeable. Reached Cox's Creek, camped and drew rations. Marched about twenty miles. Surgeon T. B. Williams has my thanks for the use of his mare to-day. Riding is preferable to walking with sore feet.

11. Started early. At 8 A. M., while the command halted, the 113th laid plans for holding an election in the evening if opportunity offered. Captains Watson, Hamilton and Shepherd were elected as judges, and the requisite clerks were appointed. Our plans miscarried, as our division commander seemed not to be in sympathy with the soldier suffrage idea. One of these days James D. Morgan will want an Ohio soldier to dip his bayonet in melted lava and cool his parched tongue. Then the Buckeye saint will refer him to the act of this date, and walk off with a canteen full of ice water.

Taking our dinner on the right bank of Elk River, we again waded the stream, and, marching on, reached a point within six miles of Athens, where we camped. Companies K and E went on picket. A hog, which was known to be disloyal, was made to take the oath, and fresh pork was a part of our suppers.

12. Reached Athens and camped east of the town at noon. Received a mail. We are waiting for a train by which we are to move on toward Stevenson.

13. Trains ran up from the east to-day, and, embarking, we moved towards Huntsville, reaching that place after dark. One car of our train ran off the track, causing some delay. This is my twenty-sixth birthday.

14. We came into Stevenson at 1:30 A. M., reached Bridgeport and crossed the Tennessee at daylight, and at noon arrived at Chattanooga. Last night was cold, and our position on top of a car was very uncomfortable.

Mitchell's Brigade camped east of town. Assisted Captain Swisher to issue wood and forage.

15. Shifted camp to a site near Fort Wood. A supply of clothing was issued to the men. These are much needed.

16. Sunday. At 9 A. M. the brigade marched to the depot, expecting to go south, but, after an hour waiting for transportation, it returned to its position near Fort Wood. At 11 P. M. the regiment drew rations for two days, and we expect to be off to-morrow.

17. We remain camped. New recruits, with shiny watch chains, glistening boots, huge knapsacks, paper collars, and with plenty of bounty money, are in and about Chattanooga in great numbers. A change will soon come over the spirit of their dreams. This is an unfavorable climate for paper collars and fantastic display.

18. The division left Chattanooga at 7 A. M., and, reaching Lee & Gordon's Mills, twelve miles south of Chattanooga, on Chickamauga Creek, camped for the night.

19. Our column moved early, marched fifteen miles southward, and halted for the night at La Fayette, Walker county, Georgia, where we camped. We have levied tribute on some country produce during the day. Hyatt, one of the men of the train, had captured a rebellious rooster, and we spent a good part of the night in getting him ready for supper. Mess No. 1 had sweet potatoes and a rabbit for supper. We are in the dark as to the object of this trip. This does not cause us to lose sleep.

20. Marched in a southeasterly course till noon; then, leaving the Summerville road on which we had been moving, we took a more westerly course, entered Broomtown Valley, crossed Chatooga Creek, and camped. We have traveled sixteen miles.

21. Our column reached Alpine at noon, crossed the State line into

Cherokee county, Alabama, and camped at a small creek, having marched twenty miles. We are living well and see no armed rebels. The surface of the country is rough.

22. Moved ahead till noon, when we halted at Gaylesville, finding one or more corps of our army in camp. Our brigade established headquarters at the house of a Mrs. Bowling, who is sick.

23. Sunday. Remained camped. Organized foraging parties are scouring in all directions for supplies. The unorganized man is at the same business, and seems to be the most successful. A couple of lads, who had captured a yoke of oxen and a buggy, were riding through camp with their fantastic outfit. The weather is clear and cool.

25. Wrote a letter to Lieutenant Colonel Warner. Meal was issued to us to-day, and, procuring an oven of the people at the house near which we are camped, we baked some bread. If the rebels can live and fight on corn dodger all the time, we ought to do so some of the time, just for variety.

27. The feed question becomes one of importance. Our foragers have had but very little success of late, and we are altogether short of supplies. An independent gang has gone out, assuring us they would have something to eat or stay out a week. They will get it.

28. Marched at 2 P. M., passing through Gaylesville, and at the end of seven miles went into camp.

29. Moved at daylight, marching eighteen miles, reaching Rome at 3 P. M. Here we get a mail, the first since the 17th inst. We are to rest here a day or two.

NOVEMBER, 1864.

1. Left Rome early this morning, and at 2 P. M. reached Kingston, having marched fifteen miles. We are expecting to be paid off soon. So be it.

The brigade headquarters are at the house of Mrs. Hall, who has two attractive daughters.

2. The weather is wet, windy and cool. Two trains pass south, loaded with artillery. We are fifty-nine miles from Atlanta and seventy-seven from Chattanooga.

3. Major Harris, Paymaster, paid off some of the troops of our division. We received pay for eight months, amounting in my case to $124. This makes $338.50 I have received since I enlisted.

4. All day the men are going about adjusting accounts and paying off old debts. A soldier is proverbially honest, and always pays his debts when he has the money; when he has no funds he pays in promises or gives his note. He is noted for his *borrowing* proclivities, but he seldom steals. I have known him to borrow the spoons of a steamboat on which he was taking a free ride, and sometimes he borrows the knives and forks when he dines with a citizen. He is very forgetful; he *always* forgets to return what he borrows. There are now in the 113th a number of coffee mills and coffee pots, Dutch ovens, iron wedges, looking glasses, hand saws, tin buckets, and other articles of every day use, that have been borrowed of the natives, and which the borrowers have forgotten to return. When we were packed ready to march from Tyner last March, my mess felt sad to be compelled to leave a Dutch oven and an iron wedge, which we could not carry. But before we moved out a rusty old citizen who came into camp paid us $1 for the two articles, and we marched off with light hearts. If the old chap had been cautious, and waited a few minutes, he could have had them a dollar cheaper, but he failed to see it.

Our men are sending their money home to their families and friends—some by the State Agent, others by draft. A very little money can be made to go a great ways with a soldier, but I notice that in the matters of saving and squandering their wages they are about like other men.

5. A number of chuck-a-luck banks are in operation in several parts of camp, and the men are risking and losing their money at a fearful rate. Some have lost all they had, while others are ahead of the game, but in the end the dealer scoops the pile. One of the rules of my life is never to bet; another is never to say "I'll bet."

Cass, a small village a short distance from Kingston, was burned to-day.

7. Yesterday was Sunday and a day of quiet in camp. The gamblers continue to ply their profession in various ways. The unwary lad, who always sees a thing "as plain as day," has been fleeced of his wages, and is making complaints which will result in checking the gaming business. It ought to have begun sooner. To-morrow is the day of the Presidential election. We intend to vote.

8. The division left Kingston at 6 A. M., reaching Cartersville at 2 P. M. and going into camp. During a halt on the way, the 113th appointed Captains J. K. Hamilton, Otway, Watson and George Mc-

Crea judges of election, and Lieutenant C. P. Garman and J. C. Doty clerks, and determined to have the vote of the regiment cast at any risk. After reaching Cass the vote was cast. Total vote cast, 241. For Lincoln and Johnson, 165; for McClellan and Pendleton, 76. There were twenty-five counties represented in the regiment, and the work of making out the returns was no trifling one. It is said that the 113th cast a larger vote for McClellan than any other Ohio regiment in the division. That will make us the pets of the division commander. The Champaign county soldiers numbered thirty-eight—Republicans 31, Democrats 7. The 98th O. V. I. gave McClellan seventeen votes.

10. In the evening I started to Atlanta on a train to do some business for Captain Swisher. I arrived at my destination at midnight, and remained in the car till morning.

12. Lieutenant Ladd returned from Atlanta, bringing the *retain* papers. All baggage is being sent rearward. A train which left for the North at noon is said to be the last that will leave. We are under orders, and will move southward. Many stores and army supplies at this place are being burned.

13. Our division moved from Cartersville at 6 A. M., and, crossing the river on a high bridge, marched half a mile and stacked arms. We then began work destroying the railroad, making a full day's work of it, and reaching from the place of beginning to Allatoona, a distance of nearly six miles. We then marched forward to Acworth, five miles further, and camped.

14. Leaving Acworth, we moved southward, passing Big Shanty during the forenoon. Captains McCrea and Swisher and Lieutenant Lippincott visited the grave of Sergeant Scott and others, who are of our command buried at Big Shanty. Peculiarly painful feelings took possession of our hearts as we marched past the graves of our comrades and as we passed the many lines of defenses which played so important a part in the summer's campaign. We marched twenty-one miles to-day.

15. The column moved at six o'clock, crossing the Chattahoochee at 8 A. M. At 3 P. M. we camped nearly two miles in an easterly direction from Atlanta. We left this vicinity forty-five days ago, have traveled several hundred miles without seeing an armed foe, and now we are on the verge of some great strategic movement—we know not what. A supply of clothing was issued this evening. I drew only a gum blanket. Sold my great coat to Captain McCrea for $8.50, and a woolen shirt to Lieutenant Chatfield for $5.

The city of Atlanta is being burned, and it is understood that all communication with the rear, northward, is at an end. Colonel Mitchell is in Ohio now, and will not share in our exploits in the immediate future.

ON TO SAVANNAH.

The army, now ready to move southward, has been divided into two great wings:

The right wing consists of the Fifteenth and the Seventeenth Corps. This wing is in command of Major General O. O. Howard.

The left wing consists of the Fourteenth and the Twentieth Corps, commanded by Major General H. W. Slocum.

The Fifteenth Corps consists of the divisions of Generals Charles R. Wood, Wm. B. Hazen, John E. Smith and John M. Corse.

The Seventeenth Corps has three divisions, under command of Major General John A. Mower and Brigadier Generals Miles D. Leggett and Giles A. Smith.

The Fourteenth Corps has three divisions, led by Brigadier Generals William Carlin, James D. Morgan and Absalom Baird.

The Twentieth Corps includes the divisions of Brigadier Generals Norman J. Jackson, John W. Geary and William T. Ward.

Kilpatrick's division of cavalry consists of two brigades, commanded by Colonels Eli H. Murray and Smith D. Atkins.

The several corps are commanded as follows:

Fifteenth Corps, Major General P. J. Osterhaus.

Seventeenth Corps, Major General Frank P. Blair, Jr.

Fourteenth Corps, Brevet Major General Jefferson C. Davis.

Twentieth Corps, Brigadier General A. S. Williams.

16. At 11 A. M. our column moved from our camp east of Atlanta, and, taking a southerly course, marched parallel with the Georgia railroad, passing through Decatur, and camping twelve miles from Atlanta. Stratton had found (?) a note book during the day, and our shelter tent was the scene of an evening concert. We thought it better to sing than weep. Our camp is in the neighborhood of Stone Mountain.

17. Starting at seven, we marched briskly till noon, when we halted and took dinner. Moved till 5 P. M., when we began destroying the railroad. Worked till dark, then marched forward three miles and camped at Conyers, thirty miles from Atlanta. Have marched eighteen miles. We made our suppers on parched corn and meat, and felt less like singing than we did last night. Captain Jones has command of the regiment.

18. Left Conyers before daylight, reaching Covington and Oxford at noon. These towns are close together, forty-one miles from Atlanta. Crossed Yellow River at 10 A. M. on a pontoon. At one o'clock we began to destroy the railroad, but at the end of two hours we again moved on. Marched three miles further and camped, having traveled sixteen miles.

19. After a hasty breakfast the division moved ahead in a heavy rain, the troops straggling much on account of a bad road. Passed through Sandtown at 10 A. M., carrying off a number of negroes. Stratton pressed in a likely looking contraband and loaded him with a heavy knapsack. It was a case of misplaced confidence, for the darkey gave him the slip, taking knapsack and all with him. Marched twenty-one miles and camped near Shady Dale, and in a thicket. Late in the evening a detail of two men from each company, one commissioned officer and one non-commissioned officer from the regiment was made. These were organized into a foraging band. Their duties consisted in procuring supplies for the command. I was detailed as the non-commissioned officer of this force. We are camped near the plantation of Matthew Whitefield, one of the wealthy planters of Georgia.

20. The 113th O. V. I. and 78th Illinois V. I. were on duty as train guards. The trains moved slowly and the men improved the time in appropriating whatever had escaped the vigilance of the troops in the advance. One fellow, lacking a jug for the purpose, filled a plug hat with molasses at Whitefield's store and carried it to his company. Everything in this store worth carrying, and some things that were not, was taken. The command camped near Eatonton Factories, having marched fifteen miles. The foragers brought in horses, mules, oxen and sheep, with plenty meal, meat, sweet potatoes and other delicacies. I shot and killed two ganders, and then remembering that time was too precious to waste in boiling them a day and night, I concluded to abandon them. Green says he went into a building to fill his canteen with molasses, and found the floor covered two inches deep with it.

21. The command deflected to the right and moved toward Milledgeville in a heavy rain and very bad roads. Camped fourteen miles from Milledgeville on Williams' farm, near Murder Creek. We have marched twelve miles. Captain McCrea's means of transportation consists of three horses and a mule. John Ganson killed a sheep, and plenty reigns.

22. Sunday. The Second Division remained halted during the day; the Third Division passed. The weather is clear and cold, and rails are growing scarcer every hour. Soldiers are not great eaters, but a mess of eight consumed nearly two hogs to-day, and they are not very hoggish, either. It snowed some in the night.

23. Marched at 5:30 A. M. and in the evening camped within two miles of Milledgeville, having marched eleven miles. I have been sick to-day and by the kindness of Dr. Williams I rode in an ambulance this afternoon. Our brigade halted for dinner on the plantation of Howell Cobb. General Sherman has been making his headquarters with the Fourteenth Corps.

24. Marching at 10 A. M. we passed through Milledgeville at noon, crossed the Oconee river and camped about seven miles from the capital. Every hour has its incidents. As we passed a house to-day a soldier asked a woman if supper was ready. She burst into tears and replied that she had not a morsel of food in the house. One day's rations of bread was issued to-night. Our way led us by Black Spring, Fair Play and Long's Bridge.

25. Started at 6 A. M., passed the camp of the third division, and at ten o'clock our advance met some resistance from a small force of rebels. At noon we halted two hours while a stream was being bridged so we might cross. Crossed and camped two miles beyond the crossing, and six miles from Sandersville. This is in Washington county.

26. Moved at six o'clock, and for two hours we were not molested. As we neared Sandersville our skirmishers and foragers met a force of the enemy which disputed our advance. Our men deployed and drove them to the suburbs of the town. Then the 113th, being in the advance of the column, were deployed in line and moved on them. Our men drove the rebels through and out of town, and then halted and stacked arms. Companies B, G, K and E go on the skirmish line, and while on this duty they captured a Sergeant of the 12th Georgia Infantry, and a fine horse. Our loss was one killed and two wounded. The one killed belonged to the 108th Ohio; Jno. A. Wood, Sergeant of Company I, 121st O. V. I. was badly wounded through the lungs. The division went into camp and the 20th Corps camped near us. S. E. Bailey, Company B, is the fortunate possessor of a blind mule, which he pressed into service recently. He comes in now and then with a full supply of poultry and other choice feed.

27. Sunday. The division moved with the second brigade in the rear. We had no particular incident to record. The foragers now comprise about ninety men out of a hundred. It is not possible to describe the nature and extent of this band of food gatherers. They do not always exercise mercy toward the citizens with whom they come in contact, but I have witnessed no acts of violence. The first soldier divides with the unfortunate citizen, taking the larger share ; the next, and the next do likewise, and by the time the whole line has passed, nothing remains worth dividing.

We crossed the Ogeechee river at 3 P. M. and camped three miles further on. We have been moving southeasterly, and have marched fifteen miles.

28. We were on our way at an early hour, reaching a point within two miles of Louisville, Jefferson county, Ga., at noon. At this point we were detained while a bridge was thrown across Rocky Comfort creek. We then marched forward, passed through Louisville, and camped a mile east of town. The foragers found a great quantity of provisions and household goods in a swamp on our left to-day. They brought in many articles not necessary to the comfort of a soldier. We have marched fifteen miles to-day.

29. Adjutant Ladd took a party out on a foraging expedition and procured pork, poultry and meal.

Richard Cox, teamster, was out with a foraging party. They were attacked by rebels, and Cox was shot, stripped of his clothing, and left for dead. He was brought into camp and cared for. He may recover. Stratton is suffering an attack of colic. We remained camped to-day.

30. Companies C, H, E, K, G and B went out a mile from camp, as a guard to a forage train consisting of six wagons.

"When within a few hundred yards of the house at which a party of rebels had been seen yesterday, we halted and prepared to throw out skirmishers. Before this was accomplished some foragers further out began to exchange shots with the foe, and sooner than it can be told a detachment of rebel cavalry came upon us, front, right and left. Their appearance was so sudden and unexpected that our party was taken at a great disadvantage.

"The enemy dashed, fired and shouted at us at a terrible rate. A ball passed through a sapling and then spent its wasted force in my stomach, but upon examination I found I was not much hurt. We were being pressed on our front, right and left, but we kept up a brisk fire and fell back gradually toward our pickets and camp.

"At the picket post we received some support, and soon the 17th

N. Y. came to our aid, giving us the opportunity of regaining what ground had been lost. Other regiments from camp came out on double-quick upon learning of our being attacked. These, and a force of our cavalry scoured the county, and soon returned to camp without getting a shot at the enemy. The affair lasted an hour and had some features about it that were worth laughing at after it was over. We lost eight men, and I presume these were all taken prisoners. One or two of our wounded were carried off by the enemy. Earnest Snyder, of Company E, was captured. Tom Hallan was in their hands for a time, but got away." [G.]

The foraging detail under command of Lieutenant C. P. Garman, made a trip into the country but found very little produce. At the residence of a wealthy lady we were entertained by her daughters with some piano music. These girls do not use tobacco. The vandal hand was very busy all day, but no outrages were committed.

DECEMBER, 1864.

1. The column again moved on; Morgan's division is marching as a train guard for the 14th Corps. The roads run through swamps and are sandy and heavy. The country is flat and only partly improved.

Captain McCrea commanded the organized company of foragers to-day. We can find plenty of hogs, cattle and sheep, but bread stuff, that which we need most, can not be found so easily. Marched ten miles and camped on the left. We are leaving Millen to our right and Wainsboro to the left. Our course since leaving Milledgeville has been nearly east, but now we bear toward the south.

2. Our division is again with the corps train. It has been a hard day on man and beast. The road is almost a continuous swamp and the heavy trains require frequent assistance. The rear of our train came in at midnight and the 113th went to bed supperless.

It is reported that six of our foragers were killed to-day. Some say their throats were cut and a card pinned to each, read, "Death to all foragers."

The foraging detail was commanded by Captain J. K. Hamilton, and the party took dinner near a large, vacant house, the property of a prominent and wealthy rebel named Byrne. Before the column had passed the house was in flames, having been set on fire by accident or design; probably the latter.

Near here Captain Hamilton's party found a large pile of sweet potatoes, guarded by a single Michigan soldier. Captain H. told us to take them; the Michigander fixed his bayonet and objected   He was at length dispossessed. Captain H. said to him, "Tell your officers that Captain Hamilton, of the 113th Ohio, took your potatoes; we must have them." We have marched ten miles, and our camp is at the crossing of the Birdsville and Wainsboro roads, and near Buckhead creek.

3. The troops moved ahead, crossing Buckhead creek during the forenoon. The column changed direction, and, after a hard day's work on account of the character of the roads, the divisions of Carlin and Morgan camped at Lumpkin's station, at the crossing of the Jacksonboro road and the Augusta and Savannah railway.

While crossing the pontoon at Buckhead, a mule loaded with sweet potatoes lost his equilibrium and fell into the stream. He was fished out by the boys, more on account of the load he carried than for their love of the animal.

Lieutenant George H. Lippincott commanded the organized regimental foragers. Crossing the creek at an early hour the party flanked to the right and then returned to the road and took dinner in a farm yard at a plantation, whose owner had gone off, leaving his family and his worldly effects at our mercy.

Later in the day we halted at the palatial residence of Mrs. Churchill, whose daughters entertained us with music. One of them sang a rebel song in our very faces, with a defiant devotion worthy of a better cause. The chorus ran thus:

> " I'd rather be a soldier's wife
> And smile upon him all his life;
> I'll wait for some brave *volunteer*,
> Who shall my youth and beauty share."

We find but few houses. These indicate by their character that the country is inhabited by two classes, the very rich and the very poor. We have marched eleven miles.

4. Sunday. Our two divisions moved in the direction of Jacksonboro. A part of the command destroyed three miles of the railroad at Lumpkin's Station, and moving ahead the whole force made an agreeable march of thirteen miles, camping on the right of the road in a grove of pine. The character of the route differs from that we have been marching over. Only an occasional plantation can be seen, the country is covered with pine timber and a tall wiry grass

grows everywhere. We saw patches of rice to-day growing in low places. This is the first many of us have ever seen.

The regimental foragers marched in command of Lieutenant W. A. M. Davis. Crossing the railroad in the direction of Wainsboro they captured some meal a mile further on. The party worked on the right flank during the forenoon and dined near a church at a spring, six miles from the railroad. Camped with their comrades at night.

5. The 113th moved with the rear part of the corps train, leaving camp after 10 A. M. The route lay through a sandy country giving evidences of poverty. After a hard day's march of fifteen miles the whole corps camped in the vicinity of Jacksonboro, and close to Brier creek.

Lieutenant John S. Skeels commanded our foraging party to-day. We reached Lawton's Mills early in the day. Our mounted foragers had already taken possession of the mill and were grinding briskly. Here we procured a light wagon, and putting upon it a load of meal proceeded forward. Flanked to the right and went into camp near the brigade at night.

6. Our regiment is marching again with the train. The sand is deep and loose and often fills our shoes. We have marched nearly parallel with the Savannah river and not far from it. Crossed Beaver-dam creek early this morning on a pontoon which had been built during last night. We have made twenty miles to-day, and our camp is in the vicinity of Hudson's Ferry, on the Savannah river. The enemy has obstructed the road in our advance by falling trees across it. These are being removed. Captain Shepherd, Company K, commanded the foragers. Soon after leaving camp we entered a house on the left. Here we found some clothing buried in a garden. Going to a room in the second story I found a double barreled shot gun which I broke round a sapling in the yard. Further on we butchered some hogs and left the meat at the roadside in charge of two men who were instructed to point it out to the 113th when they came along. At a house on the right, further on, was a young Miss from the other side of the river. She begged us to deal gently with her fellow, even her lover, if he should fall into our hands. Took dinner near a burning gin house, and again struck the road at the Middle Ground Church (Baptist). Chas. Sprague had captured a fine shell during the day, for which I paid him $5.

7. After some delay in clearing the road we again moved forward.

Our division with a pontoon train in charge of Colonel Buell, reached Ebenezer creek late in the evening and began to prepare to lay a bridge across the stream. The 113th took a position near the creek, and within a supporting distance of Colonel Buell's pontooneers. We have marched fifteen miles, and have passed several dreary swamps on either hand.

The foragers marched again in command of Captain Shepherd. We killed seventeen hogs on the left of the road, and after dressing and cutting up the meat into small pieces (leaving the hair on), we piled it at the road side on some rails, in ten equal quantities, for the ten companies of the regiment. Leaving three men in charge of the meat we moved on. When the 113th came along in the line of march the meat was pointed out to them, and each company, securing the pile to which it was entitled, carried it to the end of the day's march, when the pieces were skinned and prepared for cooking.

Late in the evening we found a large lot of sweet potatoes, and piling them into a cart, we prevailed on a cavalry man of Kilpatrick's command to haul them into camp for us. Harness? Well, the harness, cart and potatoes belonged at the same place.

8. Our column did not move till late in the forenoon, though Colonel Buell and his force worked all night to complete the bridge. When the bridge was completed the work of crossing Ebenezer began, but progressed slowly. After crossing, our brigade halted for dinner near the bridge; several shots were fired at our column from a gunboat in the river on our left. We were not harmed, but the first shot made us a little nervous. Captain Jones remarked that in all probability there was flour on board that boat, but we had better delay going for it till after dark. We can hear artillery a distance in our front. We moved ahead six miles and prepared to camp, but an order to counter march was given, and the division returned and camped near where we had taken dinner. Have marched twelve miles.

The foragers under Captain Shepherd moved off to the right, procured sweet potatoes and mutton, and then returning to the main road, had a vexatious time finding the regimental camp. The Ebenezer has two streams here; one is smaller than the other. The smaller one is spanned by a pontoon.

9. Our column moved from Ebenezer, and passing southward through a low, swampy country, reached Cuyler's plantation, where we found the enemy occupying a small fort planted in our pathway. He opened upon us in a lively manner, and for a time we were at a standstill. Two field pieces were put into position by our forces and for a while there was an artillery duel, night coming on in the meantime. In this action Lieutenant Coe, Battery I, 2d Illinois Artillery, was killed. During the afternoon a flat-boat was captured on the Savannah river on our left, it contained provisions and some wine. Some of our men came up from the boat in a condition which recalled the adage that "the way to keep the spirits up is to pour the spirits down." The regiment camped in a swamp fifteen miles from Savannah.

To-day the foragers were again under the command of Captain Shepherd. In a garden near the road we found buried a quantity of sweet potatoes, honey, meal, meat, dishes, butter and lard. This discovery was made by thrusting the ramrod of a gun into the earth in various places in the garden. Finally, the rod struck the lid of a box in which the goods were stored, and the whole was unearthed. Though we have been marching parallel with the river, and sometimes within a half mile of it for two days, we had but one glimpse of the stream, its banks being so densely covered with cypress and other trees as to hide the river entirely. We marched only eight miles.

10. The fort in our front was evacuated last night, and we moved ahead unmolested early this morning. The 113th went on a scout in the direction of the river. Returning to the main road, the 113th joined the rest of the division at Ten Mile House. Camped near the Charleston and Savannah railroad, having marched only five miles.

The foragers have been under my orders to-day. We scouted on the right of the main road, captured a portable corn mill, and carried it with us till noon, when we put it up and ground some meal. In the afternoon we crossed the road, and, after considerable effort, we reached the river, and then, returning to the road, camped with the regiment.

11. Sunday. At 8 A. M. our brigade moved toward Savannah, passed the 20th A. C., filed right, and, striking the line of the railroad, took a position on the front line, relieving troops of the 17th A. C. These go to the right. The rebels, under Hardee, are in our front.

Our protracted picnic is now at an end; we are here to stay, and sooner or later we shall hold dress parade in the streets of this historic old city. I took the foragers several miles south to the river's bank, where we procured meat, rice and potatoes. We then joined our command in the line. The rebels are shelling part of our line.

12. Our brigade was relieved this morning by troops of the Twentieth Corps. Marching some distance southward, we crossed the Savannah & Augusta railroad, and relieved the troops of the First Division, 14th A. C. Companies I, C, H and E went on the skirmish line on the bank of an old dry canal, which is said to have been made by General Jackson during the Florida War.

The foraging party repaired to the river, and, procuring a boat, crossed over a branch of the Savannah on to a large island called Argile, seven miles above the city. Then, by means of a skiff, rowed by some negroes belonging to Taylor's plantation, we crossed the eastern arm of the river which separates the island from South Carolina. We are now on the hated soil of the chief of rebel states. We began an indiscriminate slaughter of Mr. Taylor's stock. All at once the cry was heard: "The rebels are coming! the rebels are coming!" Not a few of our party turned their backs on South Carolina and made for the skiff at the bank of the river. Others of us, who were too heavily loaded to run, stood our ground, and began inquiring into the cause of the alarm. At the distance of half a mile could be seen a body of cavalrymen drawn up in line, carefully watching our movements. I assisted Lieutenant Henry Urban, 108th Ohio, to rally the men into line, and we took a position behind a dike near Taylor's rice mill. The enemy contented themselves by watching us a few minutes longer, and then rode slowly away. We then recrossed the river to the Georgia side, and made our way to camp, finding the regiment with difficulty. During the night, a cannon shot, passing through a tree above our heads, cut off a limb, which fell on our bed, but did us no harm.

13. The bread question is becoming an important one. One pound of bread for three days is our allowance. The rebels in our front are busy building forts and other offensive and defensive works. Something will be done soon that will astonish the natives.

The different corps of our army are in position as follows: The Twentieth Corps occupies the left of our line; its left rests on the Savannah river, near Williams' plantation. The Fourteenth joins the right of the Twentieth, and extends from the Augusta railroad to Lawton's plantation, beyond the canal. The Seventeenth Corps joins the right of the Fourteenth, and the Fifteenth Corps occupies the extreme right, resting on the Gulf railway.

Late this evening we received the news that General Hazen's troops have taken Fort McAllister, and such cheering as was heard along the line is seldom heard by mortal ears. This means bread and mail. The foragers remained in camp.

14. One of our guns on the line of the First Division has been throwing solid shot into the city, a distance of three miles. This is calculated to disturb their devotions to some extent.

Captain John W. Kile went with a foraging party for supplies. We proceeded to the river, and crossed over into Argyle island. Had a little skirmish with a party of rebels, who fired at us from the Carolina shore, but at such a distance as to do us no harm. We procured rice, beans and meat, and, returning to the west bank, spent the night at a rice mill near the river.

15. Rode into camp on a mule barefooted. Some miscreant stole my shoes while I slept, and I paid two dollars for a pair to replace the stolen ones. There is seldom a loss that does not have a corresponding good. I will watch this case and see where the good comes in. Ned, our cook, decamped early this morning, carrying with him considerable goods belonging to McLane, Cisco and Ray. Their curses and maledictions followed him in the direction of Shady Dale.

16. The foragers went to the river bank to-day to thresh and clean rice. They are in the charge of Corporal J. E. Sidner. There is a great quantity of rice in some of those mills, but it is in the sheaf and hull, and we Yankees are ignorant of the process of threshing and hulling it. Matters in camp are monotonous, and nearly devoid of interest. We understand that steamers and other vessels now run up the Ogeechee within six miles of our camp.

17. A large mail arrived to-day. My share is forty-seven papers and seven letters. Perhaps some got away. Nearly everybody got a letter. No mail has reached us till now since November 21st, and we have been in blissful ignorance of what has been going on in other places.

18. Sunday. The foraging party has been disbanded and the men have joined their respective companies. They have had a rare experience in the past thirty days. The weather continues warm and clear. The men are engaged in writing letters to their friends, giving a description of the grand march and of the present situation. The folks will be glad to hear from us. Lieutenant Chatfield who has been out foraging for three days, returned loaded with supplies.

20. Things are oppressively dull on our line, and have been for days past. It is feared that General Sherman contemplates an assault on these works of the enemy soon. That means death to many of us, and we dread to hear of it. General Sherman demanded a surrender of the city three days ago, but General Hardee refused. Hope he may change his mind soon.

SAVANNAH IS OURS.

21. At daylight the news sped along our line that there was no enemy in our front, and in a few minutes some of our men were inspecting the rebel works and scouting far beyond the lines held by them yesterday. An hour later we learned more of the particulars, and began to rejoice. By noon it was generally known that Hardee had evacuated the city by crossing the Savannah on a pontoon bridge during the night, and that his forces had marched toward Charleston by the Causeway road. It is a great victory; doubly great because it is bloodless.

We packed our knapsacks and held ourselves ready to move, but the day passed and night came on, and yet we did not move. The rebels left most of their heavy artillery (fifty guns it is said), for, having to cross a pontoon, it was hardly possible to move their siege pieces. They left several thousand bales of cotton.

22. We fell in at eight o'clock, and, after a tedious and provoking march, reached the site on which we camped at 3 P. M. We are camped south of the canal, one and a half miles from Savannah. We began preparations for building quarters.

24. We have been full of business in erecting quarters to live in. The nights are cool, and we do not sleep very comfortable. Some of our officers—Kile, Chatfield, McCrea, Shepherd and Lippincott—have come into possession of a rebel hospital tent, and will put it up and mess together. Our men who have visited the city are much pleased with its appearance.

25. Sunday. Christmas has come again. Last year we were on Stringer's Ridge, in Tennessee. Who dare predict where we shall be when Christmas shall come again? This is our third Christmas in the service.

Last night some one in camp began to celebrate Christmas by firing a salute. Another followed the example, and the fun spread like a contagion. Finally Companies D and E were ordered out and instructed to arrest the noisy offenders. This increased the fun, for, as the guards passed up and down the streets of camp, they were saluted with: "Lie down;" "Grab a root;" "Hide your haversacks, they are after your rice." The 113th had company inspection at 9 A. M.

Lieutenant Chatfield, J. O. Kite, John G. Ganson, John Wauk, Jackson C. Doughty and I went to the city on a pass. Some of us took dinner with members of the 66th O. V. V. I.

26. The company officers are busy with their accounts and papers of various kinds. I have been assisting Lieutenant McCrea to make "*Final Statements*" for deceased soldiers. Mike Huddleston, John Wilson and Captain Swisher started home on furlough. This may be very fine for each of them, but I have no special desire to go home, and therefore do not envy them in the least.

27. The Fourteenth Corps was reviewed by General Sherman in the city to-day. Our division left at 10 A. M., and returned at 3 P. M. All passed off well, and the men are in a good humor, an uncommon thing on review day. I remained in camp and began work on *Muster Rolls* for September and October.

31. This day closes the eventful year of 1864. As we sit in our little cotton homes and let our minds run back to that bleak New Year's Eve one year ago, when we watched for the foe at Shallow Ford in northern Georgia, and then follow our record month after month down to the present hour, it seems like an age, so thickly have events crowded one after another upon us. The young and joyous spring, the busy eventful summer, the solemn autumn, have each come and gone; and now the chilly winter is upon us. We are on the threshold of another year, whose dangers and trials are kindly hidden from us by a providential hand. Luckily for us the long and weary marches, the battles, sieges and campaigns, the hungerings and thirstings, the sickness and sufferings of the future, all are unknown to us. We have a brave and sagacious leader, a noble and confident army, a righteous cause, and a God who rules the destinies of nations and individuals. In these we will put our trust and go forward in belief that the right will triumph.

MARCHING THROUGH GEORGIA.

Bring the good old bugle, boys! we'll sing another song—
Sing it with a spirit that will start the world along—
Sing it as we used to sing it, fifty thousand strong,
  While we were marching through Georgia.

CHORUS.

Hurrah! hurrah! we bring the Jubilee!
Hurrah! hurrah! the flag that makes you free!
So we sang the chorus from Atlanta to the sea,
  While we were marching through Georgia.

How the darkeys shouted when they heard the joyful sound!
How the turkeys gobbled which our commissary found!
How the sweet potatoes even started from the ground,
  While we were marching through Georgia.—*Chorus.*

Yes, and there were Union men who wept with joyful tears,
When they saw the honored flag they had not seen for years!
Hardly could they be restrained from breaking forth in cheers,
  While we were marching through Georgia.—*Chorus.*

Sherman's dashing Yankee boys will never reach the coast!
So the saucy Rebels said; and 'twas a handsome boast—
Had they not forgot, alas! to reckon with the host,
  While we were marching through Georgia.—*Chorus.*

So we made the thoroughfare for Freedom and her train,
Sixty miles in latitude—three hundred to the main;
Treason fled before us—for, resistance was in vain,
  While we were marching through Georgia.—*Chorus.*

JANUARY, 1865.

1. Sunday. The day dawns full of hope to the American people. The war cloud which has been darkening our National sky seems to be lifting, and the sun of hope and enduring peace begins to shine. During the past few months Atlanta and Savannah have both fallen before our victorious columns, and Hood has been sorely defeated at Nashville by Thomas and his veterans. Peace to the ashes of those who have fallen, and let the living take fresh courage and stop at nothing short of an abundant and lasting peace.

2. Our work continues on rolls, papers and statements. But for this our time would be heavier than it is. A soldier longs for the excitement of the march, and thrives on campaigns and duties of an onerous character. Sometimes he enjoys a rest in camp for a short time, and then the restless spirit takes possession of him, and he chafes under the monotony of camp life, and wants to hear the *assembly* sounding.

Green made a visit to the city yesterday and attended worship at one of the churches. He says the preacher neglected to mention the soldier in his sermon, and in his prayer he failed to thank God that the city was again in the hands of the Federal government. Green was so disgusted at this that he calls the minister an old sinner, and will not again visit his church.

Stratton and Bradford built a chimney to our quarters. The thing draws well, but it is no beauty.

3. The 113th went out on a special duty this afternoon. Passing through the southern part of the city the regiment took the King's Bridge road and marched to Marshall's plantation, six miles west of the city. Here they camped to the left of the shell road, and in a grove of live oaks. Nature and art have joined hands in making the situation attractive, and we shall try to enjoy our stay here. We are guarding a large lot of mules which are feeding on the dead grass which abounds in this section.

The company officers established themselves in a long brick building which has been used as negro quarters in times past. This building is nearly 200 feet in length, and is sub-divided into small apartments.

6. The weather is warm and wet. I can hardly believe that at home our friends are riding over the frozen snow, with bells jingling and ears tingling with cold. Captain Jones, Lieutenant McCrea and Lieutenant Lippincott went bathing this afternoon.

8. Sunday. The 98th O. V. I. relieved the 113th at 11 A. M. and we returned to our former camp near the city. Our trip of five days out among the green trees and singing birds has been an enjoyable one, yet all are glad to be back.

9. The 113th, with six commissioned officers, performed duty on the fortifications near the city. There was fun in this to those of us who viewed the work from a distance. I have been very busy with my writing work for several days, and have been excused from other duties. Lieutenant McCrea visited Richard Cox at the hospital to-day. He is getting along well and will recover. Some of the men killed an aligator near camp a day or two ago. It had been tempted too far from the river by the offal of our slaughter pen. Some of the boys said it wanted to enlist.

11. Yesterday was a rainy, disagreeable day, and we kept inside our quarters to keep dry. Richard Sullivan, Company E, died in the hospital to-day. The frogs are having a vocal concert near camp. Clothing was issued to the men to-day. A colored dance was one of the attractions last night. We get an occasional mess of oysters in the shell.

12. We have been listening for some time for an order to change our camp to some other site. The order came this forenoon, and after some *little* oaths on account of the impossibility of moving our

chimneys and the probabillty of getting our camp in a worse place, we packed, marched a short distance and built our cotton city at the southern suburbs of the city on West Broad street. Kilpatrick's cavalry division is being reviewed by General Sherman.

13. We have been busy to-day with our quarters. Some of the materials of our former camp were carried up on our shoulders and used again here. We are on a dry site, somewhat better than the one we have just left. John O'Leary had his arm broken last night. A number of our officers went to theater to hear Doesticks.

14. The 113th went on the picket line about four miles west of the city and near the old line of works of the rebels. We relieved the 14th Michigan, Major Fitzgibbon commanding. A high wind prevailed all day, and our post of duty being in the open country, we suffered some discomfort. I had charge of a post and twenty-one men.

15. Sunday. We were relieved from picket at 9 A. M. by the 16th Illinois. Arriving at camp we received a large mail. We had light bread and rice for dinner. Our camp has been visited to-day by a number of ladies from the city. The sight of a Yankee soldier does not seem to throw them into fits; on the contrary they seem to enjoy the situation reasonably well. A soldier was buried in the cemetery to-day with military honors.

16. Captain Geo. A. Race, Division Inspector, condemned some camp and garrison equipage for the 113th. Company E borrowed some articles of Company H for this occasion, and had them condemned; by the time the officer reached that company they had borrowed the necessary things of us, and they were again inspected and condemned. It is so seldom that we get to play a trick on an officer, that when such a thing happens, it ought to be recorded.

17. These rebel shop-keepers have a steep list of prices. While in the city to-day I paid seventy-five cents for a crystal for my watch, and the same for a shave and cutting my hair. A day or two ago I paid thirty cents for a pound of nails, to be used in fixing our quarters. Lieutenant G. H. Lippincott will leave the regiment to-morrow to take charge of a section in a general supply train.

19. It is raining briskly. We are under orders to move, and the men stay close to camp. Some of our company officers returned to camp from the city feeling very rich; it required some effort to keep them from returning to buy the city.

Silas Mahlone, a descendant of Ham, and a cook of some reputation, got into a melee with a citizen of color down town, and Captains Shepherd, Kile, McCrea and the writer "fell in" and went to his rescue.

This being the last night in this camp, there was a removal of restrictions at company headquarters, and some unusual exercises were indulged in. Captain S. took the floor and indulged in some flights of oratory; Lieutenant M. danced a jig, and others applauded vociferously. Nothing like it will ever occur again.

It has been more than a month since we neared the outer works surrounding Savannah, and we are not displeased in having to start out on another campaign.

20. The Fourteenth Corps left Savannah early this morning, marched ten miles northward on the Augusta road, and camped in a heavy rain. Most all the men left Savannah cheerfully. We have had enough of masterly inactivity, and want to be going.

24. We are mud-bound and water-bound, and still it rains. We are halted at the camp, ten miles out from Savannah. Some fears are entertained that we may be compelled to return to Savannah and wait till the weather is more favorable.

Sergeant Ward, Green and Mahlone have been sent back to Savannah to find and bring to the regiment, Samuel I. Beck and William Cisco, who remained there without leave when the troops moved.

25. The command moved ahead at sunrise, taking the Louisville road for several miles, then filing right we moved northward, crossing field and forest, regardless of roads. Marched fifteen miles and camped in a pine woods. Mutton and beef were issued to us in the evening.

26. Our progress to-day has been exceedingly slow. The second brigade was train guard, and we had plenty of work to do in helping the wagons out of the deep holes and quicksand. The country is flat and much water stands on the surface. We built small fires of pine knots in the woods during the day, and while the weary mules dragged their heavy loads along at almost a snail's pace, we stood around our smoking fires until our faces were dusky to an extent that was amusing. Captain Jones met me during the day, and after gazing in my face for a minute, studying who I was, at length said, "Ah, I know who you are now; think you had better wash your face."

We halted at the end of a seven miles drive, camping in the vicinity of Springfield.

27. After a march of two miles we reached Ebenezer creek, finding it swollen by recent rains, and difficult to cross. But we waded in and pushed for the opposite shore. The water was very cold and small sheets of ice adhered to the chunks and logs. Soon as we had crossed our clothes began freezing and were soon stiff and uncomfortable; but building a number of big fires in the woods we danced around them, joking and cheering until we were somewhat comfortable, then moving on three miles from the creek, we camped near the house of Mr. Dasher. The grass caught fire near our tent in the night, and our bedding was partially destroyed by the fire.

28. Moved forward, and bearing to the right we reached the road on which our corps marched to Savannah last month. At noon we reached the vicinity of Sisters Ferry, which is for the present our destination. A good supply of provisions was brought in. We have marched only seven miles.

29. Sunday. The weather has moderated. We get a glimpse of the river at the ferry. It is high and out of its banks, and we shall not be able to cross for several days. The gunboat Pontiac and two transports are lying here. John Wilson and Mike Huddleston joined us, having been absent on a furlough of twenty days.

31. The 113th is on picket a half mile from camp. The jolly Lieutenant Garman entertained the men on the reserve by a number of songs, which he sang in a matchless manner. Perhaps the poet had Garman in his mind when he wrote:

> "There are those who touch the magic string,
> And noisy fame is proud to win them ;
> But some, alas, refuse to sing,
> And die with all their music in them."

Our post of duty is near the Augusta road.

FEBRUARY, 1865.

1. The 17th New York Vols. took the place of the 113th on the picket line, and we returned to camp. Captain Swisher arrived in camp from home, bringing me a pair of good socks from home. These are from my mother, way up north in Ohio. I will put them on at once, for she intends I shall wear them out tramping through rebeldom. Sergeant Ward was again sent back yesterday to find and bring up those skulkers, Beck and Cisco.

2. Small-pox has broken out in the brigade, but I learn it is under control. A large mail came to-day. I get fifty papers and several letters.

4. It rained yesterday and was a dull day. We had company inspection this afternoon by Captain Otway Watson. I had charge of Company E on inspection, Lieutenant McCrea being on fatigue duty, working the roads on the South Carolina side of the river. Ward came in with Beck and Cisco under arrest.

5. Sunday. John O'Leary starts home on a furlough. Parts of the army have been passing over the river on the pontoon here for two days. At noon we fell in, and marched to the bank near the bridge and stacked arms. At 8 P. M. we took arms, crossed the Savannah into hated South Carolina, and went into camp in a sandy bottom, two miles from the river at 10 P. M.

The troops crossing at this ferry consist of the three divisions of the Fourteenth Corps, Geary's Division of the Twentieth, and Corse's Division of the Fifteenth. Each body has an immense train, and the work of crossing a large river during high water is attended with much labor and risk. In a day or two from now all will be across in safety and then we go forward.

7. We remained motionless yesterday, had a supply of clothing issued to us, and received a mail. It was a rainy, disagreeable day.

Our late Colonel, John G. Mitchell, who has been absent since October last, joined the command to-day, and is now a Brigadier General. His commission as such is dated January 12th, 1865, and awaited his arrival. Every man of the 113th feels gratified at this promotion to a higher position in rank. General Mitchell brings with him a new flag for the 113th, on which is inscribed the names of the several engagements in which the regiment has participated, viz.: CHICKAMAUGA, CHATTANOOGA, MILL CREEK GAP, ROME, KENESAW MOUNTAIN, ATLANTA, JONESBORO, SAVANNAH.

The Second Brigade has been commanded by Lieutenant Colonel John S. Pearce, 98th O. V. I. during Colonel Mitchell's absence.

Cassiday, of Company B, issued recently the following facetious order, parodizing one issued by General Sherman :

HEADQUARTERS MILITARY DIVISION OF THE MISSISSIPPI, }
IN THE FIELD, SISTERS FERRY, S. C., Feb. 5, 1865. }
GENERAL ORDER }
    No. 10. }

The army during the ensuing campaign will subsist chiefly by foraging off the country through which it passes, and foraging parties will be governed by the following rules:

I. Each regimental commander will detail a foraging party each day while upon the march.

II. No detail shall be made to exceed the whole effective force, including negroes.

III. Not more than one thousand pack-mules will be allowed to a regiment.

IV. No soldier will be allowed to take any horses or mules that cannot walk.

V. No soldier will be allowed to take anything from a plantation which he cannot carry, unless provided with a wagon or pack-mule.

VI. No person shall carry more than two hundred pounds unless he is a negro impressed for the purpose.

VII No soldier shall carry off a grindstone weighing more than five hundred pounds, as a greater weight would injure the knapsacks.

VIII. No soldier will be allowed more than three negroes as private servants; the surplus, if any, will be sent to these headquarters, if females.

IX. Burning of property is strictly prohibited, unless accidental; and any soldier caught attempting to fire any incombustible material will be arrested

X. Foraging will be conducted with as little shooting as possible, and no soldier will be allowed to shoot anything already dead. Division and brigade commanders will see that these orders are strictly enforced. Any soldier violating the above orders will be deprived of the privilege of participating in any engagement during the present campaign, and will be summarily dismissed from the service immediately upon the expiration of his enlistment

By order of   MAJOR GENERAL W T. SHERMAN.

OFFICIAL,

(Signed) No—T. WISEMAN.   OFFICIAL,

(Signed) L. M. DAYTON,

A A. A. G.

8. Our division marched at 7 A. M., going in a northwesterly course. Our way lay through a swampy and uninhabited region of country. Went into camp near Brighton, having marched seven miles.

9. The column moved in the direction of the Augusta railroad, marched eighteen miles, and camped. The weather is chilly, and a high wind prevails. The road is good, and we have moved with ease.

10. Marched twenty miles, and camped in the vicinity of Blackville, Barnwell county, South Carolina. Geary's Division of the Twentieth Corps is camped near us. Our foragers brought in plenty potatoes and cattle. The work of destruction by fire has been carried on extensively to-day.

11. During the first mile this morning we passed a cross roads. The guide boards pointed north to Barnwell C. H., south to Burton's Ferry, east to Fiddle Pond, and west to Augusta, Ga. Halted at

9:30 A. M. to let the First Division of the Fourteenth Corps take the advance. Moved ahead at 1 P. M., crossed the Salkehatchie, and passed through Barnwell C. H., the county seat of Barnwell county. This town was mainly in ashes by the time our division entered. It is situated on the left bank of the Combahee River, which at this point is only an insignificant, sluggish stream. Camped on the right of the road, three miles northeast of town, having marched twelve miles. Foragers brought in meat and sweet potatoes in abundance, a part of which will be abandoned.

12. Sunday. Marched at daylight, going at a rapid pace. At 10:30 A. M. we reached the Charleston & Augusta railroad at Williston, thirty-eight miles from Augusta, Georgia, and ninety-nine miles from Charleston. Taking the Columbia road, we halted for dinner near a drained pond on the left. At half past three we went into camp on the right bank of the South Edisto River, having marched seventeen miles. The 113th went to work preparing a bridge on which the column will cross to-morrow.

13. The troops have a difficult time crossing the stream before mentioned. Mitchell's Brigade, being in the rear, did not cross till about noon. Continued our march in the direction of Columbia, and, having marched nine miles, we camped at Sally's Mills. A great quantity of supplies was brought in by the foragers, and we have more now than we can care for. Green's party came in with a yoke of oxen hauling a cart loaded with flour, meal, meat and sorghum.

The torch of destruction has been freely applied to-day, and we have at no time been out of sight of fire and smoke from burning buildings. It looks hard, and *is* hard, but then war means death and suffering, and the innocent often suffer with, as well as for, the guilty.

The Twentieth Corps has been on our right, and Kilpatrick's cavalry division on our left, for several days past.

14. Marched at 6 A. M. and reached the North Edisto at 11 A. M. Crossed at Horsey's Bridge, and halted on the left bank for dinner. Marched on toward Columbia, and camped in the evening eighteen miles from the city on the right of the road. Rain and sleet fell during the afternoon, and our march was more disagreeable on that account. Captain Swisher hauled my knapsack during the afternoon, for which he has the thanks of my weary body. Whole distance marched, eighteen miles.

15. Our column countermarched a mile, then started westerly on a road leading to Wateree Ferry. Some of our men straggled from their command, and several were captured, among them John Vandever, 78th Illinois. Camped on the left, four miles from Lexington, having marched eighteen miles. The 113th moved in the advance to-day, and during the afternoon we were deployed as skirmishers, and exchanged shots occasionally with the rebel cavalry.

16. Moved toward Columbia at six o'clock, and halted for dinner within three miles of the city. Rested two hours, and then about-faced and moved toward Lexington, and went into camp at sundown, having marched fifteen miles. We learn that Columbia is ours. I am sick, and have marched with difficulty.

17. Marched early. The head of our column reached the Saluda River late yesterday evening, and this morning we are crossing at Hart's Ferry on a pontoon one hundred and thirty yards long, which had been laid during the night.

We are marching a northerly course and in the direction of Winnsborough. Marched sixteen miles, and halted on the right bank of Broad River, near Alston. The day has been chilly, and a high wind prevails. A great deal of property has been burned to-day, including two mills, numerous dwellings, and a large quantity of cotton.

18. Our brigade began crossing Broad River on a flatboat soon after midnight. The 78th Illinois had already crossed, and at 3 A. M. the 113th began crossing, sixty men going at each trip. A pontoon is now being put across, but it will not be done for several hours. As the men are landed on the left bank they stack arms and prepare breakfast. The Spartanburg & Alston railroad runs parallel with the river and only a short distance from it. This is Freshley's Ferry, taking its name from Joseph Freshley, who owns a mill below the point where we crossed, and who lives (or *did* live) on the left bank, half a mile or more from the crossing.

This man is not only a prominent citizen but a prominent rebel. One of our men took from the Freshley residence an account book, which showed that Mr. Freshley was the receiver of supplies which had been levied upon the inhabitants in this section of country for the sustenance of the rebel army. I presume that to live in this part of South Carolina and not be a rebel would be an up-hill business and a dangerous experiment.

The river at this point is two hundred yards wide, and the pontoniers seem to have more difficulty in putting a bridge across than at any other place, except at Sisters Ferry, on the Savannah.

The foragers have added a three mule team to their means of transportation. With this and the ox team they manage to keep a good supply of the best the country affords. The mule team moves rapidly with the advance, but the oxen are held in reserve for emergencies.

Our entire brigade was ferried over by ten o'clock. Companies E, K and G were posted as pickets. We took a position on a high bluff, from which a fine view of the country could be had. The entire day has been occupied in crossing the river, and the whole force will not be over before to-morrow morning.

19. Sunday. Marched at 7 A. M. in a northwesterly direction. After a march of five miles, we took a left oblique course and marched three miles to the Spartanburg railroad, which we destroyed for some distance. Then, returning to the main road, we camped for the night.

20. The march was resumed in nearly a directly north course. The Second Brigade was assigned to the wagon train of the corps. The column reached Little River and camped. Our brigade marched four miles, then, turning east at a church, we marched a mile further and camped for the night. A hundred mules and horses were killed this morning, they having become used up and worthless.

21. At 8 A. M. we moved, crossing Little River at Kincaid's bridge. We marched on the Winnsborough road till within four miles of that place; then we about-faced, and, countermarching one mile, we took the Chester C. H. road, and moved three miles in that direction; then, again filing to the right, we camped, having marched twelve miles.

22. We marched at early dawn, Schellhorn in the lead discoursing plenty of good music. We struck the Charlotte & South Carolina railroad at Adger's Station, five miles from Winnsborough and seventy-two miles from Charlotte. Halted two hours and again marched north to Whiteoak; then, turning east, we went six miles further on the Camden road, and went into camp, having marched twelve miles. About noon we passed an extensive plantation, with the mansion on the left. This was on fire as we passed out of sight. Ed Campbell, who fell into the hands of the rebels when we withdrew from Willis' Mills last August, came to us to-day. Our camp is near a church and a box spring. This is Fairfield District (County.)

As we passed a chaise which stood on a hillside, I hinted to a comrade that it would look well rolling down hill. Each of us seized a hub on the upper side and away it went to the bottom of the hill. Just then Captain Watson rode up to my side and said reprovingly, "Sergeant McAdams, I did not think that of you." There was reproof enough in his tone and manner to last me a week.

23. Morgan's Division marched in the rear of the two other divisions. Mitchell's Brigade marched with the train, and the 113th entirely in the rear. It was nearly or quite noon when we pulled out, and when night came on we had moved but five miles. A heavy rain was falling, and the roads were next to impassable. Hour after hour we plodded on—moving and halting, cursing, sulking, singing, moving and halting. Thus the whole night passed, and as morning dawned we moped into camp, wet, hungry and disheartened.

The bugle was sounding the *reveille* before the last wagon halted. Eighteen hours of toil and exposure had given us an appetite for breakfast. We had marched twelve miles.

24. Remained camped till nearly noon, and many of us were about to lie down to rest when the "general" sounded, and we packed our wet duds and again moved forward. It rains.

A march of two miles brought us to the Wateree or Catawba River, which we crossed on a pontoon of thirty-three boats. The stream is narrow, deep and swift; the banks are high, and the recent rains had softened the roads leading to and from the bridge so that it looked to be impossible to cross with teams. How glad I felt that I happened not to be a mule or a teamster. This is Rocky Mount Ferry, and this pontoon was laid on the night of the 22d. The division camped two miles further on, being unable to go further on account of the condition of the roads. Have marched nearly four miles. This evening an insane soldier shot and killed George Workman, of Company B. Several of the 113th made preparations to hang the man for this deed, but Captain Kile appearing on the scene, ended the scheme. The soldier was put under a strong guard.

25. We do not move to-day. Fatigue parties are at work building corduroy roads ahead so that we may move on, but it looks very doubtful. The waters in the Catawba are on the rise, and the pontoon breaks and washes away several times a day. It is stated that Cornwallis crossed the Wateree at this ferry during the Revolution.

28. The column moved ahead to-day, and, having with great difficulty marched four miles, camped. We are in Kershaw district, and our route to-day left Liberty Hill to our right. We have corduroyed the road with rails and poles nearly the entire distance.

MARCH, 1865.

1. Marched twenty miles to-day. At noon we took dinner near Hanging Rock, and on the spot where Generals Gates and Carleton fought during the Revolution. We have crossed two streams—Lick Creek and Hanging Rock. The country is rough and the soil excessively poor.

2. A box of shoes was issued to each regiment before day. Marched early. Company E was assigned to guard and assist the wagons of the brigade headquarters. Passed through Taxahaw in Lancaster district, and camped at Lynch Creek. Distance traveled, twelve miles.

3. Marched twenty-one miles and camped at Tompson's Creek. The bridge over this creek was burned yesterday, and the Second Brigade proceeded to build a bridge and repair the roads so that we can proceed.

4. Crossed Tompson's Creek and entered North Carolina. Our brigade is in advance, with the 113th in front. As soon as we entered North Carolina, Provost Marshal Lewis placed a guard at many of the houses, and the devastating hand was stayed for a time. Before night we again entered South Carolina. Camped on the right bank of the Great Peedee River. We began at once to corduroy the road close to the river, and a pontoon will be pushed across during the night. Have marched thirteen miles. To-day President Lincoln will be reinaugurated at Washington.

5. Sunday. Lying at a halt on the bank of the Great Peedee. The construction of the pontoon goes on slowly. The day is fine. The capture of Charleston and Wilmington is reported in camp.

7. Yesterday and the day before we remained on the right bank of the Great Peedee waiting and expecting to cross. Some ice froze last night. At noon the bugle call sounded, and, packing up, we held ourselves ready to cross. One hour after another wore slowly away. Our brigade is in the rear, and the right companies of the 113th, A, F, D, I and C, held the rear, and were the last to cross. A squad under the command of Sergeant J. R. Topping were the last of the regiment. The pontoon was then lifted and loaded, ready for use at the next crossing, wherever that may be. Having crossed in safety, the 113th went into camp within a mile of the crossing, and near the line of South Carolina and North Carolina.

This crossing is near and below the town of Sneedsboro, and several miles above Cheraw, in Fairfield district, South Carolina. The pontoon on which this wing crossed consisted of forty-two canvas boats, and was three hundred and twenty paces long.

 8. The column moved ahead at an early hour, but Mitchell's Brigade, being in the rear, did not move till 8 A. M. The 113th was rear guard to the entire column. We marched on the Rockingham road till noon, entering the State of North Carolina during the forenoon. It rained nearly all day, and the men suffered much from fatigue. At noon we filed right, taking the Fayetteville road, and, moving in a northeasterly direction, made a hard day's march of twenty-three miles.

 9. The column crossed Love's Bridge over the Lumber River about midday. A resin factory was burning on the stream above the bridge, and, as our column passed over, the surface of the water under our feet was ablaze with burning resin and turpentine, presenting a sight not easily forgotten. As we halted and made preparations for supper it was raining so hard that it was next to impossible to make a fire in the ordinary way. Some of the men struck on the plan of holding a blanket over the wood while a fire was being started The project worked well. Just before noon we reached the plank road running from Cheraw to Fayetteville, and for the rest of the day we marched on this road, the first one of the kind many of us had ever seen. Marched twenty-three miles.

 10. We marched very early. A heavy cannonading can be heard on our left since daylight, and at 7 A. M. General Mitchell's Brigade filed left and moved at quick time in the direction of the firing. We reached the scene of the fighting at the distance of nearly five miles from the plank road, and learned that three divisions of Hampton's cavalry had attacked the camp of Kilpatrick at daylight.

Our arrival was too late to render any assistance, for though Kilpatrick had been surprised and driven from his camp with the loss of his headquarters, and several of his staff officers were taken prisoner, yet he rallied his men, charged the enemy in the act of harnessing the battery horses and plundering the camp, retook the artillery he had lost, and finally forced them out of camp with great slaughter. He then established his line, and held his position for an hour against the frenzied efforts of the foe to retake it.

The Union losses were four officers and fifteen men killed, sixty men wounded, and one hundred and three of all ranks taken prisoners.

We remained here three hours, viewing the bloody scene and talking with the daring men who had achieved a victory out of the jaws of a defeat.

Our brigade then returned to the plank road from which we had moved in the morning, and, following in the line of march, camped with the division fourteen miles from Fayetteville. The brigade has marched sixteen miles.

11. The brigade moved in the rear as train guard. Halted and took dinner eight miles from Fayetteville. Our dinner consisted of mush, meat and coffee. Bradford and Stratton, my messmates, disagreed about some culinary matter (perhaps the thickness or thinness of the mush) and a war of words ensued, but when the word reached us that Fayetteville was in our hands harmony was restored, and the two men, who an hour before had hurled at each other their pointed javelins of anger, now scooped mush from the same pot, peacefully.

We moved ahead and camped in the suburbs of Fayetteville, our cavalry having taken the place early in the day with but little opposition.

Fayetteville is on the right bank of Cape Fear River, at the head of navigation. It is ninety-five miles above Wilmington and one hundred and thirty miles from the ocean. We have marched twelve miles.

12. Sunday. It is intimated that we may remain here some length of time. Procuring permission, John Ganson and I went down into town and visited places of interest. The gunboat, J. Mc B. Davidson, arrived from Wilmington to-day, and now lies in the river. While in town I wrote a letter to my wife, and placed it in the hands of a member of the 13th Indiana Volunteers of the 24th A. C. Returning to camp, we find the 113th ready to move. We fell in, marched through town, crossed Cape Fear River on a pontoon one hundred and thirty steps in length, situated just below the abutments of the bridge destroyed by the rebels yesterday. Marching up the river a mile, the division camped for the night. It was now long after dark. We have marched three miles.

13. Early this morning the regiment struck tents, and, moving up the Cape Fear River three miles, went into camp in order. The troops rested and washed their clothing.

14. James O. Kite and I went back into town and spent part of the day, stopping for a while with the family of a Mrs. Clark. A mail was sent off. I procured several copies of Kelly's History of North Carolina. Presented a copy to Captain Jones, Captain Watson and Lieutenant R. E. Robinson.

15. The command moved at 9 A. M., taking the plank road in the direction of Raleigh. A heavy rain fell during the afternoon. We marched twelve miles and camped near a creek. Our advance has had continual skirmishing with the enemy during the afternoon. Heavy cannonading can be heard on our right.

16. We moved forward at daylight. The roads are very soft and next to impassable. The Twentieth Corps is in our front. About noon the troops of the Twentieth Corps in our front met and engaged a force of the enemy posted behind works with well posted artillery enfilading the approach across a cleared field. Our division was hurried forward, and was soon in position on the left of the road, well towards Cape Fear River. Companies H and E were put on the skirmish line in front of the 113th. The whole line advanced late in the afternoon, driving the enemy's skirmishers back, back, back, till their works were in sight of our skirmishers. The skirmishers of our regiment grew short of ammunition, and a supply of cartridges was brought up. Lieutenant McCrea gave them to me, and instructed me to distribute them to the rest of the line. This I did by running from tree to tree and handing them to the men as they stood concealed in the woods.

When night came on Companies K and B took the skirmish line, relieving H and E, and these returned to the main line. I took a thin supper on corn coffee, eating the grounds for dessert. During the night the enemy withdrew. This will be known as the battle of Averysboro. Our entire loss in this action was twelve officers and sixty-five men killed and four hundred and seventy-seven wounded. The losses were mainly of the Twentieth Corps. We have marched twelve miles.

17. Our brigade being a train guard to-day, did not move till after twelve o'clock. We then pulled out and dragged our slow length along, wading swamps and floundering through mud of unmeasureable depth. Crossed Black River by wading and walking logs. We crossed other streams not deserving a name. I cannot understand what such a country was made for. We reached our camping place late in the night, having marched ten miles. We are on the Goldsboro road.

18. Morgan's Division is in the advance of the column. We started early and moved without opposition till noon, when a force of the enemy disputed our right of way. A skirmish line was deployed, and behind it was formed a line of battle, the whole moving forward grandly. The line of the 113th encountered a tall paling fence, which, as we struck it, fell flat to the ground, and the line moved ahead as steadily as if on drill. The enemy gave way, and our column halted to burn a few rails and stay over night. We are twenty-eight miles from Goldsboro, and have marched ten miles.

19. The column moved with Carlin's Division of the Fourteenth Corps in the advance. At the end of a few miles he met and began to exchange shots with the enemy. The enemy struck his advance guard at an advantage, and it soon became apparent that he had met the foe in force.

BATTLE OF BENTONVILLE

The firing of the skirmishers grew fiercer and more earnest. Now the roar of the cannon sounds through the woods, and the roar of musketry begins to tell a story of force confronting force. Our column was steadily marching in the direction of the conflict. Presently a courier is seen galloping toward and meeting our column. Halting a moment with each regimental commander, he delivers his message: "General Davis instructs that you come forward as rapidly as possible without fatiguing the men."

The men were soon on a double-quick, and after twenty minutes rapid marching we passed General Davis and staff on the side of the road, on their horses, looking anxious and peering in the direction of the contending forces. Presently we filed right into the woods, and, going some distance ahead, fronted in line. A skirmish line was formed, and we were soon pressing the skirmishers of the enemy backward toward his main line. On the left, in Carlin's front, the contest was thickening every moment, but in Morgan's front the work had not yet begun. Finally, when the enemy's skirmishers would drive no further, our men began building works. Camp hatchets and a few axes were all the implements at hand, but these flew as if life and death depended on the diligence with which they were used. Providentially, or luckily, the enemy seemed to wait on our movements, as if unwilling to meet us until we were ready to meet him. At the end of forty minutes we were nearly ready. We would have been nearer ready if we had had twenty minutes more time. Logs, stumps, limbs, and everything that could be found, had been piled in our front to protect us from the enemy's attack. All at once our skirmish line came bounding over our works, telling us to be ready, for they were coming close in their rear.

Every man of us dropped to our knees in two ranks, and made ready for the contest. The woods in our immediate front were thick with brush, and the advancing foe came within short range of our guns before we could see his line. Then we opened upon him such a fire as carried destruction and death with it, and before which a man might not hope to advance and live. This was kept up for a long while, the men in the rear rank loading the guns and those in the front rank firing. Mike Huddleston, my rear rank man, shouted in my ear after we had been engaged for some time: "My God, Mack, these guns of ours are getting too hot; we had better rest." But the work went on until it became known that the rebel line had retired. As we ceased firing we listened to ascertain the situation elsewhere. The roar of cannon on our left told the story too plainly that Carlin's Division was being driven back and badly punished. But we had all we could do to care for our part of the line. During a lull in the firing Captain Watson came along, telling me to go to the front with two men and gather ammunition off the rebel dead. Taking Isaac Green and John Ganson, I proceeded into the woods, coming upon some of the dead and wounded within a few rods of our works. We performed the duty assigned to us in a rapid manner and with some success. I came upon a wounded rebel who was fatally wounded. He cried out: "Is there no help for the widow's son?" I told him he was beyond help, and that I had no time to give to his wants, but that, as he had no further use for the cartridges in his box nor for the Yankee knapsack on his back, I would relieve him of both, which I did. We were then driven back into our works by the enemy's skirmishers, and the conflict was again renewed by the foe. Again we welcomed them by a fire more fatal, if possible, than the first. Hardly had this attack terminated in the repulse of our assailants when a force of the enemy broke through our line beyond the left of Mitchell's Brigade, and, swinging round, appeared in our rear. For a moment we were confused, not knowing whether they were friends or foes, and the enemy seemed equally puzzled at the situation. Then, climbing over our works and changing front to rear, we delivered into their ranks a raking fire, which drove them back within range of Vandeveer's Brigade, where they were made prisoners. Recrossing our works, we again met the foe in our original front. Thus the day passed away, every moment fraught with incidents which can neither be recounted nor numbered.

Night came on and active operations ceased. Many of the

wounded of the foe lay near our works, and all night their cries and appeals for help rang in our ears, robbing us of sleep. About ten o'clock Captain Jones was approached by a soldier from our rear, who inquired of him if he was in command of this regiment. He was answered affirmatively. He then delivered a message to Captain Jones, instructing him to join up in a certain movement, which created some suspicion in the Captain's mind, and, scrutinizing him closely, the Captain saw in his man a rebel. Turning to me, the Captain said: "Sergeant McAdams, take charge of this man; he is in the wrong place." I took the man's equipment, and placed him under guard. This convinced us that that part of the enemy's line which had broken through ours at an early hour in the forenoon was completely cut off from the main body.

Late in the night I made an effort, at the request of Captain Jones, to bring in and care for a wounded rebel in our front. He was making piteous appeals for assistance, and his cries had awakened sympathy, even in the hearts of his enemies. I made my way to the line of pickets, told them the object of my visit, but could not prevail on them to let me pass out.

Thus every feeling of enmity gives way to pity, and the hand which was uplifted to slay an hour ago, is now ready to do deeds of mercy to the fallen foe. Near midnight, when all seemed hushed and no enemy seemed to threaten our line, we sought out the knolls and high places in the swamp through which our line ran, and spreading our beds thereon, lay down to rest, keeping our equipments on and our arms within reach, ready for a renewal of the conflict.

We were ignorant of the situation, and knew not whether the left had been overwhelmed and destroyed or had rallied and held its own; but we knew that in our front the enemy had fallen by the hundreds, and that our men were ripe and ready for more of the same sort. We had had no dinner and no supper, but no man gave that matter a moment's thought.

20. This morning there is no renewal of the fight. Our two divisions which were guarding the wagon train yesterday, and which were not engaged, are now up, and our position is impregnable.

At noon we advanced and occupied the works of the enemy in our front, changing them so as to serve our purpose in case of an attack.

Johnson's army, which was on the offensive yesterday, is now on the defensive, with Mill Creek in his rear.

The losses in our army yesterday is nine officers and one hundred and forty-five men killed, fifty-one officers and eight hundred and sixteen men wounded, and three officers and two hundred and twenty-three men taken prisoners; total, twelve hundred and forty-seven. We took sixteen hundred and twenty-five prisoners, and buried two hundred and sixty-seven of the Confederate dead.

21. Skirmishing has been brisk all along the line to-day. Toward evening fighting began in the direction of the enemy's rear, and we are led to think that General Howard is feeling them in the right place to suit us.

22. The enemy fell back last night in the direction of Smithfield, leaving his pickets, his dead and wounded, and his hospitals in our hands. This morning the road to Goldsboro is open, and we go forward. Advancing to the opposite side of the Goldsboro road, our brigade stacked arms and remained several hours.

At 1 P. M. we moved toward Goldsboro, and late in the evening went into camp, with brigade headquarters near the Neuse River, having marched eight miles. A strong wind is driving the sand into our eyes and making things disagreeable, generally.

23. The First Division of the Fourteenth Corps took the advance. Morgan's Division followed at 10 A. M., crossing the Neuse River at Cox's Bridge.

Reaching Goldsboro at sundown, we entered and passed through the town with banners floating proudly, and with Schellhorn in advance playing the music of the Union. Went into camp a mile north of town, far from wood and—rails. We have marched twelve miles.

24. Our camp is pleasantly situated, and if General Sherman wills it we are willing to stay for some time. The day is fine, and so is the sand that blows into our mess kettles and fills our eyes.

Goldsboro has been a town of some business, with a population of two thousand five hundred. It is fifty miles from Raleigh and sixty-five from Newbern. The camp was staked off, and our tents were arranged in proper order. This may mean that we are to remain here some considerable time. Many of the men are writing letters, telling the folks at home the story of our adventures, battles, marches and successes. The half will never be told.

25. There is not much restraint in Camp to-day, and many of our men are scouting about town increasing the list of adventures which they may live to relate to their grandchildren.

26. Sunday.

"Good news from home; good news for me
Has come across the dark, blue sea."

A large mail was distributed to us to-day at noon. Thank you, Postmaster Bostwick; thank you, Uncle Sam. We shall spend the remainder of the day reading letters and papers. We can endure short rations of bread, meat and coffee, but when the mail fails us we are despondent and unhappy. Wish the people at home could understand this.

28. Have suffered some with rheumatism to-day, the first time I have ever made the acquaintance of that disease. Yesterday and to-day have been dull days in camp. We have begun work on papers and reports.

30. Yesterday I made application for a furlough for twenty days. The idea struck me that I ought to go home and rusticate a few days, drink fresh buttermilk, and fatten up a little. My modest request was based on long and faithful service, with a sprinkling of rheumatism.

Captain R. D. Stinson, A. I. G., Second Division, 14th A. C., condemned some camp and garrison equipage for the 113th to-day. I noticed one thing that escaped the attention of the officer. The same articles did duty in several companies, and were repeatedly condemned by the vigilant Inspector. Such stupidity is pardonable in an officer, but an enlisted man who would do the like ought to be punished.

31. A member of the Twelfth New York Cavalry was executed near our camp to-day by shooting. He had been found guilty of an outrageous crime on the person of an old woman somewhere of late. Many of our men went to witness the execution, but I preferred not to go; I have seen more shooting than I care about. Am working on the company pay rolls.

Green, who witnessed the execution to-day, describes it as follows:

"A large field was selected for the purpose. A brigade of armed men, with fixed bayonets, formed three sides of a square, with an open grave near the center. The prisoner approached following his coffin, which was carried by four men. The ranks were opened to a distance of fifteen paces, the front rank coming to an *about face*. Between these ranks the doomed man was marched under a strong guard. He was conducted to the grave, and the two chaplains who accompanied him knelt, and one of them offered prayer, after which the prisoner's hands were tied behind him and his eyes bandaged. Then he knelt beside his coffin, and twelve of the guard fired at him at a distance of twelve paces. He fell forward on his face, dead. I do not desire to witness another scene like this."

APRIL, 1865.

1. Captain Jones, commanding the regiment, approved my application for furlough; it passed on, and received the approval of General Mitchell.

This is a fine day, and spring is upon us in all its verdure and beauty. Look backward, and see what has transpired with us since we lay at Rossville. The retrospect is so full of achievements, battles, deeds and distances, that it seems almost like a visit to dreamland. It is estimated that since the taking of Atlanta we have traveled thirteen hundred and thirty miles, and every mile has been a page of history. We hear it rumored that Richmond has been evacuated by the Confederates.

2. Sunday. We have regimental inspection. Captain Jones started home on furlough. Though it is the Sabbath, we have worked diligently on our company papers all day.

6. A dispatch has been received by General Sherman announcing the fall of Richmond. It is a fact this time. Our brigade was massed while General Mitchell read the dispatch, and then followed such cheering as seldom vibrates on mortal ears. The men are in a state of excitement bordering on insanity.

The dullest kind of monotony has prevailed in camp for days past, but this grand news breaks in on us as a light in a dark place.

9. Sunday. The wildest excitement still prevails over the news from the Potomac, and we are expecting to move on Johnson in consequence of what has occurred in and about Richmond. Companies H and E and part of K went on picket yesterday, and returned to camp this morning. My application for a furlough has returned disapproved by division and corps commanders. I have concluded to stay a while, but when I get a command I intend that every enlisted man shall have a perpetual furlough.

Sergeant Ward and I visited Goldsboro. Jenkins and Reeder, who have been absent at hospital, joined Company E to-day. Some recruits for the other companies came in.

An organized raid was made on our sutler, Nick White, in which he suffered the loss of his principal stock of goods. We are under orders to move to-morrow. We have been at this place seventeen days.

10. Before it was fairly light we were moving toward Smithfield. The Second Brigade headed the column, with 108th O. V. I. in advance. At the distance of three miles from camp we were met by the enemy, and skirmish firing began in real earnest. The 108th Ohio deployed and drove the rebels for two miles. Here he showed some determination to stand, and artillery was used on both sides. A spirited fire ensued, resulting in killing John Bensell, Company A, of the 113th.

The enemy finally gave way, and we again moved ahead by the right of companies to the front. The enemy continues his skirmishing, and Captain Frantz Fleischman, Company H, 108th Ohio, was killed. At noon Companies A, F, D and I of the 113th took the front line of march, and the remaining six companies were in reserve. Moving on a mile further, he again brought us to a halt, using artillery freely. The advance companies pressed the foe sharply, and the reserve lay on their faces awaiting the development of events. At length he gave way, and left us in possession of his position. This occurred at Holt's Mill, near Boonhill, Johnston county, and thirteen miles from Goldsboro. Camped for the night.

11. Our column resumed the march in the direction of Smithfield, the Third Division being in advance. The enemy showed less resistance than yesterday, but he was constantly in our front. We arrived at Smithfield at 4 P. M., where we encamped, having marched twelve miles. Smithfield is the county seat of Johnston county, and is twenty-six miles southeast of Raleigh. Our advance drove a force of the enemy's cavalry out of town this forenoon. They burned the bridge that crossed the Neuse River as they retreated.

12. Early this morning we received the news of Lee's surrender to General Grant at Appomattox, Virginia, on the ninth instant. This news was received by the soldiers with great joy, which was vented in deafening and prolonged cheers. The end certainly approaches. Marching in the rear, we did not move till after noon; crossed the Neuse River on a pontoon, and, marching twelve miles, camped close to Clayton, a station fourteen miles from Raleigh. Here Governor Vance, Ex-Governor Graham, and other worthies, met General Sherman and surrendered the city to him. The conqueror guaranteed protection to private property.

13. Marched at 6 A. M., passing through Clayton, and pursued our way in the direction of Raleigh. At noon we took dinner within four miles of the city, and, moving ahead, we passed through the capital on review, marched beyond the city limits, and camped for the night, having marched sixteen miles. We are favorably impressed with the beauty of Raleigh, and agree that it is a place of more beauty than we have seen elsewhere in the Confederacy.

14. A foraging party was organized this morning, consisting of twenty men and a commissioned officer. Lieutenant McCrea has command.

The column moved westward in pursuit of Johnston's army. For eight miles our way lay along a railroad running west from Raleigh. Then, filing left at a new depot, we traversed an obscure road running a snaky course through a woody district. Marched eighteen miles, and at 4 P. M. camped near the railroad in the woods. The foragers brought in plenty of bacon and meal.

15. Marched at 5 A. M. A tremendous rain fell during the forenoon, making the marching very disagreeable. We are aiming for the Cape Fear River, and on the Lockville road. At noon we found ourselves on the wrong road; then, countermarching a mile, we took a south-southeast direction, marched till 3 P. M., when we halted and camped at Avon's Ferry, on Cape Fear River. We have marched eighteen miles. Foragers brought flour, meal, meat and poultry.

16. Sunday. We continue at Avon's Ferry, waiting the arrival and the laying of a pontoon across the river. Morgan's Division is the only force at this place. The genial spring-time has clothed every tree and shrub in a robe of green.

Something is being said in camp about Johnston's surrender to General Sherman, but we cannot get the straight of it. Sergeant Flowers made our mess an evening call, and we had the usual evening concert. The foragers captured two more horses to-day, and now the majority of them are mounted.

17. Still lying at Avon's Ferry. It is now reported as a fact that, on the fourteenth instant, General Johnston communicated by flag of truce with General Sherman, requesting an armistice and a statement of the best terms under which Sherman would allow him to surrender his command. This is about all we can learn of the matter, except that active operations are suspended in both armies. We hope this is the beginning of the end.

The morning we left Raleigh, Cisco and Ray organized an independent party of two, and went on a raid. Cisco has returned, but Ray got taken in out of the wet.

Some days ago S. F. Bailey, Company B, came in after an absence of two days and nights, clad in North Carolina jeans and a white shirt. He had lost his bearings while foraging, but came in with a full load of supplies for himself and comrades

18. We still remain at Avon's Ferry. We learn that the commanders of the two armies had a personal interview at noon yesterday at Durham's Station, and that they meet again to-day to arrange terms of surrender. With this glorious news we can afford to endure the monotony of camp. Orders have been issued prohibiting foraging except for feed for the animals.

The news came to-day that President Lincoln had been assassinated, and the sad affair was made public by the following order:

"HEADQUARTERS MILITARY DIVISION OF THE MISSISSIPPI,
IN THE FIELD, RALEIGH, APRIL 17, 1865.

"The General commanding announces, with pain and sorrow, that, on the evening of the 14th instant, at the theater in Washington City, his Excellency, the President of the United States, Mr. Lincoln, was assassinated by one who uttered the State motto of Virginia. At the same time the Secretary of State, Mr. Seward, whilst suffering from a broken arm, was also stabbed by another murderer in his own house, but still survives, and his son was wounded, supposed fatally.

"It is believed, by persons capable of judging, that other high officers were designed to share the same fate. Thus it seems that our enemy, despairing of meeting us in manly warfare, begin to resort to the assassin's tools. Your General does not wish you to infer that this is universal, for he knows that the great mass of the Confederate army would scorn to sanction such acts, but he believes it the legitimate consequences of rebellion against rightful authority. We have met every phase which this war has assumed, and must now be prepared for it in its last and worst shape—that of assassins and guerrillas; but woe unto the people who seek to expend their wild passions in such a manner, for there is but one dread result. By order of

MAJOR GENERAL W. T. SHERMAN.

L. M. DAYTON,
Major and Assistant Adjutant General."

This sad announcement creates a feeling of indescribable gloom in all our hearts, and the feeling is entertained that, if we again move against the enemy, the worst deeds of the past will be humane in comparison with what will follow. Every heart is sad, all heads are bowed in mourning, and every mind is filled with thoughts of the awful crime.

20. The dullness of camp life, and the anxiety to learn the result of the conference now pending between the commanders of the two armies, bear heavily on our minds, and we think and talk of little else than the prospect of a speedy return to peace and our homes.

Sergeant Horton, Company F, Ports, Company D, and Flowers, Company C, visited our tent this evening, and we made it mutually pleasant. We expect to move from here to-morrow.

21. We broke camp at Avon's Ferry at five o'clock this morning, and are now camped at Holly Spring in Wake county, fourteen miles from our former camp. This is a small village of two stores and a very few houses. No news from the conference.

24. We have been occupied for a day or two with ordinary camp duties. The men are excessively restless under the suspense of the past few days. We want to know the best or the worst, soon. Earnest Snyder, who was captured by the enemy at Saunderville, Ga., on the 30th of last November, joined Company E to-day. Chas. Stewart, a recruit, came to the company, also.

25. We have orders to be ready to move to-morrow. It is now understood that the terms of surrender agreed upon between Generals Sherman and Johnston have been disapproved by the authorities at Washington, and that Sherman will assume the offensive at noon to-morrow.

Later: The order to move has been countermanded.

26. The company officers are at work on rolls, papers and reports, and I have been occupied in this way for a day or two past. Late this evening a rumor prevailed that Johnston had surrendered. We shall hear more about it to-morrow, perhaps.

27. All remains quiet. Late in the evening a dispatch was received confirming the rumor that Johnston had surrendered on the terms accorded to General Lee by General Grant. Good enough. Our suspense is at an end and the war is closed.

28. Last night heavy firing was heard to the northwest, and we were unable to account for it, and therefore felt some uneasiness. This morning we learn that it was a jubilee in one of our camps, the soldiers giving vent to their joy by firing off a few hundred dollars' worth of ammunition. In the language of old Casper:

> "Things like this, you know, must be,
> After a famous victory."

All necessary plans are being perfected looking to the sending of our army to Washington, from whence the commands will be distributed to their respective states.

No. 66 Special Field Order was read to the different commands, giving the plan and order of march.

HOMEWARD BOUND.

29. Our division marched from Holly Springs at five o'clock A. M., going in the direction of Raleigh, but bearing to the left we camped at Morrisville, after a march of twelve miles. The weather is fine and we have marched rapidly. Stratton, Huddleston and I went to a creek near camp and washed. We are fifteen miles nearly west of Raleigh.

30. Sunday. We do not move. The companies were mustered for pay at one P. M. Brigade drill was had in the afternoon. It is a busy day—and Sunday at that.

MAY, 1865.

1. The command left Morrisville at five o'clock this morning, marching in the direction of Richmond, Va. Crossed the Neuse river at 2:30 P. M., and marching twenty-two miles camped on the right of the road.

2. Marched early. Passed through Oxford, the county-seat of Granville county, N. C. This is a fine looking place and the ladies who appeared at the doors and balconies to witness our marching, were well-dressed and had an intelligent look, but they made no demonstrations of joy on account of our presence, a circumstance which did not destroy our appetites. Went into camp at Fishing Creek, having marched twenty-one miles. Kite and I scouted in the evening and procured biscuits and onions.

3. Marched at 5 A. M., in the direction of Richmond. Crossed Tar river, and crossing the state line into Virginia, went into camp near the Roanoke river, having marched twenty-two miles. The Fourteenth and Twentieth Corps hindered each other's progress during the day by marching on the same road.

Crossed the Roanoke at day-break at Taylor's Ferry on a pontoon 240 steps in length, passed through Boydton, the shire town of Mecklenburg county, Va. The country shows little signs of the effects of the war. Wheat is in head. Went into camp at Meherrin river, near a mill. It begins to rain.

5. Marched at 5 A. M. in a brisk rain, accompanied with thunder. The rain laid the dust and made the marching easier. Passed through Weston, the county seat of Lewis county. Crossed the Little Nottoway river at "the falls" and encamped four miles from Nottoway C. H., having marched twenty-four miles. A fine spring near camp supplied us with good water.

6. Resuming the march at an early hour we reached Nottoway C. H. at 8 A. M. Here the sick and disabled were put on board the

cars and sent on to Petersburg. Halted at the end of seventeen miles and took dinner near a small stream on our right. Pursued our march till late in the evening, and having marched thirty-two miles, went into camp at Good's Bridge, on the Appomattox. The day has been warm and hundreds of the men, unable to keep up with the column, fell out, and taking their own time came into camp late in the night. Many are cursing the officers, some are cursing their sore feet, while a very few grin and bear it good-humoredly. I have been fortunate in having a pair of good legs, and I make it a rule to stack arms with the few who hold out to the end. But there is room for complaint, there being no necessity for marching us more than twenty miles a day. The order of march says: "These columns will be conducted slowly and in the best of order, and aim to be at Richmond, ready to resume the march, by the middle of May."

7. Sunday. If I could have had my wishes gratified we would have made this a day of rest; but marching at an early hour we crossed the Appomattox and moved on toward Richmond. Crossing Swift creek about noon we took dinner on the left upon a hill near a clear stream. Stratton had captured some green onions and our mess had sumptuous fare. Pursuing our way we camped for the night within five miles of Richmond, having marched twenty-five miles. Nearly half the men are exhausted and lie scattered along the road for miles in the rear. It takes muscle and pluck to march twenty-five miles on a day like this, carrying a heavy knapsack and other accoutrements. Rations were issued this evening.

11. We have been resting three days in camp five miles from Richmond. They have been three dull days, barren of incident or accident.

At 7 A. M. we marched toward Richmond; passed through Manchester, crossed the James river and then entered the city, the late Confederate capital. We left Castle Thunder and Libby Prison on our right; passed up Seventeenth street to Main; up Main to Thirteenth; up Thirteenth to Capitol street; through Capitol to Grace; up Grace to Adams, and thence to Brooke avenue. Large crowds of citizens crowded the sidewalks to witness the movements of our column. We passed out of the city northward toward Hanover C. H., and after a tiresome march crossed the Chickahominy river and camped in the vicinity of Fair Oaks battle ground. The weather has been warm, and I am suffering from a pain in my head. Distance marched, twenty miles.

12. Rested till noon; then moving ahead we halted for a time near Hanover, C. H. This is the place where Patrick Henry made his immortal addresses during the infancy of our Republic. I am led to remark that great orators are seldom great fighters, for although the great statesman above-named uttered sentiments that quickened the life of the nation, he neglected to go to the field and share in the fighting. Now when the *next* war comes I want to enlist as a sutler or chaplain; failing in this I shall imitate Patrick Henry by staying at home and making speeches.

Passing on northward our column crossed the Pamunky river on a pontoon, and then abandoning the road, we marched across the country for some distance, camping in an open field. A board fence near our camp disappeared and set our coffee pots to boiling nicely. We have become so accustomed to building fires of rails and boards that we don't think of looking for other fuel. Drew rations for three days; then leveling off the furrows we spread thereon our virtuous couches and slept the sleep of innocence. Marched ten miles.

13. Marched early, passing into Caroline county. Camped on the right of road after a march of eighteen miles. During the afternoon we passed the headquarters of the army of Georgia and got another sight of our great leader, W. T. Sherman. We passed Chesterfield Station, and our camp is on the road to Spotsylvania, C. H. road. Chaplain Morris preached in a church near camp in the evening.

14. Sunday. We are on our way at 7 A. M., making ten miles before dinner. In the afternoon we passed New Hope church and entering Spotsylvania county camped in a pine forest with an undergrowth of cedar. Distance marched, twenty miles.

15. Resumed the march; passing through a fine country we passed the Rapidan at Raccoon Ford. This stream is about a hundred yards wide here and nearly three feet deep. We crossed by wading, and then moving ahead we went into camp in a pasture of tame grass. Here we received three days' rations, and Company H had a small pugilistic encounter between two of its members. This section has been the center of many scenes of the war, and little remains but naked fields where once was thrift and domestic comfort. Here and there a solitary family remains, as if to defy the ravages of grim-visaged war to drive them from the sacred soil. Marched eighteen miles.

16. We marched as usual. We are now about sixty miles from Alexandria. At noon we crossed the Rappahannock, taking dinner on the left bank. Moved ahead for eight miles, and camped at a small stream called Elk Creek or Devil's Run. Have been marching through a splendid country, with only an occasional inhabitant. Think we are in Stafford county, and about sixteen miles from Warrenton. We are twenty miles closer to Alexander than we were this morning.

17. At 5 A. M. our column was moving ahead, and by noon had marched eighteen miles. We struck the Orange & Alexandria railroad at Cattlett's Station, and waded Cedar Run and Broad Run. Took dinner near a small creek, where the brigade rested more than an hour. During the afternoon we passed Manasses Junction, and viewed the works erected here early in the history of the war by our armies and our enemies. These are already fast crumbling to decay, and will soon be lost to sight.

At 5 P. M. we reached the vicinity of the historic field of Bull Run, and waded the stream, which at this place is forty yards wide and nearly three feet deep. We camped on the left of the stream and on the right of the road. Have marched twenty-five miles.

18. Left our camp on the bank of Bull Run at 5 A. M. At the distance of four miles we reached Centerville, where we struck the Alexandria and Warrenton turnpike, (the first pike we had seen in marching nearly two thousand miles) passed through Fairfax C. H., and at noon halted and camped near a creek, nine miles from Alexandria. Drew rations. Distance marched, fourteen miles.

19. At eight o'clock we fell in line, and marched on the Fairfax pike as far as Hunting Creek. Waded the creek, and, abandoning all roads, we crossed the fields in a left oblique direction and went into camp near Fort Ward, two miles from Alexandria. Have marched seven miles, and, for the present, our tramp is ended. It is seventeen days since we left Holly Spring.

23. For several days past we have been quietly camped near Fort Ward, with nothing transpiring of moment. New clothing has been issued, and we are preparing for the Grand Review, which takes place to-morrow in Washington. Many of us have never seen the Capital of the United States, and we anticipate having an enjoyable time.

THE GRAND REVIEW.

24. Made preparations to march to Washington to join in the review of the armies of Tennessee and Georgia. Our division, the Second, marched in rear of the Third Division. Reaching the Potomac at noon, we crossed the Long Bridge into the city and participated in the great event. Being a stranger in the city, and occupying a place in the ranks, is the best apology which can be made for my inability to describe the grand pageant.

For miles there was a surging, admiring multitude filling the sidewalks, windows, balconies, and every conceivable spot from which a view of our column could be had. There was waving of handkerchiefs by fair hands and cheers from husky voices, together with flags, mottoes, emblems and decorations, which no one can describe with tongue or pen.

Garlands, wreaths, festoons and evergreens added beauty and brilliancy to the scene. There was little or no effort on our part to make a display. Commanding officers seemed to take pride in having the men appear in their every-day attitude of marching or fighting. The forager was on hand, with his pack mule loaded down with bacon, forage and poultry; the pioneers carried spades, hatchets and shovels, and the artillery men trundled their heavy guns, that had done duty in swamp and morass, mountain and valley. The tattered banners told of conflicts on distant battle fields, and the decimated ranks of the infantry companies told how nobly some had fought and how bravely they had fallen. This sad thought was tempered with the reflection that the toils of the living were at an end; and though many had died of disease, or on the field of battle, their death and sacrifices had brought peace to the land from one end to the other.

Passing through Pennsylvania Avenue, we marched to Georgetown, recrossed the Potomac, and occupied the camp from which we moved in the forenoon. Every man has his story to tell of how the review went off, but all admit that the half can not be told. I find it as much of a task to describe a grand review as a great battle. I have attempted both and failed.

25. Remained camped till noon, when we struck tents, marched to the Potomac, crossed on the Long Bridge, passed through Washington, and encamped two and one-half miles north of the city, near Fort Slemmer and the Soldiers' Home. This is about eight miles from our former camp.

26. A rainy, disagreeable day. Lieutenant A. M. Grafton, who has been on detached duty and absent from the regiment, joined us to-day. The rain keeps us in our tents and creates a spirit of unrest.

27. A pair of chickens roosting in the neighborhood were brought in and cared for by Craig and Snyder. Though the war is at an end,

it does not destroy our weakness for chicken pot-pie. We have been for so long accustomed to appropriating what comes within our reach that is fit to eat that we find it difficult to quit our old tricks. Then, chickens ought to know better than to roost near the camp of an Ohio regiment.

29. With better weather we are enjoying ourselves better than heretofore.

Captain Kile, Lieutenant McCrea, myself and others visited the city, and spent the day in viewing the public buildings and places of interest. Every place is crowded with soldiers, all busy seeing the sights. We soldiers seem to feel an increased interest in the Capital of the Nation.

A short distance from our camp is a National cemetery, in which are interred several thousand of our gallant dead. The inclosure is divided into sections by streets and avenues. The grave of each soldier is marked by his name, command, and date of death. It is a beautiful place and kept in the very best condition. In the western part of the grounds stands a beautiful little chapel, over the door of which is this inscription:

> "On fame's eternal camping ground
> Their silent tents are spread;
> And glory guards with solemn round
> The bivouac of the dead."

31. Since we occupied this camp there has been less effort to construct quarters than in our previous camps. The men are led to believe that our stay here will be brief, and they are content with simply pitching their shelter tents, as has been our custom when halted for the night.

The usual busy time of preparing reports, rolls, statements and accounts, has begun at the several company headquarters, and this work will go on from day to day until everything is brought up to date.

JUNE, 1865.

1. The day has been partially observed as a day of fasting and prayer. Religious services were held in some parts of camp, but the men pay very little attention to those matters. They are too anxious about getting home to think of anything besides. At the fort east of our camp a soldier of the garrison was being punished by being made to carry a log of wood back and forth before an officer's tent. Some of our regiment went over in a body, and relieved the man from duty by bringing the log into camp with them, cautioning the officers not to attempt to inflict such a punishment on a man while we remain near them. Major Sullivant is with us, but resigned a day or two ago. Lieutenant Colonel Warner is here also, and is looking reasonably well. This is the first we have seen of him since he lost his arm at Kenesaw. When we met to-day, he exclaimed: "My God, Sergeant, are you yet alive? I saw you last where I supposed no man could stay and live, and, as I had never heard of you since, I supposed you were slaughtered at Kenesaw." He then told me that while the fight was going on at Kenesaw he saw me exposed to the fire of the enemy, and, fearing that I would be killed, he motioned to me to lie down, and while doing so his right arm was struck and shattered.

Many civilians from the city of Washington visit our camp daily. They seem to look upon the men of Sherman's army as being of a peculiar species, and they watch us in our camp customs with as much interest as though they had never seen a soldier. They know something of our rough-and-tumble record, especially that of the past twelve months, and this accounts for their interest in us. The women who come into camp to peddle pies and other delicacies, bring whisky in small bottles and sell to the men on the sly. They secrete the whisky bottles under their skirts near the waist, and, when a soldier wants to purchase a flask of the "ardent," the peddler takes momentary refuge in the tent of the buyer, and then, fishing out the bottle, the trade is consummated in a moment, and the enterprising seller moves on.

3. The 98th O. V. I. started home yesterday. We have been brigaded with them so long that they seemed like brothers to us. The 113th occupied their camp after they had departed.

I spent part of the day in Washington, but saw more than any one can tell. General George H. Thomas reviewed his old corps, the Fourteenth, late this evening. We had not seen the old hero since the fatal day of Kenesaw. A short time after dark a meeting was called to nominate a delegate to attend the approaching State Republican Convention, at Columbus. Lieutenant Colonel Warner was chosen by acclamation, after which speeches were made by J. C. Doty, Company K, and John F. Chapman, Company A.

The Sanitary Commission issued pickles, onions, canned tomatoes and lemons to us to-day. I stepped into General Mitchell's tent to-day, and lying on the desk was the photograph of an infant. On the bottom margin was written: "Half is mine and half is thine." This is the portrait of the General's first baby, a girl, and he is very proud of it. Who wouldn't be?

4. Sunday. An order has been issued allowing furloughs to five *per cent.* of each regiment. I prepared an application for furlough for twenty days, having learned of the dangerous illness of my youngest sister. Religious services were held in camp in the forenoon, afternoon and evening. Secretary Seward passed through camp this afternoon, but did not stay for supper. He rolled past in a grand carriage, and did nor attract the attention that a Major General would have done. Fame is an empty bubble, anyhow.

5. In company with John O'Leary, Jeremiah Bair, D. R. Taylor, Michael Huddleston, John Wilson and others, I made a visit to Washington. We spent some time in the Post Office, Patent Office, Smithsonian Institute, and other places of interest. Captain Joseph Swisher has tendered his resignation.

6. My application for a furlough returned to-day disapproved. It passed up approved till it reached General H. W. Slocum at corps headquarters, where it was disapproved. This explanatory statement is endorsed upon it:

"This man having been mustered into service August 15th, 1862, will be discharged in a few days."

8. The men of the 113th chafe and fret because they see other regiments of the troops of 1862 starting for the states where they belong, preparatory to being mustered out and discharged. It requires a great exercise of patience not to feel that we are being overlooked and neglected. Our company officers now have all their back papers completed, and are ready to begin the final rolls. Several Ohio regiments started west to-day. The old reliable 78th Illinois left for their homes to-day. God bless their brave souls; they have done honor to their State on many well fought fields. Two posts of the Sanitary Commission are located near our camp, and to-day we received from them a good supply of pickles and lemons; also a few shirts.

The Sixth Corps was reviewed in the city to-day. Many of our officers were present, and reported an enjoyable time.

10. The resignation of Captain Swisher gives opportunity for the promotion of Lieutenant McCrea to Captain. Few officers have such a record for faithfulness as he. He has won the esteem of all with whom he has associated, and now that he is promoted we all seem to share in his good fortune. Captain Watson is promoted to Major. He has never been found wanting, though he has been often tried. I will be sorry to separate from many of these brave and good men.

11. Sunday. The 108th O. V. I. and the 121st O. V. I. started for Ohio this morning. They have both done good service for their country. It is like parting with one's family to see the regiments of the old *Second Brigade* pulling out. The 34th Illinois is still with us, but we shall soon part from them also.

General Mitchell left for home yesterday. Our brigade now consists of the 35th Indiana Volunteers, 22d Indiana Volunteers, 34th Illinois Volunteers, and the 113th O. V. I.

The brigade is commanded by Colonel Burton. We have some hopes of leaving Washington to-morrow. Chaplain Morris preached to us at three this afternoon.

HOMEWARD BOUND.

12. The 113th remained in camp during the forenoon, waiting orders and expecting every minute to march. The order came at 11 A. M.. The men cheered a cheery cheer, down came the tents, and all was soon packed and ready. At 12:30 we marched toward the city, and halted near the gas works preparatory to embarking on the cars. Here we remained waiting, waiting, waiting, until our patience was well nigh exhausted. The sun beamed down upon us with an almost blistering heat, rendering our halt on the avenue very uncomfortable. Finally we boarded a train and began moving out of the city. Before the train got out of Washington a coupling broke, and the front part of the train went on, leaving several cars and their loads in the city. The men piled out and spent the time in the city till near midnight, when the engine returned, and, coupling on to the remaining part of the train, pulled ahead and joined the other part. Thirty-five men to a car gave plenty of room. Of course restless soldiers would prefer riding on the outside rather than the inside. We left Washington with pleasure; there is no place on earth but home where we would be satisfied to stay now.

13. Our train reached the Relay House, nine miles from Baltimore, some time in the night. Here we took the Baltimore and Ohio road for Harper's Ferry, which place we reached about 11 A. M. to-day. At four this afternoon we reached Cumberland, Maryland, where we are to remain till midnight. We have passed through cities, villages and stations; climbed mountains, crossed gorges, ravines, rivers and valleys, each possessing some item of interest; but the thought which most absorbed our minds is the thought of being soon at home, freed from military restraints and permitted to go out and come in at will.

During last night a member of Company B fell from the train, and was probably killed

NOTE.—The following letter, found in the office of the Adjutant General of Ohio, gives further information in this case:

> HEADQUARTERS THIRD MARYLAND BATTALION, VET. VOLS,
> LAURAL STATION, MARYLAND, *June 14th*, 1865.
>
> *To His Excellency, the Governor of Ohio:*
>
> YOUR EXCELLENCY:—I have the honor respectfully to report to you the following:
>
> About 12 M., on the 13th instant, a train passed the station above this, called White Oak Bottom, when a soldier fell from one of the cars, who died at six o'clock and thirty minutes the same morning. He was buried with proper ceremonies by me near the Station His name seems to be Alexander Henry, Company B, 113th Ohio Volunteers, residing in Mechanicsburg, Ohio. From the loss of blood he was very weak when he gave us his name, and it remains doubtful if this is his full name and address. From a letter found on his person, signed by a lady who calls herself "Teets" and his sister, he lost two brothers in the war
>
> I take the liberty to communicate this sad news to your Excellency, in order that his family may obtain the information. His regiment was probably on the same train and on its way home.
>
> Your Excellency will greatly oblige me by a few lines informing me of his correct name, when I will see that a proper head-board is placed on his grave.
>
> I am, very respectfully,
> Your Excellency's obedient servant,
> ARTHUR O. BRICKMAN,
> *Chaplain 3d Md. Vet. Vol. Infantry, 3d Brigade, 1st Division, 9th A. C.*

14. Our train left Cumberland near midnight, and this morning found us at Piedmont, thirty-eight miles from Cumberland. Here we began to ascend the Alleghanies, reaching the top at two o'clock in the afternoon. Then for nearly twenty miles we ran on a level country, reaching Cranberry Summit, where our train was divided into four sections, with a locomotive to each. For four hours we descended a heavy grade, the scenery being of the wildest and most romantic character we have ever beheld. Reaching Grafton at six o'clock we took supper and were again moving on.

15. We ran through Clarksburg at dusk last evening and this morning at sun up we arrived at Parkersburg. Disembarking from the train, on which we had spent three nights and two days, we boarded the steamer Ella Faber. During last night we traveled one hundred and four miles, the distance from Grafton to Parkersburg. The whole distance from Washington is very nearly five hundred miles. We are done with our weary car ride and will now have a change for something better, an Ohio river steamer.

About the middle of the afternoon our bark backed out from the landing, and heading down stream moved for Louisville, our destination. As we pass Blannerhassett Island we recall the days of childhood, the school house, the old reader from which we first read of Aaron Burr and Harman Blannerhassett. How unreined ambition sometimes supplants every nobler feeling of our nature, turns our heaven to hell and leaves us full of disappointment and sorrow.

On our right are the grand, green hills of our native Ohio. The trees sway to and fro and seem to offer us a welcome to the land we love the best. How the sight quickens our pulses and how we long to stand on her shores and with the poet sing the language of our happy hearts:

"I'm with you once again, my friends,
 No more my footsteps roam;
Where it began my journey ends,
 Amid the scenes of home
No other clime has skies so blue,
 Nor streams so broad and clear,
And where are hearts so warm and true
 As those that meet me here?"

"Since last, with spirits wild and free,
 I pressed my native strand,
I've wandered many miles at sea,
 And many miles on land;
I've seen fair regions of the earth,
 With rude commotion torn,
Which taught me how to prize the worth
 Of that where I was born."

"My native land! I turn to you,
 With blessing and with prayer,
Where man is brave and woman true,
 And free as mountain air.
Long may our flag in triumph wave
 Against the world combined,
And friends a welcome—foes a grave
 Within her borders find."

16. Our boat ran cautiously during the night, and this morning we halted at Gallipolis on the Ohio shore to let some one off. Reached Cincinnati at one o'clock in the night and after a halt of thirty minutes we again moved on. The day has been pleasant and the people of the town's and cities through which we have passed have greeted us with shouts of welcome, waving of hats and handkerchiefs and with other demonstrations of joy. At Portsmouth, Gallipolis, Ripley and Maysville salutes were fired as we passed. Many of our men are hoarse from continued shouting in answer to the greetings from the shore.

17. At Louisville, Ky. Our trip down the Ohio ended at four o'clock this evening. It has been a very pleasant one to most of us, for we felt that every revolution of the wheels of the boat brought us that much nearer the end. Schellhorn's band enlivened the trip with good music, and the constantly changing scenery on either hand combined to make the time pass pleasantly. The distance from Washington to Louisville is 850 miles.

Disembarking from the Ella Faber the 113th marched through Louisville and went into camp late in the evening on the "Owl Creek Farm," in the vicinity of the fair grounds, and four miles from the city. Our passage through Louisville did not elicit a bit of enthusiasm from the citizens. This was in cool contrast with the joyous greetings we have been receiving since we left Washington. But, then, Louisville is in Kentucky.

18. Sunday. The weather is hot, but a shower to-day gave some relief. The 113th re-pitched its tents, going to a more desirable spot half a mile distant. The three other regiments of our brigade are camped near us.

19. Camp is very quiet. The men begin to talk about getting paid and are planning what they will do with their wages. Wages are due us for ten months, and when we are paid it will pile up amazingly. Many soldiers fare as well without money as with it, some do much better; but for myself, I like to have a little on hand for emergencies.

20. We have struck and pitched tents only twice to-day, and the site we now occupy is in dispute. This is a big country and there is certainly room for each of us to spread our dog tent where it will not interfere with some one else. The officers who were recently promoted were mustered to-day.

21. The troops of other commands have been paid off and the men are buying new clothes of the civilian pattern.

Government brogans are being laid aside, the slouch hat has been abandoned, and a new watch and chain adorns each lad you meet. The faro-banker is doing a live business and the chuckalucker is full of business in many places. Some of these discharged men will have only the clothes on their backs to show for their wages when they get home.

22. Ten per cent. of the men are being furloughed for ten days. Work on the final papers and muster rolls has begun, and the company officers are too busy to go to the theater at night. How unlucky. Getting paid and getting home are the leading topics now.

23. To-day the one-year men were mustered out by special order. They numbered about forty in the regiment. These and our furloughed men started homeward in a body. We have no duty to perform and the monotony of camp is becoming oppressive.

25. Sunday. We are now getting a better supply of rations than at any time in the past two years. We get hard bread, soft bread, soap, candles, beans, pickles, sugar, coffee, salt and pepper. We are told that the paymaster began paying the men of the first brigade of our division to-day. At five o'clock this evening we had dress-parade —the first since we were at Goldsboro, N. C. A roll-call this morning and inspection to day. Getting back to first principles. Several of the commissioned officers visited a certain German garden, two miles from camp. I suspect that the Teuton keeps something in his garden besides vegetables.

27. A year ago to-day we fought, bled and fled at Kenesaw. Who can ever forget that 27th day of June, 1864? What a record we have made since that day. Now all is over and friend and foe go home to fight no more.

28. Eighty men have been furloughed in the proper way, and nearly as many have *frenched* on their own account.

The authorities in the city use every effort to prevent our men from getting liquor, but it is not successful. They will get it and many disgraceful riots and melees ensue. The women peddlers of pies and cakes are closely watched and often searched on account of the fact that they bring whisky into camp and sell it to the men.

An old Dutch lady and her two daughters came into camp and gave us a serenade with several instruments. After playing a few pieces they take a collection of the crowd around them. One of the girls made an unsuccessful effort to cross the creek to collect something of a number of officers who stood on the opposite side. An over-gallant soldier took the girl in his arms and attempted to ferry her across in that way; but when part way over he lost his balance and both went down. They both floundered through amid the shouts of the delighted crowd.

30. Major Carpenter, one of the army paymasters, paid us eight months pay to-day. I received $161. This brings us up to the first of May. When we are discharged we will be paid all that is then due us. The men are busy settling debts of all kinds. We were mustered this afternoon for May and June.

A strong force is now engaged on the muster-out rolls. These are to be made in seven rolls, all alike. It requires a vast amount of careful work.

JULY, 1865.

1. Now that the men of the 113th have plenty of money they are in the city to-day spending it freely. I can not blame them for wanting to doff the blue and don citizen's dress. It seems so natural, now that peace has come, to return to our former lives and customs. I feel like I would never again like to hear the roar of cannon and the command to shoulder arms. I have taken delight in it in times past, but I am sick of martial music and of the gory glory of war.

Our men are exchanging photographs with each other in token of friendship. We realize now that in a few days we are to separate, never to meet again. The thoughts of peace and home are thus tinged with a feeling of sadness. I have been very busy for some time on the company rolls.

2. Sunday. "Don't you want to buy a rabbit?" queried the pie woman. "A what?" asked I. "A rabbit, don't you understand?" Yes, I understood it in a moment, but I suggested she had better try some one who was thirstier than I. She found a buyer for the "rabbit," and it was soon uncorked and emptied. The weather continues very hot, day and night. The churches in the city were crowded with soldiers to-day. They are laying in a stock of piety for the home visit. I have been eating too much and am on the sick list.

3. Our men are mostly in the city, and the camp looks nearly deserted. Night will bring them all in and then each will have a story of his exploits to recite, for no soldier of the 113th would think of spending a day in Louisville and not having an adventure worth telling.

4. At an early hour we received notice that the second division would be reviewed by General Sherman. A number of the men skipped for the city to avoid this exercise. The 113th took its position in the parade and bore a creditable share in the movements. At the close of the review the division was massed and General Sherman addressed the troops at some length. He referred to the long and noble service which the troops of this division had seen, to the situation one year ago to-day and to the happy circumstances by which we are now surrounded. He said that the whole division, officers and men, had no superiors as soldiers, and that the country will never be able to pay the debt of gratitude which it owes to the men who have done and suffered so much. He said he would see us no more as soldiers, but he hoped to see and know us hereafter as citizens of a great and happy country. He bade us farewell in tones full of emotion and meaning.

This is the third national anniversary which we have spent in the South, each of which has been attended with peculiar surroundings. When the next one comes we will be far from scenes like this, and surrounded by that domestic peace which years of toil and danger have taught us to prize at its true value.

This is a very hot day and we have suffered in consequence. We are nearly done with the rolls. When these are completed and approved we will be mustered out.

5. We have completed our muster-out rolls and our muster pay-rolls, and the mustering officer need wait on us no longer. We are ready. Made an ordinance return for second quarter, 1865. Late in the evening a jubilee occurred in camp, and one unaccustomed to such scenes would have concluded that the men had been to a beer garden.

6. The mustering officer for whom we have waited so long appeared at regimental headquarters at noon, and began his work by mustering out the field and staff; then came the non-commissioned staff, and finally the companies in their order, A, F, D, I, C, H, E, K, G, B. The work was finished at 2:30 P. M. We have been busy in the necessary work of packing up and preparing to start for Columbus, Ohio.

7. Early this morning we pulled down our tents, and together with our camp and garrison equipage, turned them over to the quarter-

master of the brigade. At nine o'clock we formed in line and started in the direction of Louisville. We were escorted a short distance by the 14th Michigan Infantry, who bade us farewell. We reached the wharf at the Ohio river and there remained several hours before our boat was ready. In this time many of the men fired up with liquid poison, and a disgraceful riot occurred. The drunken men determined to prevent the colored men belonging to the regiment from taking passage with us to Ohio. They resorted to violence and some of the colored men were badly hurt, but I think none of them were entirely driven off. At noon we went on board the Prima Donna, and after an hours' delay in loading some baggage, we began to move up the river. Our boat was a stern-wheel craft of the second class, having a barge in tow, and our progress was too slow to be agreeable. During the afternoon William H. Whitney, of Company E, was robbed of more than $200 by Chas. Alden, of Company C. The principal part of the money was recovered and the thief put under guard.

8. Our progress during the night was provokingly slow. We reached Lawrenceburg, Ind., shortly after daylight, and at 10:30 A. M. landed at the wharf at Cincinnati. A guard at the gang plank prevented the men from disembarking and scattering through the city.

At half-past twelve we went ashore, formed in line and marched to the Little Miami depot. Here we were loaded into a train of eleven box cars, with seats. We moved out at 1:30 P. M. As we left the city the siding on our cars yielded to the persuasive knocks of our guns, and the delighted urchins of the city gathered a good supply of kindling wood. We ran at a rapid rate, halting at Xenia and other points. At London we halted ten minutes. Here the friends of companies A. and G. gave their sons and brothers in those companies a joyous greeting, like that which awaits the rest of us, further on. As we neared Columbus, Alden, the thief, jumped from the cars and made for the woods, unpursued.

We reached Columbus at 7 P. M., and marching to Tod's Barracks on High street we stacked arms and made some inquiry for supper. The officer in command conducted us into the feed department of the barracks and showed us the bill of fare. It was not inviting, nor did it come up to our standard of a supper, such as returning soldiers deserved. Some emphatic criticisms were indulged in and many of the men left the hall in disgust. Others remained and worried down their suppers, then took to the streets for a *ratification*. They ratified and jubilated till a late hour, and then returning to the barracks shared for a time with the gray-backs which held possession. At midnight our boys declared themselves repulsed by the vermin, and retiring to the street spent the rest of the night wandering about over the city.

9. Sunday. Many of our men attended worship at the various churches, others slept the day away. Earnest Snyder, John Ganson, John Craig, Oliver Craig and I went to the Whetstone river and bathed. Captain McCrea and I invoiced ordinance belonging to Co. E. Considerable work is to be done before we can be discharged, but we will be ready to-morrow. This is certainly our last Sabbath with Uncle Sam. The pay rolls were signed to-day.

10. At noon we turned over the guns which had done our fighting for us. They were good ones and have made their mark on Rebeldom. Early in the afternoon we received our pay and final discharges, and once more we are citizens.

The majority of the men boarded the first trains leaving in the direction of their homes, but many remained over night.

Late in the afternoon, those who remained, attended a reception or welcome, given the 113th at Goodale Park, by the ladies and citizens of Columbus. It was an enjoyable occasion and reflected the feelings of the good citizens of the city toward the men who had done gallant service for the State. Speeches were made by General J. D. Cox, General John G. Mitchell, Colonel Wilcox, Colonel Warner, Colonel Jones and Honorable Henry C. Noble. A bounteous supper followed and then a tremendous rain put an end to all, and before we could find shelter we were all thoroughly wet.

The exercises of the afternoon are spoken of by the Ohio State Journal, of the 11th, as follows:

"RECEPTION OF THE 113TH, O. V. I."

"The shower yesterday afternoon was no doubt needed, as the atmosphere cooler was needed by everyone, but we are sorry to say that it came in a very bad time, and almost spoiled one of the best arranged and most complete receptions of the season.

"The 113th O. V. I., noted for prompt action throughout its term of service, arrived in the city on Saturday evening, one day sooner than expected, and somewhat disarranged the programme of those preparing for the members thereof, a formal reception.

"This disarrangement was but shortlived, and busied preparations yesterday culminated in the evening in the production of a fine collation spread upon the tables of the Park. Our citizens seemed to make amends for former neglect and were out in full force.

"This was especially true in reference to the ladies, more of them being present yesterday evening than at any other five receptions tendered our returning soldiers.

"The 113th, escorted by the band of the 18th Regulars, marched from the barracks at about five o'clock, carrying with them as trophies their two tattered flags, literally torn to pieces in service. These attracted much attention, and the boys seemed as proud of them as the people were anxious to see them.

"The tables were surrounded with an easy, orderly kind of a movement, and the veterans proceeded to enjoy the substantials and delicacies. With so much that was good before them, and with so many pleasant and pretty faces around them, to have not enjoyed the feast would have been impossible.

"After the disposition of the eatables to the satisfaction of all concerned, the boys concentrated in front of the speaker's stand and were addressed by General Mitchell, Henry C. Noble, Colonel Wilcox, Major General J. D. Cox and Lieutenant Colonel Warner. The addresses were all in good taste, brief, pointed and were most enthusiastically received. Each speaker was greeted with cheers, and after each speech came rounds of applause.

"In the midst of Colonel Warner's speech came the afore-mentioned shower and the crowd dispersed on the 'double quick' order.

"The scene was most peculiar and irresistibly funny, in spite of the dampening qualities of the rain.

"'Ye local' was among the unfortunates, and begs to be excused from talking about the weather in this connection.

"The 113th was organized at Camp Chase, October 10th, 1862. The men composing this regiment were recruited principally in Franklin, Licking, Madison and Pickaway counties, and on the 25th of October the regiment, with six hundred men, was on its way to active service. That it saw a goodly amount of this, the following names of battles in which it was engaged bear witness: Commencing at Chickamauga, then follow Wilson's Creek, Mill Creek Gap, Rome, Resaca, Kenesaw Mountain, Peachtree Creek, Atlanta, Jonesboro, Savannah, Averysboro, Bentonville, etc.

"The regiment was first commanded by Colonel James A. Wilcox, afterwards by Colonel (now General) Mitchell, and returns to its starting point in charge of Lieutenant Colonel Toland Jones."

113th REGIMENT OHIO VOLUNTEER INFANTRY.---Roster, Three Years' Service.

Rank.	Name.	Date of Rank.	Com. Issued.	Remarks.
Colonel	JAMES A. WILCOX	Dec. 28, 1862	Dec. 31, 1862	Resigned April 20, 1863.
"	JOHN G. MITCHELL	April 29, 1863	May 26, 1863	Promoted to Brigadier General.
"	DARIUS B. WARNER	Feb. 23, 1865	Feb. 23, 1865	Resigned June 6, 1865.
Lt. Colonel	TOLAND JONES	June 8, 1865	June 8, 1865	Mustered out with regiment as Lieut. Col.
"	JOHN G. MITCHELL	Sept. 2, 1862	Dec. 31, 1862	Promoted to Colonel.
"	DARIUS B. WARNER	April 29, 1863	May 6, 1863	Promoted to Colonel.
"	TOLAND JONES	Feb. 23, 1865	Feb. 23, 1865	Promoted to Colonel.
Major	OTWAY WATSON	June 8, 1865	June 8, 1865	Mustered out with regiment as Major.
"	DARIUS B. WARNER	Sept. 8, 1862	Dec. 31, 1862	Promoted to Lieutenant Colonel.
"	LYNE S. SULLIVANT	April 29, 1863	May 6, 1863	Resigned May 20, 1865.
"	ODWAY WATSON	June 8, 1865	June 28, 1865	Promoted to Lieutenant Colonel.
"	ABRAHAM L. SHEPHERD			Mustered out with regiment as Captain.
Surgeon	JAMES L. BLACK	August 9, 1862	Dec. 31, 1862	Resigned July 31, 1863.
"	ALBERT WILSON	July 31, 1863	Dec. 8, 1863	Mustered out with regiment.
Ass't Surgeon	T. C. TIPTON	Sept. 1, 1862	Dec. 31, 1862	Resigned May 11, 1863.
"	ALONZO HARLOW	Sept. 3, 1862	Dec. 31, 1862	Resigned June 8, 1863.
"	GEORGE W. KEMP	May 19, 1863	May 19, 1863	Resigned October 6, 1863.
"	H. M. HASSETT	July 20, 1863	July 20, 1863	Transferred to 121st O. V. I. as Surgeon.
Chaplain	JOSEPH MORRIS	Sept. 16, 1863	Sept. 16, 1863	Mustered out with regiment.
Captain	Toland Jones	August 11, 1862	Dec. 31, 1862	Promoted to Lieutenant Colonel.
"	David Taylor, Jr	August 12, 1862	Dec. 31, 1862	Resigned June 10, 1863.
"	Wm. C. Peck	August 12, 1862	Dec. 31, 1862	Resigned March 17, 1863.
"	Marvin M. Munson	August 12, 1862	Dec. 31, 1862	Resigned January 13, 1863.
"	John F. Riker	August 14, 1862	Dec. 31, 1862	Resigned May 15, 1863.
"	Levi T. Nichols	August 17, 1862	Dec. 31, 1862	Mustered out August 25, 1865.
"	Harrison Z. Adams	August 22, 1862	Dec. 31, 1862	Resigned January 28, 1863.
"	Lyne S. Sullivant	Nov. 13, 1862	Dec. 31, 1862	Promoted to Major.
"	Nathan Straus	Oct. 27, 1862	Jan. 6, 1863	Resigned May 17, 1863.
"	Abraham L. Shepherd	Dec. 8, 1863	Jan. 25, 1864	Promoted to Major.
"	Thomas J. Downey	Jan. 13, 1863	Feb. 4, 1863	Promoted In U. S. Colored Regiment.
"	Alvin L. Messmore	Jan. 28, 1863	Feb. 4, 1863	Declined promotion.
"	Joshua M. Wells	March 17, 1863	April 14, 1863	Killed September 20, 1863.
"	Nelson Durant	March 17, 1863	April 14, 1863	Honorably discharged November 25, 1864.
"	Otway Watson	May 16, 1864	May 16, 1864	Promoted to Major.
"	John Bowersock	May 15, 1863	May 25, 1863	Killed June 27, 1864.
"	Horatio N. Benjamin	June 10, 1863	June 23, 1863	Resigned August 30, 1864.
"	Lucius Windle	June 14, 1864	June 14, 1864	Mustered out with regiment.
"	Joseph Swisher	July 25, 1864	July 25, 1864	Resigned June 6, 1865.
"	James Kent Hamilton	July 1864	July 1864	Mustered out with regiment.
"	John W. Kile	Oct. 12, 1864	Oct. 12, 1864	Mustered out with regiment.
"	John S. Skeels	Feb. 10, 1865	Feb. 10, 1865	Mustered out with regiment.

Rank	Name	Date	Date	Remarks
Captain	Charles Garman	May 31, 1865	May 31, 1865	Mustered out with regiment.
"	George McCrea	June 8, 1865	June 8, 1865	Mustered out with regiment.
"	James R. Ladd	June 8, 1865	June 8, 1865	Mustered out with regiment.
1st Lieutenant	George H. Lippincott	June 28, 1865	June 28, 1865	Mustered out with regiment as 1st Lieut.
"	Nathan C. Vickers	August 11, 1862	August 11, 1862	Resigned January 13, 1863.
"	Thomas J. Downey	August 12, 1862	August 12, 1862	Promoted to Captain.
"	Samuel H. Hughes	August 12, 1862	August 12, 1862	Resigned February 1, 1863.
"	Frederick A. Eno	August 13, 1862	August 13, 1862	Resigned January 28, 1863.
"	Nelson Durant	August 14, 1862	August 14, 1862	Promoted to Captain.
"	John Bowersock	Sept. 3, 1862	Sept. 3, 1862	Promoted to Captain.
"	Erasmus Skerrett	Sept. 8, 1862	Sept. 8, 1862	Resigned January 26, 1864.
"	Charles C. Cox	Sept. 5, 1862	Sept. 5, 1862	Resigned May 28, 1863.
"	Alvin L. Messmore	Nov. 13, 1862	Nov. 13, 1862	Promoted to Captain.
"	George St. Clair	Dec. 31, 1862	Dec. 31, 1862	Resigned February 1, 1864.
"	Otway Watson	Jan. 28, 1863	Jan. 28, 1863	Promoted to Captain.
"	Charles Sinnett	Feb. 1, 1863	Feb. 1, 1863	Commissioned in Engineer Corps.
"	Joshua M. Wells	Feb. 13, 1863	Feb. 13, 1863	Promoted to Captain.
"	Horatio N. Benjamin	Jan. 29, 1863	Jan. 29, 1863	Promoted to Captain.
"	Julius C. Bostwick	Feb. 5, 1863	Feb. 5, 1863	Died March 16, 1864.
"	Miles C. Nolan	Oct. 27, 1862	Oct. 27, 1862	Resigned February 2, 1863.
"	Lucius Windle	March 17, 1863	March 17, 1863	Promoted to Captain.
"	George W. Holmes	March 17, 1863	March 17, 1863	Killed in action September 20, 1863.
"	Edward P. Haynes	Feb. 2, 1863	Feb. 2, 1863	Discharged March 15, 1864.
"	Aquilla Toland	April 25, 1863	April 25, 1863	Resigned January 18, 1864.
"	James Kent Hamilton	May 29, 1863	May 29, 1863	Promoted to Captain.
"	Joseph Swisher	May 15, 1863	May 15, 1863	Promoted to Captain.
"	John W. Kile	June 10, 1863	June 10, 1863	Promoted to Captain.
"	Charles Garman	Dec. 26, 1863	Dec. 26, 1863	Promoted to Captain.
"	Cyrus G. Platt	Feb. 1, 1864	Feb. 1, 1864	Killed June 15, 1864.
"	John S. Skeels	Feb. 1, 1864	Feb. 1, 1864	Promoted to Captain.
"	Wm. H. Baxter	Feb. 23, 1864	Feb. 23, 1864	Honorably discharged November 25, 1864.
"	George McCrea	June 14, 1864	June 14, 1864	Promoted to Captain.
"	James R. Ladd	June 14, 1864	June 14, 1864	Died July 4, 1861, at Chickamauga.
"	Jesse W. Dungan	June 14, 1864	June 14, 1864	Honorably discharged as 2d Lt. Oct. 8, '64.
"	Theodore D. Bentley	June 14, 1864	June 14, 1864	Killed June 27, 1864.
"	Edward Crouse	July 25, 1864	July 25, 1864	Discharged as 2d Lt. Oct. 26, 1864.
"	Jonathan Watson	July 25, 1864	July 25, 1864	Promoted to Captain.
"	George H. Lippincott	August 19, 1864	August 19, 1864	Mustered out with regiment as Reg't Q.M.
"	George W. Brigham	August 19, 1864	August 19, 1864	Mustered out with regiment.
"	James Coulths	Oct. 12, 1864	Oct. 12, 1864	Mustered out with regiment.
"	Wm. A. M. Davis	Feb. 10, 1865	Feb. 10, 1865	Mustered out with regiment.
"	David H. Chatfield	Feb. 10, 1865	Feb. 10, 1865	Mustered out with regiment.
"	Ambrose E. Grafton	Feb. 10, 1865	Feb. 10, 1865	Mustered out with regiment.
"	Wm. Grove	Feb. 10, 1865	Feb. 10, 1865	Mustered out with regiment.
"	Timothy Haley	May 31, 1865	May 31, 1865	Mustered out with regiment.
"	Benj. W. Mason	May 31, 1865	May 31, 1865	Mustered out with regiment.
"	Isaac N. Hobill	June 8, 1865	June 8, 1865	Mustered out with regiment as Adjutant.

113th REGIMENT OHIO VOLUNTEER INFANTRY.—Roster, Three Years' Service.—Continued.

RANK.	NAME.	DATE OF RANK.	COM. ISSUED.	REMARKS.
1st Lieutenant	Alex. Carpenter	June 8, 1865	June 8, 1865	Mustered out with regiment.
"	John R. Cross	June 8, 1865	June 8, 1865	Mustered out with regiment.
2d Lieutenant	Otway Watson	August 11, 1862	Dec. 31, 1862	Promoted to 1st Lieutenant.
"	John Deckey	August 12, 1862	Dec. 31, 1862	Resigned Nov. 17, 1862.
"	Joshua M. Wells	August 12, 1862	Dec. 31, 1862	Promoted to 1st Lieutenant.
"	Charles Sinnett	August 12, 1862	Dec. 31, 1862	Promoted to 1st Lieutenant.
"	Lucius Windle	August 13, 1862	Dec. 31, 1862	Promoted to 1st Lieutenant.
"	Horatio N. Benjamin	August 14, 1862	Dec. 31, 1862	Promoted to 1st Lieutenant.
"	J. C. Bostwick	August 14, 1862	Dec. 31, 1862	Promoted to 1st Lieutenant.
"	George W. Holmes	August 13, 1862	Dec. 31, 1862	Promoted to 1st Lieutenant.
"	Francis O. Scarth	August 17, 1862	Dec. 31, 1862	Resigned May 14, 1863.
"	Aquilla Toland	Jan. 14, 1863	Feb. 5, 1863	Promoted to 1st Lieutenant.
"	Chas. C. Hayes	Jan. 28, 1863		Resigned August 5, 1863.
"	Joseph Swisher	Jan. 13, 1863		Promoted to 1st Lieutenant.
"	Hiram C. Tipton	Jan. 28, 1863		Resigned March 25, 1863.
"	Edward P. Haynes	Oct. 27, 1863	March 6, 1863	Promoted to 1st Lieutenant September 20, 1863.
"	Wm. R. Hanewalt	March 25, 1863	April 25, 1863	Killed in action September 20, 1863.
"	Chas. Garman	Feb. 2, 1863	April 14, 1863	Killed September 20, 1863.
"	James S. Wheelock	March 17, 1863	April 14, 1863	Promoted to 1st Lieutenant.
"	Cyrus G. Platt	March 17, 1863	April 14, 1863	Promoted to 1st Lieutenant.
"	John S. Skeels	Feb. 1, 1863	August 25, 1863	Commission returned.
"	Jesse W. Dungan	April 29, 1863		Promoted to 1st Lieutenant.
"	John W. Kile	March 15, 1863	August 25, 1863	Promoted to 1st Lieutenant.
"	George McCrea	August 5, 1863	Feb. 20, 1864	Promoted to 1st Lieutenant.
"	James R. Ladd	Nov. 5, 1863	March 2, 1864	Promoted to 1st Lieutenant.
"	Theodore D. Bentley	Nov. 5, 1863	March 1, 1864	Promoted to 1st Lieutenant.
"	Edward Crouse	Dec. 16, 1863	Jan. 28, 1864	Promoted to 1st Lieutenant.
"	Jonathan Watson	Dec. 15, 1863	March 29, 1864	Promoted to 1st Lieutenant.
"	George H. Lippincott	March 31, 1864	March 31, 1864	Promoted to 1st Lieutenant.
"	David H. Chatfield	Nov. 5, 1863	April 6, 1864	Promoted to 1st Lieutenant.
"	Jesse W. Brigham	June 14, 1863	June 14, 1864	Promoted to 1st Lieutenant.
"	James Coultis	June 14, 1863	June 14, 1864	Killed June 27, 1864.
"	Joseph Parker	July 25, 1864	July 25, 1864	Promoted to 1st Lieutenant.
"	Wm. Grove	July 26, 1864	July 25, 1864	Promoted to 1st Lieutenant.
"	Ambrose E. Graffon	July 25, 1864	July 25, 1864	Promoted to 1st Lieutenant.
"	Wm. A. M. Davis	Oct. 12, 1864	Oct. 12, 1864	Promoted to 1st Lieutenant.
"	Timothy Haley	May 31, 1865	May 31, 1865	Promoted to 1st Lieutenant.
"	Isaac N. Hobil	May 31, 1865	May 31, 1865	Promoted to 1st Lieutenant.
"	Alex. Carpenter			Promoted to 1st Lieutenant.
"	Benj. W. Mason	June 8, 1865	June 8, 1865	Promoted to 1st Lieutenant.

[FROM OHIO IN THE WAR. By permission.]

MUSTER-OUT ROLL.

FIELD AND STAFF.
Mustered out at Louisville, Kentucky, July 6th, 1865.

COLONEL JAMES A. WILCOX—Commissioned at Columbus, Ohio, September 2, 1862; resigned April 29, 1863.

COLONEL JOHN G. MITCHELL—Commissioned at Franklin, Tennessee, May 6, 1863; promoted from Lieutenant Colonel May 6, 1863; appointed Brigadier General U. S. V. January 12, 1865.

LIEUTENANT COLONEL DARIUS B. WARNER—Commissioned at Franklin, Tennessee, May 6, 1863; promoted from Major May 6, 1863; resigned June 6, 1865, on account of wounds received June 27, 1864; Resignation accepted by General Slocum.

LIEUTENANT COLONEL TOLAND JONES—Commissioned at Washington, D. C.; promoted from Captain of Company A to date, June 7, 1865; mustered out with regiment.

MAJOR L. STARLING SULLIVANT—Commissioned at Franklin, Tennessee, May 6, 1863; promoted from Captain of Company H May 6, 1863; resigned May 30, 1865; resignation accepted by General Slocum.

MAJOR OTWAY WATSON—Commissioned at Louisville, Kentucky, June 12, 1865; promoted from Captain of Company H; mustered in as Major to date from June 12, 1865; mustered out with regiment.

SURGEON JAMES R. BLACK—Commissioned at Columbus, Ohio, August 19, 1862; resigned July 21, 1863; resignation accepted by General Rosecrans.

SURGEON ALBERT WILSON—Commissioned at Chattanooga, Tennessee, September 30, 1863; mustered out at Louisville, Kentucky, July 5, 1865.

ASSISTANT SURGEON ALONZO HARLOW—Commissioned at Columbus, Ohio, September 1, 1862; resigned May 11, 1863; resignation accepted by General Rosecrans.

ASSISTANT SURGEON THOMAS C. TIPTON—Commissioned at Columbus, Ohio, September 3, 1862; resigned June 8, 1863; resignation accepted by General Rosecrans.

ASSISTANT SURGEON GEORGE W. KEMP—Commissioned at Shelbyville, Tennessee, July 20, 1863; resigned October 13, 1863; resignation accepted by General Rosecrans.

ASSISTANT SURGEON HIRAM M. BASSETT—Commissioned at Shelbyville, Tennessee, July 20, 1863; mustered out to date, April 23, 1865, to accept commission as Surgeon of the 121st Ohio Volunteer Infantry.

CHAPLAIN JOSEPH MORRIS—Commissioned at Chattanooga, Tennessee, October 27, 1863; mustered out with regiment.

ADJUTANT CHARLES C. COX—Commissioned at Columbus, Ohio, September 8, 1862; resigned May 28, 1863; resignation accepted by General Rosecrans.

ADJUTANT JAMES K. HAMILTON—Commissioned at Shelbyville, Tennessee, June 22, 1863; mustered out to date, August 17, 1864, to accept commission as Captain of Company D.

ADJUTANT JAMES R. LADD—Commissioned at Vining's Station, Georgia; mustered out to date, June 11, 1864, to accept commission as Captain of Company H.

ADJUTANT ISAAC N. HOBILL—Commissioned at Louisville, Kentucky, June 12, 1865; promoted from Sergeant Major, date June 12, 1865; mustered out with regiment.

R. Q. M. ERASMUS SCARRITT—Commissioned at Columbus, Ohio, September 3, 1862; resigned January 30, 1864; resignation accepted by General Thomas.

R. Q. M. JOSEPH SWISHER—Commissioned at Triune, Tennessee, June 8, 1863; mustered out August 21, 1864, to accept commission as Captain of Company E.

R. Q. M. GEORGE W. BRIGHAM—Commissioned at Atlanta, Georgia, September 17, 1864; mustered out with regiment.

NON-COMMISSIONED STAFF.

SERGEANT MAJOR JOEL L. REED—Commissioned at London, Ohio, August 11, 1862; appointed Sergeant Major from Sergeant to date, June 12, 1865; mustered out at Louisville, Kentucky, July 6, 1865.

Q. M. SERGEANT WM. H. HALLIDAY—Commissioned at Columbus, Ohio, August 18, 1862; enlisted August 13, 1862, as a pri-

vate of Company B; Mustered out at Louisville, Kentucky, July
6, 1865.
COMMISSARY SERGEANT F. M. REIGEL—Commissioned at Camp
Dennison, Ohio, September 22, 1862; mustered out at Louis-
ville, Kentucky, July 6, 1865.
HOSPITAL STEWARD WM. N. YOST—Commissioned at Hebron, Ohio,
August 22, 1862; mustered out at Louisville, Kentucky, July
6, 1865.
FIRST MUSICIAN CORTLAND C. RUNYAN—Commissioned at Dayton,
Ohio, October 8, 1862; mustered out at Louisville, Kentucky,
July 6, 1865.
SECOND MUSICIAN LOYAL H. CLOUSE—Commissioned at Granville,
Ohio, August 14, 1862; mustered out at Louisville, Kentucky,
July 6, 1865.

DISCHARGED.

SERGEANT MAJOR JESSE W. DUNGAN—Commissioned at London,
Ohio, August 11, 1862; discharged to accept promotion as 2d
Lieutenant in Company A, November 5, 1863.
Q. M. SERGEANT WM. R. HANAWALT—Commissioned at Mt. Ster-
ling, Ohio; discharged to accept promotion as 2d Lieutenant in
Company G, March 25, 1863.
Q. M. SERGEANT J. W. INGRIM—Commissioned at Mt. Sterling,
Ohio, August 13, 1862; discharged on account of physical dis-
ability November 14, 1863, by order of General R. S. Granger.
COMMISSARY SERGEANT GEORGE W. BRIGHAM—Commissioned at
Hartford, Ohio, August 14, 1862; discharged to accept promo-
tion as 1st Lieutenant and R. Q. M. September 16, 1864.
SERGEANT MAJOR ISAAC N. HOBILL—Commissioned at Jackson,
Ohio, August 14, 1862; discharged to accept promotion as 1st
Lieut. Adjt. June 11, 1865.

COMPANY A.

Mustered out at Louisville, Ky., July 6, 1865.

COMMISSIONED OFFICERS.

CAPTAIN TOLAND JONES—Commissioned Captain August 11, 1862,
at Columbus, O.; promoted to Lieutenant Colonel 113th Regiment O. V. I., June 7, 1865; commanded regiment from August
28, 1864, to day of discharge.

CAPTAIN CHAS. P. GORMAN—Commissioned Captain June 8, 1865; transferred from Company I; mustered out at Louisville, Ky., July 6, 1865.
FIRST LIEUTENANT N. C. VICKERS—Commissioned First Lieutenant August 11, 1862; resigned January 13, 1863.
FIRST LIEUTENANT OTWAY WATSON—Promoted to First Lieutenant February 6, 1863; promoted to Captain Company H, 113th O. V. I., May 6, 1863. (See H Roll.)
FIRST LIEUTENANT AQUILLA TOLAND—Promoted to First Lieutenant June 6, 1863; resigned January 21, 1864.
FIRST LIEUTENANT J. R. CROSS—Promoted to First Lieutenant June 12, 1865; assigned to Company A, June 12, 1865; mustered out at Louisville, Ky., July 6, 1865.
SECOND LIEUTENANT JESSE W. DUNGAN—Promoted to Second Lieutenant November 5, 1863; wounded June 27; died July 4, 1864.
SECOND LIEUTENANT JAMES COULTIS—Promoted to Second Lieutenant July 5, 1864; promoted to First Lieutenant, Company G, August 31, 1865. (See G Roll.)
SECOND LIEUTENANT WM. A. M. DAVIS—Promoted to Second Lieutenant September 24, 1864; promoted to First Lieutenant Company B, October 21, 1864. (See B Roll.)

NON-COMMISSIONED OFFICERS

JOHN C. COBLENTZ, First Sergeant—Enrolled at London, O., August 11, 1862; mustered out July 6, 1865.
ROBERT KNIGHT, Second Sergeant—Enrolled at London, O., August 11, 1862; mustered out with the regiment July 6, 1865.
EDWIN SLAGLE, Third Sergeant—Enrolled at London, O., August 11, 1862; mustered out with the regiment.
GEORGE ELLARS, Fourth Sergeant—Enrolled at London, O., August 11, 1862; mustered out with the regiment.
CHAS. J. GOULD, Fifth Sergeant—Enrolled at London, O., August 11, 1862; promoted from Corporal to Sergeant June 12, 1865; mustered out with the regiment.
GEO. C. PHLEEGER, First Corporal—Enrolled at London, O., September 2, 1862; mustered out at Louisville, Ky., July 6, 1865.
RICHARD B. CORSON, Second Corporal—Enrolled at London, O., August 11, 1862; mustered out at Louisville, Ky., July 6, 1865.
JOSEPH E. SIDNER, Third Corporal—Enrolled at London, O., August 11, 1862; mustered out at Louisville, Ky., July 6, 1865.

SMITHFIELD JACKSON, Fourth Corporal—Enrolled at London, O., August 11, 1862; mustered out at Louisville, Ky., July 6, 1865.
JOSEPH SANDERS, Fifth Corporal—Enrolled at London, O., August 11, 1862; mustered out July 6, 1865, while absent on furlough.
JACOB MARCH, Sixth Corporal—Enrolled at London, O., August 11, 1862; mustered out with the regiment.
BENJAMIN NORRIS, Seventh Corporal—Enrolled at London, O., August 11, 1862; promoted to Corporal May 26, 1865; mustered out with the regiment.
AUSTIN SLAGLE, Eighth Corporal—Enrolled at London, O., August 11, 1862; promoted to Corporal June 12, 1865; mustered out July 6, 1865, while absent on furlough.

PRIVATES.

JOHN W. ADAMS—(Recruit) Enrolled at London, O., January 2, 1864; mustered out with the regiment.
WM. ARMSTRONG—Enrolled at London, O., August 11, 1862; mustered out with the regiment.
JOHN BOESINGER—Enrolled at Camp Chase September 2, 1862; mustered out with the regiment.
JOSEPH E. BUZZARD—Enrolled at London, O., August 11, 1862; mustered out with the regiment.
CHAS. BATES—Enrolled at London, O., August 11, 1862; mustered out with the regiment.
THOS. H. BELL—Enrolled at London, O., August 11, 1862; mustered out with the regiment.
HARVEY BRADLEY—Enrolled at London, O., January 4, 1864; mustered out with the regiment.
RILY CARTER—Enrolled at London, O., August 11, 1862; mustered out with the regiment.
JOHN F. CHAPMAN—(Veteran) Enrolled at London, O., December 21, 1863; mustered out with the regiment.
JOHN L. DALLAS—Enrolled at London, O., August 11, 1862; mustered out with the regiment.
PHILIP FIX—Enrolled at London, O., August 11, 1862; mustered out July 6, 1865, while absent on furlough.
ALFRED E. GARRET—(Veteran) Enrolled at London, O., December 9, 1863, mustered out with the regiment.
DANIEL HILDERBRAN—Enrolled at London, O., August 11, 1862; mustered out with the regiment.
JOHN N. HOWSMAN—Enrolled at London, O., August 11, 1862; mustered out with the regiment.

JOHN N. JONES—Enrolled at London, O., August 11, 1862; mustered out with the regiment.
LEVI MARCH—Enrolled at London, O., August 11, 1862; mustered out with the regiment.
WM. MARKS—Enrolled at London, O., September 9, 1862; mustered out with the regiment.
WM. MEHEGAN—(Recruit) Enrolled at London, O., January 23, 1864; mustered out with the regiment.
JOHN MILLER—(Veteran) Enrolled at London, O., January 13, 1864; mustered out with the regiment.
GEORGE MILES—Enrolled at London, O., August 11, 1862; mustered out July 6, 1865, while absent on furlough.
JOHN MCSAVANY—Enrolled at London, O., August 11, 1862; mustered out July 6, 1865, while absent on furlough.
ALEXANDER MCCOMBS—(Recruit) Enrolled at London, O., January 22, 1864; mustered out with the regiment.
ISAAC J. NORRIS—Enrolled at London, O., August 22, 1862; mustered out with the regiment.
WILLIAM ORPUT—(Recruit) Enrolled at London, O., January 4, 1864; mustered out with the regiment.
THOMAS O'NEIL—(Recruit) Enrolled at London, O., March 26, 1864; mustered out with the regiment.
JOHN H. PETERS—Enrolled at London, O., August 11, 1862; mustered out July 6, 1865, while absent on furlough.
JOHN H. PEMBERTON—(Veteran) Enrolled at London, O., March 30, 1864; mustered out with the regiment.
ALBERT T. PHIFER—Enrolled at London, O., August 11, 1862; mustered out with the regiment.
MICHAEL POWERS—Enrolled at London, O., August 11, 1862; mustered out July 6, 1865, while absent on furlough.
JOHN G. POLING—(Recruit) Enrolled at London, O., January 23, 1864; mustered out July 6, 1865, while absent on furlough.
SAMUEL POWELL—(Recruit) Enrolled at London, O., March 18, 1864; mustered out with the regiment.
JAMES RAYBURN—Enrolled at London, O., August 11, 1862; mustered out July 6, 1865, while absent sick.
JOSEPH D. RITCHARDSON—Enrolled at London, O., August 11, 1862; mustered out July 6, 1865, while absent on furlough.
SIMEON W. RODGERS—Enrolled at London, O., August 11, 1862; mustered out with the regiment.

DANIEL RIORDAN—Enrolled at London, O., August 11, 1862; mustered out with the regiment.
JOHN RIGHTSELL—Enrolled at London, O., August 11, 1862; mustered out with the regiment.
BALZER SPEACEMAKER—(Recruit) Enrolled at London, O., December 31, 1864; mustered out with the regiment.
ALEXANDER SCHAFER—Enrolled at London, O., August 11, 1862; mustered out with the regiment.
NICHOLAS SCHIMMEL—(Veteran) Enrolled at London, O., February 4, 1864; mustered out with the regiment. (Musician.)
AURELIUS SIMPSON—(Recruit) Enrolled at London, O., March 1, 1864; mustered out with the regiment.
JOHN H. TALLMAN—Enrolled at London, O., August 11, 1862; mustered out with the regiment.
WILLIAM WAIT—Enrolled at London, O., August 11, 1862; mustered out with the regiment.
ALFRED WILLET—Enrolled at London, O., August 11, 1862; mustered out with the regiment.
WILLIAM C. WARD—Enrolled at London, O., August 11, 1862; mustered out July 6, 1865, while absent on furlough.
MARK WALLACE—Enrolled at Camp Chase, September 19, 1862; mustered out with the regiment.
GEORGE W. WATSON—(Recruit) Enrolled at London, O., November 8, 1863; mustered out with the regiment.
WALTER M. WATSON—(Recruit) Enrolled at London, O., February 19, 1864; mustered out with the regiment.
JOSEPH P. WAGERMAN—(Recruit) Enrolled at London, O., December 25, 1863; mustered out July 6, 1865, while absent on furlough.
CHARLES YEATTS—(Recruit) Enrolled at London, O., March 1, 1864; mustered out with the regiment.
DANIEL YOUNG—(Recruit) Enrolled at London, O., January 2, 1864; mustered out July 6, 1865, while absent sick.
GEORGE W. PARMER—(Recruit) Enrolled as under cook, at Shelbyville, Tenn., August 6, 1863; mustered out with the regiment. Colored.
GEORGE W. VALENTINE—Enrolled as under cook, at Chattanooga, Tenn., October 31, 1863; mustered out with the regiment. Colored.

DISCHARGED.

BENJAMIN F. ALLISON—Enrolled at London, O., August 11, 1862; discharged August 8, 1863, Camp Dennison, on account of physical disability, by order of Military Commission.

JOHN BELL—Enrolled at London, O., August 11, 1862; discharged April 30, 1863, at Nashville, Tenn., on account of physical disability, by order of Major General Rosecrans.

PHILIP E. BLESH—Enrolled at London, O., August 11, 1862; discharged April 26, 1864, Camp Dennison, on account of physical disability, by order of Military Commission.

JAMES BEMIS—Enrolled at London, O., August 11, 1862; arrested October 25, 1862, Camp Chase, by civil authority, by order of Governor of Iowa. (Discharged.)

CHESTERFIELD CARTER—Enrolled at London, O., August 11, 1862; discharged February 9, 1865, Cleveland, O., on account of physical disability, by order of Major General Hooker.

THOMAS DWYER—Enrolled at London, O., August 11, 1862; discharged May 27, 1863, Nashville, Tenn., on account of physical disability, by order of Major General Rosecrans.

WILLIAM P. ECHARD—Enrolled at Columbus, O., September 8, 1864; mustered out June 22, 1865, Louisville, Ky., per order War Department.

HERBERT FAY—Enrolled at London, O., August 11, 1862; discharged November 9, 1863, Nashville, Tenn., on account of physical disability, by order of Major General Thomas. (Drummer.)

JOHN S. HARVEY—Enrolled at London, O., February 22, 1864; mustered out May 29, 1865, Camp Dennison, O., per order War Department.

ROBERT HOWLETT—Enrolled at London, O., August 11, 1862; Discharged April 27, 1865, Columbus, O., on account of insanity, by order of Major General Hooker.

MICHAEL Q. KELLY—Enrolled at London, O., August 11, 1862; discharged July 17, 1864, Bridgeport, Ala., on account of physical disability, by order of Major General Thomas.

JOHN P. LOW—Enrolled at London, O., August 22, 1862; mustered out June 2, 1865, Camp Dennison, O., per order War Department.

ROBERT MOORE—Enrolled at London, O., August 11, 1862; mustered out May 22, 1865, Nashville, Tenn., per order War Department.

JAMES McDERMOTT—Enrolled at Dayton, O., October 1, 1864; mustered out June 22, 1865, Louisville, Ky., per order War Department.

HENRY NUSSBAUM—Enrolled at London, O., August 11, 1862; discharged January 12, 1864, Nashville, Tenn., on account of physical disability, by order Major General Grant.

JOHN H. PEMBERTON—Enrolled at London, O., August 11, 1862; discharged June 8, 1863, Nashville, Tenn., on account of physical disability, by order Major General Rosecrans.

EZRA PAUGH—Enrolled at London, O., August 11, 1862; discharged April 8, 1865, Columbus, O., of wound received June 27, 1864.

JOHN REESE—Enrolled at London, O., August 22, 1862; discharged July 9, 1863, Nashville, Tenn., on account of physical disability, by order Major General Rosecrans.

GEORGE H. ROLAND—Enrolled at London, O., August 11, 1862; discharged April 13, 1863, Nashville, Tenn., on account of physical disability, by order Major General Rosecrans.

JOHN C. SOUTHRON—Enrolled at London, O., August 11, 1862; discharged February 11, 1863, Columbus, O., on account of physical disability, by order J. R. Black, Regimental Surgeon.

JOHN SIMPSON—Enrolled at London, O., August 11, 1862; mustered out May 26, 1865, Camp Dennison, O., per order War Department.

WILLIAM WOODMAN—Enrolled at London, O., August 22, 1862; discharged April 19, 1865, Columbus, O., of wound received June 27, 1864, at Kenesaw Mountain, by Major General Hooker.

TRANSFERRED.

JOHN H. ANDERSON—Enrolled at London, O., August 11, 1862; transferred to V. R. C. April 30, 1864, per order War Department.

ABNER D. CARTER—Enrolled at London, O., August 11, 1862; transferred to V. R. C. November 21, 1864, per order War Department.

WILLIAM FORD—Enrolled at London, O., August 11, 1862; transferred to V. R. C. January 15, 1864, per order War Department.

TIMOTHY HALEY—Enrolled at London, O., August 11, 1862; transferred to Co. F March 25, 1865, promoted to First Lieutenant.

HENRY McCANN—Enrolled at London, O., August 11, 1862;

transferred to U. S. Engineer Corps, Chattanooga, Tenn., by order Major General Thomas, August 15, 1865.

ISAAC G. NEFF—Enrolled at London, O., August 22, 1862; transferred to V. R. C. February 17, 1864, per order War Department.

JOEL L. READ—Enrolled at London, O., August 11, 1862; transferred to Regt. Staff June 12, 1865, as Sergeant Major, by order Lieutenant Colonel Jones.

BENONI RAY—Enrolled at London, O., August 11, 1862; transferred to V. R. C. April 30, 1864, per order War Department.

KILLED.

JOHN C. BENTZEL—Enrolled at London, O., August 11, 1862; killed April 10, 1865, Holt's Mills, N. C.

EVERETT W. JACKSON—Enrolled at London, O., August 22, 1862; killed June 27, 1864, Kenesaw Mountain, Georgia.

LOUIS H. KENNEDY—Enrolled at London, O., February 23, 1864; killed June 27, 1864, Kenesaw Mountain, Georgia.

JOHN WEBER—Enrolled at London, O., September 2, 1862; killed in action July 19, 1864, Peachtree Creek, Georgia.

DIED.

HENRY J. BECKMAN—Enrolled at London, O., August 22, 1862; died March 5, 1863, Franklin, Tenn., of disease.

WILLIAM BEAR—Enrolled at London, O., August 11, 1862; died March 18, 1863, Franklin, Tenn., of disease.

PETER BROWN—Enrolled at London, O., October 11, 1862; died June 6, 1863, at Nashville, Tenn., of disease.

ALEXANDER BRADLEY—Enrolled at London, O., October 11, 1862; died July 29, 1864, Chattanooga, Tenn., of wounds received at Kenesaw Mountain, Ga., June 27, 1864.

ROBT. R. BALENGER—Enrolled at London, O., August 11, 1862; died August 12, 1864, at Nashville, Tenn., of wounds received at Kenesaw Mountain, Ga., June 27, 1864.

WM. T. COHRAN—Enrolled at London, O., August 11, 1862; died March 14, 1863, at Nashville, Tenn., of disease.

LYMAN CARTER—Enrolled at London, O., August 11, 1862; died March 21, 1863, Franklin, Tenn., of disease.

JAMES W. CARR—Enrolled at London, O., August 22, 1862; died March 22, 1863, at Nashville, Tenn., of disease.

FRANCIS M. CRABB—Enrolled at London, O., August 6, 1862; died September 2, 1863, at Nashville, Tenn., of disease.

JESSE N. CANNON—Enrolled at London, O., August 11, 1862; died September 20, 1863, at Chickamauga, Ga., of wound.
JOHN J. CLOUD—Enrolled at London, O., August 11, 1862; died October 15, 1864, at Kingston, Ga., of wounds received at Kenesaw Mountain, Ga.
THOMAS COWLING—Enrolled at Camp Chase August 11, 1862; died April 13, 1865, at Newbern, N. C., of wounds received in action March 19, 1865.
JAMES S. HARVEY—Enrolled at London, O., October 11, 1862; died January 20, 1863, at Muldrough Hill, Ky., of disease.
WM. E. HUGHES—Enrolled at London, O., December 22, 1863; died July 29, 1864, at Chattanooga, Tenn., of wounds received at Kenesaw Mountain, Ga.
ARCHIBALD MORSE—Enrolled at London, O., August 22, 1862; died September 1, 1864, at Chattanooga, Tenn., of chronic diarrhœa.
GEO. T. RENO—Enrolled at London, O., August 22, 1862; died January 26, 1863, at Muldrough Hill, Ky., of disease.
EUGENE SMITH—Enrolled at London, O., August 11, 1862; died March 11, 1863, at Louisville, Ky., of disease.
JOHN B. SULSOR—Enrolled at London, O., August 11, 1862; died July 14, 1864, at Nashville, Tenn., of wounds received at Kenesaw Mountain, Ga., June 27, 1864.
FRED. WEBER—Enrolled at London, O., January 4, 1862; died January 14, 1865, at Savannah, Ga., of acute dysentery.
WM. R. WARD—Enrolled at London, O., August 11, 1862; died September 20, 1863, at Savannah, Ga., of acute dysentery.

DESERTED.

CHAS. J. FRITZ—Enrolled at London, O., August 11, 1862; deserted January 27, 1863, at Louisville, Ky.
AARON W. HIBBER—Enrolled at London, O., August 11, 1862; deserted January 27, 1863, at Louisville, Ky.
LOUIS MEADE—Enrolled at London, O., August —, 1862; deserted January 27, 1863, at Louisville, Ky.

COMPANY F.

Mustered out at Louisville, Ky., July 6, 1865.

COMMISSIONED OFFICERS.

CAPTAIN L. T. NICHOLS—Commissioned at Columbus, O., August 17, 1862; absent on detached services in Ohio since February 12, 1864; mustered out at Louisville, Ky., July 6, 1865.

FIRST LIEUTENANT NELSON DURANT—Commissioned at Columbus, O., August 13, 1862; promoted from First Lieutenant to Captain and assigned to Company I, April 21, 1863; mustered out.

FIRST LIEUTENANT L. S. WINDLE—Commissioned at Franklin, Tenn., April 21, 1863; promoted from First Lieutenant to Captain and assigned to Company C, July 14, 1864; mustered out with company.

FIRST LIEUTENANT J. R. LADD—Commissioned at Vining's Station, Ga., June 25, 1864; transferred to Field and Staff Roll September 20, 1864; mustered out with Company. (See Field and Staff Roll.)

FIRST LIEUTENANT T. HALEY—Commissioned at Goldsboro, N. C., March 25, 1865; mustered out with Company; transferred from A.

SECOND LIEUTENANT J. L. WHEELOCK—Commissioned at Franklin, Tenn., April 21, 1863; killed in battle at Chickamauga September 20, 1863.

SECOND LIEUTENANT EDW. CROUSE—Commissioned at Columbus, O., November 5, 1863; killed in battle at Kenesaw Mountain June 27, 1864.

NON-COMMISSIONED OFFICERS.

P. I. HORTON, First Sergeant—Enrolled at McKean, O., August 22, 1862; absent on furlough in Ohio; mustered out with Company.

E. J. CARLILE, Sergeant—Enrolled at Newark, O., August 19 1862; mustered out with Company.

WM. H. THRALL, Sergeant—Enrolled at Hartford, O., August 14, 1862; mustered out with Company.

C. A. COFFROTH, Sergeant—Enrolled at Columbus, O., August 21, 1862; mustered out with Company.

T. E. OSBURN, Sergeant—Enrolled at Franklin, O., August 22, 1862; mustered out with Company.

E. N. THRALL, Corporal—Enrolled at Hartford, O., August 14, 1862; absent on furlough in Ohio; mustered out with Company.
JOHN DENUNE, Corporal—Enrolled at Columbus, O., August 19, 1862; mustered out with Company.
R. B. STADDEN, Corporal—Enrolled at Madison, O., August 22, 1862; mustered out with Company.
LEANDER PANCOAST, Corporal—Enrolled at Camp Zanesville, O., October 13, 1862; absent on furlough in Ohio; mustered out with company.

PRIVATES.

LEVI AGLER—Enrolled at Columbus, O., August 22, 1862; mustered out with company.
GEO. W. BROOKS—Enrolled at McKean, O., August 22, 1862; mustered out with company.
ROBERT BALLENGER—Enrolled at Columbus, O., August 22, 1862; mustered out with company.
ALONZO N. BROWN—Enrolled at Camp Chase, O., September 27, 1862; mustered out with company.
ALBERT C. CADY—Enrolled at Johnstown, O., August 22, 1862; mustered out with company; wounded at Chickamauga, Ga., by a shell, from the effects of which he died at Johnstown, O., April 14, 1872, aged 27 years. He had a good record as a soldier.
JACOB S. CLOUSE—Enrolled at Johnstown, O., August 22, 1862; mustered out with company.
OLIVER GREEN—Enrolled at Johnstown, O., August 22, 1862; absent on furlough; mustered out with company.
JOHN Q. HOWARD—Enrolled at Monroe, O., August 22, 1862; mustered out with company.
HENRY S. HOWELL—Enrolled at McKean, O., August 22, 1862; mustered out with company.
JAMES HOURIGAN—Enrolled at Columbus, O., August 22, 1862; mustered out with company. (Irish.)
JOHN W. LAYMAN—Enrolled at Newark, O., August 22, 1862; mustered out with company.
CHAS. G. LARRABEE—Enrolled at Camp Chase, O., August 22, 1862; mustered out with company.
JOHN PERRIN—Enrolled at McKean, O., August 22, 1862; mustered out with company.
T. M. STEADMAN—Enrolled at Franklin, O., August 22, 1862; mustered out with company.

JOHN A. SMALLY—Enrolled at Newark, O., August 22, 1862; absent without leave from the 14th of November, 1862, to December 2d 1864; sentenced by General Court Martial to forfeit all pay and allowances for time absent; mustered out with company.
TULLER WILLIAMS—Enrolled at Johnstown, O., August 22, 1862; mustered out with company.
JACKSON STEVENSON—Enrolled at Franklin, Tenn., March 3, 1863; mustered out with company. (Cook.)
WILLIAM POINTER—Enrolled at Franklin, Tenn., March 3, 1863; mustered out with company. (Cook.)

KILLED.

THOS. DISPENNET, Corporal—Enrolled at Franklin, O., August 22, 1862; killed September 20, 1863, at battle of Chickamauga, Ga.
IBBOTSON HENRY—Enrolled at Newark, O., September 20, 1862; killed September 20, 1863, at battle of Chickamauga, Ga.
WESLEY MURPHY—Enrolled at Madison, O., August 22, 1862; killed September 20, 1863, at battle of Chickamauga, Ga.
LYMAN LINCOLN, Sergeant—Enrolled at Hartford, O., August 20, 1862; killed June 27, 1864, at battle of Kenesaw Mt. Ga.
URIAH A. McCOMB—Enrolled at Hartford, O., August 14, 1862; killed August 8, 1864, at Atlanta, Ga. (Musician.)
S. J. OGILVIE, Corporal—Enrolled at Hartford, O., August, 14, 1862; missing since battle of Chickamauga, Ga., September 20, 1863.

DIED.

DEVER COFFMAN—Enrolled at McKean, O., August 20, 1862; died March 2, 1863, Franklin, Tenn.; dropsy of the heart.
AMOS RICH—Enrolled at Columbus, O., August 22, 1862; died March 23, 1863, Franklin, Tenn.; typhoid fever.
JOHN GRAY—Enrolled at Mary Ann, O., August 22, 1862; died April 14, 1863, Franklin, Tenn.; congestive fever.
J. D. D. STEVENS—Enrolled at Hartford, O., August 14, 1864; died June 1, 1865, Franklin, Tenn.; chronic diarrhea.
WM. H. LARRABEE—Enrolled at Newark, O., August 22, 1862; died August 15, 1863, Louisville, Ky.; disease unknown.
M. D. L. PARR, First Sergeant—Enrolled at Newark, O., August 22, 1862; died November 23, 1863, in the Tennessee river by drowning. (See reference to this in Knapsack.)
WM. H. LANE, Corporal—Enrolled at Hartford, O., August 15, 1862; died December 31, 1863, at Annapolis, Md., Variola. (See prison sketch in Knapsack.)

HENRY BLADE—Enrolled at Franklin, O., August 20, 1862; died July 12, 1864, Chattanooga, Tenn.; wounds received in action at Kenesaw Mt., Ga., June 27, 1864.

ANDREW J. SHAW—Enrolled at Madison, O., August 22, 1862; died July 20, 1864, Chattanooga, Tenn.; wounds received in action at Kennesaw Mt., Ga., June 27, 1864.

J. G. KIRKPATRICK—Enrolled at Columbus, O., January 18, 1864; died October 6, 1864, Nashville, Tenn.; chronic diarrhea.

GEORGE SMART—Enrolled at Johnstown, O., August 14, 1862; died of chronic diarrhea, November 27, 1864, on board the hospital steamer D. A. January.

VINCENT LAKE—Enrolled at Washington, August 22, 1862; died December 10, 1864, Camp Dennison, O.; typhoid fever.

ISAAC BAILY—Enrolled at Hartford, O., August 22, 1862; died April 28, 1865, Washington, D. C.; softening of the brain.

DISCHARGED.

JOHN SCALLY—Enrolled at Columbus, O., August 20, 1862; discharged December 20, 1863, Millitary Commander at Columbus, O., by reason disability.

GEO. W. ALLISON—Enrolled at Columbus, O., August 20, 1862; discharged March 18, 1863, by General Rosecrans, Nashville, Tenn.; disability.

M. H. PORTER, Corporal—Enrolled at Newark, O., August 20, 1862; discharged April 9, 1863, by General Rosecrans, Franklin, Tenn.; disability.

HENRY L. THRALL—Enrolled at Hartford, O., August 15, 1862; discharged May 18, 1863, by Surgeon certificate, Louisville, Ky.; disability.

BENJAMIN SHAFFER—Enrolled at Columbus, O., August 22, 1862; discharged June 2, 1863, Surgeon certificate, Nashville, Tenn.; disability.

JOHN E. RICE—Enrolled at Columbus, O., August 22, 1862; discharged July 3, 1863, Surgeon certificate, Louisville, Ky.; disability.

JOHN RENCH—Enrolled at Columbus, O., August 22, 1862; discharged July 28, 1863, by Military Commander, Camp Dennison, O.; disability.

THOS. J. PARR, Corporal—Enrolled at Franklin, O., August 18, 1862; discharged August 18, 1863, by General Rosecrans, Nashville, Tenn.; physical disability.

HENRY S. W. BUTT—Enrolled at Johnstown, O., August 22, 1862; discharged June 5, 1865, at Camp Chase, O., by order War Department.

PHILO HOUSE—Enrolled at Newark, O., August 22, 1862; discharged by Colonel M. Mundy, Louisville, Ky., September 7, 1863; physical disability.

JOSEPH JACKSON—Enrolled at Johnstown, O., August 22, 1862; discharged December 31, 1863, by Colonel Wm. Wallace, Columbus, O.; permanent disability from wounds received September 20, 1863, at Chickamauga, Ga.

EDGAR D. HORTON, Corporal—Enrolled at McKean, O., August 20, 1862: discharged February 24, 1864, at Columbus, O., of disability from wounds received in right hand, September 20, 1863, at Chickamauga, Ga.

THOMAS DAVIS—Enrolled at Columbus, O., August 14, 1862; discharged July 31, 1864.

THOMPSON P. FREEMAN—Enrolled at Johnstown, O., August 15, 1862; discharged April, 1864, Camp Dennison. Wound in hand at Chickamauga.

JOHN C. BALL—Enrolled at Johnstown, O., August 22, 1862; discharged June 30, 1864, by Maj. Gen. Heintzleman, at Columbus, O., of wounds received September 20, 1863, at Chickamauga, Ga.

JASPER EVANS—Enrolled at Jonhstown, O., August 19, 1862; discharged August 3, 1864.

GEO. W. CLARK—Enrolled at Camp Chase, O., October 4, 1862; discharged August 30, 1864, by Maj. Gen. Heintzlemar. at Columbus, O.; physical dissability.

JOHN J. OGILVIE, Sergeant—Enrolled at Hartford, August 14, 1862; discharged December 14, 1864, by Maj. Gen. Hooker at Columbus, O., of wounds received at Kenesaw Mt., June 27, 1864.

JOHN LILLIBRIDGE—Enrolled at Granville, O., August, 20, 1862; discharged June 2, 1865, Camp Dennison, O., Maj. Gen. Hooker.

ESAU RICE—Enrolled at Camp Chase, O., September 16, 1862; discharged June 7, 1865, at Columbus, O., by Maj. Gen. Hooker. Lost a leg.

JOHN R. ELLIS—Enrolled at Madison, O., August 22, 1862; date of discharge not given.

Company F.]   *History of the 113th O. V. I.*   191

DESERTED.

AMOS BARTHOLOMEW—Enrolled at McKean, O., August 22, 1862; deserted February 1, 1863, at Portland, Ky.

SAMUEL M. DAVIDSON—Enrolled at Newark, O., August 20, 1862, deserted February 1, 1863, at Portland, Ky.

M. DELLAPLANCE—Enrolled at Franklin, O., August 22, 1862; deserted November 10, 1862, at Camp Zanesville, O.

JAMES LOVE—Enrolled at Newark, O., August 21, 1862; deserted February 1, 1863, at Portland, Ky.

JOEL ELLIS—Enrolled at Newark, O., August 22, 1862; deserted November 6, 1862, at Camp Zanesville, O.

THOMAS W. LARRABEE—Enrolled at Newark, O., August 22, 1862; deserted November 29, 1862, at Camp Zanesville, O.

WM. T. REED—Enrolled at Madison, O., August 22, 1862; deserted December 14, 1862, at Camp Zanesville, O.

BENTLY ECHELBARGER—Enrolled at Newark, O., August 22, 1862; deserted December 14, 1862, at Camp Zanesville, O.

ROBERT McGEASY—Enrolled at Newark, O., September 11, 1862; deserted November 18, 1862, at Camp Zanesville, O.

TRANSFERRED.

GEO. H. WINSLOW—Enrolled at Hartford, O., August 22, 1862; transferred September 20, 1863, to V. R. C. by general order of War Department.

EZRA L. WHITEHEAD—Enrolled at Johnstown, O., August 22, 1862; transferred December 29, 1863, to V. R. C. by general order of War Department.

JONAS WILLIAMS—Enrolled at Franklin, O., August 18, 1862; transferred April 10, 1864, to V. R. C. by general order of War Department.

SYLVESTER FRYE—Enrolled at Franklin, O., August 18, 1862; transferred July 27, 1864, to Vet. Eng. Corps by general order of War Department

JACOB LOWN—Enrolled at McKean, O., August 22, 1862; transferred July 27, 1864, to Vet. Eng. Corps by general order of War Department.

ISAAC EVANS—Enrolled at Johnstown, O., August 12, 1862; transferred February 15, 1864, to V. R. C. by general order of War Department.

JOHN R. CROSS, Sergeant—Enrolled at Johnstown, O., August 22, 1862; promoted from First Sergeant to First Lieutenant, June 12, 1865, assigned to Company A, 113th Regiment.

GEO. W. BRIGHAM, Corporal—Enrolled at Hartford, O., August 14, 1862; promoted from Corporal to Commissary Sergeant September 25, 1862, and transferred to Field and Staff roll. Discharged as Regt. Q. M.

COMPANY D.

Mustered out at Louisville, Ky., July 6, 1865.

COMMISSIONED OFFICERS.

CAPTAIN MARVIN M. MUNSON—Commissioned at Granville, O., August 12, 1862; resigned January 21, 1863.

CAPTAIN THOS. J. DOWNEY—Commissioned at Franklin, Tenn., February 7, 1863; resigned August 10, 1864; resignation accepted by General Thomas. Served as Col. U. S. C. T.

CAPTAIN J. K. HAMILTON—Commissioned at Atlanta, Ga., August 18, 1864; mustered out at Louisville, Ky., July 6, 1865.

FIRST LIEUTENANT F. A. ENO—Commissioned at Granville, O., August 12, 1862; resigned January 31, 1863; resignation accepted by Major General Rosecrans.

FIRST LIEUTENANT CHAS. SINNET—Commissioned at Franklin, Tenn., February 7, 1863; transferred November 7, 1864, to fiirst regiment V. V. U. S. Engineers.

FIRST LIEUTENANT B. W. MASON—Commissioned at Washington, D. C., June 8, 1865; mustered out at Louisville, Ky., July 6, 1865; wounded at Chickamauga, Ga., September 20, 1863; wounded June 27, 1864, at Kenesaw Mt., Ga.

SECOND LIEUTENANT CHAS. C. HAYS—Commissioned at Franklin, Tenn., February 7, 1863; resigned August 8, 1863; resignation accepted by Major General Rosecrans.

NON-COMMISSIONED OFFICERS.

JAMES S. PORTS, First Sergeant—Enrolled at Granville, O., August 20, 1862; mustered out with company.

MOSES GOODRICH, Sergeant—Enrolled at Granville, O., August 20, 1862; absent on furlough since June 26, 1865; mustered out with company.

JAMES PARTRIDGE, Sergeant—Enrolled at Granville, O., August 20, 1862; absent on furlough as exchanged prisoner of war since March 18, 1865; mustered out with company.

ALFRED JONES, Sergeant—Enrolled at Liberty, O., August 20, 1862; mustered out with company.
BURTON HUSON, First Corporal—Enrolled at Granville, O., August 20, 1862; mustered out with company.
HENRY JEWELL, Corporal—Enrolled at St. Albans, O., August 20, 1862; absent on furlough since June 30, 1865; mustered out with company.
WARREN C. ROSE, Corporal—Enrolled at Granville, O., August 12, 1862; mustered out with company; taken prisoner at Chickamauga.
ELIAS THOMAS, Corporal—Enrolled at Granville, O., August 20, 1862; mustered out with the company.
RUFUS MERRILL, Corporal—Enrolled at St. Albana, O., August 20, 1862; mustered out with company.
ANDREW J. CHAMBERS, Corporal—Enrolled at Granville, O., August 20, 1862; mustered out with company.
WM. H. HARMAN, Corporal—Enrolled at St. Albans, O., February 1, 1864; absent on furlough since June, 26, 1865; mustered out with company.
CHAS. D. PARKER, Corporal—Enrolled at Granville, O., August 20, 1862; absent on furlough since June 26, 1865; mustered out with company.

PRIVATES.

JOHN BROWN—Enrolled at St. Albans, O., January 26, 1864; mustered out with company.
LEROY S. BANCROFT—Enrolled at Granville, O., August 20, 1862; mustered out with company.
HENRY C. CASE—Enrolled at Granville, O., August 20, 1862; mustered out with company.
CHARLES M. CARRIER—Enrolled at Granville, O., August 20, 1862; absent on furlough since June 27, 1865; mustered out with company.
DAVID N. CONRAD—Enrolled at Liberty, O., August 20, 1862; mustered out with company.
JOHN J. CHRYSTLAR—Enrolled at St. Albans, O., January 27, 1864; absent sick at Louisville, Ky., since June, 17, 1865; mustered out with company.
MILLIGAN DUNN—Enrolled at Fallsburg, O., August 22, 1862; mustered out with company.

JOHN F. DENSOR—Enrolled at Liberty, O., August 22, 1862; mustered out with company.
THOMAS J. EVANS—Enrolled at Granville, O., August 20, 1862; mustered out with company.
SHEPARD R. FULTON—Enrolled at Granville, O., August 20, 1862; mustered out with company.
GEORGE W. FLAHARDA—Enrolled at Harrison, O., August 22, 1862; mustered out with company. Died near Plain City, O., July 17, 1883.
RODNEY FLAHARDA—Enrolled at Harrison, O., August 27, 1862; mustered out with company.
GEORGE A. GRAVES—Enrolled at Granville, O., August 20, 1862; mustered out with company.
HEMAN L. HOBART—Enrolled at Granville, O., August 20, 1862; mustered out with company.
EZRA D. HUMMELL—Enrolled at St. Albans, O., August 20, 1862; mustered out with company.
THOMAS A. JONES—Enrolled at Granville, O., August 20, 1862; mustered out with company.
JAMES MERRILL—Enrolled at Granville, O., August 20, 1862; absent on furlough since June 26, 1865; mustered out with company.
JOHN NORTON—Enrolled at St. Albans, O., January 22, 1864; mustered out with company.
THOMAS NORTON—Enrolled at St. Albans, O., February 20, 1864; mustered out with company.
WM. R. NEWBERRY—Enrolled at Granville, O., August 20, 1862; mustered out with company.
HENRY C. PAIGE—Enrolled at Granville, O., August 20 1862; mustered out with company.
JACOB PITTS—Enrolled at St. Albans, O., August 20, 1862; mustered out with the company.
WILLIAM PORTS—Enrolled at Granville, O., August 20, 1862; absent on furlough since June 26, 1865; mustered out with company.
GILMAN ROSE—Enrolled at Granville, O., August 20, 1862; mustered out with company.
THEODORE G. WARDEN—Enrolled at Granville, O., August 20, 1862; mustered out with company.
WM. F. WILLIAMS—Enrolled at Granville, O., August 20, 1862; mustered out with company.
HIRAM WILLIAMS—Enrolled at St. Albans, O., August 22, 1862; mustered out with company.

LEWIS WILLIAMS—Enrolled at St. Albans, O., August 20, 1862; mustered out with company.
GEORGE A. WILSON—Enrolled at Granville, O., August 20, 1862; mustered out with company.

KILLED.

JOSEPH W. GOODING, Sergeant—Enrolled at Granville, O., August 20, 1862; killed in the battle of Chickamauga, Ga., September 20, 1863.
LYMAN B. PRATT, Corporal—Enrolled at Granville, O., August 20, 1862; killed in battle of Chickamauga, Ga., September 20, 1863.
GUILFORD D. HASLIP—Enrolled at Granville, O., August 11, 1862; killed in battle of Chickamauga, Ga., September 20, 1863.
DANIEL ROSE, Corporal—Enrolled at Granville, O., August 12, 1862; killed in battle of Chickamauga Ga., September 20, 1863.
JESSE H. TUCKER—Enrolled at St. Albans, O., August 20, 1862; killed in battle of Chickamauga, Ga., September 20, 1863.
HIRAM PAIGE—Enrolled at Granville, O., August 20, 1862; killed in battle of Chickamauga, Ga., September 20, 1863.
DAVID R. DUNN—Enrolled at Fallsburg, O., August 22, 1862; killed in the battle at Chickamauga. Ga., September 20, 1863.
ISAAC S. MINTON—Enrolled at Granville, O., August 22, 1862; killed in battle at Chickamauga, Ga., September 20, 1863.
MACY MANN—Enrolled at St. Albans, O., February 1, 1864; killed in battle at Jonesboro, Ga., September 1, 1864.

DIED.

JASPER GILLESPIE, Corporal—Enrolled at Bennington, O., August 20, 1862; died February 10, 1863, at Nashville, Tenn., of brain fever.
ARTHUR P. WRIGHT—Enrolled at St. Albans, O., August 20, 1862; died February 20, 1863, at Nashville, Tenn., of brain fever.
HENRY A. WELLS—Enrolled at Liberty, O., August 20, 1862; died February 27, 1863, Nashville, Tenn., of typhoid fever.
ALBERT ROSE—Enrolled at Granville, O., August 24, 1862; died March 3, 1863, at Nashville, Tenn., of rheumatism.
WM. C. MASON, Corporal—Enrolled at St. Albans, O., August 22, 1862; died March 14, 1863, at Franklin, Tenn., of brain fever.
JOHN MOREHEAD—Enrolled at McKean, O., August 22, 1862; died April 18, 1863, at Nashville, Tenn., dysentery.
WM. J. MINTON—Enrolled at Granville, O., August 22, 1862; died September 2, 1863, at Wartrace, Tenn., flux.

SOLOMON PRIEST—Enrolled at Jersey, O., August 20, 1862; died October 10, 1863, at Chattanooga, Tenn., of wounds received in battle.
SAMUEL L. ROSE, Sergeant—Enrolled at Granville, O., August 20, 1862; died October 21, 1863, at Chattanooga, Tenn., of wounds received in battle of Chickamauga.
JOHN T. CHEEK—Enrolled at St. Albans, O., August 20, 1862; died October 17, 1863, at Nashville, Tenn., of wounds received in battle.
MADISON C. MESSENGER, Sergeant—Enrolled at Harrison, O., August 22, 1862; died November 16, 1863, at Chattanooga, Tenn., of wounds received in battle.
SAMUEL RICHARDS—Enrolled at Granville, O., August 22, 1862; died June 2, 1864, at Jeffersonville, Ind, of rheumatism.
LORENZO BARRICK—Enrolled at St. Albans, O., August 20, 1862; died July 26, 1864, at Nashville, Tenn., of typhoid fever.
EDWARD WILLIAMS—Enrolled at St. Albans, O., January 28, 1864; died November 20, 1864, at Nashville, Tenn., of chronic diarrhea.
RICHARD BROWN—Enrolled at Columbus, O., September 23, 1864; died April 23, 1865, at Alexandria, Va., of spinal affection.

DISCHARGED.

JOHN WAMSLEY—Enrolled at Granville, O., August 20, 1862; discharged June 2, 1863, at Louisville, Ky., by order of Amsthel, discharge officer.
ABRAHAM BARKLEY—Enrolled at St. Albans, O., August 22, 1862; discharged December 14, 1863, at Murfreesboro. Tenn., by order of A. E. Ottis.
HENRY C. CARLOCK—Enrolled at St. Albans, O., August 22, 1862; discharged May 17, 1864, at Camp Dennison, O., by order of Major General Heintzleman.
W. H. H. AVERY—Enrolled at Granville, O., August 12, 1862; discharged November 1, 1863, at Chattanooga, Tenn., by order of Major General Thomas.
JAMES R. LADD, 1st Sergeant—Enrolled at St. Albans, O., August 25, 1862; discharged June 24, 1864, at Vinings' Station, Ga., by order of Maj. Gen'l. Palmer.
ELIAS W. SHOWMAN,—Enrolled at Granville, O., August 21, 1862; discharged April 6, 1864, at Nashville, Tenn., by order of Maj. Gen'l Thomas.

ANDREW J. POWELL—Enrolled at Granville, O., August 20, 1862; discharged January 9, 1864, at Nashville, Tenn., by order of Maj. Gen'l. Thomas.

GEORGE F. NELSON—Enrolled at Granville, O., August 20, 1862; discharged September 27, 1863, Nashville, Tenn., by order of Maj. Gen'l Thomas.

ALVIN DRAKE—Enrolled at Columbus, O., September 23, 1864; discharged June 22, 1865, at Louisville, Ky., by order of Sec. War.

RICHARD CHIDISTER—Enrolled at St. Albans, O., January 28, 1864; discharged September 8, 1864 at Camp Dennison, O., by order of Maj. Genl. Hientzleman.

JOHN EGGLESTON—Enrolled at St. Albans, O., January 28, 1864; discharged May 25, 1865, at Columbus, O., by order of Sec. War.

ENOS. JEWELL—Enrolled at St. Albans, O., August 20, 1862; discharged October 19, 1865, at New Albany, Ind., by order of Maj. Gen'l. Rosecrans.

HORATIO H. KNEELAND—Enrolled at Granville, O., August 29, 1862; discharged September 30, 1863, at Nashville, Tenn., by order of Maj. Gen'l. Rosecrans.

WM. H. STARR—Enrolled at Granville, O., August 18, 1862; discharged October 28, 1864, at Nashville, Tenn., by order of Maj. Genl. Thomas.

F. J. CRESSEY, Sergeant—Enrolled at Granville, O., August 20, 1862; discharged December 14, 1863, at Chattanooga, Tenn., by order of Maj. Gen'l Thomas.

DESERTED.

JERRY OWEN—Enrolled at Zanesville, O., October 1, 1862; deserted December 11, 1862, at Camp Zanesville, O.

GEORGE W. BOWIE—Enrolled at St. Albans, O., August 22, 1862; deserted February 1, 1863, at Portland, Ky.

GEORGE L. DEVILBLISS—Enrolled at St. Albans, O., August 22, 1862; deserted February 1, 1863, at Portland, Ky.

JOHN E. EVANS—Enrolled at Granville, O., August 20, 1862; deserted February 2, 1863, at Salt Creek, Ky.

CHAS. M. MARSHELL—Enrolled at Zanesville, O., December 13, 1862; deserted March, 31, 1865, on the campaign through S. C.

TRANSFERRED.

GEORGE GARDNER—Enrolled at Granville, O., August 20, 1862; transferred to V. R. C. November 14, 1863, Camp Dennison, O., by order of Secretary of War.

LOYAL H. CLOUSE—Enrolled at Granville, O., August 19, 1862; transferred to Regt. Non-Commissioned Staff, March 12, 1864, by order of Colonel Mitchell. (Bugler.)

STILLMAN CLARK—Enrolled at St. Albans, O., August 20, 1862; transferred to V. R. C. October 26, 1863, at Cincinnati, O., by order of Secretary of War.

ISAAC T. EVANS, Corporal—Enrolled at Granville, O., August 22, 1862; transferred to V. R. C. December 12, 1863, at Nashville, Tenn., by order of Secretary of War.

THOS. H. MCBRIDE—Enrolled at Bennington, O., August 20, 1862; transferred to V. R. C. June 26, 1864, at Nashville, Tenn., by order of Secretary of War.

SAMUEL H. WILCOX—Enrolled at Granville, O., August 18, 1862; transferred to V. R. C. June 27, 1864, at Murfreesboro, Tenn., by order of Secretary of War.

ALBERT KNEELAND—Enrolled at Granville, O., August 20, 1862; transferred to V. R. C. December 14, 1863, at Murfreesboro, Tenn, by order of Secretary of War.

COMPANY I.

Mustered out at Louisville, Ky., July 6, 1865.

COMMISSIONED OFFICERS.

CAPTAIN NATHAN STRAUS—Commissioned at Columbus, O., September 6, 1862; resigned March 17, 1863; resignation accepted by order of Major General Rosecrans.

CAPTAIN NELSON DURANT—Commissioned at Franklin, Tenn., April 21, 1863; honorably discharged from the service of the U. S. on account of physical disability, by special order No. 416 War Department November 25, 1864.

CAPTAIN JOHN S. SKEELS—Commissioned at Goldsboro, N. C., April 1, 1865; transferred from company C; mustered out at Louisville, Ky., July 6, 1865. (See Roll C.)

FIRST LIEUTENANT MILES C. NOLAN—Commissioned at Columbus, O., September 6, 1862; resigned February 2, 1863; resignation accepted February 2, 1863, by order of General Wright, Commanding Department of the Ohio.

FIRST LIEUTENANT ED. T. HAYNES—Commissioned at Franklin, Tenn., May 2, 1863; dishonorably discharged from the service March 15, 1864, by order Major General Thomas, Commanding Department of the Cumberland.

FIRST LIEUTENANT WM. GROVE—Commissioned at Avon's Ferry, N. C., April 10, 1865; mustered out at Louisville, Ky., July 6, 1865.

SECOND LIEUTENANT CHAS. P GARMAN—Commissioned at Franklin, Tenn., May 2, 1863; appointed First Lieutenant and transferred to company A, by order of Regimental commander, March 1, 1864.

SECOND LIEUTENANT T. D. BENTLY—Commissioned at Columbus, O., November 5, 1863; honorably discharged from the service of the U. S. on account of physical disability (caused by wounds received in battle) by special order No. 338, War Department, November 25, 1864.

NON-COMMISSIONED OFFICERS.

ARTHUR C. NASH, First Sergeant—Enrolled at Dayton, O., October 4, 1862; mustered out with company.

A. STRAUS, Sergeant—Enrolled at Mansfield, O., September 6, 1862; absent on furlough; mustered out with company.

CALEB GRAY, Sergeant—Enrolled at Columbus, O., September 29, 1862; absent on furlough; mustered out with company.

PRESTON GOAD, Sergeant—Enrolled at Dayton, O., December 25, 1863; mustered out with company.

CHAS. V. MCCALLA, Sergeant—Enrolled at Cincinnati, O., October 17, 1862; mustered out with company.

WESLEY STRAUS, Corporal—Enrolled at Dayton, O., January 7, 1864; mustered out with company.

J. C. AMBROSE, Corporal—Enrolled at Cincinnati, O., October 30, 1862; absent on furlough; mustered out with company.

ALFRED BLAKE, Corporal—Enrolled at Dayton, O., January 28, 1864; mustered out with company.

PRIVATES.

JOHN ARMATROUT—Enrolled at Harrisburg, O., September 17, 1862; mustered out with company.

OSCAR E. BASSETT—Enrolled at Dayton, O., February 11, 1864; absent sick in hospital.
HENRY CARR—Enrolled at Columbus, O., February 10, 1864; mustered out with company.
RALPH CRAIG—Enrolled at Dayton, O., March 18, 1864; mustered out with company.
JOHN DORAN—Enrolled at Columbus, O., November 14, 1862; absent sick in hospital; mustered out with company.
SOLOMON H. DAVIS—Enrolled at Dayton, O., October 2, 1862; mustered out with company.
FRANCIS DUFFY—Enrolled at Cincinnati, O., October 11, 1862; mustered out with company.
JEFFERSON DODSON—Enrolled at Harrisburg, O., October 9, 1862; absent sick in hospital.
ANDREW J. ENGLAND—Enrolled at Harrisburg, O., September 15, 1862; absent sick in hospital.
PRESTON B. FISHER—Enrolled at Dayton, O., October 20, 1862; absent sick in hospital.
PETER FAIRL—Enrolled at Camp Dennison, O., November 22, 1862; mustered out with company.
DAVID GITTINGS—Enrolled at Columbus, O., November 11, 1862; mustered out with company.
HENRY GREENACHEL—Enrolled at Cincinnati, O., November 17, 1862; mustered out with company.
HENRY HOUCK—Enrolled at Cincinnati, O., October 15, 1862; mustered out with company.
WILLIAM HUGHES—Enrolled at Harrisburg, O., September 15, 1862; mustered out with company.
WILLIAM HUNTER—Enrolled at Cincinnati, O., October 1, 1862; absent sick in hospital.
JOHN J. HAHN—Enrolled at Dayton, O., January 23, 1864; mustered out with company.
ANDREW KROMER—Enrolled at Columbus, O., September 15, 1862; mustered out with company.
PETER MITTLESTETTER—Enrolled at Dayton, O., September 22, 1862; absent on furlough; mustered out with company.
WILLIAM MCCAIN—Enrolled at Dayton, O., October 8, 1862; mustered out with company. (Muleteer.)
HUGH MCCARNEY—Enrolled at Sandusky, O., December 17, 1863; absent sick in hospital.

JOHN J. MYERS—Enrolled at Dayton, O., January 11, 1864; mustered out with company.
JOHN MCHU—Enrolled at Dayton, O., January 13, 1864; absent sick in hospital.
PATRICK MORRIS—Enrolled at Sandusky, O., December 17, 1863; mustered out with company.
ELWOOD T. NICKOLS—Enrolled at Harrisburg, O., September 15, 1862; absent sick in hospital.
H. RAMSBOTHAM—Enrolled at Dayton, O., September 26, 1862; mustered out with company.
WM. H. TAYLOR—Enrolled at Cincinnati, O., October 11, 1862; mustered out with company.
JAMES L. TURNER—Enrolled at Harrisburg, O., September 14, 1862; mustered out with company.
JEFFERSON WALES—Enrolled at Columbus, O., October 3, 1862; mustered out with company.
CHAS. WILSON—Enrolled at Cincinnati, O., October 1, 1862; mustered out with company.
LOUIS WHARTON—Enrolled at Dayton, O., January 21, 1864; absent sick in hospital.
HIRAM HEATH—Enrolled at Zanesville, O., November 4, 1862; mustered out; erroneously dropped from rolls as prisoner of war since August 28, 1864.
EVANS COLUMBUS (Colored under-cook)—Enrolled at Shelbyville, Tenn., July 7, 1863; mustered out with the company.

KILLED.

WM. MCMANUS—Enrolled at Urbana, O., January 27, 1864; killed in action May 9, 1864, at Buzzard Roost, Ga.
GEORGE KELSEY—Enrolled at Cincinnati, O., October 15, 1862; killed in action September 1, 1864, at Jonesboro, Ga.
WILLIAM KOLTMAN—Enrolled at Cincinnati, O., October 1, 1862; killed in action March 16, 1865, at Averysboro, N. C.

DIED.

NICHOLAS MARTIN—Enrolled at Cincinnati, O., October 23, 1862; died February 18, 1863, at Muldrough's Hill, Ky., froze to death.
JACOB KELSING—Enrolled at Columbus, O., September 15, 1862; died April 27, 1863, at Franklin, Tenn.; congestion of the brain.

Anthony Dreher—Enrolled at Columbus, O., September 18, 1862; died April 28, 1863, at Louisville, Ky., of inflammatory rheumatism.

James England—Enrolled at Harrisburg, O., October 17, 1862; died July 28, 1863, at New Albany, Ind., of typhoid fever.

Rudolph Webber—Enrolled at Columbus, O., September 19, 1862; died August 13, 1863, at Camp Dennison, O., of general debility.

Charles West—Enrolled at Columbus, O., September 12, 1862; died March 19, 1864, at Rossville, Ga., of general debility.

Francis Leehey—Enrolled at Cincinnati, O., October 13, 1862; died June 28, 1864, at Field Hospital, Marietta, Ga., of wounds received in action on the day before.

Thomas Sweeney—Enrolled at Dayton, O., January 24, 1864; died June 30, 1864, at Big Shanty, Tenn., of disease.

John Rooks—Enrolled at Dayton, O., February 13, 1864; died July 8, 1865, at Chattanooga, Tenn., of wounds.

Franklin Elliott—Enrolled at Cincinnati, O., October 30, 1862; died July 6, 1864, at Kingston, Ga., of wounds.

Wm. H. Coblentz, Corporal—Enrolled at Dayton, O., October 4, 1862; died August 19, 1864, at Chattanooga, Tenn., of wounds.

Wm. McKnight—Enrolled at Cincinnati, O., October 21, 1862; died August 23, 1864, at Nashville, Tenn., of wounds.

Michael Kehoe, Corporal—Enrolled at Dayton, O., October 25, 1862; died August 21, 1864, at Nashville, Tenn., of wounds.

Henry Bracke, Sergeant—Enrolled at Cincinnati, O., October 2, 1862; died September 5, 1864, at Atlanta, Ga., of wounds received at the battle of Jonesboro, Ga.

William Collins—Enrolled at Dayton, O., January 18, 1864; died September 11, 1864, at Atlanta, Ga., of disease.

John H. Duncan—Enrolled at Dayton, O., October 6, 1862; died October 15, 1864, at Chattanooga, Tenn., of disease.

Jesse Curtis—Enrolled at Dayton, O., January 4, 1864, died October 31, 1864, at Atlanta, Ga., of disease.

Wm. H. Barlett—Enrolled at Dayton, O., February 10, 1864; died July 22, 1864, at Hospital No. 1, Nashville, Tenn., of wounds received in action.

Jacob Meyers, Corporal—Enrolled at Camp Dennison, O., September 13, 1862; died July 6, 1864, at Chattanooga, Tenn., of wounds received in action.

CHARLES STORMS—Enrolled at Sandusky, O., December 15, 1863; died July 25, 1864, Second Brigade Hospital, Second Division 14th, A C., of disease.

JOHN D. SNYDER—Enrolled at Columbus, O., September 20, 1862; died September 1, 1864, in Ambulance Hospital, of disease.

DISCHARGED.

WM. H. HOBLITT—Enrolled at Dayton, O., October 9, 1862; discharged June 13, 1863, at Cincinnati, O., by order of Colonel Burbank, commanding post.

GEO. W. JOHNSON—Enrolled at Columbus, O., September 18, 1862; discharged February 21, 1863, at Camp Dennison, O., by order of Colonel Burbank, commanding post.

SAMUEL GESTER—Enrolled at Columbus, O., October 30, 1862; discharged March 13, 1863, at Nashville, Tenn., by order of General Rosecrans.

WILLIAM LOHIG—Enrolled at Dayton, O., October 29, 1862; discharged March 12, 1863, at Nashville, Tenn., by order of General Rosecrans.

ANTHONY HUBER—Enrolled at Dayton, O., October 27, 1862; discharged April 10, 1863, at Nashville, Tenn., by order of General Rosecrans.

GEO. W. JEWELL—Enrolled at Dayton, O., October 9, 1862; discharged April 10, 1863, at Nashville, Tenn., by order of General Rosecrans.

CHRISTIAN EICHNER—Enrolled at Dayton, O., October 24, 1862; discharged April 20, 1863, Nashville, Tenn., by order General Rosecrans.

HENRY CARROLL—Enrolled at Camp Dennison, O., November 20, 1862; discharged May 11, 1863, Nashville, Tenn,, by order General Rosecrans.

WM. ARMATROUT—Enrolled at Harrisburg, O., September 15, 1862; discharged August 3, 1863, at Camp Dennison, O., by order of military commander.

JOHN BARRY—Enrolled at Cincinnati, O., September 20, 1862; discharged April 3, 1865, at Quincy, Ill., by order of S. F. Cooper, V. R. Corps Military assistant.

LOUIS DIEHL—Enrolled at Camp Dennison, O., October 10, 1862; discharged September 17, 1864, at Camp Dennison, O., by order of Major General Heintzelman.

FRANCIS F. HENDY—Enrolled at Cincinnati, O., October 11, 1862; discharged February 18, 1865, at Cincinnati, O., by order of Major General Hooker, for wounds received in battle at Kenesaw Mountain, Ga. (Sergeant.)

JAMES KELLS, Sergeant—Enrolled at Dayton, O., October 21, 1862; discharged March 21, 1865, at Camp Dennison, O., by order of Major General Hooker.

JOHN F. ROCKAFIELD, Corporal—Enrolled at Dayton, O., October 4, 1862; discharged March 21, 1865, at Camp Dennison, O., by order of Major General Hooker.

PATRICK OMELIA—Enrolled at Cincinnati, O., October 16, 1862; discharged April 17, 1865, at Camp Dennison, O., by order of Major General Hooker.

PETER BYE—Enrolled at Columbus, O., September 18, 1862; discharged May 30, 1865, at Camp Dennison, O., by order of the Surgeon in charge.

WILLIAM T. JOHNSON—Enrolled at Cincinnati, O., October 1, 1862; discharged May 23, 1865, at Camp Dennison, O., by order of the Surgeon in charge.

JOHN B. MILLER—Enrolled at Dayton, O., January 2, 1864; discharged May 23, 1865, at Camp Dennison, O., by order of the Surgeon in charge.

DAVID PARCELLS—Enrolled at Harrisburg, O., September 15, 1862; discharged May 6, 1865, at Columbus, O., by order of Major General Hooker.

JOSEPH SHERMAN—Enrolled at Dayton, O., September 10, 1862; discharged at Franklin, Tenn.; no record of time of discharge given.

WILLIAM SELLS—Enrolled at Harrisburg, O., September 15, 1862; mustered out of service of the U. S. June 9, 1865, pursuance to general order No. 77, Par. 6, Adjutant General's office, dated April 28, 1865, at Washington, D. C.

DESERTED.

JOHN ARMATROUT—Enrolled at Harrisburg, O., September 15, 1862; deserted December 2, 1862, at Camp Dennison, O.

JOHN DONAHOE—Enrolled at Camp Dennison, O., October 19, 1862; deserted December 2, 1862, at Camp Dennison, O.

R. H. BROMAGE—Enrolled at Dayton, O., October 7, 1862; deserted December 29, 1862, at Camp Dennison, O.

RUDOLPH BOLEN—Enrolled at Camp Dennison, O., September, 15 1862; deserted December 15, 1862, at Camp Dennison, O.

CHAS. H. BASCOMB—Enrolled at Cincinnati, O., November 1, 1862; deserted December 28, 1862, at Camp Dennison O.

T. BURGHOORST—Enrolled at Camp Dennison, O., November 22, 1862; deserted January 23, 1863, at Camp Laura, Ky.

ELIAS O. BRACKE—Enrolled at Columbus, O., November 4, 1862, deserted February 10, 1863, at Nashville, Tenn.

JOSEPH CAMPBELL—Enrolled at Cincinnati, O., October 21, 1862; deserted December 4, 1862, at Camp Dennison, O.

LEWIS COLLINS—Enrolled at Cincinnati, O., October 31, 1862; deserted December 5, 1862, at Camp Dennison, O.

WILLIAM FINLEY—Enrolled at Cincinnati, O., October 23, 1862; deserted December 15, 1862, at Camp Dennison, O.

JAMES HOWITT—Enrolled at Cincinnati, O., October 15, 1862; deserted December 23, 1862, at Camp Dennison, O.

JASPER HAUSER—Enrolled at Camp Dennison, O., November, 17, 1862; deserted December 13, 1862, at Camp Dennison, O.

HENRY KING—Enrolled at Cincinnati, O., October 30, 1862; deserted December 14, 1862, at Camp Dennison, O.

MICHAEL KAYS—Enrolled at Cincinnati, O., October 5, 1862; deserted February 1, 1863, at Louisville, Ky.

JAMES LEAS—Enrolled at Columbus, O., September 19, 1862; deserted February 5, 1863, at Dover, Tenn.

JOHN LANER—Enrolled at Camp Dennison, O., September 15, 1862; deserted December 13, 1862, at Camp Dennison, O.

LOUIS MANTLE—Enrolled at Harrisburg, O., September 20, 1862; deserted December 14, 1862, at Camp Dennison, O.

HENRY MASSMAN—Enrolled at Cincinnati, O., November 17, 1862; deserted December 23, 1862, at Camp Dennison, O.

RICHARD MCCOHEY—Enrolled at Cincinnati, O., November 22, 1862; deserted December 23, 1862, at Camp Dennison, O.

JOHN S. RHOADS—Enrolled at Dayton, O., September 11, 1862; deserted February 1, 1863, at Louisville, Ky.

BERNARD D. SHUTE—Enrolled at Cincinnati, O., October 21, 1862; deserted December 2, 1862, at Camp Dennison, O.

HENRY STONE—Enrolled at Cincinnati, O., October 21, 1862; deserted December 9, 1862, at Camp Dennison, O.

PETER SKELLY—Enrolled at Cincinnati, O., September 28, 1862; deserted December 24, 1862, at Camp Dennison, O.

NATHAN T. VAUGHAN—Enrolled at Cincinnati, O., August 1862; deserted December 28, 1862, at Camp Dennison, O.

THOMAS WILLIAMS—Enrolled at Cincinnati, O., October 20, 1862; deserted December 2, 1862, at Camp Dennison, O.

HENRY WILBURN—Enrolled at Cincinnati, O., October 23, 1862; deserted December 1, 1862, at Camp Dennison, O.

JOHN YOUNG—Enrolled at Cincinnati, O., November 17, 1862; deserted December 1, 1862, at Camp Dennison, O.

SAMUEL H. ROWE—Enrolled at Dayton, O., January 18, 1864; deserted November 17, 1864, at or near Atlanta, Ga.

RUSSELL CHARLES—Enrolled at Harrisburg, O., November 14, 1862; deserted November 17, 1864, at or near Atlanta, Ga.

FRANK ALLEN—Enrolled at Dayton, O., January 15, 1864; deserted January 16, 1864, at Dayton, O.

WILLIAM HAGARTY—Enrolled at Dayton, O., January 26, 1864; deserted January 26, 1864, at Dayton, O.

J. H. HAMILTON—Enrolled at Dayton, O., January 11, 1864; deserted January 11, 1864, at Dayton, O.

JOHN MARSHALL—Enrolled at Dayton, O., February 15, 1864; deserted February 15, 1864, at Dayton, O.

JOHN MCGRATH—Enrolled at Dayton, O., January 28, 1864; deserted January 28, 1864, at Dayton, O.

FRANK NOLAN—Enrolled at Dayton, O., December 4, 1863; deserted December 4, 1863, at Dayton, O.

THOMAS WHITE—Enrolled at Hamilton, O., September 10, 1862; deserted January 27, 1863, at Colesburg, Ky.

THADDEUS SPRAGUE—Enrolled at Cincinnati, O., October 20, 1862; arrested as a deserter from the Twenty-First Kentucky Volunteer Infantry, October 24, 1864.

TRANSFERRED.

C. C. RUNYAN, Musician—Enrolled at Dayton, O., October 6, 1862; transferred September 4, 1863, to Non-Commissioned Staff of 113th O. V. I., by order of Colonel Mitchell commanding.

LOUIS MANGUS—Enrolled at Columbus, O., October 1, 1862; transferred to the Invalid Corps, March 22, 1864, by order of Secretary of War.

RUDOLPH ANKENY—Enrolled at Columbus, O., September 15, 1862; transferred to First U. S. Engineer Regt. by order of Secretary of War, August 13, 1864.

JOHN CLARK—Enrolled at Dayton, O., October 4, 1862; transferred to First U. S. Engineer Regt., August 13, 1864, by order of Secretary War.

JOHN N. PRICE, Sergeant—Enrolled at Dayton, O., September 23, 1862; transferred to First U. S. Engineer Regt., August 13, 1864, by order of Secretary War.

F. M. RIEGEL, Corporal—Enrolled at Dayton, O., September 22, 1862; transferred to Non-Commissioned Staff, September 15, 1864, as Commissary Sergeant, by order of Regimental Commander at Atlanta, Ga.

WILLIAM QUINN—Enrolled at Harrisburg, O., September 15, 1862; transferred to Vet. Reserve Corps, January 15, 1865, by order of Secretary of War.

WM. W. DAVIS—Enrolled at Columbus, O., September 12, 1862; absent since February 12, 1865, prisoner of war.

COMPANY C.

Mustered out at Louisville, Ky., July 6, 1865.

COMMISSIONED OFFICERS.

CAPTAIN WM. C. PECK—Commissioned at Columbus, O., August 12, 1862; resigned March 17, 1863.

CAPTAIN JOSHUA M. WELLS—Commissioned at Franklin, Tenn., April 19, 1863; killed at the battle of Chickamauga, Tenn., September 20, 1863.

CAPTAIN LUCUS S. WINDLE—Commissioned near Marietta, Ga., June 25, 1864; mustered out at Louisville, Ky., July 6, 1865.

FIRST LIEUTENANT SAMUEL A. HUGHES—Commissioned at Columbus, O., August 12, 1862; resigned January 28, 1863.

FIRST LIEUTENANT GEORGE W. HOLMES—Commissioned at Franklin, Tenn., April 19, 1863; died of wounds received in battle, September 20, 1863.

FIRST LIEUTENANT JOHN S. SKEELS—Commissioned at Chattanooga, Tenn., February 1, 1864; promoted to Captain; transferred to Company I, April 1, 1865.

FIRST LIEUTENANT A. M. GRAFTON—Commissioned at Washington, D. C., May 26, 1865; promoted from First Sergeant Company E; transferred May 26, 1865; mustered out at Louisville, Ky., July 5, 1865.

NON-COMMISSIONED OFFICERS.

JOHN L. FLOWERS, First Sergeant—Enrolled at Columbus, O., August 13, 1862; promoted First Sergeant from Second Sergeant May 17, 1865; absent on furlough.

JAMES R. TOPPING, Sergeant—Enrolled at Worthington, O., August 12, 1862; mustered out with Company.

GEO. A. PINGREE, Sergeant—Enrolled at Worthington, O., August 12, 1862; absent on furlough; mustered out with Company.

M. V. B. LITTLE, Sergeant—Enrolled at Clinton, O., August 19, 1862; promoted from Corporal May 17, 1865; mustered out with Company.

NELSON FOOS, Sergeant—Enrolled at Columbus, O., August 13, 1862; promoted from Corporal May 17, 1865; mustered out with Company.

ALBERT FIELD, Corporal—Enrolled at Clinton, O., August 20, 1862; absent in hospital since June 22, 1864.

ELIAS J. BEERS, Corporal—Enrolled at Clinton, O., August 18, 1862; absent in hospital since June 27, 1864.

CHAS. C. CLEMENTS, Corporal—Enrolled at Orange, O., August 21, 1862; absent on furlough; mustered out with Company.

JONAS ORDERS, Corporal—Enrolled at Jackson, O., August 12, 1862; absent on furlough; mustered out with Company.

THOS. GOLDSMITH, Corporal—Enrolled at Jackson, O., August 21, 1862; mustered out with Company.

JAMES T. BAKER, Corporal—Enrolled at Clinton, O., August 20, 1862; promoted from the ranks to date, April 17, 1865; absent on furlough; mustered out with Company.

WM. SIMMONS, Corporal—Enrolled at Blendon, O., August 21, 1862; promoted from the ranks to date May 17, 1865; mustered out with Company.

GEO. B. LOMERSON, Corporal—Enrolled at Jackson, O., August 12, 1862; promoted from the ranks to date May 17, 1865; mustered out with Company.

PRIVATES.

CHARLES ALDEN—Enrolled at Columbus, O., November 16, 1863; returned prisoner of war; mustered out with Company.

JAMES M. ANDERSON—Enrolled at Jackson, O., August 12, 1862; absent in hospital since June 22, 1864; absent on furlough; mustered out with Company.

JOHN W. BAKER—Enrolled at Clinton, O., August 22, 1862; mustered out with Company.
WM. E. BACON—Enrolled at Dublin, O., August 12, 1862; absent on furlough; mustered out with Company.
JOHN BRENNAN—Enrolled at Columbus, O., January 4, 1864; mustered out with Company.
MINOR CRIPPIN—Enrolled at Sharon, O., August 13, 1862; absent in hospital since February 12, 1863.
WM. E. FEARING—Enrolled at Jackson, O., August 12, 1862; mustered out with Company.
DAVID J. GREEN—Enrolled at Clinton, O., August 21, 1862; mustered out with Company.
THEODORE G. GANTZ—Enrolled at Jackson, O., August 12, 1862; as nurse at general field hospital, August 2, 1864.
HENRY GILES—Enrolled at Dayton, O., September 10, 1864; mustered out with Company.
HIRAM HARTER—Enrolled at Sharon, O., August 20, 1862; mustered out with Company.
PATRICK HALLARAN—Enrolled at Springfield, O., December 3, 1863; mustered out with Company.
JOHN E. LAFLER—Enrolled at Sharon, O., August 13, 1862; mustered out with Company.
WILLIAM LUKE—Enrolled at Columbus, O., November 16, 1863; mustered out with Company.
HIRAM V. MALOTT—Enrolled at Jackson, O., August 13, 1862; mustered out with Company.
MICHEAL MURPHY—Enrolled at Green County, O., February 3, 1864; mustered out with Company.
CHRISTIAN ORTMAN—Enrolled at Zanesville, O., October 24, 1862; mustered out with Company.
JOSHUA PRIEST—Enrolled at Jackson, O., August 12, 1862; mustered out with Company.
ISAAC PECK—Enrolled at Sharon, O., August 21, 1862; mustered out with Company.
ROBERT PEOPLES—Enrolled at Jackson, O., August 22, 1862; mustered out with Company.
JAMES PARKS—Enrolled at Osborne, O., February 8, 1864; absent in hospital since June 27, 1864.
JOSEPH RIDGWAY—Enrolled at Jackson, O., August 13, 1862; mustered out with Company.

ADAM M. RANNEBERGER—Enrolled at Perry, O., August 13, 1862; mustered out with Company.
STEPHEN SMITH—Enrolled at Jackson, O., August 12, 1862; mustered out with Company.
GEO. SUNDERLAND—Enrolled at Clinton, O., August 20, 1862; mustered out with Company.
FERNANDO SWIGER—Enrolled at Jackson, O., August 15, 1862; mustered out with Company.
MARTIN SCANTLIN—Enrolled at Urbana, O., February 5, 1864; mustered out with Company.
MICHAEL SHARKEY—Enrolled at Green County, O., February 8, 1864; absent in hospital since June 27, 1864.
DANIEL WEYGANDT—Enrolled at Jackson, O., August 12, 1862; mustered out with Company.
CHARLES WRIGHT—Enrolled at Perry County, O., August 21, 1862; sick in hospital.
HENRY WILSON—Enrolled at Sandusky. O., December 10, 1863; absent in hospital since June 27, 1862.
WILLIAM ZINN—Enrolled at Clinton, O., August 21, 1862; mustered out with Company.

DIED.

JOHN G. PERKINS—Enrolled at Columbus, O., August 22, 1862; died at Nashville, Tenn., February 15, 1863, of disease of the brain.
JOHN A. WEYGANDT—Enrolled at Jackson, O., September 13, 1862; died at Franklin, Tenn., February 20, 1863, disease of the brain.
WM. ANDERSON—Enrolled at Sharon, O., August 16, 1862; died at Franklin, Tenn., March 9, 1863, of consumption.
JOHN ROYAL—Enrolled at Jackson, O., August 15, 1862; died at Nashville, Tenn., March 9, 1863, of measles.
WM. MELLON—Enrolled at Jackson, O., August 13, 1862; died at Franklin, Tenn., March 27, 1863, of typhoid fever.
JOHN H. PRICE—Enrolled at Jackson, O., August 18, 1862; died at Franklin, Tenn., April 1, 1863, of brain fever.
GEO. HARTER—Enrolled at Sharon, O., August 20, 1862; died at Franklin, Tenn., April 8, 1863, of congestion of the lungs.
JAMES M. CLEMENTS—Enrolled at Orange, O., August 20, 1862 died at Franklin, Tenn., April 11, 1863, of camp fever.

JOHN E. WILLIAMS—Enrolled at Perry, O., August 15, 1862; died at Franklin, Tenn., April 16, 1863, of disease of the heart.
THOS. SPILLMAN—Enrolled at Jackson, O., August 13, 1862; died at Nashville, Tenn., June 4, 1863, of diarrhœa.
WM. H. H. GOLDSMITH—Enrolled at Jackson, O., August 13, 1862; died at Nashville, Tenn., June 22, 1863, of typhoid fever.
JOHN BOYER—Enrolled at Jackson, O., August 12, 1862; died at Stevenson, Ala., October 21, 1863, from wounds received in battle.
SAMUEL H. BURWELL.—Enrolled at Camp Zanesville, O., August 15, 1862; died at Covington, Ky., January 3, 1864, of small-pox.

KILLED.

WM. J. KAARAN, Corporal—Enrolled at Sharon, O., August 15, 1862; killed at Chickamauga, Ga., September 20, 1863.
MOROLOUS WILCOX—Enrolled at Liberty, O., August 21, 1862; killed at Chickamauga, Tenn., September 20, 1863.
LEWIS C. BAKER—Enrolled at Camp Zanesville, O., November 15, 1862; killed at Chickamauga, Ga., September 20, 1863.
TITUS CHAMBERLIN—Enrolled at Perry, O., August 22, 1862; killed near Marietta, Ga., June 27, 1864.
JOHN MARTIN—Enrolled at Green County, O., February 8, 1864; killed near Marietta, Ga., June 27, 1864.
HIRAM WILCOX—Enrolled at Clinton, O., August 18, 1862; killed near Marietta, Ga., June 27, 1864.
JAMES HISER, Corporal—Enrolled at Perry, O., August 21, 1862; died at Louisville, Ky., February 26, 1864, of a gun-shot wound received in battle.
ANDREW CONNOLLEY—Enrolled at Osborne, O., February 10, 1864; died at Nashville, Tenn., July 15, 1864, of wounds received in action.
ANSON W. BENEDICT—Enrolled at Columbus, O., November 16, 1863; died at Kingston, Ga., August 28, 1864, of dysentery.
ROBERT BRITTIN—Enrolled at Clark County, O., January 19, 1864; died at Lookout Mountain, Tenn., October 11, 1864, of chronic diarrhœa.
WM. CUNNINGHAM—Enrolled at Dayton, O., January 14, 1864; died near Savannah, Ga., December 14, 1864, of diarrhœa.
DAVID NEAL—Enrolled at Jackson, O., September 18, 1862; died at Nashville, Tenn., August 30, 1864, from wounds received in action.

JAMES ABBOTT—Enrolled at Columbus, O., November 16, 1863; died at Savannah, Ga., December 30, 1864, of chronic diarrhœa.

MISSING IN ACTION.

PETER GERBA—Enrolled at Camp Zanesville, O., November 10, 1862; missing in action September 21, 1863.

DISCHARGED.

LEVI TUCKER—Enrolled at Clinton, O., August 22, 1862; discharged at Columbus, O., for disability, by Captain Dod, February 20, 1863.

MORRIS PERCELL—Enrolled at Hamilton, O., August 21, 1862; discharged at Nashville, Tenn., March 13, 1863; rupture; order of Major General Rosecrans.

JOHN L. B. WISWELL—Enrolled at Perry, O., August 14, 1862; discharged at Nashville, Tenn., March 14, 1863, by order of Major General Rosecrans.

BENTON HISER—Enrolled at Perry, O., August 21, 1862; discharged at Columbus, O., March 28, 1863, by order of Captain Dod.

WILBER C. BOOTH, Corporal—Enrolled at Columbus, O., August 13, 1862; discharged at Nashville, Tenn., May 1, 1863, by order of Major General Rosecrans.

EDWARD W. BISHOP—Enrolled at Sharon, O., August 12, 1862; discharged at Nashville, Tenn., June 4, 1863, by order of Major General Rosecrans.

THOS. SPILLMAN—Enrolled at Jackson, O., August 13, 1862; discharged at Nashville, Tenn., June 4, 1863, of chronic diarrhœa.

WM. H. LANGSTAFF—Enrolled at Columbus, O., August 21, 1862; discharged at Camp Dennison, O., June 23, 1863; order of military commander.

GEORGE LEMON—Enrolled at Jackson, O., August 22, 1862; discharged at Nashville, Tenn., July 13, 1863, by order of Major General Rosecrans.

WM. HICKMAN—Enrolled at Sharon, O., August 20, 1862; discharged at Camp Dennison, O., June 23, 1863, by order of military commander.

JOHN CASEY—Enrolled at Franklin, Tenn., May 1, 1863; discharged at Chattanooga, Tenn., December 22, 1863, special order War Department No. 529.

GEORGE MUZZY—Enrolled at Sharon, O., August 20, 1862; discharged at Louisville, Ky., July 23, 1863; disability, by order of Major General Rosecrans.
JOHN W. WHITE—Enrolled at Sharon, O., August 16, 1862; discharged at New Albany, Ind., February 22, 1865; disability, by order of Major General Rosecrans.
JOHN A. GLENN, Sergeant—Enrolled at Columbus, O., August 21, 1862; discharged at Columbus, O., May 17, 1865, from wounds received in action, by order of Major General Hooker.
JOHN W. BRINK, Corporal—Enrolled at Jackson, O., August 12, 1862; discharged at Camp Dennison, O., May 20, 1865, from wounds received in action, by order of Major General Hooker.
WM. P. SOUDER, Sergeant—Enrolled at Worthington, O., August 21, 1862; wounded June 27, 1864; discharged at Camp Dennison, O., May 26, 1865; mustered out by order of War Department; disability, by order of Adjutant General, May 18, 1865.
JAMES SULLIVAN—Enrolled at Sandusky, O., December 10, 1863; discharged at Camp Dennison, O., May 29, 1865; disability, by order of Adjutant General of Ohio, May 18, 1865.
ISAAC N. STROHM—Enrolled at Clinton, O., August 18, 1862; discharged at Louisville, Ky., June 15, 1865, by order of Adjutant General of Ohio, May 18, 1865.

TRANSFERRED.

JOHN W. ROCKY—Enrolled at Clinton, O., August 21, 1862; transferred at Zanesville, O., December 6, 1862, by order of Colonel James A. Wilcox.
BARNETT TOLLIVER—Enrolled at Columbus, O., August 20, 1862; transferred at Bridgeport, Ala., November 1, 1863, by order of Secretary of War.
ELIJAH THRAILKILL—Enrolled at Jackson, O., August 15, 1862; transferred at Nashville, Tenn., September 1, 1863, to invalid corps, Adjutant General order 302.
SAMUEL LIPPERT—Enrolled at Jackson, O., August 12, 1862; transferred at Nashville, Tenn., September 1, 1863, to invalid corps, Adjutant General order 301.
WILLIAM H. SMITH—Enrolled at Clinton, O., August 19, 1862; transferred at Nashville, Tenn., September 3, 1863, to invalid corps, Adjutant General order 321.

CHAS. MORGAN—Enrolled at Perry, O., August 15, 1862; transferred at Nashville, Tenn., January 28, 1864, to invalid corps, Adjutant General order 24.

JAMES WRIGHT—Enrolled at Clayborn, O., August 22, 1862; transferred at Nashville, Tenn., November 1, 1863, to invalid corps, Adjutant General order 352.

CLARK W. COTTRELL—Enrolled at Urbana, O., February 12, 1864; transferred at Rossville, Ga., April 6, 1864, by order of Major L. S. Sullivant.

ROBT. S. SMITH—Enrolled at Clinton, O., August 16, 1862; transferred at Nashville, Tenn., July 27, 1864, to Engineer Corps, by order of Major General Thomas.

GILBERT W. BRINK—Enrolled at Jackson, O., August 12, 1862; transferred at Nashville, Tenn., May 1, 1864, to Invalid Corps, Adjutant General order 188.

FRANCIS KIBBY—Enrolled at Worthington, O., August 15, 1862; transferred at Nashville, Tenn., May 1, 1864, to Invalid Corps, Adjutant General order 188.

LEMUEL SPILLMAN—Enrolled at Jackson, O., August 13, 1862; transferred at Nashville, Tenn., May 1, 1864, to Invalid Corps, Adjutant General order 188.

SAMUEL SPILLMAN—Enrolled at Jackson, O., August 13, 1862; transferred at Nashville, Tenn., March 15, 1864, to Invalid Corps, Adjutant General order 93.

ISAAC N. HOBILL—Enrolled at Jackson, O., August 14, 1862; transferred at Rossville, Ga., April 25, 1864, by order of Lieutenant Colonel Warner.

WM. A. M. DAVIS, Sergeant—Enrolled at Worthington, O., August 21, 1862; transferred at Atlanta, Ga., September 23, 1864, by order of Captain Jones.

GEORGE WEBER—Enrolled at Clinton, O., August 18, 1862; transferred at Nashville, Tenn., April 10, 1864, to Invalid Corps Paymaster, General Circular 150.

JOHN MURPHY—Enrolled at Osborne, O., February 10, 1864; transferred at Columbus, O., January 24, 1865, to Invalid Corps Paymaster, General Circular 183.

DESERTED.

AUGUSTA MAIKS—Enrolled at Columbus, O., August 18, 1862; deserted at Camp Chase, O., October 28, 1862.

Company H.]   *History of the 113th O. V. I.*   215

WASHINGTON O'NEIL—Enrolled at Jackson, O., August 22, 1862; deserted at Portland, Ky., February 1, 1863.
JAMES SMILEY—Enrolled at Clinton, O., August 18, 1862; deserted at Nashville, Tenn., February 9, 1863.
JOHN C. WAITZ—Enrolled at Jackson, O., August 13, 1862; deserted at Camp Chase, O., April 25, 1863.
GEO. F. SHAPLY—Enrolled at Columbus, O., November 24, 1863; deserted while being transferred to regiment.
CROMWELL W. PORTER—Enrolled at Erie County, O., December 21, 1863; deserted while being transferred to regiment.
JAMES COADY—Enrolled at Clark County, O., January 19, 1864; deserted near Atlanta, Ga., August 14, 1864.
THOS. BRENNAN—Enrolled at Sandusky, O., December 10, 1863; deserted near Atlanta, Ga., August 14, 1864.
JOHN FRANKLIN (colored under cook)—Enrolled at Chattanooga, Tenn., October 1, 1863; deserted at Kenesaw Mountain, June 22, 1864.
ROBERT VALENTINE (colored under cook)—Enrolled at Chattanooga, Tenn., October 1, 1863; deserted at Savannah, Ga., January 20, 1865.

COMPANY H.

Mustered out at Louisville, Ky., July 6, 1865.

COMMISSIONED OFFICERS.

CAPTAIN L. S. SULLIVANT—Commissioned at Zanesville, O., November 13, 1862; promoted to Major May 6, 1863, *vice* Major D. B. Warner, promoted.
CAPTAIN OTWAY WATSON—Commissioned at Triune, Tennessee, May 16, 1863; promoted to Major June 12, 1865, *vice* Major L. S. Sullivant, resigned.
CAPTAIN JAMES R. LADD—Commissioned at Washington, D. C., June 11, 1865; promoted to Major June 12, 1865, *vice* Otway Watson, promoted; absent on leave since July 2, 1865; mustered out at Louisville, Ky., July 6, 1865.
FIRST LIEUTENANT GEORGE SINCLAIR—Commissioned at Zanesville, O., September 16, 1862; resigned February 6, 1864; resignation accepted by Major General Thomas.
FIRST LIEUTENANT CYRUS G. PLATT—Commissioned at Chattanooga, Tennessee, February 24, 1864; killed June 15, 1864, near Kennesaw Mountain.

FIRST LIEUTENANT D. H. CHATFIELD—Commissioned at Goldsboro, North Carolina, March 15, 1865; mustered out at Louisville, Kentucky, July 6, 1865; transferred from Company E; died at home, near Woodstock, O., August 19, 1869, aged 36 years.
SECOND LIEUTENANT GEORGE W. HOLMS—Commissioned at Zanesville, O., August 30, 1862; mustered out to accept a commission as First Lieutenant of Company C, April 19, 1863.

NON-COMMISSIONED OFFICERS.

WILLIAM ROMOSIER, First Sergeant—Enrolled at Franklinton, Ohio, August 23, 1862; absent on furlough since June 27, 1865; mustered out with Company.
WILLIAM H. BRUNK, Second Sergeant—Enrolled at Dublin, O., August 12, 1862; absent on detached service since February 12, 1864; mustered out with Company.
DAVID O. MULL, Sergeant—Enrolled at Franklinton, O., August 22, 1862; absent wounded since June 27, 1864; lost right arm at Kenesaw; left arm wounded same time.
ROBERT E. LENNON, Sergeant—Enrolled at Zanesville, O., October 11, 1862; mustered out with Company.
GEORGE ASHTON, Sergeant—Enrolled at Columbus, O., September 12, 1862; mustered out with Company.
GEORGE W. PRITCHARD, Corporal—Enrolled at Dublin, O., August 21, 1862; mustered out with Company. Taken prisoner at Chickamauga.
J. CARRIER, Corporal—Enrolled at Dublin, O., August 11, 1862; absent wounded since September 20, 1863.
WILLIAM H. HOLMES, Corporal—Enrolled at Franklinton, O., August 22, 1862; mustered out with Company.
J. R. BRUNK, Corporal—Enrolled at Dublin, O., August 3, 1862; mustered out with Company.
HENRY DEWITT, Corporal—Enrolled at Camp Chase, O., August 22, 1862; absent sick since June 27, 1864. Captured at Kenesaw.
CHAS. H. SPRAGUE, Corporal—Enrolled at Dublin, O., August 12, 1862; absent on furlough since June 25, 1865; mustered out with Company.
JAMES MCMANEES, Corporal—Enrolled at Franklinton, O., August 12, 1862; mustered out with Company.
HUGH H. MITCHELL, Corporal—Enrolled at Dublin, O., August 8, 1862; mustered out with Company.

PRIVATES.

LEWIS ANDREWS—Enrolled at Dublin, O., August 6, 1862; mustered out with Company.

NOAH C. BRETTON—Enrolled at Dublin, O., August 11, 1862; absent sick in Columbus, O., since December 1, 1864.

FRANK BUTTLES—Enrolled at Columbus, O., August 12, 1862; mustered out with Company.

JOHN ELFERT—Enrolled at Zanesville, O., October 11, 1862; mustered out with Company.

HENRY B. FLANNER—Enrolled at Columbus, O., October 11, 1862; absent sick since January 1, 1863.

PETER S. FRANCES—Enrolled at Columbus, O., February 11, 1864; absent on furlough since June 27, 1865.

WM. S. GRACE—Enrolled at Dublin, O., August 14, 1862; absent sick since September 29, 1864; mustered out by General Order No. 77 of War Department.

JAMES GOODEN—Enrolled at Zanesville, O., December 9, 1862; mustered out with Company.

DAVID HUDSON—Enrolled at Dublin, O., August 14, 1862; mustered out with Company.

SAMUEL HOLT—Enrolled at Urbana, O., March 4, 1865; mustered out with Company.

CHAS. H. JENKINS—Enrolled at Franklinton, O., August 23, 1862; mustered out with Company.

PETER L. JONES—Enrolled at Zanesville, O., December 9, 1862; mustered out with Company.

JAMES A. KELLER—Enrolled at Columbus, O., June 14, 1863; mustered out with Company.

WILLIAM KELLER—Enrolled at Franklinton, O., August 17, 1862; absent on furlough since June 25, 1865.

LORENZO KATES—Enrolled at Worthington, O., August 21, 1862; absent wounded since June 27, 1864.

AUGUSTUS LESHITE—Enrolled at Franklinton, O., August 14, 1862; mustered out with Company.

JESSE LUMBARD—Enrolled at Franklinton, O., November 14, 1862; mustered out with Company.

GARLAND MCKIENSEY—Enrolled at Columbus, O., July 20, 1863; mustered out with Company.

WILLIAM MOCK—Enrolled at Dublin, O., August 20, 1862; absent sick since September 13, 1863.

MICHAEL MOONEY—Enrolled at Columbus, O., September 10, 1862 ; absent on furlough since June 27, 1865 ; mustered out with Company.
ENOCH E. MULFORD—Enrolled at Zanesville, O., October 10, 1862 ; mustered out with Company.
JESSE MUSSLEMAN—Enrolled at Columbus, O., September 13, 1862 ; absent on furlough since June 30, 1865 ; mustered out with Company.
HENRY PFOUTCH—Enrolled at Columbus, O., February 14, 1864 ; absent on furlough since June 9, 1865. (Musician.)
DANIEL ROBBINS—Enrolled at Zanesville, O., November 12, 1862 ; mustered out with Company.
JOHN ROMOSIER—Enrolled at Franklinton, O., August 20, 1862 ; absent on furlough since June 25, 1865.
MANUEL STULTS—Enrolled at Dublin, O., August 13, 1862 ; mustered out with Company.
THOMAS VANSISE—Enrolled at Camp Chase, O., September 12, 1862 ; mustered out with Company.
JOSEPH TWIGG—Enrolled at Dublin, O., August 21, 1862 ; mustered out with Company.
CICERO WILLIAMSON—Enrolled at Camp Chase, O., August 2, 1862 ; mustered out with Company.
GERARD A. WING—Enrolled at Dublin, O., August 6, 1862 ; mustered out with Company.
NATHANIEL B. YEAZLE—Enrolled at Columbus, O., July 20, 1863 ; mustered out with Company.
DAVID POINTER (under-cook)—Enrolled at Franklin, Tenn., March 2, 1863 ; mustered out with Company.
POMPEY POINTER (under-cook)—Enrolled at Chattanooga, Tenn., October 31, 1863 ; mustered out with Company.

KILLED.

CALVIN D. CHELLIS, Corporal—Enrolled at Dublin, O., August 12, 1862 ; killed September 20, 1863, at Chickamauga, Ga.
JOHN W. CARTER, Corporal—Enrolled at Camp Chase, O., August 22, 1862 ; killed in action June 27, 1864, at Kenesaw Mountain, Georgia.
JAMES ELLIS—Enrolled at Columbus, O., October 20, 1862 ; killed in action September 20, 1863, at Chickamauga, Ga.
FREEMAN DULEN—Enrolled at Dublin, O., August 15, 1862 ; killed in action June 27, 1864, at Kenesaw Mountain, Ga.

MICHAEL O'CONNELL—Enrolled at Camp Chase, O., August 22, 1862; killed in action June 27, 1864, at Kenesaw Mountain, Ga.
ANDREW J. RHODES—Enrolled at Franklinton, O., August 11, 1862; killed in action June 27, 1864, at Kenesaw Mountain, Ga.
EUGENE H. PALIN—Enrolled at Camp Chase, O., August 12, 1862; killed in action June 27, 1864, at Kenesaw Mountain, Ga.
JOHN McCAULY—Enrolled at Zanesville, O., November 11, 1862; killed in action September 20, 1863, at Chickamauga, Ga.
ELISHA STETLER—Enrolled at Camp Chase, O., August 19, 1862; killed in action June 27, 1864, at Kenesaw Mountain, Ga.

DIED.

WILLIAM SINSEL—Enrolled at Dublin, O., August 12, 1862; died February 9, 1863, in hospital at Louisville, Ky., of brain fever.
GODFREY SNYDER—Enrolled at Camp Chase, O., August 21, 1862; died March 30, 1863, in hospital at Nashville, Tenn., of camp fever.
THOMAS PERRY—Enrolled at Dublin, O., August 21, 1862; died January 12, 1863, in hospital at Franklin, Tenn., of chronic diarrhea.
BENJ. F. TOWNSEND—Enrolled at Camp Chase, O., October 11, 1862; died August 8, 1863, in hospital at Murfreesboro, Tenn., of chronic diarrhea.
JOSEPH BELL—Enrolled at Columbus, O., October 18, 1862; died July 12, 1864, in hospital at Dalton, Ga., of pneumonia.
FRANCIS M. CLOUD—Enrolled at Camp Chase, O., August 23, 1862; died June 30, 1864, in hospital at Big Shanty, Ga., of wounds received at Kenesaw.
VOLNEY HOLYCROSS—Enrolled at Zanesville, O., November 14, 1862; died November 1, 1863, in hospital at Bridgeport, Ala., of chronic diarrhea.
E. C. KIMBROUGH—Enrolled at Morgantown, Tenn., December 6, 1863; died March 9, 1865, in hospital at Wilmington, N. C., of disability.
GEORGE WILSON—Enrolled at Dublin, O., September 10, 1862; died September 6, 1864, in hospital at Columbus, O., of wounds.

DISCHARGED.

JOHN McNAMARA, Corporal—Enrolled at Zanesville, O., October 11, 1862; discharged January 30, 1864, at Columbus, O., by order of Major General Hientzleman.

MORRIS HAFEY, Musician—Enrolled at Columbus, O., September 9, 1862; discharged November 22, 1863, at Chattanooga, Tenn., by order of Major General Halleck.

ROBERT CRAMER—Enrolled at Dublin, O., August 15, 1862; discharged April 27, 1863, at Columbus, O., by order of Medical Director.

BAZIL GREEN—Enrolled at Camp Chase, O., August 21, 1862; discharged December 30, 1862, at Columbus, O., by writ of Habeas Corpus.

THOMAS HATFIELD—Enrolled at Columbus, O., September 29, 1862; discharged December 30, 1862, at Zanesville, O., by certificate of Surgeon.

JOSEPH HAGUE—Enrolled at Dublin, O., August 11, 1862; discharged April 20, 1863, at Quincy, Illinois, by Medical Director U. S. A.

JESSE KENT—Enrolled at Zanesville, O., November 11, 1862; discharged May 26, 1865, at Camp Dennison, O., by order of War Department.

HENRY LEESHITE—Enrolled at Camp Chase, O., August 18, 1862; discharged December 30, 1862, at Columbus, O., by writ of Habeas Corpus.

WILLIAM KEEHN—Enrolled at Camp Chase, O., August 16, 1862; Discharged January 7, 1865, at Columbus, O., by order of Major General Hooker.

JONATHAN LOOKER—Enrolled at Camp Chase, O., October 16, 1862; discharged December 26, 1863, at Madison, Ind., by order of Medical Director U. S. A.

JONATHAN MOATS—Enrolled at Camp Chase, O., August 19, 1862; discharged May 15, 1864, at Madison, Ind., by order of Surgeon's certificate.

DANIEL HILER—Enrolled at Dublin, O., August 8, 1862; discharged July 8, 1863, at Shelbyville, Tenn., by order of General Rosecrans.

JOHN ULRY—Enrolled at Zanesville, O., November 1, 1862; discharged May 21, 1863, at Nashville, Tenn., by order of Major General Rosecrans.

RUSSELL RHODES—Enrolled at Franklinton, O., August 2, 1862; discharged May 7, 1865, at Columbus, O., by order of Major General Hooker.

SAMUEL RHINEHART—Enrolled at Columbus, O., September 30, 1864; discharged; mustered out June 22, 1865, Louisville, Ky., by General Order of War Department, May 18, 1865.

THOMAS WATSON—Enrolled at Dayton, O., August 9, 1864; mustered out June 22, 1865, Louisville, Ky., by General Order of War Department, May 18, 1865.

CYRUS H. TURNER—Enrolled at Dublin, O., August 22, 1862; discharged April 22, 1863, Franklin, Tenn., by order of Major General Rosecrans.

DESERTED.

LORENZO DULEN—Enrolled at Dublin, O., August 12, 1862; deserted January 28, 1863, at Louisville, Ky.

FREDERICK DUVALL—Enrolled at Dublin, O., August 15, 1862; deserted December 13, 1862, Zanesville, O.

HENRY FIKE—Enrolled at Camp Chase, O., August 22, 1862; deserted December 14, 1864, Zanesville, O.

JACOB GARDNER—Enrolled at Zanesville, O., December 10, 1862; deserted December 15, 1862, Camp Dennison, O.

WILLIAM JOHNSON—Enrolled at Zanesville, O., November 20, 1862; deserted December 21, 1862, Camp Dennison, O.

WILLIAM K. JOHNSON—Enrolled at Zanesville, O., November 21, 1862; deserted December 21, 1862, Camp Dennison, O.

ROBERT MILLER—Enrolled at Zanesville, O., November 22, 1862; deserted December 16, 1862, Camp Dennison, O.

JOHN W. ROCKY—Enrolled at Camp Chase, O., August 21, 1862; deserted December 14, 1862, Camp Zanesville, O.

JOHN ROSS—Enrolled at Zanesville, O., November 25, 1862; deserted December 14, 1862, Zanesville, O.

JAMES VALENTINE—Enrolled at Zanesville, O., November 10, 1862; deserted December 20, 1862, Camp Dennison, O.

JOHN WETHERBY—Enrolled at Camp Chase, O., August 21, 1862; deserted June 28, 1863, Louisville, Ky.

THOMAS WOOD—Enrolled at Zanesville, O., December 10, 1862; deserted December 15, 1862, Camp Dennison, O.

J. M. MORRISON—Enrolled at Dublin, O., August 15, 1862; deserted July 25, 1864, near Atlanta, Ga.; supposed deserted to the enemy; received notice of his exchange.

LEONARD KEETZLEMAN—Enrolled at Dublin, O., August 11, 1862; deserted July 25, 1864, near Atlanta, Ga.; supposed deserted to the enemy; received notice of his exchange; serving life sentence in Ohio Penitentiary since November, 1882.

TRANSFERRED.

WM. GROVE, First Sergeant—Enrolled at Columbus, O., September 12, 1862; transferred April 10, 1865, at Goldsboro, N. C., to Company I, 113th O. V. I., and promoted to First Lieutenant.

JAMES L. BLAKELY—Enrolled [at Columbus, O., August 15, 1862; transferred December 18, 1862, at Zanesville, O., to Company B, by order of Colonel James A. Wilcox.

A. J. McCLELLAND—Enrolled at Dublin, O., August 12, 1862; transferred February 15, 1864, at Louisville, Ky., by order of Secretary of War, to Invalid Corps.

JEROME L. ROBY—Enrolled at Zanesville, O., December 5, 1862; transferred December 18, 1862, at Zanesville, O., to Company B, by order of Colonel James A. Wilcox.

DANIEL McEOWEN—Enrolled at Camp Chase, O., August 21, 1862; transferred February 15, 1864, at Madison, Ind., by order of Secretary of War, to Invalid Corps.

LEANDER PANCOST—Enrolled at Zanesville, O., October 31, 1862; transferred December 18, 1862, at Zanesville, O., to Company F, by order of Colonel James A. Wilcox.

HARRISON KELLER—Enrolled at Camp Chase, O., August 13, 1862; transferred July 25, 1864, at Chattanooga, Tenn., to Engineer Corps, by order of Secretary of War.

JAMES HUNTER—Enrolled at Dublin, O., August 14, 1862; transferred February 18, 1864, at Madison, Ind., to Invalid Corps, by order of Secretary of War.

COMPANY E.

Mustered out at Louisville, Ky., July 6, 1865.

COMMISSIONED OFFICERS.

CAPTAIN JOHN F. RIKER—Commissioned at St. Paris, O., August 14, 1862; resigned May 15, 1863.

CAPTAIN JOHN BOWERSOCK—Commissioned at Franklin, Tenn., June 1, 1863; killed in action near Marietta, Ga., June 27, 1864; buried at St. Paris, Ohio. Original First Lieutenant.

CAPTAIN JOSEPH SWISHER—Commissioned near Atlanta, Ga., August 3, 1864; resigned June 5, 1865; promoted to the rank of Major. Original First Sergeant.

Company E.] *History of the 113th O. V. I.* 223

CAPTAIN GEO. MCCREA—Commissioned at Louisville, Ky., June 12, 1865; promoted from First Lieutenant June 12, 1865; commanding company mustered out at Louisville, Ky., July 6, 1865; was made Second Sergeant at the original company organization.

FIRST LIEUTENANT ALEXANDER CARPENTER—Commissioned at Louisville, Ky., June 12, 1865; promoted from First Sergeant June 12, 1865; mustered out with Company. (See B roll.)

SECOND LIEUTENANT H. N. BENJAMIN—Commissioned at Columbus, O., August 14, 1862; promoted from Second Lieutenant to First Lieutenant; transferred to Company B, 113th O. V. I., January 13, 1863; wounded at Chickamauga, Ga., September 20, 1863. (See B roll.)

NON-COMMISSIONED OFFICERS.

J. N. HALL, First Sergeant—Enrolled at St. Paris, O., August 16, 1862; original Fourth Sergeant; prisoner of war, captured at Chickamauga, Ga., September 20, 1863; remained a prisoner of war nineteen months and eight days. (See Hall's Prison Life.)

M. L. STRATTON, Sergeant—Enrolled at St. Paris, O., August 16, 1862; mustered out with Company; original Second Corporal.

F. MCADAMS, Sergeant—Enrolled at Urbana, O., August 15, 1862; mustered out with Company; promoted to Sergeant at Whitehall, Ga., September 26, 1864.

WM. M. GRAFTON, Sergeant—Enrolled at St. Paris, August 22, 1862; promoted from Corporal to date May 27, 1865; mustered out with Company.

J. O. KITE, Sergeant—Enrolled at Westville, O., August 21, 1862; promoted from First Corporal July 1, 1865; absent on furlough; mustered out with Company.

ERNEST SNYDER, Corporal—Enrolled at Zanesville, O., November 13, 1862; mustered out with Company. (German.) Taken prisoner at Sandersville, Ga.

J. H. GIRARD, Corporal—Enrolled at Camp Chase, O., October 17, 1862; absent on furlough; mustered out with Company.

J. H. JOHNSON, Corporal—Enrolled at Urbana, O., August 22, 1862; mustered out with Company.

JOHN G. GANSON, Corporal—Enrolled at Urbana, O., March 28, 1864; mustered out with Company. (Recruit.)

J. MERICA, Corporal—Enrolled at St. Paris, O., August 17, 1862; promoted from private May 27, 1865; mustered out with Company.

PRIVATES.

JESSE ABBOTT—Enrolled at Zanesville, O., November 20, 1862; absent sick since September 20, 1863, at Camp Dennison, O.; wounded at Chickamauga, and left in the hands of the enemy.

HARRISON H. ALSTADT—Enrolled at Urbana, O., March 8, 1865; mustered out with Company. (Recruit.)

PRICE T. BOWMAN—Enrolled at St. Paris, O., August 22, 1862; mustered out with Company.

SAMUEL BISHOP—Enrolled at St. Paris, O., August 20, 1862; absent on furlough; mustered out with Company.

ANTHONY BISHOP—Enrolled at St. Paris, O., August 22, 1862; mustered out with Company.

LEONARD BISHOP—Enrolled at Camp Chase, O., October 16, 1862; mustered out with Company.

SAMUEL I. BECK—Enrolled at St. Paris, O., August 22, 1862; mustered out with Company.

WM. C. BRINNON—Enrolled at Mechanicsburg, O., August 18, 1862; mustered out with Company. (Deceased.)

SULLIVAN W. BUCK—Enrolled at Zanesville, O., November 11, 1862; absent sick since November 10, 1864.

JESSE BROWN—Enrolled at Urbana, O., February 10, 1864; absent on furlough; mustered out with Company. (Recruit.)

JEREMIAH BAIR—Enrolled at Columbus, O., February 17, 1864; mustered out with Company. Recruit and veteran. (Musician.)

WILLIAM CISCO—Enrolled at St. Paris, O., August 17, 1862; mustered out with Company.

JOHN H. CRAIG—Enrolled at Urbana, O., March 28, 1864; mustered out with Company. (Recruit.)

MILTON G. DOAK—Enrolled at Mechanicsburg, O., August 16, 1862; absent on furlough; mustered out with Company; died near Mechanicsburg, O., February 21, 1873, aged 30 years.

ISAAC GREEN—Enrolled at Urbana, O., August 17, 1862; mustered out with Company; shared in all the engagements, campaigns and marches of the regiment.

ELIJAH GABRIEL—Enrolled at St. Paris, O., August 20, 1862; absent sick since September 20, 1863, at Camp Dennison, O.; wounded at Chickamauga.

THOS. HALLAN—Enrolled at St. Paris, O., August 16, 1862; absent on furlough; mustered out with Company.

MICHAEL HUDDLESTON—Enrolled at St. Paris, O., August 16, 1862; mustered out with Company.

WILLIAM HOOR—Enrolled at Urbana, O., August 15, 1862; absent sick since November 10, 1864, Chattanooga, Tenn.

WM. HOFFMAN—Enrolled at Zanesville, O., November 15, 1862; absent sick since November 10, 1864, Chattanooga, Tenn.

RICHARD HOWELL—Enrolled at Urbana, O., February 16, 1864; mustered out with Company. (Recruit.)

JOHN M. HEMPHILL—Enrolled at Urbana, O , February 27, 1864; mustered out with Company. (Recruit and musician.)

WILLIAM JENKINS—Enrolled at St. Paris, O., August 19, 1862; mustered out with Company.

JOHN O'LEARY—Enrolled at St. Paris, O., August 22, 1862; mustered out with Company. (Blacksmith.)

PAUL LEHMAN—Enrolled at Zanesville, O., November 13, 1862; absent on furlough; mustered out with Company. (German.)

HENRY MCALEXANDER—Enrolled at St. Paris, O., August 22, 1862; mustered out with Company.

JAMES MIRANDA—Enrolled at St. Paris, O., August 18, 1862; mustered out with Company.

WM. S. MOTT—Enrolled at St. Paris, O., August 16, 1862; absent on furlough at Columbus, O.; mustered out pursuant to General Order No. 17 War Department; captured at Chickamauga, Ga., September 20, 1863; died years later from the effects of his imprisonment. Original Fifth Sergeant.

JOHN A. MCLANE—Enrolled at Urbana, O., February 16, 1864; was a prisoner of war; exchanged January 1, 1865; mustered out with Company. (Recruit.)

GEORGE NICKOLS—Enrolled at Zanesville, O., October 20, 1862; mustered out with Company.

CYRUS PARMER—Enrolled at Zanesville, O., November 13, 1862; mustered out with Company; wounded at Kenesaw.

FREDRICK PENCE—Enrolled at St. Paris, O., August 22, 1862; mustered out with Company.

ANTHONY RAY—Enrolled at Zanesville, O., November 15, 1862; mustered out with Company.

JACOB REEDER—Enrolled at St. Paris, O., August 19, 1862; mustered out with Company.

THOMAS J. SCOTT—Enrolled at St. Paris, O., August 14, 1862; sentenced by General Court Martial to forfeit all pay and allowances from August 24, 1864, to June 2, 1865; mustered out with Company.

DUTTON SWIGER—Enrolled at St. Paris, O., August 17, 1862; mustered out with Company.
RICHARD SHELLHORN—Enrolled at Columbus, O., February 24, 1864; mustered out with Company. (Musician and recruit.)
HENRY SILLBACH—Enrolled at Columbus, O., February 29, 1864; mustered out with Company. (Recruit and musician.)
JOHN W. TAYLOR—Enrolled at Urbana, O., August 20, 1862; mustered out with Company.
DANIEL R. TAYLOR—Enrolled at Columbus, O., February 27, 1864; mustered out with Company. (Musician.)
WILLIAM VINCENT—Enrolled at Urbana, O., February 5, 1864; mustered out with Company. (Recruit.)
JOHN WILSON—Enrolled at St. Paris, O., August 16, 1862; mustered out with Company.
DANIEL WALKER—Enrolled at St. Paris, O., August 16, 1862; absent on furlough; mustered out with Company.
JOHN WANK—Enrolled at Camp Chase, O., October 15, 1862; absent on furlough; mustered out with Company.
JOHN WOLF—Enrolled at Columbus, O., February 4, 1864; mustered out with Company. (Recruit and musician.)
WM. H. WHITNEY—Enrolled at Urbana, O., November 28, 1863; mustered out with Company. (Recruit.)
HENRY GILL—Enrolled at Shelbyville, Tenn., July 25, 1863; mustered out with Company. (Colored Cook.)

KILLED.

HENRY C. SCOTT, Sergeant—Enrolled at St. Paris, O., August 16, 1862; killed in action near Marietta, Ga., June 27, 1864. Original First Corporal.
WILLIAM G. CARPENTER—Enrolled at St. Paris, O., August 19, 1862; killed in action at Chickamauga, Ga., September 20, 1863. Original Fifth Corporal.
ROLVIN HUDDLESTON—Enrolled at St. Paris, O., August 18, 1862; killed in action at Chickamauga, Ga., September 20, 1863.
FRANKLIN RUSSELL—Enrolled at Camp Chase, O., September 25, 1862; killed at Chickamauga, Ga., September 20, 1863.
ANTHONY SCHIMMEL—Enrolled at Westville, O., August 22, 1862; killed in front of Atlanta, Ga., August 7, 1864.
JACOB HESS—Enrolled at Urbana, O., November 28, 1863; killed at Kenesaw, Ga., June 27, 1864.

DIED.

PETER BAKER, Corporal—Enrolled at St. Paris, O., August 19, 1862; 'died at Nashville, Tenn., August 15, 1864, of wounds received near Marietta, Ga., June 27, 1864; wounded at Chickamauga, Georgia.

H. H. WALLBURN, Corporal—Enrolled at Urbana, O., August 15, 1862; died at Nashville, Tenn., March 5, 1863; aged twenty-four years. Buried at Treacle's creek, four miles north of Mechanicsburg. Original Sixth Corporal.

WM. H. PORTSMAN, Corporal—Enrolled at Urbana, O., August 19, 1862; died at Nashville, Tenn., March 5, 1863. Buried at Union Chapel, sixth miles east of Urbana. Original Eighth Corporal.

ANDREW J. WARD—Enrolled at Zanesville, O., November 11, 1862; died at Nashville, Tenn., July 18, 1863.

PETER MILLER—Enrolled at St. Paris, O., August 22, 1862; died at Murfreesboro, Tenn., December 9, 1863, chronic diarrhea.

ANDREW HELLER—Enrolled at Urbana, O., August 20, 1862; died in the field hospital, Ga., August 13, 1864.

GEORGE CONRAD—Enrolled at Westville, O., August 22, 1862; died at Nashville, Tenn., May 10, 1863.

REASON B. PARKER—Enrolled at Zanesville, O., November 15, 1862; died at Nashville, Tenn., February 21, 1863, of inflammation of brain.

GEO. W. SLONAKER—Enrolled at St. Paris, O., August 22, 1862; died at Nashville, Tenn., March 20, 1863.

GEO. A. BAKER—Enrolled at St. Paris, O., August 20, 1862; died at Nashville, Tenn., March 20, 1863.

JOSEPH WARNER—Enrolled at Urbana, O., February 16, 1864; died at Jeffersonville, Ind., September 24, 1864, of typhoid fever.

RICHARD SULLIVAN—Enrolled at Urbana, O., August 15, 1862; died at Savannah, Ga., January 11, 1865, acute disentary.

U. S. McROBERTS—No record of his enlistment given; died at his home in Ohio, September, 1862. Buried at Moorefield, Clark county.

JOSIAH McDOWELL—Enrolled at Zanesville, O., November 4, 1862; died in prison hospital at Danville, Va., April 16, 1864, scorbutis. Taken prisoner at Chickamauga.

PETER McDOWELL—Enrolled at Jackson, O., February 18, 1864; died on the way to his regiment, March 13, 1864, Nashville, Tennessee.

DISCHARGED.

ISRAEL G. POWELL, Corporal—Enrolled at Urbana, O., August 18, 1862; discharged from hospital at Nashville, Tenn., April 7, 1863, by order of General Rosecrans. Disability. Original Seventh Corporal.

ROCKWELL H. SEELY, Corporal—Enrolled at St. Paris, O., August 17, 1862; discharged at Tyner's Station, Tenn., February 17, 1864, by order of General Thomas. Disability. Original Fourth Corporal.

DAVID BEATY, Corporal—Enrolled at St. Paris, O., August 19, 1862; discharged at Camp Chase, O., July 30, 1864, by order of General Heintzelman. Cause—from wounds received in action September 20, 1863.

JOHN F. BARGER—Enrolled at St. Paris, O., August 18, 1862; discharged from hospital at Franklin, Tenn., April 13, 1863, by order Gen'l Rosecrans; physical disability.

JAMES L. EDMISTON—Enrolled at St. Paris, O., August 22, 1862; discharged from hospital at Franklin, Tenn., April 15, 1863, by order of Gen'l Rosecrans.

JAMES HULING—Enrolled at St. Paris, O., August 17, 1862; discharged from hospital at Nashville, Tenn., April 18, 1863, by order Gen'l Rosecrans.

FLEMING H. KYSER—Enrolled at St. Paris, O., August 17, 1862; discharged from hospital at Nashville, Tenn., April 18, 1863, by order Gen'l Rosecrans.

ABRAHAM G. SMITH—Enrolled at Adams township, O., August 22 1862; discharged from Muldrough's Hill, Ky., January 21, 1863, by order of Col. Wilcox, commanding 113th Regt.

HENRY D. SHANLEY—Enrolled at Urbana, O., August 22, 1862; discharged from Chattanooga, Tenn., May 26, 1865, by Tel. Order War Department May 3, 1865.

HERBERT N. NORMAN—Enrolled at Urbana, O., February 12, 1864; discharged from Chattanooga, Tenn., May 26, 1865, by Tel. Order War Department.

SOLOMON BRADFORD—Enrolled at Columbus, O., August 15, 1864; discharged at Louisville, Ky., June 26, 1865, by order War Department May 18, 1865. (One year man.)

RICHARD COX—Enrolled at St. Paris, O., August 22, 1862; discharged at Camp Dennison, O., June 21, 1865, by Tel. Order War Department May 18, 1865. Wounded at Louisville, Ga.

WM. G. MCALEXANDER—Enrolled at Camp Chase, O., October 15, 1862; discharged at Camp Dennison, O., June 17, 1863, by order of Lient. Col. Neff, Commanding Post.

REUBEN GARDNER—Enrolled at Urbana, O., August 15, 1862; discharged at Nashville, Tenn., June 18, 1863, by order of Gen'l Rosecrans. Died at his home in Mutual, O., July 9, 1863, aged 24 years. Native of New York.

FELIX L. ROCK—Enrolled at Urbana, O., August 22, 1862; discharged at Nashville, Tenn., June 11, 1863, by order of Gen'l Rosecrans.

SAMUEL SCOTT—Enrolled at St. Paris, O., August 19, 1862; discharged at Nashville, Tenn., May 11, 1863, by order of Gen'l Rosecrans.

JOHN LOOKER—Enrolled at St. Paris, O., August 22, 1862; discharged at Nashville, Tenn,, May 11, 1863, by order Gen'l Rosecrans.

WARREN KEYES—Enrolled at Mechanicsburg, O., August 16, 1862; discharged at Columbus, O., April 29, 1863, by order War Department.

JOSEPH H. RILEY—Enrolled at St. Paris, O., August 22, 1862; discharged at Nashville, Tenn., April 23, 1863, by order Gen'l Rosecrans.

CYRUS T. WARD, Sergeant—Enrolled at Urbana, O., August 22, 1862; discharged at Washington, D. C., June 17, 1865, by Tel. Order of War Department May 3, 1865. Original Third Corporal.

DESERTED.

FERDINAND STICKLER—Enrolled at Union township, O., August 22, 1862; deserted at Camp Dennison, O., November 24, 1862.

FREDERICK W. FASSET—Enrolled at Zanesville, O., November 18, 1862; deserted at Camp Zanesville, O., November 25, 1862.

WILLIAM MILLER—Enrolled at Zanesville, O., November 20, 1862; deserted at Camp Zanesville, O., November 25, 1862.

JOHN RILEY—Enrolled at Zanesville, O., November 15, 1862; deserted at Camp Zanesville, O., December 11, 1862.

GEORGE SMITH—Enrolled at Zanesville, O., November 25, 1862; deserted at Camp Zanesville, O., December 19, 1862.

L. S. PARISH—Enrolled at Canaan, O., January 30, 1864; deserted on the way to his regiment; date unknown.

JACOB FUDGE—Enrolled at St. Paris, O., August 22, 1862; deserted at Rome, Ga., May 23, 1864.

DANIEL R. BAKER—Enrolled at Columbus, O., February 27, 1864; deserted at Rome, Ga., May 23, 1864.
ISAAC L. GREY—Enrolled at Urbana, O., February 16, 1864; deserted at Rome, Ga., May 23, 1864.
CLARK W. COTTRELL.—Enrolled at Urbana, O., February 12, 1864; deserted April, 1865.
STEPHEN CARRIGG—Enlisted, but never mustered; deserted at Camp Chase, O., 1862.
JOSEPH SWEENY—Enlisted, but never mustered; deserted at Camp Chase, O., 1862.
THOMAS SCUDDER—Enlisted, but never mustered; deserted at Camp Chase, O., 1862.
MICHAEL CANE—Enlisted, but never mustered; deserted at Camp Chase, O., 1862.
JOSEPH FISHER—Enlisted, but never mustered; deserted at Camp Chase, O., 1862.
JAMES HURLY—Enlisted, but never mustered; deserted at Camp Chase, O., 1862.

TRANSFERRED.

D. H. CHATFIELD, Corporal—Enrolled at Urbana, O., August 22, 1862; promoted from 4th Corporal to 2d Lieutenant, and transferred to Co. H, 113th O. V. I., by order Col. D. B. Warner, November 5, 1863. Original private.
ASA KITE, Corporal—Enrolled at St. Paris, O., August 22, 1862; transferred to V. R. C. March 24, 1864, by order War Department.
A. M. GRAFTON, First Sergeant—Enrolled at St. Paris, O., August 16, 1862; promoted from 1st Sergeant to 1st Lieutenant May 26, 1865, and transferred to Co. C, 113th O. V. I., by order Lieut. Col. Jones. Original Third Sergeant.
WM. FROMME—Enrolled at St. Paris, O., August 22, 1862; transferred to 1st U. S. Volunteer Engineers, July 27, 1864, by order of Col. Wm. E. Merrill. A native of Germany and had seen service in his own country. Discharged Sept. 26, 1865. Born June, 1823. Died Feb. 13, 1873.
WILLIS HUDDLESTON—Enrolled at St. Paris, O., August 22, 1862; transferred to V. R. C. April 30, 1863, by order War Department.
S. E. SMITH—Enrolled at St. Paris, O., August 22, 1862; transferred to 1st U. S. Volunteer Engineer, July 29, 1864, by order of Col. Wm. E. Merrill.

JOHN BOLT—Enlistment and muster unknown; received from depot by error; transferred to the 82d O. V. I., September 13, 1864, by order of Capt. Jones, Commanding 113th Regiment; descriptive list was never received.

GEORGE CARROLL—Enlistment and muster unknown; received from depot by error; transferred to the 82d O. V. I., September 13, 1864, by order Capt. Jones, Commanding 113th Regiment; descriptive list was never received.

SAMUEL HALTERMAN—Enrolled at St. Paris, O., August 22, 1862; transferred to V. R. C., April, 1, 1865, by order War Department.

PERRY D. VINCENT—Enrolled at Zanesville, O., November 19, 1862; transferred to Invalid Corps, September 30, 1863, by order War Department.

DAVID WALKER—Enrolled at St. Paris O., August 16, 1862; transferred to V. R. C., March 15, 1865, by order War Department; transfer No. 4 A. G. O., March 13, 1865.

COMPANY K.

Mustered out at Louisville, Ky., July 6, 1865.

COMMISSIONED OFFICERS.

CAPTAIN A. L. SHEPHERD—Commissioned at Columbus, O., December 8, 1863; on leave of absence. Mustered out.

FIRST LIEUTENANT WM. H. BAXTER—Commissioned at Rossville, Ga., March 14, 1864; discharged November 25, 1864, by order of War Department, special order 416. Wounded at Kenesaw, Ga., June 27, 1864.

FIRST LIEUTENANT GEO. H. LIPPINCOTT—Commissioned at Holly Springs, N. C., December 1, 1864; promoted from Second Lieutenant December 1, 1864; mustered out at Louisville, Ky., July 6, 1865. Wounded at Kenesaw Mountain, Ga., June 27, 1864.

NON-COMMISSIONED OFFICERS.

O. H. BARBER, First Sergeant—Enrolled at Urbana, O., December 28, 1863; mustered out with Company. Injured by a shell at Kenesaw Mountain, June 27, 1864.

C. T. BAXTER, Sergeant—Enrolled at Urbana, O., February 17, 1864; mustered out with Company.

GEORGE L. TIESTER, Sergeant—Enrolled at Urbana, O., December 28, 1863; mustered out with Company.
WM. BARNES, Sergeant—Enrolled at Urbana, O., December 22, 1863; mustered out with Company.
CYRUS GUY, Sergeant—Enrolled at Urbana, O., December 16, 1863; mustered out with Company.
WM. H. GROVES, Corporal—Enrolled at Urbana, O., December 23, 1863; mustered out with Company.
J. W. CLABAUGH, Corporal—Enrolled at Urbana, O., December 27, 1863; mustered out with Company. Wounded at Kenesaw.
J. R. ROGERS, Corporal—Enrolled at Urbana, O., December 16, 1863; mustered out with Company.
ALEXANDER MICHEALS, Corporal—Enrolled at Mechanicsburg, O., December 20, 1863; mustered out with Company.
G. W. HUPP, Corporal—Enrolled at Columbus, O., February 29, 1864; mustered out with Company.
GEO. GABRIEL, Corporal—Enrolled at Urbana, O., December 8, 1863; mustered out with Company.

PRIVATES.

MICHAEL AGNEW—Enrolled at Urbana, O., January 14, 1864; mustered out with Company.
CHAS. M. BOON—Enrolled at Urbana, O., December 28, 1863; mustered out with Company.
FRANCIS BLONDIN—Enrolled at Urbana, O., December 26, 1863; mustered out with Company.
JAMES A. BLAKE—Enrolled at Urbana, O., December 28, 1863; mustered out with Company.
FREDERICK BOHER—Enrolled at Madison county, O., January 29, 1864; absent wounded since June 27, 1864.
JOHN BAILEY—Enrolled at Urbana, O., December 23, 1863; mustered out with Company.
THOMAS CONWAY—Enrolled at Urbana, O., January 14, 1864; mustered out with Company.
EDWARD CAMPBELL—Enrolled at Delaware, O., January 6, 1864; mustered out with Company.
WILLIAM CRAIG—Enrolled at Urbana, O., January 4, 1864; mustered out with Company.
OLIVER CRAIG—Enrolled at Mechanicsburg, O., December 24, 1863; mustered out; had served in the Sixty-Sixth O. V. I. formerly; wounded.

R. M. J. COLEMAN—Enrolled at Urbana, O., January 23, 1865; mustered out with Company.

LEWIS DAVIS—Enrolled at Columbus, O., January 12, 1864; absent sick at Rome, Ga., since June 2, 1864.

JOHN E. DAVIS—Enrolled at Mechanicsburg, O., December 23, 1863; absent wounded at Camp Dennison, O., since June 27, 1864.

CHAS. N. DAVIS—Enrolled at Urbana, O., December 16, 1863; mustered out with Company.

J. C. DOUGHTY—Enrolled at Urbana, O., December 22, 1863; absent in Ohio on furlough; mustered out with Company.

RAPER ELLSWORTH—Enrolled at Urbana, O., January 23, 1863; absent in Ohio on furlough; mustered out with Company. (Musician.)

HENRY E. FAY—Enrolled at Urbana, O., December 26, 1863; absent sick in hospital at Louisville, Ky., since June 18, 1865.

OLVERD B. FAY—Enrolled at Urbana, O., January 16, 1864; absent sick in hospital at Louisville, Ky., since June 18, 1865.

LEVI FAY—Enrolled at Urbana, O., March 28, 1864; mustered out with Company.

SYLVESTER FOY—Enrolled at Columbus, O., January 11, 1864; mustered out with Company.

JOHN FARLEY—Enrolled at Urbana, O., January 1, 1864; absent sick at Nashville, Tenn., since July 14, 1864.

SIMON GABRIEL—Enrolled at Urbana, O., December 8, 1863; mustered out with Company.

W. S. GEARHEART—Enrolled at Columbus, O., February 10, 1864; mustered out with Company.

PHILIP A. HUFF—Enrolled at Urbana, O., December 23, 1863; mustered out with Company.

ABNER C. HUPP—Enrolled at Columbus, O., December, 16, 1863; mustered out with Company.

JACOB HUBEN—Enrolled at Urbana, O., December 23, 1863; mustered out with Company.

PERRY C. HOWARD—Enrolled at Urbana, O., December, 28, 1863; absent without leave since June 1, 1865; wounded in the arm at Kenesaw, June 27, 1864.

BENJAMIN F. IRWIN—Enrolled at Urbana, O., December 16, 1863; mustered out with Company.

JAMES KELLY—Enrolled at Columbus, O., January 22, 1864; absent on detached service since June 3, 1864; mustered out with Company.

JOHN W. LESSENGER—Enrolled at Mechanicsburg, O., December 24, 1863; absent in Ohio on furlough; mustered out with Company.
JOHN C. MILLER—Enrolled at Urbana, O., December 22, 1863; mustered out with Company.
PATRICK MALONE—Enrolled at Urbana, O., January 16, 1864; mustered out with Company.
THOMAS MOODY—Enrolled at Urbana, O., December 28, 1863; absent at Cincinnati, O., since June 27, 1864; mustered out with Company. Wounded at Kenesaw.
GEO. W. NEGLEY—Enrolled at St. Paris, O., December 17, 1863; mustered out with Company.
WILLIAM A. NEER—Enrolled at Mechanicsburg, O., December 15, 1863; mustered out with Company.
CHARLES ODELL—Enrolled at Mechanicsburg, O., December 22, 1863; absent sick since May 12, 1865.
DANIEL ROUTT—Enrolled at Urbana, O., January 18, 1864; mustered out with Company.
JOHN RANDALL—Enrolled at Urbana, O., January 23, 1864; mustered out with Company.
JOSEPH RIDER—Enrolled at Urbana, O., January 15, 1864; mustered out with Company.
JOHN W. SNYDER—Enrolled at Urbana, O., December 28, 1863; mustered out with Company.
JASPER C. SHEPHERD—Enrolled at Mechanicsburg, O., December 23, 1863; mustered out with Company.
THOS. E. SHEPHERD—Enrolled at Urbana, O., December 16, 1863; absent sick at Louisville, Ky., since June 27, 1864. (Musician.)
JOHN SPANGERBERGER—Enrolled at Springfield, O., December 31, 1863; mustered out with Company.
CHARLES SMITH—Enrolled at Urbana, O., December 21, 1863; mustered out with Company.
EDWARD SHELLHORN—Enrolled at Urbana, O., January 27, 1864; mustered out with Company. (Musician.)
HARMAN SILBAUGH—Enrolled at Columbus, O., February 29, 1864; mustered out with Company. (Musician.)
GEO. W. SWARTS—Enrolled at Urbana, O., December 16, 1863; mustered out with Company.
CHARLES STEWART—Enrolled at Urbana, O., January 23, 1865; mustered out with Company. (Recruit.)

JOHN W. TWAY—Enrolled at Mechanicsburg, O., December 15, 1863; mustered out with Company.
JAMES H. TARBUTTON—Enrolled at Urbana, O., February 29, 1864; mustered out with Company.
JOHN WALKER—Enrolled at St. Paris, O., December 23, 1863; mustered out with Company.
WILLIAM WALKER—Enrolled at Urbana, O., December 8, 1863; mustered out with Company.
JAMES WALKER—Enrolled at Urbana, O., December 30, 1863; absent wounded since June 27, 1864; mustered out with Company.
JOHN H. WALKER—Enrolled at Urbana, O., December 19, 1863; mustered out with Company.

KILLED.

EYRA ALLEN, Corporal—Enrolled at Urbana, O., December 21, 1863; killed June 27, 1864, at battle of Kenesaw Mountain, Ga.
STEPHEN V. BARR—Enrolled at Urbana, O., February 27, 1864; killed June 27, 1864, at battle of Kenesaw Mountain, Ga.
WILLIAM COPPIN—Enrolled at Salem, O., December 24, 1863; killed June 27, 1864, at battle of Kenesaw Mountain, Ga.
HIRAM HANCOCK—Enrolled at Urbana, O., January 21, 1862; killed June 27, 1864, at battle of Kenesaw Mountain, Ga.
LEVI ROMINE—Enrolled at Urbana, O., January 16, 1864; killed June 27, 1864, at battle of Kenesaw Mountain, Ga.
JOSEPH WILKINSON—Enrolled at Springfield, O., December 31, 1863; killed June 27, 1864, at battle of Kenesaw Mountain, Ga.
LEMUEL P. JONES—Enrolled at Salem, O., December 22, 1863; killed June 27, 1864, at battle of Kenesaw Mountain, Ga.
JOHN H. BRICKER—Enrolled at Urbana, O., January 26, 1864; killed July 4, 1864, near the Chattahoochee River, Ga.
BOOKER R. DURNELL.—Enrolled at Urbana, O., December 24, 1863; missing at battle of Kenesaw Mountain, Ga., June 27, 1864. Nothing definite can be stated, but he was either killed and buried as unknown, or was taken prisoner and died in prison.

DIED.

HECTER MORRIN—Enrolled at Urbana, O., December 24, 1863; died June 30, 1864, at Big Shanty, Ga., of wounds received at battle of Kenesaw Mountain, Ga., June 27, 1864.

HENRY C. BRITTON—Enrolled at Mechanicsburg, O., December 15, 1863; died July 6, 1864, at Chattanooga, Tenn., of disease.
JOSEPH H. NEWCOMB—Enrolled at Urbana, O., December 16, 1863; died July 24, 1864, at Nashville, Tenn., of wounds received in battle of Kenesaw Mountain, Ga., June 27, 1864. (Musician.)
LEVI HEMINGER—Enrolled at Urbana, O., December 30, 1863; died August 1, 1864, at Chattanooga, Tenn., of wounds received in battle of Kenesaw Mountain, Ga., June 27, 1864.
LEVI ELLIOTT—Enrolled at Urbana, O., December 28, 1863; died August 12, 1864, at Nashville, Tenn., of disease.
PATRICK FIELDS—Enrolled at Urbana, O., January 12, 1864; died August 19, 1864, at Nashville, Tenn., of wounds received at battle of Kenesaw Mountain, Ga., June 27, 1864.
ROBERT R. OSBORNE—Enrolled at Urbana, O., December 16, 1863; died August 22, 1864, at Chattanooga, Tenn., of wounds received in battle of Kenesaw Mountain, Ga., June 27, 1864.
AZRO MANN, Sergeant—Enrolled at Urbana, O., December 16, 1863; died October 31, 1864, at Nashville, Tenn., of disease.
JAMES MCMAHAN—Enrolled at Woodstock, O., December 26, 1863; died November 30, 1864, at Jeffersonville, Ind., of disease.
MONROE ELLIOTT, First Sergeant—Enrolled at Urbana, O., December 29, 1863; died February 4, 1865, at Savannah, Ga., of acute diarrhea.
GEORGE PEOBLES—Enrolled at Urbana, O., December 26, 1863; died April 18, 1865, at Baltimore, Md., of chronic diarrhea.

DISCHARGED.

OSCAR C. MORROW—Enrolled at Urbana, O., December 28, 1863; discharged February 17, 1865, at Camp Dennison, O., by order of War Department.
MARTIN MOONEY—Enrolled at Columbus, O., January 26, 1864; discharged March 2, 1865, at Camp Dennison, O., by order of War Department.
ALFRED KILBORN—Enrolled at Urbana, O., December 16, 1863; discharged April 14, 1865, at Columbus, O., by order of War Department.
EBENEZER WILLIAMS—Enrolled at Mechanicsburg, O., December 16, 1863; discharged May 29, 1865, at Columbus, O., by order of War Department.

WILLIAM M. SMITH—Enrolled at St. Paris, O., January 4, 1864; discharged May 26, 1865, at Camp Dennison, O., by order of War Department.

STEPHEN W. RIDDLE—Enrolled at Mechanicsburg, O., December 15, 1863; discharged May 29, 1865, at Columbus, O., by Order of War Department.

HARVEY F. SULLIVAN—Enrolled at Mechanicsburg, O., December 23, 1863; discharged June 3, 1865, at Camp Dennison, O., by Order of War Department.

JAMES V. ROBERTS—Enrolled at Mechanicsburg, O., December 16, 1863; discharged June 9, 1865, at Camp Dennison, O., by Order of War Department.

ARTEMUS L. NASH—Enrolled at Mechanicsburg, O., December 19, 1863; discharged June 9, 1865, at Fortress Monroe, Va., by Order of War Department.

DESERTED.

MARTIN MAYER—Enrolled at Urbana, O., December 23, 1863; deserted March 29, 1864, enroute to the regiment.

ALEXANDER McGILOERY—Enrolled at Urbana, O., January 25, 1864; deserted March 29, 1864, enroute to the regiment.

THOS. MANNING—Enrolled at Urbana, O., December 23, 1863; deserted March 29, 1864, enroute to the regiment.

PATRICK O. RILEY—Enrolled at Urbana, O., January 26, 1864; deserted March 29, 1864, enroute to the regiment.

PETER TROSSEL—Enrolled at Urbana, O., December 31, 1863; deserted August 31, 1864, near Atlanta, Ga.

COMPANY G.

Mustered out at Louisville, Ky., July 6, 1865.

COMMISSIONED OFFICERS.

CAPTAIN HARRISON Z. ADAMS—Commissioned at Mt. Sterling, O., August 22, 1862; resigned January 25, 1863. (Minister.)

CAPTAIN A. L. MESSMORE—Commissioned at Franklin, Tenn., February 7, 1863; mustered out at Louisville, Ky., July 6, 1865.

FIRST LIEUTENANT J. C. BOSTWICK—Commissioned at Franklin, Tenn., February 7, 1863; promoted to First Lieutenant from Second, February 7, 1863; died March 15, 1864, at Columbus, O.

FIRST LIEUTENANT JAMES COULTAS—Commissioned at Whitehall, Ga., August 31, 1864; mustered out at Louisville, Ky., July 6, 1865.
SECOND LIEUTENANT H. C. TIPTON—Commissioned at Franklin, Tenn., January 28, 1863; promoted from Second to First Lieutenant January 28, 1863; resigned March 25, 1863.
SECOND LIEUTENANT WM. R. HANEWALT—Commissioned at Franklin, Tenn., May 1, 1863; promoted from Q. M. Sergeant to Second Lieutenant, May 1, 1863; killed in action at Chickamauga, Ga., September 20, 1863.

NON-COMMISSIONED OFFICERS.

A. W. DAVIS, First Sergeant—Enrolled at Mt. Sterling, O., August 13, 1862; absent on furlough since June 27, 1865; mustered out with Company.
J. J. RIGGIN, Sergeant—Enrolled at Mt. Sterling, O., August 13, 1862; absent on furlough since June 25, 1865; mustered out with Company.
JOHN A. SMITH, Sergeant—Enrolled at Mt. Sterling, O., August 13, 1862; mustered out with Company.
O. W. LOOFBOURROW, Sergeant—Enrolled at Mt. Sterling, O., August 13, 1862; mustered out with Company.
F. A. WICKELL, Sergeant—Enrolled at Mt. Sterling, O., August 13, 1862; promoted from Corporal to Sergeant, April 1, 1865; mustered out with Company.
JOHN A. LAKE, First Corporal—Enrolled at Mt. Sterling, O., August 12, 1862; mustered out with Company.
H. B. BRILEY, Corporal—Enrolled at Mt. Sterling, O., August 13, 1862; on detached service at Columbus, O., since February 12, 1864; mustered out with Company.
J. W. DENNISON, Corporal—Enrolled at Mt. Sterling, O., August 13, 1862; mustered out with Company.
W. S. TAMMADGE, Corporal—Enrolled at Mt. Sterling, O., August 13, 1862; mustered out with Company.
JOHN W. BEALE, Corporal—Enrolled at Mt. Sterling, O., August 13, 1862; mustered out with Company.
HARRY HAGANS, Corporal—Enrolled at Columbus, O., March 30, 1864; mustered out with Company.
GEO. M. NEFF, Corporal—Enrolled at Mt. Sterling, O., August 13, 1862; absent on furlough since June 27, 1865; mustered out with Company.

W. S. DAVIS, Corporal—Enrolled at Mt. Sterling, O., August 13, 1862; promoted from private to Corporal April 1, 1865; mustered out with Company

PRIVATES.

JOHN W. ALKIRE—Enrolled at Mt. Sterling, O., August 13, 1862; mustered out with Company.

DANIEL W. ANDERSON—Enrolled at Harrisburg, O., February 2, 1864, mustered out with Company.

RUFUS BARCUS—Enrolled at Columbus, O., March 23, 1864; mustered out with Company.

AUGUSTUS BOYLER—Enrolled at Mt. Sterling, O., August 13, 1862; mustered out with Company.

BENJAMIN BOSTWICK—Enrolled at Harrisburg, O., December 30, 1863; on detached duty at Brigade Headquarters; absent sick since April 22, 1864.

WILLIAM C. BOSTWICK—Enrolled at Mt. Sterling, O., August 13, 1862; mustered out with Company. Served as regimental postmaster.

ANDREW BURGET—Enrolled at Camp Chase, O., September 25, 1862; mustered out with Company.

SAMUEL BUSICK—Enrolled at Mt. Sterling, O., August 13, 1862; absent sick at Camp Chase, O., since November 30, 1864.

EDWARD BLAIN—Enrolled at Circleville, O., July 23, 1864; mustered out with Company.

J. C. CHAFFIN—Enrolled at Camp Chase, O., September 20, 1862; mustered out with Company.

JOHN I. COOK—Enrolled at Mt. Sterling, O., August 13, 1862; mustered out with Company.

JOHN N. CRABB—Enrolled at Columbus, O., January 13, 1864; mustered out with Company.

W. S. DELENGER—Enrolled at Camp Chase, O., September 20, 1862; mustered out with Company.

WILLIAM DEFABAUGH—Enrolled at Mt. Sterling, O., August 13, 1862; absent on furlough since June 26, 1865; mustered out with Company.

TITUS ENGLAND—Enrolled at Harrisburg, O., February 3, 1864; mustered out with Company.

ROBERT FOSTER—Enrolled at Camp Chase, O., September 20, 1862; mustered out with Company.

JOSEPH FORD—Enrolled at Mt. Sterling, O., August 13, 1862; mustered out with Company.

JAMES GARDNER—Enrolled at Harrisburg, O., February 20, 1864; absent on furlough since June 25, 1865; mustered out with Company.
GEORGE HARTINGER—Enrolled at Harrisburg, O., February 21, 1864; mustered out with Company.
SAMUEL HOOVER—Enrolled at Mt. Sterling, O., August 13, 1862; mustered out with Company.
CHAS. H. KANEASTER—Enrolled at Harrisburg, O., February 9, 1864; mustered out with Company.
MARTIN LEONARD—Enrolled at Columbus, O., February 10, 1864; mustered out with Company.
JESSE LOW—Enrolled at Harrisburg, O., March 9, 1864; absent sick at Annopolis, Md., since April 20, 1865.
ANDREW MITCHELL—Enrolled at Mt. Sterling, O., August 13, 1862; absent sick at Annapolis, Md., since April 25, 1865; taken prisoner at Chickamauga, September 20, 1863.
DAVID MADDEN—Enrolled at Mt. Sterling, O., August 13, 1862; absent sick at Camp Dennison, O., since May 10, 1863.
JOSEPH McARTY—Enrolled at Cleveland, O., February 10, 1864; mustered out with Company.
ZERO McINTIRE—Enrolled at Camp Chase, O., September 20, 1862; absent on furlough since June 30, 1865; mustered out with Company.
ANTHONY S. MORGAN—Enrolled at Mt. Sterling, O., August 13, 1862; on detached services as hospital nurse since January 23, 1864; mustered out with Company.
JOHN O'DAY—Enrolled at Mt. Sterling, O., August 13, 1862; absent on furlough since June 28, 1865; mustered out with Company.
HARRISON RIGGIN—Enrolled at Mt. Sterling, O., August 13, 1862; mustered out with Company. (Wounded.)
JEROME L. ROBY—Enrolled at Zanesville, O., December 5, 1862; mustered out with Company.
JACOB SEIGLE—Enrolled at Harrisburg, O., November 24, 1863; mustered out with Company.
JAMES J. SHEEDERS—Enrolled at Mt. Sterling, O., August 13, 1862; mustered out with Company.
THORNTON SMITH—Enrolled at Mt. Sterling, O., August 13, 1862; absent on furlough since June 30, 1865; mustered out with Company.
THOMAS SMITH—Enrolled at Mt. Sterling, O., August 13, 1862; absent sick at Camp Dennison, O., since December 25, 1863.

WM. H. SMITH—Enrolled at Mt. Sterling, O., August 13, 1863; absent on furlough since June 25, 1865; mustered out with Company.

JOHN SOUTHARD—Enrolled at Mt. Sterling, O., August 13, 1862; mustered out with Company.

ELIAS STREETS—Enrolled at Columbus, O., January 22, 1864; absent sick at Chattanooga, Tenn., since June 15, 1864.

JAS. A. TAMMADGE—Enrolled at Mt. Sterling, O., August 13, 1862; mustered out with Company.

ALEXANDER TAINER—Enrolled at Mt. Sterling, O., August 13, 1862; mustered out with Company.

JOSIAH TIMMONS—Enrolled at Mt. Sterling, O., August 13, 1862; mustered out with Company.

WM. H. TIMMONS—Enrolled at Columbus, O., February 1, 1864; mustered out with Company.

ABRAHAM TRIMBEE—Enrolled at Urbana, O., December 2, 1862; mustered out with Company.

SAMUEL WALKER—Enrolled at Mt. Sterling, O., August 13, 1862; mustered out with Company.

ABRAM WRIGHT—Enrolled at Harrisburg, O., February 20, 1864; mustered out with Company.

FREDRICK YOUNG—Enrolled at Mt. Sterling, O., August 13, 1862; absent sick at Nashville, Tenn., since June 21, 1864.

KILLED.

ABRAHAM DENNISON—Enrolled at Mt. Sterling, O., August 13, 1862; killed September 20, 1863, at Chickamauga, Ga.

JOSEPH PARKER, Sergeant—Enrolled at Mt. Sterling O., August 13, 1862; killed June 27, 1864, at Kenesaw Mountain, Ga.

LEVI GRIFFIN—Enrolled at Mt. Sterling, O., August 13, 1862; killed June 27, 1864, at Kenesaw Mountain, Ga.

LEVI THOMAS—Enrolled at Mt. Sterling, August 13, 1862; killed July 19, 1864, at Peachtree Creek, Ga.

J. W. HALLAWAY—Enrolled at Columbus, O., March 15, 1864; missing November 30, 1864, Louisville, Ga.

DIED.

DAVID MITCHELL, Sergeant—Enrolled at Mt. Sterling, O., August 13, 1862; died September 22, 1863, at Chickamauga, Ga., of wounds.

THOS. PETERSON, Corporal—Enrolled at Camp Chase, O., September 22, 1862; died August 20, 1864, at Andersonville, Ga., of wounds.

A. A. TALBOT, Corporal—Enrolled at Mt. Sterling, O., August 13, 1862; died December 24, 1864, at Savannah, Ga., of wounds.

JOHN W. ROGERS—Enrolled at Mt. Sterling, O., August 13, 1862; died December 5, 1862, Camp Zanesville, O., of measles.

ROBT. H. McCLEAN—Enrolled at Mt. Sterling, O., August 13, 1862; died February 3, 1863, at Louisville, Ky., of diarrhea.

HENRY GILLINWATERS—Enrolled at Mt. Sterling, O., August 13, 1862; died February 17, 1863, Nashville, Tenn., of pneumonia.

ISAAC TIMMONS—Enrolled at Mt. Sterling, O., August 13, 1862; died April 13, 1863, at Nashville, Tenn., no cause given.

GRIFFIN DENNISON—Enrolled at Mt. Sterling, O., August 13, 1862; died March 18, 1863, Nashville, Tenn., of icterus.

JOHN W. MILLER—Enrolled at Mt. Sterling, O., August 13, 1862; died April 18, 1863, at Franklin, Tenn., of diarrhea.

PERRY GERRARD—Enrolled at Mt. Sterling, O., August 13, 1862; died April 23, 1863, at Nashville, Tenn., of chronic diarrhea.

ALEXANDER E. BRAGG—Enrolled at Mt. Sterling, O., August 13, 1862; died May 28, 1863; Madison Co., O., of chronic diarrhea.

JAMES L. RIGGIN—Enrolled at Mt. Sterling, O., August 13, 1862; died June 27, 1863, Nashville Tenn., of pneumonia.

MERRIL SMITH—Enrolled at Mt. Sterling, O., August 13, 1862; died October 10, 1863, Chattanooga, Tenn., of wounds.

SAMUEL THORTON—Enrolled at Mt. Sterling, O., August 13, 1862; died November 14, 1863, Chattanooga, Tenn., chronic diarrhea.

ANDREW MILLER—Enrolled at Mt. Sterling, O., August 13, 1862; died November 15, 1863, Chattanooga, Tenn., of wounds.

OTHO W. NIGH—Enrolled at Mt. Sterling, O., August 13, 1862; died February 7, 1864, Murfreesboro, Tenn., chronic diarrhea.

JACOB FOSTER—Enrolled at Camp Chase, O., September 23, 1862; died at Nashville, Tenn., chronic diarrhea. Date not given.

CHAS. ROSENDALE—Enrolled at Columbus, O., February 11, 1864; died June 1, 1864, Big Shanty, Ga., diarrhea.

JAMES COOKEY—Enrolled at Harrisburg, O., February 3, 1864; died September 27, 1864, Jeffersonville, Ind., diarrhea.

HEZEKIAH SUVER—Enrolled at Harrisburg, O., February 12, 1864; died June 24, 1864, Rome, Ga., chronic diarrhea.

WM. H. BRASKET—Enrolled at Harrisburg, O., December 7, 1863; died April 1, 1864, Chattanooga, Tenn., pneumonia.

WM. H. HUNT—Enrolled at Mt. Sterling, O., August 13, 1862; died July 16, 1864, Andersonville, Ga., dysentery.

DANIEL D. MILLER—Enrolled at Mt. Stearling, O., August 13, 1862; died March 25, 1863, Nashville, Tenn., diarrhea.

DISCHARGED.

JOHN W. INGRIM, Sergeant—Enrolled at Mt. Sterling, O., August 13, 1862; discharged November 14, 1863, Nashville, Tenn., by order of Major General Thomas.

CLARK S. WHITE, Sergeant—Enrolled at Mt. Sterling, O., August 13, 1862; discharged March 29, 1864, Camp Chase, O., by order of Major General Heintzleman; died March 7, 1876, from effects of a wound received at Chickamauga.

EDWIN DEYO, Corporal—Enrolled at Mt. Sterling, O., August 13, 1862; discharged June 24, 1864, Camp Dennison, O., by order of War Department.

JAMES S. ABERNATHY—Enrolled at Mt. Sterling, O., August 13, 1862; discharged January 9, 1863, Columbus, O., by order of War Department.

JOHN J. BISHOP—Enrolled at Mt. Sterling, O., August 13, 1862; discharged February 16, 1863, Columbus, O., by order of War Department.

JOHN W. HARNESS—Enrolled at Mt. Sterling, O., August 13, 1862; discharged March 5, 1863, Nashville, Tenn., by order of Major General Rosecrans.

SAMSON M. STONE—Enrolled at Mt. Sterling, O., August 13, 1862; discharged March 11, 1863, Columbus, O., by order of War Department.

BENJAMIN O. KELLER—Enrolled at Mt. Sterling, O., August 13, 1862; discharged March 15, 1863, Nashville, Tenn., by order of Major General Resecrans.

ROBERT FORD—Enrolled at Mt. Sterling, O., August 13, 1862; discharged April 18, 1863, Franklin, Tenn., by order of Major Gen. Rosecrans.

ALFRED IVY—Enrolled at Mt. Sterling, O., August 13, 1862; discharged May 16, 1863, Franklin, Tenn., by order of Major General Rosecrans.

HENRY STRAWBRIDGE—Enrolled at Mt. Sterling, O., August 13, 1862; discharged May 14, 1863, Columbus, O., by order of Brigadier General Mason.

THOMAS HAYS—Enrolled at Mt. Sterling, O., August 13, 1862; discharged June 16, 1863, Louisville, Ky., by order of War Department.
HARVEY STRAIN—Enrolled at Mt. Sterling, O., August 13, 1862; discharged June 24, 1863, Louisville, Ky., by order of Colonel McMondy.
WILEY CREATH—Enrolled at Mt. Sterling, O., August 13, 1862; discharged June 24, 1863, Louisville, Ky., by order of Colonel McMondy.
CREIGHTON THOMAS—Enrolled at Mt. Sterling, O., August 13, 1862; discharged July 31, 1863, Nashville, Tenn., by order of Medical Board.
EPHRIM PARKER—Enrolled at Mt. Sterling, O., August 13, 1862; discharged September 9, 1863, Louisville, Ky., by order of War Department.
JOHN W. RIGGIN—Enrolled at Mt. Sterling, O., August 13, 1862; discharged September 24, 1863, Camp Dennison, O., by order of Military Post Commandant.
DAVID HISSON—Enrolled at Columbus, O., March 21, 1862; mustered out May 6, 1865, at Columbus, O., in pursuance of General order No. 77, War Department.
JOHN M. CREATH—Enrolled at Mt. Sterling, O., August 13, 1862; mustered out May 26, 1865, at Camp Dennison, O., in pursuance of General order No. 77, War Department.
JAMES GRAY—Enrolled at Harrisburg, O., February 10, 1864; mustered out May 13, 1865, at Nashville, Tenn., in pursuance of General order No. 77, War Department.
THOMAS CLIFTON—Enrolled at Camp Chase, O., September 20, 1862; mustered out May 13, 1865, at Nashville, Tenn., in pursuance of General order No. 77, War Department.
ELIJAH ROBY—Enrolled at Mt. Sterling, O., August 13, 1862; mustered out June 9, 1865, at Cincinnati, O., in pursuance of General Order No. 77, War Department.
CHAS. WILLIAMSON—Enrolled at Harrisburg, O., December 5, 1863; discharged February 3, 1865, at Columbus, O., by order of Major General Hooker.

DESERTED.

GIBSON SAWTELL—Enrolled at Camp Chase, O., October 14, 1862; deserted January 16, 1863, at Camp Summit, Ky.

JAMES BELT—Enrolled at Madison County, O., February 1, 1864; deserted October 11, 1864, near Athens, Ala.

ELNATHAN BELT—Enrolled at Columbus, O., August 30, 1864; deserted October 11, 1864, near Athens, Ala.

ANDREW MCARTY—Descriptive list never received; deserted August 29, 1864, near Atlanta, Ga.

AUGUST EPHART—Enrolled at Harrisburg, O., February 14, 1864; deserted January 14, 1865, at Camp Dennison, O.

THOMAS NOLAND—Enrolled at Columbus, O., March 25, 1864; deserted March 28, 1864, at Columbus, O.

RICHARD MILLER—Enrolled at Madison County, O., January 13, 1864; deserted February 1, 1864, at Columbus, O.

JOHN IRVING—Enrolled at Columbus, O., March 25, 1864; deserted March 28, 1864, at Columbus, O.

JAMES HAYS—Enrolled at Columbus, O., February 27, 1864; deserted March 12, 1864, at Columbus, O.

TRANSFERRED.

EDWARD CROUSE—Enrolled at Camp Chase, O., August 13, 1862; transferred to Company C, April 18, 1864, at Rossville, Ga., by order of Lieutenant Colonel D. B. Warner.

NEHEMIAH MATLOCK—Enrolled at Mt. Sterling, O., August 13, 1862; transferred to V. R. C. October 29, 1864, at Louisville, Ky., by order of Secretary of War.

JONAS DEVO—Enrolled at Mt. Sterling, O., August 13, 1862; transferred to V. R. C. January 15, 1864, at Louisville, Ky., by order of Secretary of War.

HENRY SHUMLEFEL—Enrolled at Mt. Sterling, O., August 13, 1862; transferred to V. R. C. January 15, 1864, at Louisville, Ky., by order of Secretary of War.

JAMES A. BAKER—Enrolled at Mt. Sterling, O., August 13, 1862; transferred to V. E. Corps July 29, 1864, at Nashville, Tenn., by order of Secretary of War.

WM. M. MORGAN—Enrolled at Camp Chase, O., September 8, 1862; transferred to V. R. C. April 1, 1865, at Camp Dennison, O., by order of Secretary of War.

COMPANY B.

Mustered out at Louisville, Ky., July 6, 1865.

COMMISSIONED OFFICERS.

CAPTAIN DAVID TAYLOR, JR.—Commissioned at Columbus, O., August 12, 1862; resigned June 10, 1863.
CAPTAIN HORATIO N. BENJAMIN—Commissioned at Shelbyville, Tenn., July 13, 1863; promoted from First Lieutenant July 13, 1863; resigned August 26, 1864. Original Second Lt. Co. E.
CAPTAIN JOHN W. KILE—Commissioned at Alpine, Ga., October 21, 1864; promoted from First Lieutenant October 21, 1864; mustered out at Louisville, Ky., July 6, 1865.
FIRST LIEUTENANT THOS. DOWNEY—Commissioned at Columbus, O., August 12, 1862; promoted to Captain of Company D, 113th Regiment, O. V. I., January 13, 1863.
FIRST LIEUTENANT WM. A. M. DAVIS—Commissioned at Alpine, Ga., October 21, 1864; mustered out at Louisville, Ky., July 6, 1865.
SECOND LIEUTENANT JOHN DICKEY—Commissioned at Columbus, O., August 12, 1862; resigned November 17, 1862.
SECOND LIEUTENANT FRANCIS O. SCARTH—Commissioned at Zanesville, O., November 17, 1862; promoted from First Sergeant November 17, 1862; resigned May 4, 1863.
SECOND LIEUTENANT JONATHAN WATSON—Commissioned at Columbus, O., November 15, 1863; promoted from First Sergeant November 15, 1863; discharged October 26, 1864, by Special Order No. 336, War Department. Declined promotion.

NON-COMMISSIONED OFFICERS.

MILLEN HAYS, First Sergeant—Enrolled at Columbus, O., August 14, 1862; promoted from Second Sergeant June 12, 1865; mustered out with Company.
JOHN WARNER, Sergeant—Enrolled at Columbus, O., August 22, 1862; mustered out with Company.
WILLIAM DURANT, Sergeant—Enrolled at Columbus, O., August 22, 1862; absent on furlough, mustered out.
GEO. F. WHEELER, Sergeant—Enrolled at Columbus, O., August 22, 1862; absent on furlough; mustered out.
NATHANIEL N. MASON, Sergeant—Enrolled at Columbus, O., August 22, 1862; promoted from First Corporal June 12, 1863; mustered out with Company.

ISAAC COLLINS, Corporal—Enrolled at Columbus, O., August 15, 1862; mustered out with Company.

PETER H. WHITEHEAD, Corporal—Enrolled at Columbus, O., August 15, 1862; on detached service in Ohio since February 12, 1864; mustered out.

SYLVESTER BAILY, Corporal—Enrolled at Columbus, O., August 12, 1862; mustered out with Company.

CHAS. R. HERRICK, Corporal—Enrolled at Columbus, O., August 22, 1862; sick in hospital at Columbus, O., since October 1, 1864; wounded in front of Resaca.

JOHN BYRNE, Corporal—Enrolled at Columbus, O., August 22, 1862; sick in hospital at Columbus, O., since January 8, 1865; wounded at Kenesaw June 27, 1864, in right fore-arm.

ISAAC SLOCUMB, Corporal—Enrolled at Columbus, O., August 22, 1862; sick in hospital at Columbus, O., since January 4, 1864.

PRIVATES.

BENJAMIN ANDERSON—Enrolled at Columbus, O., August 21, 1862; mustered out with Company.

JOSIAH W. BERGER—Enrolled at Columbus, O., August 22, 1862; absent on furlough; mustered out.

WM. BURCHIN—Enrolled at Columbus, O., August 21, 1862; mustered out with Company.

BENJAMIN BURD—Enrolled at Columbus, O., August 22, 1863; absent on furlough; mustered out.

JAMES F. BEARD—Enrolled at Columbus, O., August 22, 1862; mustered out with Company.

JAMES A. BLAKELY—Enrolled at Columbus, O., August 16, 1862; hospital nurse at Chattanooga, Tenn., June 26, 1864.

THOMAS BARRESFORD—Enrolled at Urbana, O., December 8, 1863; sick in hospital at Lookout Mt., Ga., May 22, 1864.

FREDRICK BORBICK—Enrolled at Columbus, O., February 23, 1864; mustered out with Company.

WM. H. CASSIDAY—Enrolled at Columbus, O., August 22, 1862; absent on furlough at Columbus, O.; mustered out.

BAZIL CONWAY—Enrolled at Columbus, O., August 22, 1862; mustered out with Company.

HENRY M. CAPELL—Enrolled at Columbus, O., August 10, 1862; mustered out with Company.

JOHN V. CHAPIN—Enrolled at Columbus, O., August 22, 1862; sick in hospital at Jeffersonville, Ind., May 22, 1864.

Josephus Conant—Enrolled at Columbus, O., August 15, 1862; absent on furlough at Columbus, O.; mustered out.
Wm. C. Cramer—Enrolled at Columbus, O., August 22, 1862; mustered out with Company.
Geo. W. Crane—Enrolled at Columbus, O., August 15, 1862; mustered out with Company.
James Conway—Enrolled at Columbus, O., February 23, 1864; mustered out with Company.
Isaac Cary—Enrolled at Columbus, O., February 18, 1864; mustered out with Company.
Chas. Debou—Enrolled at Columbus, O., August 22, 1862; absent on furlough at Columbus, O.; mustered out.
Alva J. Darnell—Enrolled at Columbus, August 22, 1862; absent on furlough at Columbus, O.; mustered out; died December 11, 1868.
James W. Dunlap—Enrolled at Columbus, O., August 22, 1862; mustered out with Company.
John Fry—Enrolled at Columbus, O., August 22, 1862; absent on furlough at Columbus, O.; mustered out.
Henry Feller—Enrolled at Madison, O., January 20, 1864; absent on furlough at Columbus, O.; mustered out.
Elisha Himrod—Enrolled at Columbus, O., August 22, 1862; mustered out with Company.
Samuel Hoover—Enrolled at Columbus, O., August 22, 1862; mustered out with Company.
Wm. D. Hicky—Enrolled at Urbana, O., December 3, 1865; sick in hospital at Goldsboro, N. C., since April 9, 1865.
James Hamilton—Enrolled at Urbana, O., December 8, 1863; mustered out with Company.
Stephen H. Howell—Enrolled at Clark County, O., January 19, 1864; mustered out with Company.
William Hesser—Enrolled at Columbus, O., February 11, 1864; mustered out with Company.
Patrick Jones—Enrolled at Urbana, O., November 24, 1863; mustered out with Company.
William Jacobs—Enrolled at Urbana, O., November 8, 1863; mustered out with Company.
Samuel Looker—Enrolled at Columbus, O., August 22, 1862; mustered out with Company.
Chas. C. Latham—Enrolled at Urbana, O., December 3, 1863; sick in hospital No. 2 at Nashville, Tenn., October 8, 1864.

CHARLES LOWE—Enrolled at Urbana, O., December 29, 1863; mustered out with Company.
JOSEPH LOWE—Enrolled at Urbana, O., December 29, 1863; mustered out with Company. (Musician.)
WILLIAM LOWE—Enrolled at Urbana, O., January 4, 1864; mustered out with Company.
JOSEPH MILLER—Enrolled at Columbus, O., August 22, 1862; mustered out with Company.
LYMAN W. MARSH—Enrolled at Columbus, O., August 22, 1862; absent on furlough at Columbus, O.; mustered out.
ROBERT L. MOORE—Enrolled at Columbus, O., February 1, 1864; mustered out with Company.
WILTON OSBORN—Enrolled at Columbus, O., August 22, 1862; mustered out with Company.
JOHN PATTERSON—Enrolled at Columbus, O., August 15, 1862; mustered out with Company.
PETER REEVES—Enrolled at Columbus, O., August 22, 1862; mustered out with Company.
GEORGE REI—Enrolled at Columbus, O., August 22, 1862; mustered out with Company.
ROLLIN REED—Enrolled at Columbus, O., August 22, 1862; mustered out with Company.
ELIAS REMALY—Enrolled at Columbus, O., August 22, 1862; mustered out with Company.
WILLIAM REJESTER—Enrolled at Columbus, O., August 22, 1862; mustered out with Company.
JOHN SCUREMAN—Enrolled at Columbus, O., August 22, 1862; absent on furlough at Columbus, O.; mustered out.
JUDSON SWISHER—Enrolled at Columbus, O., August 22, 1862; mustered out with Company.
RUSSEL B. STEWART—Enrolled at Columbus, O., August 22, 1862; mustered out with Company.
ADAM SNIDER—Enrolled at Columbus, O., January 16, 1864; mustered out with Company.
THEBOLT SNIDER—Enrolled at Madison, O., January 1, 1864; mustered out.
JACOB SNIDER—Enrolled at Columbus, O., February 24, 1864; mustered out with Company.
JAMES SAVELY—Enrolled at Columbus, O., February 24, 1864; mustered out with Company.

ANDREW VANHOUTEN—Enrolled at Columbus, O., August 21, 1862; mustered out with Company.
SOLOMON VANHORN—Enrolled at Columbus, O. February 18, 1864; mustered out with Company.
JAMES WHITE—Enrolled at Urbana, O., November 25, 1863; mustered out with Company.
JOHN WILSON—Enrolled at Urbana, O., November 28, 1863; mustered out with Company.
DAVID YOST—Enrolled at Columbus, O., August 22, 1862; mustered out with Company.
CHAS. F. YOST—Enrolled at Columbus, O., August 22, 1862; mustered out with Company.
JOHN A. ZELLHEART—Enrolled at Columbus, O., August 22, 1862; absent on furlough at Columbus, O.; mustered out.

KILLED.

WM. LAMBERT—Enrolled at Columbus, O., August 22, 1862; killed at the battle of Chickamauga, Ga., September 20, 1863.
JOHN J. SMITH—Enrolled at Columbus, O., August 22, 1862; killed at the battle of Chickamauga, Ga., September 20, 1863. (See sketch.)
AMOS D. LEADY—Enrolled at Columbus, O., August 22, 1862; killed at the battle of Kenesaw Mountain, Ga., June 27, 1864.
GEO. WORKMAN—Enrolled at Urbana, O., Nov. 23, 1863; killed near Rocky Mountain, South Carolina, by an insane soldier, February 24, 1865. (See sketch in Knapsack.)
ALEXANDER HENRY—Enrolled at Urbana, O., November 25, 1863; killed near White Oak Bottom, Maryland, by falling from the cars, June 12, 1865. (See record in the body of this work under June 13, 1865.)

MISSING IN ACTION.

SAMUEL E. CRANE—Enrolled at Columbus, O., August 15, 1862; missing September 20, 1863, at the battle of Chickamauga, Ga.
WM. THOMAS—Enrolled at Urbana, O., November 24, 1863; missing June 27, 1864, at the battle of Kenesaw Mountain, Ga.

DIED.

ALBERT A. HODGE—Enrolled at Columbus, O., August 22, 1864; died February 21, 1863, of disease, in Hospital No. 21, Nashville, Tenn.

ALFRED PARKER, Corporal—Enrolled at Columbus, O., August 22, 1862; died March 5, 1863, of disease, in Hospital No. 9, Nashville, Tenn.
AUSTIN E. CAPEL.—Enrolled at Columbus, O., August 22, 1862; died March 7, 1863, of disease, in Hospital No. 21, Nashville, Tenn.
JOHN E. DOVIL.—Enrolled at Columbus, O., August 22, 1862; died March 8, 1863, of disease, at Louisville, Ky.
LUCIUS RITCHIE—Enrolled at Columbus, O., August 22, 1862; died March 13, 1863, of disease, in Hospital No. 9, Nashville, Tenn.
ARTHUR WHARTON—Enrolled at Columbus, O., August 22, 1862; died April 18, 1863, of disease, at Regimental Hospital, Franklin, Tenn.
JACOB WILLIAMSON—Enrolled at Columbus, O., August 15, 1862; died April 21, 1863, of smallpox, in Hospital No. 11, Nashville, Tenn.
JOHN RAGER—Enrolled at Columbus, O., August 22, 1862; died May 1, 1863, of disease, in Hospital No. 16, Nashville, Tenn.
JOHN M. WHITEHEAD—Enrolled at Columbus, O., August 15, 1862; died June 11, 1863, of chronic diarrhea, at Franklin, Tenn., aged 19 years.
GEO. RUSH—Enrolled at Columbus, O., August 22, 1862; died July 23, 1863, of congestive chills, in Regimental Hospital, Shelbyville, Tenn.
CHRISTOPHER SOWERS—Enrolled at Columbus, O., August 15, 1862; died August 25, 1863, of chronic diarrhea, at Hospital No. 1, Nashville, Tenn.
LEWIS H. BELL, Sergeant—Enrolled at Columbus, O., August 13, 1862; died October 10, 1863, at Chattanooga, Tenn., of wounds received at the battle of Chickamauga, Ga., September 20, 1863.
HENRY H. KRAMER—Enrolled at Columbus, O., August 22, 1862; died October 12, 1863, at field hospital, Chattanooga, Tenn., of wounds received at the battle of Chickamauga, Ga., September 20, 1863.
JOHN A. SINNETT—Enrolled at Columbus, O., August 15, 1862; died January 14, 1864, of chronic diarrhea at Division Hospital No. 10, Chattanooga, Tenn.
ELIJAH CRAMER—Enrolled at Columbus, O., February 1, 1864; died August 27, 1864, of congestive chills, in Field Hospital near Atlanta, Ga.

PILLOW WILLIAMS—Enrolled at Columbus, O., February 6, 1864; died September 10, 1864, of acute bronchitis, in Hospital No. 1, Nashville, Tenn.

HENRY ROBBINS—Enrolled at Columbus, O., August 15, 1862; died July 1, 1864, at Big Shanty, Ga., of wounds received at the battle of Kenesaw Mt., Ga., June 27, 1864.

NATHAN H. SMITH—Enrolled at Columbus, O., August 13, 1862; died September 29, 1864, of disease of the heart, at Camp Dennison, O.

HENRY S. GINGRY—Enrolled at Urbana, O., December 22, 1863; died September 2, 1864, at Chattanooga, Tenn., of wounds received while on duty near Atlanta, Ga., August 9, 1864.

HENRY H. LEEF—Enrolled at Columbus, O., August 18, 1862; died October 30, 1864, of disease, at Atlanta, Ga.

JOHN C. BERGER—Enrolled at Columbus, O., February 27, 1864; died October 22, 1864, of chronic diarrhea, at Chattanooga, Tenn., aged 28 years; was in action at Kenesaw, Ga., June 27, 1864, and Jonesboro, Ga., September 1, 1864.

WALLACE HOGARTH—Enrolled at Urbana, O., November 20, 1863; died March 20, 1865, at field hospital near Bentonville, N. C., of wounds received at the battle of Bentonville, N. C.

DAVID L. GREEN—Enrolled at Columbus, O., August 12, 1862; died December 30, 1864, of chronic diarrhea, at Hospital No. 2, Nashville, Tenn.

DISCHARGED.

EDWARD FRISTOE—Enrolled at Columbus, O., August 22, 1862; discharged January 31, 1863, at Columbus, O., for physical disability, by order of Captain A. B. Dodd.

ABRAM SWARTZ—Enrolled at Columbus, O., August 22, 1862; discharged March 22, 1863, at Nashville, Tenn., for physical disability, by order of General Rosecrans.

SAMUEL S. WELLS, Hospital Steward—Enrolled at Columbus, O., August 22, 1862; discharged April 28, 1863, at Franklin, Tenn., for physical disability, by order of General Rosecrans.

JOHN C. GREEN, Corporal—Enrolled at Columbus, O., August 21, 1862; discharged April 14, 1863, at Columbus, O., for physical disability, by order of Captain A. B. Dodd.

ADAM M. RAREY, Corporal—Enrolled at Columbus, O., August 22, 1862; discharged April 15, 1863, at Nashville, Tenn., for physical disability, by order of General Rosecrans.

ENOS W. ROBB—Enrolled at Columbus, O., August 15, 1862; discharged April 25, 1863, at Franklin, Tenn., for physical disability, by order of General Rosecrans.

OLIVER W. CROW—Enrolled at Columbus, O., August 22, 1862; discharged August 27, 1863, at Nashville, Tenn., for physical disability, by order of General Rosecrans.

JOHN W. WILLIAMS—Enrolled at Columbus, O., August 22, 1862; discharged June 14, 1864, at Camp Dennison, O., for physical disability, by order of General Heintzleman.

WESLEY MOORE—Enrolled at Columbus, O., August 22, 1862; discharged April 30, 1864, at Bridgeport, Ala., by order of General Thomas.

SAMUEL B. STREET—Enrolled at Columbus, O., August 14, 1862; discharged February 4, 1865, at Tripler Hospital, Columbus, O., on account of wounds received at the battle of Kenesaw Mountain, Ga., June 27, 1864, by order of General Hooker.

PETER EALY—Enrolled at Columbus, O., August 14, 1862; discharged May 11, 1865, at Columbus, O., for anchylosis of right ankle, by order of General Hooker.

JOSEPH LAMPIT—Enrolled at Urbana, O., December 3, 1863; discharged May 26, 1865, at Camp Dennison, O., by order of Adjutant General of Ohio, dated May 3, 1865.

RICHARD B. HARRISON—Enrolled at Columbus, O., August 22, 1862; discharged May 26, 1865, at Camp Dennison, O., by order Adjutant General of Ohio, dated May 3, 1865.

EDWARD I. HILL—Enrolled at Urbana, O., December 3, 1863; discharged May 9, 1865, at Camp Dennison, O., by order Adjutant General of Ohio, dated May 3, 1865.

EDWARD B. WHITEHEAD, Corporal—Enrolled at Columbus, O., August 21, 1862; discharged May 9, 1865, at Columbus, O., on account of wounds received at the battle of Kenesaw Mountain June 27, 1864, by order of General Hooker.

WM. DITMAS—Enrolled at Dayton, O., September 22, 1864; discharged June 23, 1865, at Louisville, Ky., by War Department order, May 18, 1865.

HENRY PATTERSON—Enrolled at Dayton, O., September 21, 1864, discharged June 23, 1865, at Louisville, Ky., by War Department order, May 18, 1865.

ALEXANDER CARPENTER, First Sergeant—Enrolled at Columbus, O., August 14, 1862; discharged June 11, 1865, at Louisville, Ky., to accept promotion as First Lieutenant of Company E, 113th O. V. I.

DESERTED.

GEORGE PETERS—Enrolled at Columbus, O., August 22, 1862; deserted August 29, 1862, at Camp Chase, O.

ASA BLOVELT—Enrolled at Columbus, O., August 22, 1862; deserted September 20, 1862, at Camp Chase, O.

CYRUS MILLER—Enrolled at Columbus, O., August 21, 1862; deserted November 16, 1862, at Zanesville, O.

JACOB ALMIRE—Enrolled at Columbus, O., August 22, 1862; deserted September 15, 1862, at Camp Chase, O.

JOSEPH GERMAN—Enrolled at Urbana, O., December 5, 1863; deserted August 29, 1864, near Atlanta, Ga.

TRANSFERRED.

WM. N. YOST, Hospital Steward—Enrolled at Columbus, O., August 22, 1862; transferred to non-commissioned staff September 30, 1863, by order of Lieutenant Colonel D. B. Warner, commanding 113th O. V. I.

WM. H. HALLIDAY, Sergeant—Enrolled at Columbus, O., August 15, 1862; transferred to non-commissioned staff as Quartermaster Sergeant, December 13, 1863.

ENOCH A. NEEDLES—Enrolled at Columbus, O., August 13, 1863; transferred to V. R. C. April 10, 1864, by order of Secretary of War.

ISRAEL GAYMAN—Enrolled at Columbus, O., August 13, 1862; transferred to 1st U. S. V. V. Engineers, July 27, 1864, by order of Colonel W. E. Merril.

JOHN FARLEY—Enrolled at Urbana, O., January 1, 1864; transferred April 6, 1864, to Company K, 113th Regiment, or by order of Major L. S. Sullivant, commanding 113th O. V. I.

JOHN BOLT—Muster and descriptive rolls not received; transferred April 10, 1864, to Company E, 113th O. V. I., by order of Major L. S. Sullivant, commanding 113th O. V. I.

GEO. CARROLL—Muster and descriptive rolls not received; transferred April 10, 1864, to Company E, 113th O. V. I., by order of Major L. S. Sullivant, commanding 113th O. V. I.

JACOB F. HEES—Enrolled at Urbana, O., November 28, 1863; transferred April 28, 1864, to Company E, 113th O. V. I., by order of Major L. S. Sullivant, commanding 113th O. V. I. Killed at Kenesaw.

WM. H. WHITNEY—Enrolled at Urbana, O., November 28, 1863; transferred April 28, 1864, to Company E, 113th O. V. I., by order of Major L. S. Sullivant, commanding 113th O. V. I.

ABRAHAM TRIMBEE—Enrolled at Urbana, O., December 2, 1863; transferred April 28, 1864, to Company G, 113th O. V. I., by order of Major L. S..Sullivant, commanding 113th O. V. I.

HERBERT NORMAN—Enrolled at Urbana, O., February 12, 1864; transferred April 28, 1864, to Company E, 113th O. V. I., by order of Major L. S. Sullivant, commanding 113th O. V. I.

DAVID EVANS—Enrolled at Columbus, O., August 22, 1862; transferred January 1, 1865, to V. R. C., Washington, D. C., by order of the Secretary of War.

FREDERICK L. STIRES—Enrolled at Columbus, O., August 22, 1862; transferred January 1, 1865, to V. R. C., Washington, D. C., by order of the Secretary of War.

HENRY S. BINKLEY—Enrolled at Columbus, O., August 22, 1862; transferred to 5th U. S. Cavalry, November 16, 1862.

WM. H. BROWN—Enrolled at Columbus, O., August 22, 1862; transferred to 5th U. S. Cavalry, November 16, 1862.

WM. DELLINGER—Enrolled at Columbus, O., August 22, 1862; transferred to 5th U. S. Cavalry, November 16, 1862.

LINCOLN STEPHENSON—Enrolled at Columbus, O., August 22, 1862; transferred to 5th U. S. Cavalry, November 16, 1862.

WM. STEWART—Enrolled at Columbus, O., August 22, 1862; transferred to 5th U. S. Cavalry, November 16, 1862.

ROLL OF HONOR.

NAMES OF SOLDIERS OF THE 113TH REGIMENT, O. V. I., WHO ARE BURIED IN NATIONAL CEMETERIES.

NOTE. Some of these were removed and re-interred at their former homes.

PETER BROWN, Private—Company A; died June 6, 1863; buried in Section C, grave No. 284, in National Cemetery, at Nashville, Tenn.

THOS. COWLING, Corporal—Company A; died April 13, 1865; buried in Section 17, grave No. 111, in National Cemetery, at Newbern, North Carolina.

J. W. CARR, Private—Company A; died March 22, 1863; buried in Section E, grave No. 487, in National Cemetery, Nashville, Tenn.

W. T. COCHRAN, Private—Company A; died March 14, 1863; buried in Section E, grave No. 256, in National Cemetery, Nashville, Tenn.

F. M. CRABB, Private—Company A; died September 3, 1863; buried in Section D, grave No. 511, in National Cemetery, Nashville, Tenn.

LYMAN CARTER, Private—Company A; died March 20, 1863; buried in Section 4, grave No. 376, in National Cemetery, Chattanooga, Tenn.

D. G. DON, Private—Company A; died May 16, 1865; section and grave number not given; buried in New Cemetery, Newbern, N. C.

JOHN BERGER, Private—Company B; died October 21, 1864; buried in Section G., grave No. 13, in National Cemetery, Chattanooga, Tenn.

JOHN BREGGS—Company B; died at Columbus, O., February 21, 1864; sent home for burial.

H. H. CASMER, Private—Company B; date of death not given; buried in Section D, grave No. 954, in National Cemetery, Chattanooga, Tenn.

WM. ANDERSON, Corporal—Company C; died March 7, 1863; buried in Section —, grave No. 381, in National Cemetery, at Murfreesboro, Tenn.

ROBERT BRITTON, Private—Company C; died November 11, 1864; buried in Section F, grave No. 627, in National Cemetery, Chattanooga, Tenn.

JOHN BOYER, Private—Company C; died October 21, 1863; buried in Section H, grave No. 695, in National Cemetery, Chattanooga, Tenn.

ANDREW CONNOLEY, Private—Company C; died July 15, 1864; buried in Section J, grave No. 62, in National Cemetery, Nashville, Tenn.

J. F. CHEEK, Private—Company D; died October 17, 1863; buried in Section E, grave No. 1,145, in National Cemetery, Nashville, Tenn.

WM BRASKETTE, Private—Company E; died March 1, 1864; buried in Section C, grave No. 425, in National Cemetery, Chattanooga, Tenn.

GEORGE CONARD, Private—Company E; died May 11, 1863; buried in Section E, grave No. 864, in National Cemetery, Nashville, Tenn.

GEORGE A. BAKER, Private—Company E; died March 20, 1863; buried in Section D, grave No. 598, in National Cemetery, Nashville, Tenn.

HARRY BLADE, Private—Company F; died July 12, 1864; buried in Section E, grave No. 674, in National Cemetery, Chattanooga, Tenn.

ED. CROUSE, Second Lieutenant—Company F; died June 27, 1864; buried in Section C, grave No. bbb, in National Cemetery, Marietta, Ga.

JAMES COOKSEY, Private—Company G; died September 27, 1864; buried in Section B, grave No. 92, in National Cemetery, New Albany, Ind.

A. DENNISON, Sergeant—Company G; date of death not given; buried in Section D, grave No. 962, in National Cemetery at Chattanooga, Tenn.

G. DENNISON, Private—Company G; died March 17, 1863; buried in Section E, grave No. 674, in National Cemetery, Nashville, Tenn.

J. BELL, Private—Company H; died July 12, 1864; buried in Section K, grave No. 134, in National Cemetery, Chattanooga, Tenn.

J. H. BURWELL, Private—Company H; died January 3, 1864; buried in Section B, grave No. 36, in Linden Grove Cemetery, Covington, Ky.

C. CHILLES, Corporal—Company H; date of death not given; buried in Section D, grave No. 960, in National Cemetery, Chattanooga, Tenn.

F. M. CLOUD, Private—Company H; died June 30, 1864; buried in Section J, grave No. 96, in National Cemetery, Marietta, Ga.

W. H. H. COBLENTZ, Private—Company I; died August 1, 1864; buried in Section F, grave No. 258, in National Cemetery, Chattanooga, Tenn.

WM. COLLINS, Private—Company I; died September 11, 1864; buried in Section J, grave No. 38, in National Cemetery, Marietta, Ga.

JESSE CURTIS, Private—Company I; died October 31, 1864; buried in Section G, grave No. 1180, in National Cemetery, at Marietta, Ga.

E. W. JACKSON, Private—Company A; died June 27, 1864; buried in Section I, grave No. 262, in National Cemetery, Marietta, Ga.

L. H. KENNEDY, Private—Company A; died June 27, 1864; buried in Section I, grave No. 263, in National Cemetery, Marietta, Ga.

HENRY GINGERY, Private—Company B; died September 2, 1864; buried in Section F, grave No. 525, in National Cemetery, Chattanooga, Tenn.

DAVID L. GREEN, Private—Company B; died December 30, 1864; buried in Section G, grave No. 508, in National Cemetery, Nashville, Tenn.

A. A. HODGE, Private—Company B; died February 21, 1863; buried in Section E, grave No. 499, in National Cemetery, Nashville, Tenn.

WM. KAUSON, Corporal—Company C; date of death not given; buried in Section D, grave No. 961, in National Cemetery, Chattanooga, Tenn.

W. H. H. GOLDSMITH, Private—Company C; died June 22, 1863; Section and grave No. not given; buried in National Cemetery, Nashville, Tenn.

J. S. GILLESPIE, Private—Company D; died February 10, 1863; buried in Section B, grave No. 718, in National Cemetery, Nashville, Tenn.

W. H. HUNH, Private—Company D; died July 16, 1864; grave No. 3,420, in National Cemetery, Andersonville, Ga.

ANDREW HELLER, Private—Company E; died August 13, 1864; buried in Section I, grave No. 37, in National Cemetery, Marietta, Ga.

J. G. KIRKPATRICK, Private—Company F; died October 6, 1864; buried in Section E, grave No. 2,805, in National Cemetery, Nashville, Tenn.

JOHN GRAY, Private—Company F; died April 14, 1863; buried in Section +, grave No. 9, in Stone River National Cemetery, Murfreesboro, Tenn.

JACOB FOSTER, Private—Company G; died April 30, 1864; buried in Section J, grave No. 99, in National Cemetery, Nashville, Tenn.

P. GOFFY, Private—Company G; died August 1, 1864; grave No. 4,445, in National Cemetery, Andersonville, Ga.

PERRY GERARD, Private—Company G; died April 22, 1863; buried in Section C, grave No. 347, in National Cemetery, Nashville, Tenn.

H. GILLENWATER, Private—Company G; died February 25, 1863; buried in Section E, grave No. 386, in National Cemetery, Nashville, Tenn.

LEWIS GREEN, Sergeant—Company G; died June 27, 1864; buried in Section I, grave No. 27, in National Cemetery, Marietta, Ga.

W. R. HANAWALT, Lieutenant—Company G; date of death not given; buried in Section D, grave No. 964, in National Cemetery, Chattanooga, Tenn.

VOLNEY HOLVCROSS, Corporal—Company H; died October 12, 1863; buried in Section L, grave No. 334, in National Cemetery, Chattanooga, Tenn.

ELISHA KIMBALL, Private—Company I; date of death not given; grave No. 1,851, in National Cemetery, Wilmington, N. C.

MICHAEL KEHAL, Corporal—Company I; died August 21, 1864; buried in Section F, grave No. 470, in National Cemetery, Chattanooga, Tenn.

JACOB KELSING, Private—Company I; died April 28, 1863; buried in Section K, grave No. 274, in Stone River National Cemetery, Murfreesboro, Tenn.

LEVI HEMMINGER Private—Company K; died August 1, 1864; buried in Section F, grave No. 126, in National Cemetery, Chattanooga, Tenn.

E. T. JONES, Private—Company K; died June 27, 1864; buried in Section I, grave No. 24, in National Cemetery, Marietta, Ga.

WM. LAMBERT, Private—Company B; date of death not given; buried in Section D, grave No. 959, in National Cemetery, Chattanooga, Tenn.

A. PARKER, Corporal—Company B; died March 5, 1863; buried in Section E, grave No. 752, in National Cemetery, Nashville, Tenn.

JOHN RAGER, Private—Company B; died May 1, 1863; Section and grave No. unknown; buried in National Cemetery, Nashville, Tenn.

J. ROYAL, Private—Company C; died March 9, 1863; buried in Section E, grave No. 1,084, in National Cemetery, Nashville, Tenn.

DAVID NEAL, Private—Company C; died August 30, 1864; buried in Section E, grave No. 2,920, in National Cemetery, Nashville, Tenn.

J. G. PERKINS, Private—Company C; died February 14, 1863; grave and Section No. unknown; buried in National Cemetery, Nashville, Tenn.

M. C. MESSINGER, Corporal—Company D; date of death not given; buried in Section A, grave No. 67, in National Cemetery, Chattanooga, Tenn.

L. PRATT, Private—Company D; date of death not given; buried in Section D, grave No. 958, in National Cemetery, Chattanooga, Tenn.

A. ROSE, Private—Company D; died March 3, 1863; Section and grave No. unknown; buried in National Cemetery, Nashville, Tenn.

PETER MILLER, Private—Company E; died December 9, 1863; Section and grave No. unknown; buried in Stone River National Cemetery, Murfreesboro.

J. McDOWELL, Private—Company E; died April 16, 1864; Section and grave No. unknown; buried in Danville, Va., a prisoner of war.

PETER McDOWELL, Private—Company E; died March 13, 1864; buried in Section E, grave No. 1,093, in National Cemetery, Nashville, Tenn.

R. B. PARKER, Private—Company E; died February 22, 1863; buried in Section E, grave No. 382, in National Cemetery, Nashville, Tenn.

FRANKLIN RUSSEL, Private—Company E; date of death not given; buried in Section D, grave No. 956, in National Cemetery, Chattanooga, Tenn.

W. H. LANE, Private—Company F; died December 31, 1863, in U. S. General Hospital, Division No. 1; buried at Annapolis, Md.; had been a prisoner.

U. A. McComb, Private—Company F; died August 8, 1864; buried in Section E, grave No. 758, in National Cemetery, Marietta, Ga.

DAVID MITCHELL, Private—Company G; date of death not given; buried in Section D, grave No. 963, in National Cemetery, Chattanooga, Tenn.

OTHO W. NIGH, Private—Company G; died February 7, 1864; Section and grave No. unknown; buried in Stone River National Cemetery, Murfreesboro, Tenn.

D. D. MILLER, Private—Company G; died March 25, 1863; Section and grave No. unknown; buried in National Cemetery, Nashville, Tenn.

F. PETERSON, Corporal—Company G; died August 30, 1864; grave No. 7,329, in National Cemetery, Andersonville, Ga.

JOSEPH PARKER, Lieutenant—Company G; died June 27, 1864; buried in Section C, grave No. ccc, in National Cemetery, Marietta, Ga.

J. L. RIGGIN, Private—Company G; died June 27, 1863; Section and grave No. unknown; buried in National Cemetery, Nashville, Tenn.

CHARLES ROSENDALE, Private—Company G; died June 1, 1864; buried in Section H, grave No. 409, in National Cemetery, Marietta, Ga.

R. H. McLEAN, Private—Company G; died February 3, 1863; buried in Section B, range 9, grave No 22, in Cave Hill National Cemetery, Louisville, Ky.

J. PRICE, Private—Company H; date of death not given; buried in Section D, grave No. 957, in National Cemetery, Chattanooga, Tenn.

JACOB MEYER, Corporal—Company I; died July 7, 1864; buried in Section E, grave No. 535, in National Cemetery, Chattanooga, Tenn.

WM. McMANAS, Private—Company I; died May 3, 1864; buried in Section K, grave No. 423, in National Cemetery, Chattanooga, Tenn.

WM. McKNIGHT, Private—Company I; died August 4, 1864; buried in Section H, grave No. 605, in National Cemetery, Nashville, Tenn.

JOHN ROOKS, Private—Company I; died July 8, 1864; buried in Section E, grave No. 566, in National Cemetery, Chattanooga, Tenn.

JAMES MCMAHAN, Private—Company K; died November 30, 1864; buried in Section I, grave No. 71, in soldiers' lot, Jeffersonville, Ind.

AZRO MANN, Private—Company K; died October 31, 1864; buried in Section E, grave No. 2,860, in National Cemetery, Nashville, Tenn.

HECTOR MORRIN, Private—Company K; died June 30, 1864; buried in Section J, grave No. 101, in National Cemetery, Marietta, Ga.

J. H. NEWCOMB, Private—Company K; died July 24, 1864; grave and Section No. unknown; buried in National Cemetery, Nashville, Tenn.

R. R. OSBORN, Private—Company K; died August 22, 1864; buried in Section F, grave No. 359, in National Cemetery, Chattanooga, Tenn.

LEVI ROMINE, Private—Company K; died June 27, 1864; buried in Section I, grave No. 261, in National Cemetery, Marietta, Ga.

JOHN WEBER, Private—Company A; died July 19, 1864, buried in Section G, grave No. 1,351, in National Cemetery, Marietta, Ga.

M. F. BUSHFIELD, Private—Company A; date of death not given; original burial, Franklin Tenn.; removed to National Cemetery, Columbia, in Section K, grave No. 49.

LYMAN CARTER, Private—Company A; died March 20, 1863; original burial, Franklin, Tenn.; removed to National Cemetery, Columbia, in Section N, grave No. 21.

NATHAN H. SMITH, Private—Company B; died October 1, 1864; Section and grave number unknown; buried in National Cemetery, Denison.

PHILO WILLIAMS, Private—Company B; died September 10, 1864; buried in Section F, grave No. 166, in National Cemetery, Nashville, Tenn.

SIMON WARNER, Private—Company C; died August 29, 1864; buried in Section C, grave No. 140, in National Cemetery, Marietta, Ga.

HIRAM WILCOX, Private—Company C; died June 27, 1864; buried in Section I, grave No. 2, in National Cemetery, Marietta, Ga.

J. E. WILLIAMS, Private—Company C; died April 15, 1863; buried in Section 4, grave No. 367, in Stone River National Cemetery, Murfreesboro, Tenn.

WM. ANDERSON, Corporal—Company C; died March 17, 1863; original burial, Franklin, Tenn.; removed to National Cemetery Columbia, in Section N, grave No. 26.

JOHN WILLIAMS, Private—Company C; died April 15, 1863; original burial, Franklin, Tenn.; removed to National Cemetery, Columbia, in Section N, grave No. 12.

WM. MELLEN, Private—Company C; died March 26, 1863; original burial, Franklin, Tenn.; removed to National Cemetery, Columbia, in Section K, grave No. 33.

JOHN H. PRICE, Private—Company C; died April 4, 1864; original burial, Franklin, Tenn.; removed to Columbia, in Section K, grave No. 39.

W. C. MASON, Private—Company D; died March 24, 1863; original burial, Franklin, Tenn.; removed to National Cemetery, Columbia, in Section N, grave No. 29.

EDWARD WILLIAMS, Private—Company D; died November 20, 1864; buried in Section E, grave No. 2,869, in National Cemetery, Nashville, Tenn.

A. P. WRIGHT, Private—Company D; died February 16, 1863; buried in Section E, grave No. 1,231, in National Cemetery, Nashville, Tenn.

H. A. WELLS, Private—Company D; died February 20, 1863; Section and grave unknown; buried in National Cemetery, Nashville, Tenn.

ANTHONY SCHIMMEL, Private—Company E; died August 7, 1864; buried in Section E, grave No. 759, in National Cemetery, Marietta, Ga.

HENRY C. SCOTT, Sergeant—Company E; died June 27, 1863; buried in Section J, grave No. 79, in National Cemetery, Marietta, Georgia.

A. J. WARD, Private—Company E; died July 18, 1863; buried in Section C, grave No. 342, in National Cemetery, Nashville, Tenn.

JOHN GRAY, Private—Company F; died April 14, 1863; original burial, Franklin, Tenn.; removed to National Cemetery, Columbia, in Section K, grave No. 9.

AMOS RICH, Private—Company F; died March 25, 1863; original burial, Franklin, Tenn.; removed to National Cemetery, Columbia, in Section K, grave No. 36.

M. SMITH, Private—Company G; died October 19, 1863; buried in Section D, grave No. 953, in National Cemetery, Chattanooga, Tenn.

Hezekiah Suver, Private—Company G; died March 26, 1864; buried in Section E, grave No. 130, in National Cemetery, Chattanooga, Tenn.

Wm. Sinsel, Private—Company H; died February 9, 1863; buried in Section B, range 12, grave No. 62, in Cave Hill National Cemetery, Louisville, Ky.

G. Snyder, Private—Company H; died March 17, 1863; Section and grave No. unknown; buried in National Cemetery, Nashville, Tenn.

B. F. Townsend, Private—Company H; died August 19, 1863; buried in Section E, grave No. 355, in Stone River National Cemetery, near Murfreesboro, Tenn.

Geo. H. Wilson, Private—Company H; died at Columbus, O., September 5, 1864; Section and grave No. unknown; buried in Rees' graveyard, east of Columbus.

Thos. Perry, Private—Company H; died June 2, 1863; buried in Section I, grave No. 94, in National Cemetery, Columbia.

S. Thompson—Company I; date of death not given; buried in Section A, grave No. 84, in National Cemetery, Chattanooga, Tenn.

Randolph Weber, Private—Company I; died August 13, 1863; Section and grave No. unknown; buried in National Cemetery, Camp Dennison, O.

Chas. West, Private—Company I; died March 19, 1864; buried in Section A, grave No. 41, in National Cemetery, Chattanooga, Tenn.

Jacob Kelsing, Private—Company I; died April 28, 1863; buried in Section I, grave No. 84, in National Cemetery, Columbia.

H. Wilburn, Corporal—Company I; died March 5, 1863; Section and grave No. unknown; buried in National Cemetery, Nashville, Tenn.

J. Wilkinson, Private—Company K; died June 27, 1864; buried in Section I, grave No. 8, in National Cemetery, Marietta, Ga.

OUR KNAPSACK.

OUR KNAPSACK.

[Under this head have been arranged anecdotes, sketches, incidents, and other matter pertaining to camp, field and bivouac, which have been mainly contributed by members of the command. That this department will prove to be full of interest to the members of the regiment and to their descendants to remote generations, there can be no doubt.]

PRISON LIFE.

A STORY OF CAPTURE, IMPRISONMENT AND SUFFERING IN REBEL PRISONS OF THE SOUTH.

By J. N. HALL, ONE HUNDRED AND THIRTEENTH O. V. I.

In writing the following narrative of prison life, I shall begin at the battle at which I was captured, the bloody field of Chickamauga, which was fought on the 19th and 20th of September, 1863.

We had been following the rebel army under Bragg all the way from Shelbyville to Chattanooga, and had about given up the hope of his giving us battle. Our corps, under General Gordon Granger, had pitched our tents near Rossville, an insignificant village, near five miles south of Chattanooga, and were now resting from the tiresome marches of the several days previous. On the third day after our halt, the division (Steedman's) to which we were attached, started on a reconnoisance in the direction of Ringgold and Tunnel Hill, a distance of nearly twenty miles from our camp. The Confederates were reported to be in that direction with a strong force, and the object of our movement was to ascertain his position and strength.

Late in the afternoon, and within three miles of Ringgold, we encountered the outposts of the enemy, driving them in, and appropriating their half-cooked supper of yams and sweet potatoes, which we found cooking in iron kettles.

Halting about a mile from town, we placed six pieces of artillery in a commanding position, and, for a time, paid our compliments to our enemies after the cast iron fashion. I was sent with a squad of men to the top of a hill on our left to ascertain and report any aggressive demonstration of the foe, but nothing occurred of importance. Our division, having accomplished the object of the trip, began to fall back toward Rossville late in the evening, and I was ordered to move in the rear with my squad. The Confederates, ascertaining that we were falling back, pressed our rear, and for several miles, and until darkness came on, a brisk skirmish fight was kept up, in which our loss was three killed and eight or ten wounded. We had now reached a scope of heavy timber, and were permitted to move on unmolested. Coming at length to a level piece of bottom land, through which runs the stream Chickamauga, we forded the stream and went into camp on the edge of the prairie near a strip of timber. It was now nearly ten o'clock at night, and our camp fires were soon blazing in the necessary preparations for supper and rest. During the afternoon I had had the misfortune to lose my darkey who carried my haversack and blankets, but Captain Bowersock generously shared with me his rations, and, supper being over, we stretched ourselves on the ground with our feet to the fire, congratulating ourselves that we might rest for the remainder of the night. Our enemies had calculated otherwise, for, just as Morpheus was escorting us into the dim land of dreams, we were startled by the report of a cannon shot, and the whiz of a shell filled the air above our heads. This was followed by others in rapid succession, until the air seemed alive with screaming, screeching, exploding, deadly missiles. To spring to our feet, seize our arms and extinguish our fires, was but the work of a few seconds. All was confusion for a time, but, changing our position for another that seemed to promise security, we again lay down and rested unmolested till dawn.

Returning to the vicinity of Rossville, our former camp, we remained the greater part of the day, and being within a few miles of the battle, which opened early in the morning, we could hear the roar of cannon and the din of battle as it progressed. This was Saturday, September 19th, the first day of the conflict. None of us comprehended the extent of the engagement now pending, nor did we realize that the day and the morrow would be fraught with the mighty events that have since passed into history.

About dusk we received orders to march immediately, and, leaving our tents and personal effects in charge of a light guard, we were soon moving at a quick pace in the direction of Chickamauga Creek and the fatal field. At the distance of six miles we halted, and spent the night without fires, though the night was frosty and cold.

The sun had scarcely risen the next (Sunday) morning, when the opening roar of cannon to the southeast of us told that the bloody work of the day had begun. After a hurried breakfast we fell in line and advanced about two miles to the east, where we halted and threw out a line of pickets. As the day advanced the roar of cannon became incessant, and the noise of musketry was a deafening accompaniment. We could see the sulphur smoke of battle, and its locality indicated to us the position of the deadly combatants. We were all on the tip-toe of excitement; some seemed anxious to go forward and share in the struggle with the foe; others shrank and grew pale; but truth compels me to say that in the hours that followed, the timid and the bold fought with equal bravery.

About half past nine o'clock the bugle called us to arms, and we were hurried at double quick toward the scene of battle. Presently we came to where the dead and wounded lay scattered over the field, the surgeons busy attending to the latter. This was a trying moment, for, as we were hurried along, we crossed a level, open piece of ground, and the enemy appearing in the woods on our left, opened a deadly artillery fire upon us, and, strange as it may appear, our line crossed that space of several hundred yards and not a man was injured. Striking the timber again, we came very nearly entering the enemy's lines. General Steedman rode up, his horse covered with a heavy lather of sweat, and gave orders to file to the right. We hurried through a corn field and took our position in the timber. Stray balls were flying around with a continual spatter. In five minutes after coming to a halt we were ordered to charge up the rising ground in our front. Obeying, we met the flying remnant of a regiment of our troops, who were being swept by the enemy from the position to which we were advancing; but on we went, and, reaching the summit, we met the enemy in overwhelming numbers. Now came the tug of war. Grape, canister, shot, shell, and other death-dealing projectiles, made of our ranks a harvest of death, and in five minutes nearly one-fourth of our regiment was either killed or wounded. Utter destruction awaited us. We wavered, gave way, and fled down the hill in disorder. Reaching a somewhat sheltered position we halted, and, re-forming, lay down in line of battle. Shells and cannonballs were doing their deadly work, cutting trees and large branches which, in their fall, sent consternation and sometimes death into our ranks. One limb in its fall killed two men.

Our division was now occupying the brow of a hill, with orders to hold it to the very last moment. The men hugged the ground, loading and firing continually, each man as fast as he could. The deafening roar of musketry and the boom of cannon drowned, in a great measure, the shrieks of the wounded and dying. Every moment was heard the dull thud which told that another had been killed or wounded. A few yards to my right stood a man behind a tree a foot in diameter. He was loading and firing at will, intent on killing all he could. But the brave fellow's earthly career was cut short by a cannon ball which struck the tree four feet from the ground, cutting the tree off, and killing the man so suddenly that he never knew how he was struck.

We held our position till nearly sundown. Nearly half the men in our company and the regiment were killed, wounded or missing, and at each successive moment our ranks were melting under the terrific fire of death which continued to assail us. We had done all that brave men could do to hold our position, and further stay here seemed death to the remainder. At length an order was received to fall back, and the field with our gallant dead and wounded was left to the foe. After proceeding a short distance I turned aside in company with comrade Clark, of Company B, and, as we again turned to run and rejoin our retreating column, Clark was struck by a ball and

instantly killed. I caught him in my arms and laid him on the
ground, and, being unable to render him any assistance in his last
moments, except at the risk of my life, I again ran forward. As I
ran down the hill I came near to a poor fellow whose leg had just
been shot away midway between the knee and foot. He begged me
for God's sake to stop, and though the balls were flying thick and
fast, I could not refuse him. I tied up his leg as well as I could,
and, as I rose to run again, my canteen dropped to the ground.
Stooping to pick it up, I noticed that the strap was cut asunder by a
ball, and this made me decide to let the canteen take care of itself,
and hurried forward as fast as I could run.

Reaching the gulch at the foot of the hill, I discovered that our
forces had been re-enforced, or had been able to re-form, and were
now in position on the opposite side of the gulch, on the high
ground, and were opening fire on the advancing rebels. This placed
me under the fire of friend and foe, and doubled my danger.

Two others, left by their commands, were trying to find shelter behind a double tree which grew in the gulch. While I argued with
them that there was room for a third, one of them was shot through
the hips. I then concluded that I did not want the place, and at
once started down the gulch, hoping to reach a place of safety by
flanking friend and foe.

I plunged into the thick undergrowth, feeling that I had hopes of
escape, but I ran right into a regiment of Confederates lying concealed in the thick undergrowth. A half dozen muskets were pointed
at me, and I was ordered to surrender. I had no alternative to do
otherwise, and accepted the situation.

I saw that the regiment or brigade into whose midst I had run was
bent on some particular object, for they were creeping along cautiously,
and lying close to the ground. I asked my captors if I might stand
behind a tree, which would shelter me from the fire of our own troops,
being a prisoner, I did not wish to be killed by my friends. To this
they consented, and for a brief time a friendly oak protected me.
The balls from our troops were flying dangerously near, and the
dead and wounded of both armies were to be seen all around me.
At length there came a momentary lull in the firing, but this was
followed by a storm of shot, shell and musketry poured into the ranks
of the rebels by the Union troops, almost annihilating them. They
fell back, leaving large numbers of their dead and wounded, and
also leaving me behind the tree to care for myself. I hesitated how
to proceed, but concluded to pursue my flight down the gulch in the
bare hope of finding an open space through which I might escape
the foe and rejoin my retreating friends. I had proceeded but a short
distance when I ran into a second line of the enemy, and was again
a prisoner. It was now sundown, and the work of that bloody Sabbath was drawing to a close; the fighting ceased to be general, and
the enemy at once took the best means of securing the hard-earned
fruits of the day's conflict. I was hurried to the rear and joined to
a squad of near two hundred other prisoners, and as night came on,

we remained on the field under a strong guard. I dare not recall the feelings that robbed me of slumber during that long night. I would not recall them if I could. One of the most painful recollections of one who has gone through a battle, is that of the friends lying wounded and dying, and who need that help which he is utterly unable to give. I suffered this and much more, for, as the weary hours wore away, the pangs of defeat and the consciousness that we had fallen into the hands of a merciless enemy, added to the terror of our situation.

The next morning most of the Union prisoners who were not wounded, were set to the work of caring for the wounded Union troops, who, being unable to leave the field, had fallen into the hands of the rebels. Nearly all the wounded of both armies were yet on the field, and in general, uncared for. There was a vast number of each class, and the work of collecting them together and giving the necessary attention to each man, was a task a hundred fold greater than could be performed. This was Monday morning, and the battle had raged for the two days before, over an area of field and woods of several miles in extent. We prisoners were permitted to care for our wounded as best we could, but the most we could do for them was to bring them water and give them such acts of attention as our limited means afforded. Hundreds died, who, with proper medical attention in time, might have lived and recovered. It is probably due to our foes to say that their time was fully employed in the care of their own wounded, and that the inattention given to ours, was a necessity, and beyond their control. We collected fifty or more of our comrades together, and placed them in an old house and shed adjoining. This house, and its surroundings, showed many evidences of the conflict, as several holes were to be seen in it which had been made by cannon balls. It stood in what had been a cornfield, but the fences and the crop and nearly everything but the naked house and the ground on which it stood, had been swept away by the battle.

Besides this house, there were numbers of other places on various parts of the field of battle where our wounded were collected and cared for by the well prisoners, if such attention as we were able to give them, might be called care and attention. By Tuesday, after Sunday's battle, we had many more wounded on our hands than we could possibly attend to, yet many perished for lack of attention. The rebels were still busy attending *their* wounded and burying *their* dead ; our dead being as yet unburied, the work of decay had set in and the stench produced thereby was insufferable. This state of affairs made the condition of our unfortunate comrades the more deplorable, for to be compelled to inhale the tainted atmosphere was, of itself, horrible.

The family who owned the house we were occupying, and who had been driven from it by the battle, returned on Tuesday following the battle. Everything of a personal character, except the house, had been destroyed or swept away by the contending armies, and the situation upon the return of the family was anything but inviting and agreeable. The old lady, a tall, angular woman, with a Roman nose and dark penetrating eye, was fired with malicious rage towards the Yankees. Coming into the house and finding the floor covered with the suffering wounded, she gave vent to her feelings in a tirade which I shall never wish to hear repeated, and which I can never forget. "Oh, you wretches," said she, "I am glad to hear you groan. If I durst, I would set fire to the house and burn it over your heads." And I think she would have done so, but for fear of the guards, who, I must say, treated us kindly. A brave soldier, let him fight on whatever side he may, is always magnanimous and merciful to his captive. It is the dastard and coward who uses this opportunity to inflict upon his helpless captive a humiliation or insult.

On Wednesday, September 23d, I got permission to go over that part of the battlefield on which the 113th had fought on Sunday afternoon, thinking I might find some of my comrades of the regiment who were yet alive, and to whom I might be of some service. I found every bush and tree bearing the marks of the conflict; every object was marked with grape, cannon and rifle balls; even the small twigs had been cut down, and the forest appeared as though a mighty whirlwind had swept through it. I counted on one tree the marks of forty shots, and the wonder is that any man could stand in such a place and live for a moment.

I found our dead here and there, lying where they fell—sometimes singly, sometimes in groups, all unburied. I recognized the faces of a number of the 113th, among the dead; many of the wounded were yet alive, but all I could do for the poor fellows was to give them a drink of water. Captain Joshua M. Wells, Company C, 113th O. V. I., was still alive, having been shot through the left lung. He was fully conscious, and expressed hopes of recovery. Giving what attention I could, I returned to our hospital at the old house, and giving an old man two dollars, I had the Captain brought in and placed where I could give him attention. Here I gave him all possible care, but under the circumstances very little extra care could be bestowed upon a single one.

Captain Wells lived till the following Sunday, September 27th, and met death like a heroic Christian soldier. While I attended him, he expressed a great desire that his body should be sent home to his family at Columbus, O., in case of his death. I assured him it should be done if possible, but I felt utterly powerless to do so. The Captain's body was laid in a grave prepared by my hands; I also marked his grave by a headboard, cutting thereon his name, company and regiment. I afterwards wrote to his widow, giving her an account of the incidents of his closing hours, and of the sad rites I had performed. Some months later, when the Federal troops obtained possession of the battlefield, the body was exhumed and sent home in a good state of preservation.

For a week following the Captain's death we remained in this place, continually burdened with the care of the wounded and the burial of the dead. Up to this time, fourteen days after the conflict, the dead

J. N. HALL.

were not all buried, and the stench arising from the decaying bodies, surpassed all description, and I am inclined to think caused the speedy death of many of our wounded.

An exchange of wounded prisoners on both sides, was now effected by, and between General Rosecrans and General Bragg. We prisoners who had remained thus in care of the sick, had allowed ourselves to hope that we would be included in the exchange; but we were doomed to disappointment, for, on the day following, we were mustered into line, our name, company and regiment listed, and we were marched to a station on the railroad between Chattanooga and Ringgold, where we were loaded in box cars, a hundred men to each car, and sent south to Atlanta. Remaining two days at Atlanta, we were again loaded on a train and sent to Richmond, Va., arriving at our destination about the 10th or 12th of October, 1863.

None of us had believed that our imprisonment would last but a few days, and had expected nearly every day before leaving northern Georgia, to be exchanged and returned to our commands. Upon arriving at Richmond, we were marched across two long bridges, which span the James river, below the falls, and thence down a street running parallel with the river, and thence into the famous building known as Libby.

Libby stood on the bank of the James. It was a long, brick building, with basement and two stories, and had probably been used as a wholesale tobacco house. The long way of the building was up and down the river, or, in other words, the building stood with its side to the river. On its end front was the sign "Libby & Son." Nearly four hundred of us were quartered on the lower floor of this building on our arrival, and the same evening we had issued to us, a small piece of brown bread and a half pint of thin soup to each man—not half enough to satisfy our appetites. Piling ourselves upon the hard floor, we rested well for the night, for the journey of several hundred miles had been one of fatigue and unrest.

Next morning the prison was visited by two Confederate officials, accompanied by half a dozen guards, and the work of robbing the prisoners of their money in a business-like manner began. We were told to surrender our money to the officers for safe keeping; that an account of it would be kept for us and the amount returned to us whenever we left the prison. We were also told that those who refused to surrender their money voluntarily, would be searched, and all money thus found would not be returned. Having thirty-three dollars, I thought I would divide with them; so pulling off my boot, I secreted twenty dollars therein. When my turn came to "stand and deliver," I handed over thirteen dollars, and all was satisfactory. One of my fellow prisoners had four hundred dollars in gold, all of which he handed over to these robbers. Nearly every one of us had more or less money, and by the time they were through taking care of it for us, they had a considerable pile of greenbacks, and they seemed thoroughly satisfied with the amount realized, for not a man was searched, and the few who had the good sense to keep their money, saved it all. Not a cent of this money was ever returned, nor was there any intention of returning it when it was taken. It was a cowardly, heartless theft. The second day we received our rations in kind and quantity like the first, but as before, the quantity was far short of our necessities, and after eating the whole quantity, we were almost as hungry as before.

The next day we were marched out of Libby and put into another prison known as "Pemberton's Building." This prison stood further east than Libby, and on the opposite side of the street. It was a large three story brick, with a cellar the full size of the foundation; a brick partition divided it into two nearly equal apartments. Before we were put into this prison, it was already full of prisoners, but we were crowded in among the rest, and now it was with great difficulty that we could find room to lie down. I, with others of my comrades, found a place on the third floor. The men on each floor drew their rations separately, and according to the number of men on each. One of our number was appointed to receive the rations for all the men on one floor, after which a sub-division was made to squads of twenty-five men, and then these twenty-five would sub-divide, giving to each man his portion with exactness, for even a crumb is a matter of contention among starving men. Our rations were cooked and prepared for us in the basement of Libby prison, and each day a certain number of men were detailed from each floor to go after them. Our rations now consisted of a very small piece of old bacon, boiled, a half pint of thin soup made of the water in which the bacon was boiled, a small piece of bread. This was not sufficient for one good meal a day, and our hunger was never satisfied. As soon as our food, which was intended for three meals, was issued to us, we ate it all in one, and then hungered till the same hour the next day. I have been so hungry that when I got my soup, thickened with skippers which came out of the meat in boiling, that I never pretended to separate the skippers from the soup, but greedily swallowed skippers and soup together, and thought it excellent. We all did the same in this respect. Every atom of food was precious in our eyes, and being continually hungry, our minds and conversation dwelt upon things we wished to eat. It appeared to us that if we could only have had enough to eat, that notwithstanding our loathsome confinement, we would have been the happiest creatures alive.

Nearly every day flying reports of an exchange were circulating among the prisoners, and our hopes were alternately buoyed and depressed by these groundless reports, originating—nobody knew where; and yet for all this, they served to keep us hopeful. But as day after day passed and no exchange came, I began to despair of being speedily exchanged, and began to look about and devise means and mature plans of escape. These thoughts I kept to myself, but it was several days before I struck a plan that was at all practical.

There was quite a trade, in a small way, kept up between the prisoners on the inside and the guards on the outside of the building. This was in violation of orders, and whatever was done in this line must be done with the utmost caution. I had already made several little trades with one of the guards, resulting in quite an intimate acquaintance, and the thought suggested itself that if I could induce this guard to sell me a Confederate uniform, I might by this means effect my escape. I approached the guard very cautiously at first, telling him that my clothes were about gone, and that I did not know what I would do for more, and finally ventured to ask him how much he would charge me for a pair of gray pants and a roundabout. At first he was disinclined to sell this kind of goods, fearing that by some means it might be found out, and he made to suffer. He made many excuses, saying he did not know where he could get them for me. I assured him that there would be no danger, and promised him eternal secrecy. At last he agreed that for ten dollars in greenbacks he would bring me the required articles when he came on guard again that night at one o'clock. I returned to my place on the floor and waited with impatience for the intervening hours to wear away. I feared to lie down, knowing that if I fell asleep I might miss my appointment with the guard.

At last I heard the guards sing out their accustomed cry. "Twelve o'clock and all's well." One more hour to wait and then I should know of my success or failure. That hour seemed almost an age, but at length came the cry, "One o'clock and all's well." I waited a few minutes and then crept cautiously down stairs to the window near which the guard was stationed. I found him all right, and told him in a low whisper to pass the clothes to me through the iron bars of the window, and I would pass the money to him in the same manner. The exchange was quickly made, and I hurried back up stairs to my sleeping companions. After roll call next morning, I put on my suit of gray and began to plan for the future. I have before stated that we procured our rations ready cooked in the basement of Libby prison across the street, and at some distance westward. When the time came to draw our rations, I contrived to be detailed for that purpose, and picking up a wooden bucket, I fell in line with the rest. A guard was always on duty to prevent any attempt to escape, and therefore my chances were desperate, but it could be no worse if I failed. Generally when the cook house was reached, we had to wait sometime before receiving our rations, and at these times the guards and prisoners were apt to be engaged in little trades of various kinds, and the guards were likely, on such occasions, to relax their watchfulness. It was at such a time as this, that I hoped to find a chance to escape. Watching my opportunity while the attention of the guard was drawn on some little trade, and at the same time watching for the Confederate officers, I handed my bucket to a companion with a sly nudge and look which meant silence, I slipped out of the ranks. I did not attempt to leave immediately, but stood around with some Confederate soldiers who were off of duty, and who were watching the prisoners out of curiosity. I asked one of the bystanders how long since these fellows had been captured, and made some further remark about threshing the Yankees. When the squad began drawing their rations, I sauntered slowly and carelessly up the street, passing "Castle Thunder" on my way. This building stood on the same side of the street as Libby, and two hundred yards or more further west, and not far from the river. It was a three story brick building, and was now filled with Confederate soldiers, probably deserters and those who refused to enter the rebel ranks. Being dressed in all respects as a rebel soldier, I did not attract any particular attention. As I passed on I met numbers of officers and soldiers, greeting them with the true military salute. I wandered towards the upper part of the city, intending to get out of town in the dusk of the evening. I was fearful of pursuit, for I did not know how soon I would be missed from the prison. I was risking all on one desperate chance of escape, and was, therefore, in no frame of mind to enjoy the sights of that part of Richmond through which I was passing. I stopped at a small provision store kept by an Irish woman in the suburbs of the city. I bought two dollars worth of cheese and crackers, paying for the same in Confederate money, and got about enough for a full meal. I would have eaten it all on the spot, but was fearful of exciting the curiosity of the old woman by eating too greedily.

As the sun began to sink behind the western hills, I walked out of the city, but it was dusk before I had passed beyond the last houses of the outskirts; indeed it seemed to me that the houses of the city reached a great way into the country, and every moment I feared I might meet some one who would inquire where I was from and where I was going. These were two questions which I prefered not to answer. Fortunately I saw no one who was inclined to be inquisitive.

As soon as darkness set in I left the gravel turnpike and struck out into the fields on my right. I was entirely ignorant of the country, but I knew I could not remain in or near the city long undiscovered, and I must go somewhere. The night being cold and chilly, I had to keep continually on the move to keep from suffering with cold. If I had desired to start a fire, I had no means to do so, therefore exercise was a necessity. I stumbled into ditches, scratched my face and hands with brambles, crossed fences and kept floundering along without any definite knowledge as to where I was going, but my plan was to pursue a northwesterly course from Richmond. I somehow thought this route would be clearest of enemies, and that I might be fortunate enough to slip through the lines of the enemy and get into our own lines and be safe.

A short time before daylight I entered a heavy forest, and as day began to break, I sat down, for, by this time, I was well nigh exhausted. I now ate what little food I had and waited for the sun to rise, that by that means I might be able to shape my course. I was now far out of sight of the city, and sincerely hoped I might always remain so.

As the sun came up I shaped my course and moved ahead through the woods, moving slowly and cautiously; in fact I could not have hurried if I had desired to do so. About ten o'clock I emerged from the woods onto a plantation. I could see the mansion of the planter about a mile to the right, and a little to the left of the mansion and several hundred yards distant, were the quarters of the slaves. The day was pleasant, it being the time of year when the nights are cold and the days pleasant.

Lying down behind a log, I was soon sound asleep. As near as I could judge, I slept till about two o'clock in the afternoon, when I was awakened by the barking of a dog. I aroused myself in some alarm, and looking around I saw a fierce looking canine within a few yards of me, barking savagely as though he had found something. Rubbing my eyes, I peered about that I might be able to see the dog's master, and saw an old gray haired negro with an ax on his shoulder, and a heavy piece of a dogwood sapling under his arm. He spoke to the dog to be still, and eyed me with a half-frightened look. In a moment I saw that concealment was out of the question, and the best thing I could do would be to make friends with my sable visitor. The old man seemed very shy, but I spoke kindly to him, called him uncle, and told him that being exceedingly tired, I had lain down to rest and had fallen asleep. He told me he was the slave of Major Brown, and that his master was in the army, as was also a younger son of his master, but that there was one of the sons at home. He asked me if I was not a soldier, too. I admitted that I was. He said he had heard that the Yankees were a very bad kind of men, and that they would coax the poor black man from home and then roast and eat him. I told him that I had no doubt but that many of them were very bad people. He told me the distance to Richmond was eleven miles, and that there was a camp of troops some seven or eight miles west of us. I told him I wanted to go home to see my mother, and that if these soldiers or any one else knew I was here, they would not let me go, and that he must tell no one of having seen me. I told him then that he had better go home and that I would lie down and rest a while longer. As soon as he was out of sight, I thought it unsafe to remain here longer, so I hurried away, keeping in the skirts of the woods next to the plantation on my left.

Further on I reached a road running westward, and followed it for half a mile or more, but becoming fearful of meeting Confederate soldiers, or of being seen by them, I struck off into the woods on my right, as the safest plan to escape observation. Traveling till near sundown, I came out into the open country again. The country through which I had traveled during the day was rough, hilly and broken, but now I found myself on the edge of what appeared to be a highly cultivated valley, with mansions and negro quarters stretching out before me as far as the eye could reach. I was now nearly exhausted from hunger and fatigue, and lying down, I rested till after dark, determined on procuring something to eat, by some means, at any risk. Before night came on, I had observed some negro huts in the distance, and to these I made my way, urged on by a gnawing hunger which grew keener with each passing moment.

I went first to a shanty where I could see glimmerings of light through the cracks and crevices in the wall, but upon approaching nearer, the noise of laughter and confusion from within made me hesitate to enter, and I determined to call at one or more of the other shanties near by; but at these there was no response to my knock, and I was compelled to return to the first. The hungry voice within would not be hushed, and prudence having surrendered to necessity, I could only make known my desperate condition and take the consequences. I knocked boldly at the door. The noise within at once ceased, and the door was opened by a burly darkey, who, upon seeing me, started back in some trepidation. At a glance I saw within a number of negro women, young girls and children, besides four negro men, but last and worst, there were four rebel soldiers in the party. Retreat was not to be thought of. I therefore walked boldly in without showing the fear that I felt. The soldiers were considerably startled at the situation, and I think they took me to be one of their men bent on the arrest of their party. Comprehending what might be passing through their minds, I concluded the best thing to do was to play a bold hand, so I remarked to them that we had caught each other this time, but it would never do for one soldier to blow on another.

It was but a short time till things were again moving on as usual, yet I could see that I was the object of suspicion, and the soldiers kept an eye on me, which showed a lack of confidence. Before my arrival one of the negroes had been playing the fiddle and the soldiers and wenches had been dancing, but my coming had dampened the enjoyment of the hour.

I asked one of the women for something to eat, and showed her a bone ring which I had made while in prison, promising it to her if she would get me what I wanted to eat. She set before me a good sized piece of corn bread and a small piece of bacon, which I ate with great relish, thinking it as palatable a mess as I had ever eaten.

I intended as soon as I finished eating to step quietly out of the house and make my escape; but fate had decided otherwise, for, just as I swallowed the last mouthful, there came a loud knock at the door, and, before anyone from within could open the door, it was flung open from without, and in stepped a Confederate sergeant, followed by eight soldiers with fixed bayonets. There was no chance of escape, for the only door to the room was guarded by two of the soldiers. The squad proceeded to arrest the four rebel soldiers and myself.

The negroes were kicked and cuffed shamefully, while we were threatened with severe punishment when we reached camp. The four Confederates arrested with me were known to the sergeant and his party, and I soon learned from their conversation that they had evaded duty and absented themselves from camp early in the morning. I was the extra man unaccounted for. The sergeant asked me what regiment I belonged to, and, knowing that it would be useless to tell anything but the truth, I told him I was a member of Company E, 113th O. V. I. He did not at once comprehend, and said that he knew of no such regiment about there. I did not feel inclined to enlighten him further just then, knowing that all I could say would do no good. The five of us were securely bound together, while the negroes were ordered to their respective quarters, a command they obeyed with alacrity. We were now marched off in single file in the direction of the rebel camp, which I think was about three miles distant from the place of our capture. We reached camp about one o'clock A. M., and spent the remainder of the night in a guard house, closely guarded.

When daylight appeared I had an opportunity of looking about me and of becoming acquainted with my surroundings. The camp was situated in a grove of small timber, and the troops numbered, perhaps, three regiments. I learned from my fellow prisoners that these troops were stationed here for the purpose of caring for and feeding up a lot of cavalry horses.

About seven o'clock we were furnished with a light breakfast, consisting of corn bread and beef, after which we were ordered out under a guard to perform fatigue duty. I told the sergeant who had charge of the guards over us that, as I did not belong to that command, it was unjust to compel me to do such duty. I was fearful that if I waited to be found out by force of circumstances I might be taken for a spy, in which case my punishment would be death. I told the sergeant to request his captain to come and see me, as I had something of importance about which I wished to speak. The captain, a tall, well made man, with black whiskers, made his appearance, and desired to know why I wanted to see him. I told the story of my escape and recapture, withholding nothing. He seemed much surprised, and, promising to report my case to the colonel in command, went away. After a time two guards came and conducted me before the colonel.

There were several officers present when I was taken into the presence of the colonel, all of whom looked upon me with doubt and suspicion. The colonel questioned me very closely as to how I made my escape, where I had at first been taken, and many other questions which I do not recall, all of which I answered truthfully. After this I was returned to the guard house. I felt ill at ease, for, though I had told a straight and truthful story, I could see that I was not more than half believed. About two o'clock that afternoon a lieutenant came to the guard house and told me that they had concluded to send me to Richmond, and if I had not told the truth I would have a quick passage to the other world. This gave me relief, for at Richmond I felt confident I could establish the truthfulness of my story and my innocence in being a spy. The lieutenant and two guards then started with me to Richmond. We were all mounted on mules, I riding beside the lieutenant and the two guards in our rear. We soon became somewhat acquainted, and fell into a lively conversation on the topics of the war, North and South. I told him of my services as a soldier, and of being captured, and many other incidents, in all of which he seemed interested. He, in turn, recounted some of his experience in the C. S. A., and our talk became animated and pleasant, both of us wishing the war at an end, so we could be at our respective homes—he in North Carolina and I in Ohio.

It began to grow dark before we reached the city; I was taken before the military officer in command of the city, and from there was taken to the city jail, into which I was thrust. The cell was dark, damp and loathsome. Here I spent the night, supperless. Next morning I was given a light breakfast of corn bread and soup, after which I was taken out and conducted under guard to the office of the commanding general. Here I was closely questioned in the presence of several officers in regard to the plan and means of escape, and here, as before, I told a plain and truthful tale, knowing that the truth would serve me better than a lie. The general asked me if I could name anyone in the prison by whom I could establish my identity. I mentioned the names of Ed. Wright and Thomas Hinton. They were sent for and confronted me. They were much surprised at seeing me, as well as being thus called from the prison in this manner, for what purpose they knew not.

These two men were questioned separately and very closely, and their statements regarding me coincided so completely that all present were fully convinced that I had told a true story. The general lectured me soundly for my ingratitude in trying to escape from such kind friends, and said that, as a punishment, I should be sent to the dungeon for twenty-four hours.

I was accordingly taken to the city prison, and thrust into an underground cell with an iron door. The cell was musty and without ventilation; the air was damp and stifling. In a corner was an old straw mattress, falling to pieces with age and filth. As soon as the guard had closed and locked the massive iron door, the intense darkness of the cell became oppressive beyond description. Not the faintest gleam of light could find its way into this abode of inky darkness. The darkest night was as brilliant sunshine compared with this dungeon. The thought of remaining here twenty-four hours was tormenting, and the fear that I might be forgotten entirely, and left to die a dreadful death of hunger and thirst, filled my mind with frightful fancies. None but those who have passed through a similar experience can have the least idea of, the tormenting doubts which assail a person in the position I then was. Hour after hour dragged slowly away. I became feverish and desperately thirsty; my only thought now was water. If I only could have one good drink of water I thought I could endure my situation in comfort.

At length, worn out with my own thoughts, I cast myself upon that couch of filth, and thought to wear away a part of my sentence in sleep. A restless sleep at length came over me, in which I dreamed of running streams of limpid water, at which I was drinking but could not slake my thirst. I awoke from my feverish sleep with a dull, heavy pain in my head, and with my thirst more tormenting than before. I was now really sick. I could not tell how long I had been in this horrible place, but short as the time really was it seemed to me almost an age. At length I heard the rattle of keys in the door. It was flung open, and there stood the guard and the turnkey of the prison to conduct me beyond these hated walls. Staggering to my feet, I was soon in the upper daylight, and was breathing the pure, invigorating air of heaven. It was some time before I could accustom my eyes to the glare of the sun. There was plenty of water in the prison yard, of which I drank and bathed my face, feeling much refreshed. I was then conducted by two guards to my old prison, and was again locked within its walls. Those who knew me in the prison crowded around me, asking a thousand questions; I promised to tell them all at a future time, but for the present I needed rest. I went up stairs to my old place and lay down. Some of the prisoners gave me something to eat, and I fell asleep and slept till next morning. I awoke feeling much refreshed, and though my trip to the country had not resulted as I desired, I felt that I had had some valuable experience.

Time now moved on without incident for some days. Our rations were barely sufficient to sustain life, but never enough to appease our hunger. Such of us as had money, or some other means of traffic, could sometimes effect a trade with the guards, and thereby procure a little extra to eat. At length, as if by accident, we found in one part of the prison, securely locked from our reach, a quantity of wheat bran, which could be reached by tying a tin cup to a long stick and fishing it to within our reach. By stealing this bran we were able to make mush by boiling the bran in our little tin buckets, but, lacking salt, our mush was very unpalatable. I have heretofore stated that the building had a brick wall passing up through the center. There were prisoners on both sides, but they were kept separate and not allowed to communicate with one another; but by drilling holes through the brick walls this restriction was avoided and friendly relations established.

We now ascertained that those in the other department had plenty of salt, an article of which we on our side were sadly in need, and by increasing the size of the holes in the wall to admit a spoon we were able to transport a spoonful of salt at a time, a circumstance that added much to our comfort, and traffic in salt grew active. Finally it leaked out that the salt we were buying from our fellow prisoners was found in quantity in a room of the basement on their part of the building. This induced us to prospect under our part of the building. Back next the water closet was a small passage or entry. With the aid of a hatchet which had been smuggled into the prison, we tore up the floor of this entry and sent a man below to explore. He soon returned with the news that the cellar under our part of the building was a big strike—a regular bonanza. A doorkeeper was appointed, secrecy was enjoined on all, and the utmost caution was used to prevent our good news from spreading to the authorities. Only a few were permitted to go down for sugar at a time. The men would take off their worn and dirty drawers, tie the ankles in a knot, and watch patiently for a turn to descend into the cellar for sugar. Then, filling these lousy, filthy garments with sugar, would return to their places. Every available article that would hold sugar was brought into use. Needles and thread were found and sacks made out of everything possible, and these filled till every man on our side of the house was plentifully supplied and had sugar to sell. On the other side they had plenty of salt, but no sugar; on our side there was a glut of sugar and a demand for salt. A brisk trade ensued in these two commodities and was carried on by way of the holes in the wall before mentioned.

The sugar and salt added much to our comfort; the sugar served to deaden our appetites and also to sweeten our bran mush; while the salt added made it quite palatable. The routine of prison duties were somewhat ofter the following order: The first thing after getting up of a morning was lousing, that is, we would pull off our clothing, give them a careful inspection and kill all the lice we could find. These were not a few; I think that on the average each man would kill from three hundred to four hundred of these parasites each day, and by the next morning there would be as many more to share the same fate. After "lousing" came roll-call and after roll-call we could steal sugar and trade with our friends for salt, or occupy our time in some other way. From one till two in the afternoon was our time to draw rations, but no more of our number were allowed to go out in a Confederate uniform as I had done. We ate our dinner about three o'clock in the afternoon; then we would sit around and talk of home, or of an exchange, or of what grand dinners we would have when we get out of prison. We usually lay down in our sleeping places as soon as dark came on, for, being without fire or lights, we kept early hours. A rule had been established among us that no one should go down for sugar except in the night, for there was danger of being discovered in the day-time.

The prison was so crowded that when the men all lay down the floor space was entirely occupied, and this led to more or less trouble between the occupants of the lower floor and those of the second and third floors. Those of the first or lower floor claimed a sort of monopoly in the sugar trade, and finally became so arrogant as to say that we from the second and third floors had no right to come down during the night to get sugar, and they would suffer it no longer.

The feeling increased from day to day and many personal encounters ensued between the monopolists on the lower floor and the occupants of the other two floors. Open rupture threatened, and my partner and I, seeing the storm coming in the distance, managed to accumulate a stock of sugar ahead, for under the heated animosity existing among the men, our sugar plot would soon be made known to our captors.

About the end of the third week following the discovery of our sugar mine, the crisis was reached. The men of the two upper floors said, with emphatic profanity, that they would go down in the night and get what sugar they wanted; and those of the first floor declared with equal emphasis that they would not suffer their dominions to be invaded and their dreams disturbed by intruders. So when night came on the occupants from above went below as they had promised to do, and during the whole night there was nothing but fighting and quarreling. Those from above filled their haversacks, drawers, and the like with sugar, and in attempting to return to their places they were set upon by the others, who attempted to rob them of their sugar, or, failing in this, they would rip open the sacks and other things used in carrying the sugar, and the contents were scattered on the floor.

This state of things lasted all night, and resulted in the unnecessary destruction of hundreds of pounds of sugar, so that in the morning the floor where the scene had occurred was covered with a coat of sticky taffy, the heat of the room having reduced the sugar to a half-melted state, so that in walking over the floor one's feet would stick at every step. Further concealment was now out of the question, and from the condition of affairs we felt satisfied we would have to face the music. We had now killed the goose that laid the sweet egg. It is unaccountably strange to see how very foolish men act at times, but it has been so and will so remain.

When the Confederate officers came in next forenoon to call the roll, as was their custom, they at once discovered that something unusual had occurred; their feet would stick to the floor, and they soon made the discovery that we had been stealing their sugar. A rumor ran through the prison that all of us were now to be searched, and such as were found with sugar in their possession would be tied up by the thumbs as a punishment, but these reports proved to have no foundation in fact. No one was searched nor punished, and those who had sugar were permitted to keep it. The Confederates estimated that they lost $20,000 worth of sugar and salt, but I am inclined to think that the real loss would not reach over $6,000.

The basement of our prison was emptied of these articles the same day of this discovery, and the immediate result to us was that both rose rapidly in value, the demand exceeding the supply. Sugar which could be had for nothing yesterday, is to-day worth $2.50 per pint; salt rose proportionately.

Our rations were now cut down for a week as a punishment, and as a consequence we suffered much. Day succeeded day and one week wore into another without much note until about the first of December, when we were taken out of this prison and transferred to Danville, Va., about one hundred and fifty miles southwest of Richmond and about four miles from the North Carolina line. Danville is a place of 3,000 or 4,000 inhabitants, situated on the Dan River. The Dan River Canal and the railroad leading to Richmond run through the city. Several thousand of the prisoners at Richmond were at this time, December, 1863, moved to Danville. We were quartered in large brick buildings which before the war had probably been used as tobacco warehouses. These buildings were numbered from one to six, and situated in various sections of the city.

I was put in No. 4, a large brick building covered with a tin roof. Most of these prisons were covered in the same manner. I occupied, with many others, the lower floor. On the south side of our prison was a tier of small rooms which may have been used as offices in times of peace. In one of these little rooms I and four comrades were quartered, there being two floors above us, and each filled to its utmost capacity.

At the west end of this building was a stockade inclosing the end of the prison, and here was the privy and a well of water. A strong guard was placed on the outside of the prison, but there were no guards on the inside, therefore we had the freedom of the space where the well of water was. Our rations at Danville were more than they had been at Richmond, and we all felt benefited by the change, but withal we drew only enough for an ordinary meal, and this was insufficient to satisfy the cravings of our appetites. The guards here were less vigilant than those who had guarded us at Richmond.

Prisoners confined as we were are ever restless and uneasy, planning some scheme to deceive their guards or plotting at some means to escape. Every day there were rumors of an exchange of prisoners, and we were always making calculations on being exchanged within a month's time. Many of the boys spent much of the time in making trinkets which they sold to the guards. These consisted of finger rings, tooth-picks, and breast pins, made of bone or gutta percha. By this means something to eat was purchased.

After we had been at Danville a week the occupants of our room tore up the floor and found that it was about four feet above the level ground. Here we found pieces of plank, scraps of iron and tin and a few nails, which had been used in the construction of the building.

We determined to keep this matter to ourselves, and the five of us at once began to plan to escape by tunneling out. The foundation of our prison was of stone, and was sunk eighteen inches below the surface. Along the south side of the prison ran a wide street, and on the opposite side was a dwelling house, with garden attached. We calculated that the street was sixty feet wide, and that the whole distance we would have to tunnel would be seventy-five feet. We possessed ourselves of an old hatchet and with what we had we at once began operations. Besides the hatchet we had two or three case knives and some scraps of iron. Nine o'clock in the morning was the time for roll call, at which time we would be in our places, and the planks down. We made our bed over the loose planks, and our blankets were so spread as to conceal any defects in the floor. While two of us went below to work a strict watch was kept above to prevent surprise and discovery.

With the utmost diligence very little progress could be made. We were compelled to dig down under and below the foundation before we could make a start at tunneling, but by the end of a week we had made a fair beginning. We concluded to lighten the labor by taking others into the secret; and accordingly four others, in whom we had the utmost confidence, were initiated into the plot and made acquainted with our plans and purposes. We toiled day after day nearing the accomplishment of a project, which, if successful, would be life and liberty. We never went below to work till after roll call in the morning. This we considered the safer plan, for we knew not what minute they might come in upon us. By the end of the second week our numbers had grown to fifteen, as each of our original number had his particular friend whom he wished to favor, and every day an additional man was let into the secret. As soon as roll call was over in the morning two of our number would go down and work for an hour, while one, pretending to be sick, would spread his blankets on that part of the floor through which we went down, thus guarding against interruption and discovery. When the hour was up two others would go below and take the places of the first two, and thus the work went on till dark, when it was suspended till the next day. We managed to make our exchanges so as not to attract the attention of the other prisoners, for to have made known our aim and object to all the prisoners, would have insured its failure. In making the tunnel one of our number would creep into the excavation, dig the dirt and fill it into a flour sack, which had come into our possession. This sack had attached to it two ropes, by means of which it was worked to and fro. When the sack was full it was pulled backward and its contents emptied out under the prison floor. It was then pulled back and refilled. In this way we worked till days grew into weeks, and six weeks had elapsed since we started our tunnel. We had made our way under the very feet of our guards, and passed under one of the busy streets of the city. Wagons and carts and throngs of people passed over our heads, but heeding not their din we bent every effort to one coveted end.

We were rapidly approaching a completion of our work, and all were in the best of spirits. A few more days and we would be able to go out whenever we considered the opportunity favorable. The number interested in the tunnel had now increased to near sixty. Just how so many came to be let into the scheme I never could well tell. By a careful measurement the tunnel was one hundred and twelve feet long, and we felt confident that we were far enough into the garden to insure our escape if the nights were dark, but unluckily for us the moon just at this time was full, and we were compelled to delay our final effort to escape until the dark of the moon. We, however, made all the necessary preparations so as to be fully ready when the time should arrive. Each day some of our number would go down into the tunnel to work a little and see that all was right. All our plans were discussed and to-morrow night was fixed upon as the time for our escape. We had barely finished laying our plans when a squad of soldiers led by a lieutenant came into the building and ordered us to pack our effects and move to the upper floors. This was as a clap of thunder in a clear sky to all who were interested in the tunnel. It dawned upon us in a moment that we had been betrayed, but by whom we could not tell. We were all crowded up on the second and third floors, and then our captors began walking around on the first floor in order to discover any loose planks. When they reached the little room we had occupied they found what they very probably already knew to be there, namely, the loose plank which we had used as a doorway to our work. Then followed some bitter and loud profanity. They then procured a light, and, going below, explored our work from end to end to their entire satisfaction. A squad of negroes were then brought, and put to work filling up the tunnel. From a window in the upper story we watched them, as they followed our subterranean channel across the street and into the garden where it terminated. We could see that we had gone a sufficient distance into the garden to have made our escape, and would certainly have done so but for the base treachery of some one. The tunnel was now filled with stone, and then covered with dirt. A guard was now placed on the first floor, and the prisoners were all kept on the second and third floors. This made us so crowded that it was with great difficulty we found space to lie down. No more of us were allowed to remain on the first floor, but ten were allowed to go down at a time, under guard, to get water and for other necessary purposes, and when these ten returned another ten were allowed to go in the same manner, and this going by tens was kept up day and night, the prisoners being required to fall in line and await their turns. In addition to the guard kept on the first floor, there was also one stationed in the little back yard where the well of water was situated; and, besides these, there was a strong guard at regular intervals around the prison building. Escape seemed next to, if not absolutely impossible, but prisoners confined as we were are ever restless, and ready at all times to resort to desperate means to gain their freedom.

About three weeks after the discovery of our tunnel, ten prisoners went below at night in the usual manner to procure water. When they reached the back yard, which I have before described, one of them approached the guard and asked him if he wanted to trade for a gutta percha finger ring. (The guards were always on the trade when they had the opportunity.) The guard replied that he did not know, and wanted to see the ring. While the guard was looking at the ring and dickering about the price, a prisoner approached him from bedind and dealt him a heavy blow on the head, felling him to the ground. Another prisoner had stationed himself near a small gateway, which had formerly been used as a passage way in and out, but which of late had been securely barred by heavy oak planks nailed cross-wise. As soon as the guard was knocked down, the prisoner at the gate began to knock off these plank, using for the purpose an old ax with which he had provided himself before coming down stairs.

The result was that ten made their escape through the guards no the outside of the prison. The guard who was knocked down began screaming as if suffering from a horrible night-mare, and the guard on the lower floor of the prison was so shocked with fear that more than fifty of us prisoners, rushing down stairs, passed by him without opposition. We surmised that a break for liberty was being made, and we all rushed for the place of exit. But the alarm had been sounded to guards on the outside, and on our reaching the gate we were met by a company of Confederate soldiers with fixed bayonets, who made us hurry back up stairs about as fast as we had come down. Nine of the ten men who made their escape were captured and returned to prison; of the tenth I never learned of his recapture or successful escape.

Soon after this last occurrence I was taken sick with typhoid fever, and for nearly a week I lay in my place on the floor suffering intensely. The hum of conversation and other necessary noises of the prison greatly aggravated my suffering, and as I was without medical attention my condition became alarming. I was at length moved out of prison and placed in a hospital nearly a mile from the town. Here I enjoyed the comforts of a clean bed and pure air, and besides was given some attention by the doctors. I remained very low for about three weeks—so low that a part of the time I was unconscious of what was passing around me. Finally, my strong constitution enabled me to weather the storm, and I was in a fair way of recovering my accustomed good health; my appetite returned and I was able to be up a part of each day and walk about the ward.

I began to congratulate myself on a rapid recovery, but one evening about a week after I commenced moving about, I felt so ill of a sudden that I was scarcely able to reach my bed, and my fever seemed to have returned with all its original malignity. I thought that by some means I had taken a relapse, and I began to think that I would soon be paroled into the next world. After taking my bed I became violently delirious, and I have a vivid recollection of that terrible night of scorching fever. I imagined myself in a hundred different fearful positions. At one time I seemed to be cut up into numerous pieces, placed in a wheel and whirled round with lightning velocity; then I would suffer from some other hallucination. The next morning my fever abated somewhat, and I felt better. When the doctor made his customary morning round he looked at me a moment and then directed the nurses to carry me out of the ward, and telling me at the same time that I had the small-pox, and that it would not do for me to stay there. A little while before this the small-pox had broken out among the prisoners at Danville, and I had in some manner been exposed to it. The nurses carried me to an old out-building which had the siding partly knocked off of it, and which was situated at some distance from the rest of the buildings. Here were already a dozen or more prisoners with the same disease, furnishing the company which misery is said to love. I now realized that my situation was a desperate one, and I nerved myself to endure and suffer much. On the following day several other small-pox patients were brought in, and at the end of the third day our number had increased to forty, thus crowding the old building to its utmost capacity, and creating a picture of sickness and suffering that would appall the stoutest heart. We were crowded and piled together in a manner that would have been very uncomfortable to men in health. Some of our number had the disease in its most malignant form; most of these died. Others were afflicted in a milder form and a majority of these soon recovered. All night long was heard the moaning of the sick and the ravings of the delirious. Much less attention was paid us than our suffering condition demanded; we were left to get well or die, as the case might be, and those who recovered did not owe their recovery to careful nursing. Sometimes a patient would become delirious, get out of bed and walk out into the cold and snow barefoot, and would have to be brought back. Such cases as this invariably died. Those who died during the night were suffered to remain with us till morning and then carried out for burial. Our dead numbered three, sometimes four each night. It was indeed a charnel-house of death and misery; life and death struggled for the mastery, and death usually won. Those who escaped death and recovered did so by passing through the most trying scenes and by being blessed with constitutional vigor that defied the ravages of disease. Fortunately for myself I had the disease in its mildest form, and on that account weathered through. The small-pox at length spread to the main prisons in the town, and the pest houses being already full to overflowing, many suffered and died of the disease without being removed from the prison, and the cases of small-pox became so general as to excite very little attention.

After about four weeks I had so far recovered as to be able to go about, and my appetite was so improved that I could have eaten much more than I did if I could have had it; and sometimes I was fortunate enough to have given me the rations of some other unfortunate comrade who was too sick to eat, and in this manner I sometimes met the demands of my appetite. I have no means of knowing the number of deaths from this disease, but there were a great many. Having no means of guarding against the contagion, and being crowded closely together in unventilated rooms, teeming with stench, dirt and filth, our condition invited the disease, and in the majority of cases it could not be otherwise than fatal. After a time I was returned to the hospital from which I was taken when attacked with the small-pox; here I was allowed two light meals a day, consisting of bread and soup, but in no case was this sufficient to satisfy my hunger. Some days later I was placed in another hospital nearer town and was appointed ward-master in the same. This hospital had two wards below and two above, and all were filled with sick. The worst cases were in the ward to which I was assigned, and my duties were such that I had four assistants under me. The number of patients under my charge was usually sixty, and the deaths were often six in a day. As soon as one died and was carried away this place was supplied with another patient.

Over our hospital, as a sort of general superintendent, was a Confederate officer named Daffan. This Daffan passed through the wards each day, gathering up the property of the dead men, saying that he had to account to our government for all the property of the dead. A short time previous to this, the federal government had supplied the prisoners with many articles of clothing, besides blankets and many articles of comfort, and many of us had good pants, shoes, blouses and shirts. Whenever one of the men died, Daffan would come around inquiring for the "effects" of the deceased, as he called them, and everything of value was gathered together and handed over to old Daffan. He was particular to impress on our minds that he had to account to our government for all these things. We knew all the time that he was lying to us in this matter, but it would not help the matter to tell him of it. Several times we put the good clothing on the bodies of the dead and they were buried with these on. This displeased Daffan very much, who said it was all a needless waste, and threatened me that if I allowed the like to occur again he would have me returned to prison. The old fiend said that a man was just as well off by being buried in his old clothes, and no better off for being buried in his best, and that our federal authorities would be greatly displeased when they learned of this waste. I regarded this as a piece of cool impudence on the part of Daffan, to think that I would believe a story so full of deceit and falsehood, but I kept from expressing what I thought, for I knew that anything I might say would do no good, and would only aggravate him to inflict some indignity upon me.

I had now recovered my accustomed health, and by a better supply of food was improving daily, having the opportunity of keeping myself more cleanly than I could do in the prison. Daffan made his usual rounds, demanding of the attendants the effects of the dead. Of the number of dangerously sick was a Dutchman who occupied a cot in one of the tiers near the center. Across the aisle from him lay a patient who had on a pair of good shoes, an article of which the Dutchman was entirely destitute. When this man died the Dutchman insisted so hard that I should let him have the shoes, that I told him that I was liable to get into trouble if I let him have them, but if he would get up and get them himself I would pretend that I knew nothing of it, and I would offer no objections. This he did, and the coveted shoes were placed under his own bunk. When Daffan came in to take possession of this man's effects he overlooked the shoes, and the Dutchman remained in peaceable possession of them.

It was reported and generally believed in the hospital, that this Dutchman had four or five hundred dollars in greenbacks stowed away somewhere about his person, and Daffan had said to one of the nurses that the old man had better give that money over to him for safe keeping till he got well. On the night of the third day after the shoes had changed owners, while one of the nurses and I were seated quietly by the stove, we heard the labored breathing of the Dutchman, and taking a light we went to his bed and found that he was indeed dying. He survived but a few minutes after we first heard his heavy breathing. Our custom was that when a patient died the body was placed in a suitable position, and if at night, the remains were left on the cot till morning. It was a singular fact that nearly three-fourths of the deaths occurred in the night, but why this was so I could never determine.

At the time of the death of this Dutchman only myself and one attendant were up, and we performed the necessary work of preparing the body for burial on the following morning. The nurse and I talked over the matter of the wealth of the deceased, and both expressed a desire to know the truth of the report of his keeping a large amount of money about him. We concluded that if we found it that we could use it to as good advantage as Daffan could, and we made dilligent search in the bed and clothing of the dead man, hoping to gain possession of the reputed wealth, and disappoint Daffan by keeping it ourselves. Our search was rewarded by finding only a few dollars of Confederate money and some trinkets of very little value. We were now satisfied that the report about his having a great quantity of greenbacks was a hoax, and we confessed ourselves disappointed. The next morning the body was removed in the customary manner by placing it in the dead-house. Daffan came into the hospital the next morning, and learning of the death of the Dutchman, made inquiry for his effects. I gave him all that had been found, and noticed that Daffan appeared much disappointed. He asked if we did not find a quantity of greenbacks, and we assured him that nothing of the kind had rewarded our search. He remarked that it was very strange indeed, and we read in his looks that he suspicioned me of having the dead man's money, but he went out of the ward and did not return immediately. In a short time, however, he came back accompanied by four soldiers with fixed bayonets, and, after telling me that I was suspected of having the dead man's cash, he ordered them to search me thoroughly. They proceeded to a careful inspection of every possible and impossible place about my person where money could or could not be concealed; they ripped open the collar of my overcoat, but the imaginary lost treasure was nowhere to be found. Then they turned their attention to my straw mattress and pillow, and straw after straw of both these articles was made to undergo careful scrutiny. Then other parts of the ward were carefully searched, but nothing was found, for the reason that there was nothing to find. Notwithstanding the fact that I had been vindicated by the result of this search, I was from this time on a marked man, and under the ban of suspicion. I was immediately deprived of my position as ward master, and was made to perform duties of the most menial kind, and every effort was put forth to inflict upon me some humiliation and insult. After a few days I was sent back to my old prison in town. I had been at the hospital over three months, and in that time had suffered both from typhoid fever and small-pox, but had recovered from both, so that now I was much improved in my general health, and was looking and feeling better than at any time since the beginning of my imprisonment. Spring was now close at hand, for as near as I can remember it was about the middle of March, or perhaps a little later.

Many changes had taken place in the prison during my absence; many had sickened and died. Some of my special friends had been carried out to the hospital, and of the many, but a few had returned. From the hospital they had been carried to the deadhouse, and from thence to the dwelling place of the martyred dead, to join the unreturning throng.

The small-pox continued to prevail in the prison, but it had become much milder in its character, and was now much less dreaded than formerly. Our captors still maintained a strong guard on the lower floor and in the back yard, and but three persons were permitted to go down stairs and out to the well at a time. So many had died in the three months of my absence that the prison was much less crowded than when I left. The chances for escape by the back gate or by tunneling, were now hopeless, and I soon settled down in my old place, made some new acquaintances in place of many of the old ones who had died, and resigned myself to whatever awaited me.

Our rations had become extremely light—barely enough to keep us ravenously hungry all the time, and to keep our minds and conversation dwelling on imaginary feasts, which we were to enjoy in the future. In the beginning of our imprisonment, and for months following our capture, we had allowed ourselves to hope for a speedy exchange; but now that months were lengthened into years, hope was succeeded by dispair, and we no longer allowed ourselves to encourage a hope of release in this way. The only thing left for us to do to obtain freedom from our prison life, was to plan and perfect an escape. Being carefully guarded day and night, this was no easy task, and required strategy and daring of a superior kind. Adjoining our prison was another building, the roof of which covered about one-third of the window on the north side of our prison, and this seemed to offer a possible chance of escape. If we could manage to saw the bars off which covered this window, remove the glass and crawl out upon the roof of this addition, there was a chance of jumping to the ground, a distance of ten or fifteen feet from the eaves. By choosing a dark night, and making the effort so suddenly as to surprise the guards, it was thought to be barely practicable, but our situation was so gloomy that our desperation nerved us for the trial. Consulting among ourselves, we concluded that if a number should undertake it at a time, crawl out on this roof, jump off, and attempt to escape by running, there was a possibility of some of our number escaping. The work of sawing off the bars must be done on the same night of our attempted escape, for to remove the bars and let the work remain to be completed at a future time, would have been fatal to the plot. The undertaking required the strictest secrecy. The first steps were taken by making a number of case knives into saws.

The leader in this matter was a shrewd Irishman named John Foy. Ed. Mitchell, another Irishman, Tom Hinton, my partner, and myself, were the originators and prime movers in the work. One part of our plan was to keep our scheme to ourselves until the arrival of the night when it was to be carried out, and then make it generally known, and induce as many to join us as dared to do so, thus increasing our individual chances of escape. We determined to wait for a dark, rainy night, for on such a time our guards were less vigilant than on other occasions. It was not long till a favorable night arrived, and we set to work with a will to execute what we had been so long and hopefully planning. Soon as we began sawing at the window-bars it became known in the prison that an attempt to escape was to be made that night, and about fifty or sixty of the prisoners expressed their intention of making the effort along with us. We sawed away at the bars by turns until about half past eleven o'clock at night, when we succeeded in removing one bar, making an opening sufficiently large for a man to crawl through, and nothing was now left but to determine who should follow. By this time more than one-half the number who had been so ready to escape with us, had experienced a change of purpose, and had gone off and laid down, preferring to bear their present terrible misfortunes, rather than to attempt what seemed a barely possible chance of bettering their condition. To us who had originated the plan, this determination on the part of our comrades, had no effect tending to change our purpose, for we had reckoned the cost and weighed the risks before we began. The rain which had been falling during the early part of the night now ceased, and glimpses of bright sky could be seen here and there through the clouds. It appeared to us that it was a remarkably light night, being cloudy and no moon at all. Now that the night began to grow lighter, thus decreasing our chances of escaping unobserved by the guards, we began to debate whether to go on with our half executed project or to abandon it altogether. To us prisoners, situated in a dark room, and full of fears and anxiety, every outside object seemed magnified; indeed I sometimes seemed to think that the light itself was magnified. Our numbers, too, were fast decreasing, and out of the many who were so ready to go at the beginning, scarcely a dozen remained firm to their original intention. Counseling over the matter we tarried till half past twelve or one o'clock. If we failed to go now, our work would be discoved in the morning, and we would, in all probability be made to suffer for what we had already done. At last Foy, who was standing nearest the window, turned to the rest of us and said in a whisper, that if any of us would follow, he would creep out. We told him to go on and we would be with him.

He crept out, Mitchell followed, then Hinton, and then myself. Our plan was to reach the roof and all remain quietly on the same until all who made the attempt were ready, then to drop to the ground, and each for himself, escape as best he could. I handed my haversack to the one who was to follow me; it contained a piece of corn bread, which was to be my subsistence until fortune supplied something more. In creeping out I fancied I made much more noise than any of those who preceded me, and on reaching the roof I could see the dim outlines of my three adventurous companions who had crept out in advance of me, each crouching closely to the roof to avoid being observed by the guards who were pacing to and fro in the darkness, but a few feet below. I turned round in a half-straightened position to reach my haversack, and in doing so I made a cracking noise on the roof, which alarmed my comrades, and they commenced jumping from the building to the ground below. In a moment the guards began firing and shouting the alarm at the top of their voices, and the utmost excitement prevailed both inside and outside of the prison. The shouts of the guards and the reports of their guns were anything but music to our ears. I had not yet jumped, and if it had been possible I should have returned to the prison in the same manner I had escaped, but in doing so I would be compelled to crawl back slowly, and the guards, being now fully aware of our place of escape, would have riddled me with musket shots.

A train of thought ran through my mind with lightning rapidity, and I saw that my safest plan of action was to jump to the ground, imitating the example of my comrades and share their fate. I accordingly leaped off the building into the darkness below, striking on my feet and falling heavily forward unto my knees and hands. I jumped right over the heads of three of the guards, and so close to them that they could have touched me with their guns. Each of the three fired at me, but strange to say, neither shot took effect, the darkness of the night and the confusion of the moment rendered their aim unsteady, the balls overshooting me. The flash of their pieces blinded me, and I was somewhat shocked by striking the ground, but before they could lay hold of me, I sprang forward and made my escape. They were probably of the opinion that their shots had killed me, and they being in no haste to secure a dead man, I had the better chance of getting away. In my haste and fright I ran across the street and came in collision with a plank fence, for though I knew the fence to be there, I was too much excited to remember it at that moment. The force with which I struck the fence knocked me down, and I was for some minutes too much stunned to proceed. All was excitement and confusion in and about the prison. I was now on the opposite side of the street from the prison and knew nothing of the fate of my comrades. As soon as I was somewhat recovered I commenced crawling along the fence in order to get away from the immediate vicinity of the prison. I continued to crawl until I came to a corner of the fence opposite prison No. 3, when I was able to turn to the left and to move on, still crawling and hugging the ground with the utmost caution, to prevent the guards from No. 3 seeing me. Having passed No. 3, I raised to a half-standing position, and by so doing attracted the attention of the guards of No. 4. These called out, "Here goes one of them," and began firing at me. I sprang into the street and ran as fast as I could. The alarm brought nearly twenty guards in pursuit of me, and with yelling, shooting and running, the chase soon became more interesting than agreeable to me.

I would trip and fall on my knees, then gathering myself up again and hurry on, realizing each moment that my pursuers were gaining on me, and the shots from their guns whistled uncomfortably close to me. Just as I was on the point of giving up, I came to a ditch, over which was a short bridge, under which I took refuge, sinking myself as far as possible into the mud and water with which it was filled. My pursuers, owing to the darkness, failed to notice my jumping into the ditch, and so proceeded further on, crossing the bridge under which lay their victim, or jumping the ditch above and below. After they had passed I sunk myself deeper into the mud and there rested for some time; meanwhile the guards, having lost track of their game, returned, cursing and swearing and wondering at what had become of me. After all was quiet I commenced crawling down the ditch, fearing all the time that if I left the ditch I would be discovered and retaken. I proceeded in this way till I reached the mouth of the ditch where it emptied into the canal. The canal and river being on one side and the town on the other, made my progress somewhat uncertain. I could not cross the river, and to pass through the city, even at night, would be attended with great danger. I at length moved on, creeping as I went, with the canal and river on my right and the town on my left; finally, I came to a house, back of which was a high plank fence inclosing a garden. This fence ran so near the canal that I could not go back of it, and if I went in front I would strike the street and be in danger of being seen. The fence was too high for me to climb, and under the circumstances I hesitated what to do. I halted for a time, debating with myself how to proceed. While thus considering, I saw at a short distance a creeping form approaching me, which at first I feared might be one of the pursuing guards, but my second thought led me to hope it might be one of my comrades, and acting upon this conclusion I crept toward it. It proved to be my dear friend Hinton, and though we met under the darkest circumstances, the meeting was a joyous one to both.

We congratulated each other on our fortunate meeting and for a time consulted as to future plans. Hinton could tell very little of the fate of Foy and Mitchell, but said that when the first shots were fired at the prison he heard some one say he was shot, but could not tell which it was. Hinton's wrist was badly sprained and swollen, and was paining him very much; this was the result of his jump from the prison. We determined to cross the street in our front and pass up another one leading to the suburbs in a western direction, and finally out of town.

The canal and river shut off our escape in that direction, and we felt certain that to remain here till daylight would result in our recapture. We therefore walked out across the street in our front and passed up another one to the outer edge of the town, without meeting or seeing a single person, and without being seen. Once or twice we were bayed at by some dogs that ought to have been asleep at this untimely hour. Reaching a pike entering town from the west, we struck out in a brisk walk and soon left the town with its hated prisons far behind us. We congratulated ourselves anew, and began to think ourselves real heroes.

We soon concluded that it was very risky to travel on the pike and we took to the fields on our left, leaving the river and canal on the right. The rain of the past few days had saturated the earth, and the fields through which we made our way were mirey in the extreme, making our progress slow and difficult. The fields were inclosed with high picket fences, similar to those bound around gardens in the North, and we were often compelled to creep through holes in the fence, and sometimes we tore off the pickets in order to proceed in a direct course. Being very much exhausted with the labors and excitement of the early part of the night, and having but little vigor and strength in the beginning, we found ourselves almost completely worn out, and though we desired to go as far before day as possible, we were at length forced to halt and rest.

The great difficulty of traveling through the fields and the greater ease of traveling on the pike, induced us at length to return to the pike, intending, when daylight came, to abandon the pike, return to the fields and conceal ourselves. We had reached the pike and were moving along finely, when all at once several gruff voices ordered us to halt, at the same time the clicking noise which accompanies the cocking of muskets gave emphasis to the command. Our strength was so near exhausted that we could barely walk; therefore, escape by flight was not to be thought.

Blinded by the darkness, we had run into a squad of the enemy's pickets who were guarding a ferry on the river, and had approached to within a few feet of them before we were halted. We had no knowledge of a ferry at this place, and were not suspecting the presence of the enemy's pickets. I think the guards were placed here more to intercept rebel deserters than to recapture escaping prisoners. These guards had already been notified of the escape of prisoners from the town and were on the lookout for us. Our captors taunted us on the failure of our effort to escape, and said, "You-ens might have known you could not get away from we-uns." We bore their taunts with meek submission, not deigning a reply. A sergeant and four men were detailed to take us back to town. On the way I suffered much from thirst, and asked the guards to allow me to lie down at a pool and drink. This they refused to do, fearing perhaps that in some way I might effect my escape again. It was broad day light when we reached town. I was covered with mud from head to foot, my hair was matted with mud and dirt, and I had lost my hat, and altogether I presented a sorrowful plight. One Moffitt, a major in rank, commanded at Danville at this time, and to his headquarters we were taken. The major had not got out of bed, but presently he made his appearance, looking sour and cross. He was a small man, having dark, penetrating eyes, and an ugly Roman nose, and was altogether such a man as a prisoner would prefer not to meet before breakfast. He eyed us with a look that threatened annihilation, and then said viciously, "I will make you fellows pay for causing us all this trouble." The sergeant was then ordered to take us up to the prison and leave us on the lower floor till further orders. The sergeant obeyed, placing us on one side of the building and under the care of a lank, long-haired son of chivalry as guard, telling the guard that we were a desperate couple and to shoot us upon the slightest effort to escape. The guard placed himself in a valiant attitude, and pointing his long, dirty finger at us said : " Now, Yank, you attempt to move and I will put a ball through you in a moment." We assured him that we knew escape was impossible, and therefore we should not attempt it. As soon as the sergeant had gone out our guard told us to lie down and rest if we wished ; that he was just doing that bully talking in the sergeant's presence for effect, and that he had no desire or intention to harm us.

The other prisoners were coming down stairs and returning continually on their trips for water, and all availed themselves of getting to see us, as we were objects of curiosity. The guard was instructed to allow no conversation between us and the other prisoners, though we prevailed on him to let our friends from up stairs bring us something to eat. They brought us some corn bread and sassafras tea, which was a real treat to us. Upon inquiry we learned that our comrade Mitchell, who had attempted to escape with us the preceding night, had been shot through the left breast, and was now lying up stairs alive, but not expected to recover; and in an hour after we were placed under guard in the prison, Foy was brought in. He had a badly sprained ankle, the result of jumping from the building. He had succeeded in getting out of town, but found himself unable to travel. After daylight a negro came across him and Foy offered the negro $10 if he would feed and care for him until he would be able to travel. This the negro, through fear, refused to do, but went away and informed the Confederates where he was to be found. He was accordingly captured and brought in. They now had us all four, and we were in a sorry plight. Hinton had a sprained wrist, Foy a sprained ankle and Mitchell was fatally shot. I had escaped serious injury, but was very stiff and bruised in jumping from the roof to the ground. Soon after Foy was brought in the three of us were taken into the middle of the street and bucked. This punishment was inflicted upon us in plain view of the men in both prisons. We were placed about midway between the two buildings, the object being to make the lesson an impressive one to the other prisoners and to humiliate us at the same time. Old soldiers know what bucking means, but the ordinary reader needs some explanation. The hands are tied together in front, then the body is bent down and the knees bent up, while the arms pass down the outside of the knees. Then a stick is thrust under the knees and over the arms, and the work is done. When a man is bucked he is utterly helpless, and the position of the body is so cramped that the situation becomes unendurably painful. In this case the cords were tied very tight on our wrists, which greatly increased our suffering, and our hands and arms were soon very much swollen. I began to study up a plan of relief from my painful position, and thought of a hundred different ways but all seemed useless. After suffering for two hours my limbs became numb with the pain I was enduring. All at once a thought struck me which seemed to be the thing, and I concluded to try it. Whirling myself on to my back I commenced struggling with a *fit*. I had seen many persons in fits and I hoped to accomplish something by a close imitation of the genuine. I rolled up my eyes with a stony, vacant stare, grated my teeth, worked the spittle into a froth and forced it into the corners of my mouth, and so contorted my limbs and body as to closely resemble the symptoms of fits. This attracted the attention of the guards at once, and one of them inquired of the others what it meant. The reply was that he did not know, but he believed the fellow was in a fit. Another suggested that they ought to untie me, for in that condition he feared I would soon die. The result was as I had planned it should be; they came to me, cut the cords that bound me and then left me to "come to" at my leisure. I found it more difficult to recover from than to simulate the fit, but I managed to do so with fair success. After rolling upon the ground for a short time in apparent unconsciousness, I raised myself to a sitting posture and looked around me in a half idiotic manner, pretending not to understand what had happened. At length I sat up and seemed to be recovering consciousness. My companions and the guards were completely taken in by my acting, and as I began to recover they approached me and plied me with numerous questions, all of which I answered in a foolish manner. The guard asked me if I was subject to these spells. I answered that I guessed I was, but that I did not know. Finally the lieutenant turned to Foy and asked him if I was subject to fits. Foy answered promptly that I was. This settled the matter for the time, and the lieutenant walked away. I now felt that I had accomplished a point and made a good thing of it by my little acting, and began to congratulate myself on its success. I now by signs communicated to Foy that it was all "put on," and that it was done for a purpose. I must have been detected in this, for the lieutenant, who had been watching me closely, approached me and said: "Young man, I guess you have been playing 'possum' on us." He then ordered the guards to tie me up again. To this I did not protest, for, having been untied for more than an hour, I felt that it was quite an item in my favor. We were kept tied till late in the afternoon, and then cut loose and left for a time to ourselves till we were sufficiently recovered to walk, when we were taken back to our former places in the prison. We were cautioned not to repeat our effort to escape, and were threatened with worse punishment in case we did. Our hands and wrists were swollen, and our legs and bodies sore from the effects of our long and painful punishment, and it required all our efforts to walk.

Our daring comrade, Mitchell, died from the effects of his wound on the third day after being brought in.

Viewing this effort to escape, after all the circumstances are made plain, I am of the opinion that our guards were made acquainted with our plans, and that these were communicated to them by spies in the prison, who were sharing imprisonment for the only purpose of keeping watch over our conduct and of reporting to the rebels any attempt on our part to escape. These represented themselves to us as captives from the Union army. If our captors had not been apprised of our intentions to escape, there would not have been so many at that particular point where we hoped to find the fewest, and these would not have been prepared to shoot with such promptness as they did when we commenced jumping from the building. But for this espionage on the part of our enemies, we would have certainly taken them by surprise and rendered our escape possible. I am now fully convinced, that after our first effort to escape, that spies were kept in our prison day and night, and that our sayings and doings were reported to the authorities.

From this time until our removal there there was not the slightest chance to escape; every avenue leading to liberty was carefully watched and strongly guarded.

Our rations all this time were hardly enough to sustain us from one day till the next, and but for the hopes of liberation and return to home, friends and plenty, our desperate circumstances would have driven us mad.

All the endearments of home—the companionship of friends—the social and family ties and the many blessings from which we seemed forever separated, were the topics of our conversation by day and the subject of our dreams at night.

About the first of April, 1864, rumors circulated through the prison to the effect that we were soon to be sent to some other point. We regarded this as good news, for it seemed to us that a change might result in improving our condition, while it seemed impossible that it could make it worse.

We grew to hate the name of Danville, and longed for the day when we could forever shake its dust from our feet and start for some other place, we cared not where. That long-looked-for day came at last.

About the first of May the first load of prisoners was taken from Danville, and those left behind were ignorant of their destination, but learned after a short time that they had been sent to a prison somewhere in Georgia. A week later the occupants of our prison received orders to leave. We were permitted to take all our little personal effects, but as none of us were possessed of a great quantity of goods this favor was not of much value to us.

Some of us had blankets and overcoats; some had neither. Many had parted with their clothing from time to time for something to eat, and many of this class had barely clothing to hide their nakedness, and not enough for their comfort, even in that mild climate. We were loaded into box cars, about a hundred in a car, and this necessitated considerable crowding. We passed a number of towns and villages on the route, the names of which I cannot recall. We traveled all night after leaving Danville, only stopping now and then to let other trains pass, and to procure water. Our crowded condition made the trip tiresome and disagreeable, but we endured it patiently, hoping that a change to a new prison would bring us relief in some way.

The second day our train collided with another train loaded with negroes; the engines were badly crushed, but no one on board was injured. We were delayed several hours while procuring another engine, and again we moved on. During the second night we halted near a village of considerable size; here we got off the train and spent the night in camp near the track. I was so worn out with travel that I did not care to make an attempt to escape, but slept soundly all night. Next morning we again moved on our way, and late in the day passed through Macon, in the state of Georgia, and the same night reached Andersonville, a station about sixty miles south of Macon. We remained in the cars till daylight, and were then unloaded and had a small supply of food issued to us. This consisted of corn bread and meat, but miserable in quality and meager in quantity. Following the advice of an inspired writer, we ate what was set before us and asked no questions. Andersonville consisted of a few railroad buildings and about a half a dozen dwelling houses.

After we had eaten what had been furnished us we were ordered into line that a count might be made to ascertain if any had escaped. The commandant of this prison at this time was Captain Wirtz, who for his inhuman brutality in the treatment of prisoners, was afterward hung at Washington. Wirtz was a devil in the shape of a man; a libel on the human race, and the date of his death ought to be celebrated all over the land with bonfires and illuminations. He came out of his quarters near by, passed down our line with his hands clasped behind his back, eyeing us closely, but said not a word. He looked to be fifty-five years old, had a vicious, restless eye, sunk far into his head. He was tall and spare made, with a slight stoop in his shoulders. He was not an American, but his looks gave him the appearance of a native of one of the German states. His look was cross, sour and forbidding, and he was altogether the fiend in appearance that he proved to be in fact.

Before we were marched to the prison enclosure our names, companies and commands were carefully registered. The prison grounds at this time contained about twelve thousand men and was situated nearly half a mile from the station. The prison was encircled by a stockade built by first digging a ditch four or five feet deep round the enclosure. Into this ditch were planted heavy hewn timbers, reaching above the surface twenty feet, and firmly set in the ditch and the dirt packed in closely to hold them in their place, firm and solid. On the top of this stockade, at a distance of twenty yards from each other, was a number of platforms, or sentry posts, where the guards were stationed when on duty, and on the outside at each platform was a rude stairway which led from the ground to the platform, and which was for the purpose of assisting the guard to reach his post of duty. On the inside of this stockade at a distance of ten feet from and parallel with it, ran the "dead line."

This dead line was a row of posts set in the ground at intervals of ten or twelve feet apart, on the tops of which a narrow plank was nailed. The guards were instructed to shoot any prisoner who should approach nearer to the stockade than this dead line. A small stream of water ran through the stockade near the center. From this stream the prisoners procured all the water they used. This was warm and disagreeable to the taste and was unfit for use. A few trees grew in the inclosure, and the stumps of many more were to be seen here and there. When we entered the stockade the men already there flocked around us and asked us a multitude of questions concerning our capture and imprisonment, and many other questions concerning the progress of the war, which we could not answer. We were not supplied with tents nor any other means of protection after coming here, and the supply of these things which we brought with us was totally insufficient for our actual needs; we were, therefore, left to shift for ourselves in this matter, each man taking care of himself, as a rule, in the construction of his habitation.

Sometimes a number would associate together in a club, and by each contributing a piece of tent, a bit of blanket or cloth, they managed to provide better means of shelter than could have been done singly. But there were many who had nothing of any kind out of which to construct what might shelter them from the scorching sun by day or the chilly air by night. To this class the burning sun and heavy dews added much to their other hardships. Four other prisoners joined me in the construction of quarters, and we chose a location in the eastern part of the stockade, but a few feet from the dead line, and on the south side of the creek. We dug down into the sand nearly two feet, and with our blankets and some pieces of canvas, which one of our number was fortunate enough to have in his possession, we managed to construct a very respectable looking tent compared with the others about us. There was a guard-post opposite to where we had located our tent. This spot had been selected by us on account of its commercial advantages, for being thus situated we could trade with the guards when any trading was to be done.

Before leaving Danville I had taken the precaution to lay in a stock of tobacco, and in fixing up our tent I placed the tobacco near by where it attracted the attention of a prisoner passing by. He inquired to know if I would sell it, and at what price. I told him I would take a dollar a plug for it, and he said that he would take it all at that price. I declined to sell it all at that time, but allowed him to take three plugs, for which he paid me three dollars in greenbacks. Another prisoner standing by said to me that I could have got three dollars a plug for it as well as one dollar. I thought this very strange, for this same tobacco could be bought at Danville for twenty-five cents a plug. I now began to realize that prices ranged much higher here than at Danville. Soon after this first sale a guard came on duty at the post nearest our tent with a bunch of onions for sale. These I bought and placed them in small piles for sale again. In a short time I had sold seven dollars worth of onions and had some left for our own use, which made us a light mess. Our prison experience had taught us valuable lessons of economy, and every atom of food was made to answer to its fullest extent.

Our arrival at Andersonville was about the middle of May, 1864, and the weather was already oppressively warm. Being unaccustomed to the climate of this latitude we suffered more from heat than we would otherwise have done. Our rations at first consisted of about two-thirds of a pint of unsifted corn meal, a half pint of raw beans and a small piece of meat; the latter, however, we did not receive but two days out of the three. We drew our rations at ten or eleven in the forenoon; then having to cook them, we could not get our dinner sooner than about one o'clock. Though the rations we drew were designed by our captors to make us three meals, we invariably ate the whole quantity for one, and if this one meal had been sufficient to satisfy our appetites we would have thought ourselves fortunate. Wood for cooking purposes was a scarce article, and to procure enough for our needs we dug the roots from the ground, hacked up the stumps, and it was not long until every stump, root, chip and splinter within the stockade had been gathered and consumed. In cooking we usually boiled our beans first till they were soft; then our meat was sliced thin and put in; afterwards our meal was added and stirred, making what we called "loblolly." When a number messed and cooked together the food was carefully divided, giving to each man his exact share of the mess.

My first trade with the guards having resulted so favorably, I determined to continue to traffic with the guards who came on duty at the post nearest our tent, and besides furnishing our mess with something extra, I soon began to accumulate money ahead.

Additional prisoners were being brought in nearly every day; these had more or less money, and while their money lasted they bought whatever they could find to eat, regardless of the price. Anything fit to eat sold at a fabulous price, and tobacco was not an exception. The following prices were obtained: three flour biscuits, $1.00; three eggs, $1.00; a pint of flour, $1.00; onions ranged from 75 cts. to $1.25 each; fresh pork, $2.00 a pound; potatoes were bought of the guards at $35 a bushel, and afterwards retailed singly; coffee brought $5 per pound. These prices were on a Greenback basis, Confederate money being at ten cents on the dollar. The daily additions being made to our numbers soon brought on a crowded condition of the prison, resulting in much discomfort and additional suffering. In a vast crowd like this there are always a variety of characters, and it may not seem strange that vice in its worst forms should have representatives, and that the depraved and baser elements in such a multitude should assert itself.

Here was the sneak thief, the gambler, the highwayman, the murderer, experts in every vice in the catalogue, and these made it necessary to keep a careful watch on everything of value, night and day. Theft, robbery and other heinous crimes were committed in open day, and were alarmingly frequent.

There were two main streets running through the prison grounds— one on the north side and one on the south, the creek running between the two. These streets on either side were lined with the tradesmen who bought from the guards in large quantities, and afterwards retailed in smaller quantities to their fellow prisoners. These dealers occupied small stands at various places all over the ground. At one place could be seen a dealer selling flour at a dollar a pint; near him could be seen the dealer in onions and potatoes. Another one could be seen at another place with eggs, biscuits and the like. Our lowest class of merchants dealt in soup bones. These bones, after being first carefully picked, were sawed or cut into small pieces, so as to show the marrow to advantage. Then some wretched soldier, hatless, his pants worn off to the knees and his shirt sleeves worn off to the elbows, would take these bones, and standing in a commanding position would yell out at the top of his voice: "Here is your nice, fine, rich soup bones for sale. Walk right up and buy the best."

My numerous trades with the guards resulted in my becoming personally known to many of them, and this was a great advantage to us in our provision traffic. By careful buying and selling I not only kept the mess constantly supplied with many extras, but had accumulated over two hundred dollars; I had been singularly prosperous in all I had undertaken. The grounds were becoming more and more crowded every day, for hardly a day passed that did not add to our numbers, and as the season advanced the weather became excessively hot and much sickness was the result. The water which we were compelled to drink and make general use of was warm and dirty. There was always a large number of men at the creek washing and getting water, and the consequence was that the water was made unfit for use except for washing. This led to the digging of wells in various parts of the grounds. The surface being sandy for fifteen or twenty feet made digging quite easy, and better water was reached at a depth of twenty-two feet than could be had at the creek. Many of these wells soon became useless by caving in. Our supply of fuel had become exhausted; every tree, stump and root had been used, and now and then small squads were allowed to go out under guard to bring in a supply of wood. Going out for wood was considered quite a favor, and he who happened to be so fortunate as to be detailed for that purpose was to be congratulated, for in so doing he found many an opportunity of getting some nice bit to eat in some manner or other; or, if he failed in this, he could breathe the pure air and rest his wearied eyes on green fields, and listen to the song of the free, happy birds. On such occasions he was wont to wish that he had the wings of the wind that he might fly away to a land of beauty, wealth and happiness, leaving behind the horrid scenes of that worse than horrid prison pen.

The prevailing diseases among the sick were scurvy and chronic diarrhea, and to such an extent had these and other complaints grown that the hospitals on the outside were sufficient for the accommodation of less than one-fourth of those who needed such accommodation, and consequently hundreds, for lack of needed attention and medical treatment, were left to die inside of the stockade. Each morning the bodies of such that had died during the preceding night, were carried out to the dead-house. Here they were piled in wagons like so many logs of wood, and hauled to the place of burial, where they were placed, side by side, in long, deep trenches, and covered with dirt. No such thing as a coffin or box was used to enclose these bodies, and their funeral rites were things only to be thought of, but not to be observed. The Union prisoners were employed in the work of digging these trenches and in covering up their dead comrades. Even the duty of carrying a dead comrade outside of the stockade was esteemed a favor, and I have known men to pay $5 for the privilege of carrying a corpse to the dead-house. The reason of this was that in returning from such duty each man was permitted to bring in a load of wood for his own benefit. Notwithstanding the prevailing death-rate, our prison continued to become more and more crowded, and the whole available space inside the dead-line was taken up, and the whole area was a moving mass of struggling, suffering humanity; we were so densely packed that in attempting to move around we had to pick our way with caution through the throng. The grounds were at length enlarged by the addition of eight acres to the inclosure, making the total area near twenty acres, and yet this addition, though it gave us some relief, left us very much crowded.

By July 1st, 1864, it was estimated that our numbers reached twenty-five thousand, a figure rather below than above the real number, I have no doubt. With increasing numbers the morals of the prison seemed to become more and more corrupt. Person and property was safe nowhere; robberies and petty theiving occurred day and night; no one was safe from the attacks of the human vultures who preyed upon their weaker and more unfortunate brethren. About the first of July our captors began cooking our rations on the outside of the prison, thus avoiding the necessity of sending us out for wood under guard. Instead of corn meal, as before, we received corn bread, made from unsifted meal, and without salt. Our beans were also cooked for us, and about every other day we were furnished with a very small bit of meat to each man. It is truly astonishing what a small quantity of food it takes to sustain human life, and how tenacious we cling to life, even when it seems to offer nothing but suffering. Our circumstances illustrated this point to an extent we never before dreamed of. We had among us men of all grades and dispositions; all the walks of life had representatives, and misery and wretchedness paid no respect to the one more than to the other. Squalid misery stalked abroad at midday, nor stayed its hand in the darkness of the night. Men who had been brought up in affluence and elegance, shared the wretchedness of the lowest born of his comrades. The poorer and most destitute—those without tent, blanket or other means of comfort, wandered about the pen seeking for stray cumbs of food that might fall in their way. Old potato parings, stray beans, or any other morsel were eagerly sought for and devoured. Their sharpened visages and haggard looks told a tale of starvation and want that can not be told by tongue or pen. To alleviate the sufferings of those around us seemed next to impossible; we were all in the same desperate condition, and if there were those who seemed to fare better than the rest, they were such as resorted to trade and made special efforts to improve their condition. An effort to relieve one would cause a thousand others, as destitute as the one, to ask for relief on as good grounds. On the south side of the creek the grounds had become very miry. The filth from the higher grounds had accumulated in this quarter, and it became a quagmire, and millions of maggots squirmed and worked in this filthy offal, presenting a sight, which when seen, can never be recalled except with a shudder of disgust.

Constant association with sickness, suffering and death had made us somewhat callous in our feelings toward our fellow sufferers, and many had allowed this feeling of indifference to get full possession of them, leaving no room for sympathy or pity. With each of us it was such a struggle for existence, that self-preservation ruled our every act and dictated our very thoughts. The weaker and more destitute were the first victims of disease and death. It seemed in many cases, that when hunger and disease had done their work, the starving victim would wander off to to the creek, and there he would fall, or sinking into the swampy soil, would there lay until death ended a life of misery. No helping hand was reached out to aid him. Every finer and nobler feeling seemed paralyzed, and the one thought of self-preservation checked every feeling of humanity. Death was doing his work on the right and on the left, and it was a common thing to pass by a dying man in our walks around the different parts of the prison. Lying in the hot sun, unattended, and usually unknown, the sufferer would struggle with the grim monster until struggling ended in surrender. Hundreds were passing by but no one cared to waste his time or his pity on a dying man. Inspectors passed through our prison every day, making search for any attempt at tunneling out that we might make, and if a tunnel was begun it was usually detected before progressing far.

One tunnel, however, escaped detection, and this was projected about twenty yards from the stockade. A party of prisoners were pretending to be engaged in digging a well, and after reaching a depth of fifteen feet a tunnel was begun and pushed vigorously toward the outer side of the stockade. When the inspectors made their daily rounds the diggers would be found in the bottom of their well hard at work, and the inspectors looked in approvingly, or passed on without a suspicion of the scheme on hands. The work progressed, undiscovered by the rebels, until the workmen had passed under the stockade, and preparations were being made for a grand exit in a short time. Unluckily for the enterprise the two men who were working in it, one morning about sun up, struck too near the surface and the crust caved in on them. Being on the outside they sprang out and ran for life and liberty. They were seen by the guards, who fired many times at them, but so far as we could see they were unhurt, and I never learned of their recapture.

Now and then some poor, unfortunate prisoner would wander unthoughtedly over the dead line and suffer the consequences, for the established rule was to shoot the offender without warning—a rule that was enforced with fiendish delight by our guards. How many met death in this way I know not, but the number was not a few.

Some of the guards would fire on a prisoner whenever they could find any kind of a plea for so doing, but others were more humane and only enforced the rigorous rules of the prison because it was their duty.

Before the middle of July the number of prisoners at Andersonville reached twenty-five thousand, and with increasing numbers the want, destitution, sickness and death grew more and more dreadful. Mention has been previously made of the moral depravity and consequent crimes resulting from time to time. Robberies were occurring daily and it was apparent that measures must be taken to bring the offenders to justice; but how to proceed to reach that end was a question not easily answered, and for a time longer we endured what we could not remedy. Money grew scarcer and scarcer, for the reason that it was being continually sent outside the prison and none of it was being returned. This state of affairs was aggravated by the fact that it was almost impossible to trade with the guards. The prison authorities finally established a trading-post inside the prison, and here we were compelled to do whatever trading we did do, but as very few of the prisoners had any money, our patronage to the established store was exceedingly light. Up to the time at which our trading with the guards was prohibited, I had, from a small beginning, increased my capital to two hundred and forty dollars, besides expending a large amount for such extras as money would buy. But now my money began to decrease, for every day I was put to some expense without any income, and under this state of things my money was rapidly disappearing.

Among the prisoners in the stockade there were about thirty negroes; these were taken out daily to perform labor on the outside, and were brought in at night. With a view to replenishing my wasted finances I gave one of these colored men forty-five dollars, telling him to buy with it anything that could be eaten, and bring it into the prison with him, and that I would pay him for all his trouble.

This he agreed to do. That night when the colored squad was brought in I went to their quarters and found the man with whom I had intrusted my money, and made inquiry of his success. He reported that he had purchased several articles of food with the money, but that the Confederate guards at the gate had forced him to give it all to them. Here was forty-five dollars gone at one fell swoop, and my spirits fell to a low state. I waited several days, and seeing no other means of renewing my trade, I gave fifteen dollars to another man of the colored squad, instructing him to buy and bring in something to eat. But he came in with a report similar to the first, bringing neither money nor food. Not caring to invest further in this line of speculation, I gave up further effort and waited for something to turn up, contenting myself by economizing, as well as I could, the money I had remaining. The adage, " misfortunes come in pairs," now verified itself, for following the loss of my money I was attacked with scurvy, a disease that had already carried to the grave hundreds of my fellow prisoners. Very few who were victims of the scurvy ever recovered, and I naturally supposed I would go with the majority. Our situation was such that it was nearly impossible to procure the necessary remedies for the disease; therefore, when a man was taken down with the scurvy he usually remained in his tent or lay out in the open air unattended till he died. Captain Wirtz, who had charge of the prison, usually rode through the stockade twice a day, but none of the prisoners were allowed to speak to him during these visits, and we were even denied the right to represent our grievances in a petition to our friends or our enemies. Misery and suffering that can not be told was our common lot, and though it be retold a thousand times there remains that which is too shocking to tell and too inhuman to be believed. Death was making rapid inroads in our ranks every day, for at least fifty were carried to the graveyard every day. It was a common sight to see men lying in the hot sand, forsaken and alone, unable to help themselves, sweltering in the burning sun, and slowly but surely dying.

We were forsaken, even by those who should have been our friends, for our government at Washington, by the advice and policy of Secretary Stanton, refused to exchange us, or to give an equal number of rebel prisoners for us in return; for they said: " We will not give healthy, robust Confederates in our hands, who are fit for the front, for a like number of half-starved and half-dead men who will never be fit for service ; it is policy to let them stay where they are, even if they should all die." This might have been "policy," but to say the least, it was very heartless policy.

Crime of various kinds continued to grow more and more frequent; indeed it became known that an organized band existed in the prison, the known object of which was plunder. This band numbered several hundred, and they were pledged to support and protect each other from any punishment resulting from their misdemeanors. Now and then one of the band would be caught in some offense, and would be punished by shaving one side of his head; sometimes bucking was added to this punishment. But it appeared that the principals were never caught in this way. If they were detected in their deeds they seemed to be strong enough to defy punishment. It was the little, one-horse starvling who was caught and made to suffer. The arrival of fresh prisoners was generally followed by a series of robberies, for this class of men brought into the prison more or less money, and the thieves usually fell upon them and rendered them penniless, sometimes beating them besides. On one occasion a newly arrived prisoner showed desperate resistance when attacked by members of the gang, and the result was he was very dangerously stabbed by the free-booters.

This brutal act created a feeling of indignation on the part of the order-loving prisoners. But being weak, half-starved and unorganized, and each man being compelled to make a desperate effort to support life, he had little thought of redressing the wrongs of others so long as he, himself, remained unmolested; and thus three hundred or four hundred desperadoes, well organized, were able to hold in awe the other thousands who loved peace and good order.

Following the stabbing above mentioned it was resolved that further forbearance would only result in greater outrages, and therefore a few of us determined to draw up and sign a petition to Wirtz, setting forth the state of affairs of outlawry as they existed in the stockade. We prevailed on a Confederate lieutenant to bear our petition to Captain Wirtz, asking that immediate attention be given the same. Next day Captain Wirtz and several other Confederate officers came into the stockade and held several conferences with the prisoners in various parts of the grounds, making diligent inquiry into the nature of the offenses, and, as far as possible, tried to ascertain the number and names of the offenders. Such information was furnished them as fully satisfied them that the complaints in our petition were properly founded. On the following day a Confederate captain and lieutenant came into the enclosure with a detachment of soldiers, armed and equipped. A police force of near four hundred of the honest prisoners was then detailed and organized. Then a call was made to all who were in any way acquainted with the facts concerning the commission of crimes, to come forward and make it known.

Now that they were to be protected, there were plenty of witnesses, and no lack of testimony touching the outrages. These proceedings came upon the thieves unexpectedly, and caused them great consternation. They had not expected this righteous outburst of long-delayed retribution, and knew not what to do. The worst of them were hunted in every part of the prison. The robber element had suddenly come to grief. More than forty of the ring-leaders and principals were arrested and taken outside the prison under a strong guard.

Here the trial was held. Captain Wirtz said to us: "Now, you can try these men in your own way, and if they be found guilty of the crimes of which they stand charged, they shall suffer just punishment, and you shall be protected in your decision."

A jury of twelve was then impaneled from among the prisoners, and a judge having the proper legal qualifications to decide the points of law which might arise, was also chosen. The accused were provided with good counsel and the prosecution was conducted by legal talent of no ordinary kind.

The trial then proceeded, being on the outside of the prison and under a strong Confederate guard. It lasted nine days and was characterized by great fairness and impartiality. The accused had an array of testimony to prove their innocence, but with every effort that could be brought forth in their behalf there was much damaging testimony given against them. At the close of the trial the jury retired twenty-four hours, and upon being called for a verdict they decided that thirty-five of the accused should run the gauntlet on the inside of the stockade, and that six of the number, whom they found by the evidence to be the principals, should be publicly hanged.

The punishment by running the gauntlet should take place immediately, and those who were to suffer in this manner were divided into two parties, and one party was taken to each of the two main entrances to the stockade. Here were ranged long lines of prisoners on either side of a space a few feet in width and extending far into the prison grounds. As the culprits ran between these lines they were pelted, kicked and otherwise assaulted by such of the prisoners as were quick enough to reach them. Many of the offenders were badly beaten, and it was reported that two of them died from the effect of their injuries. Those who were condemned to suffer death by hanging were allowed ten days of preparation to meet their fate, but they were kept under a strong guard outside the prison during this time. Thieves from this time forward fared roughly, for the prisoners were now well organized, having a police force of four hundred men, who diligently sought out and arrested any prisoner reported guilty of crime. When it became known that sure and severe punishment would follow the commission of a crime, the offenses from which the inoffensive and helpless ones had suffered, grew very rare.

The scurvy from which I had been suffering grew worse, and I was now barely able to walk about, but I tried to keep my spirits up and made strong efforts to continue on my feet, for I felt that if I once gave up I should certainly die. The scurvy affected us in two different forms: in one class of cases the limbs of the patient would swell and become of a dark crimson color, and if the swollen flesh were pressed with the finger the impress would remain some time. In the other cases the flesh hardened and shrank up, turning to a dark brown color. The sense of feeling was lost in some cases. In the last named cases the flesh would feel like hard, dry wood, and the joints would be more or less swelled. In both cases the gums swelled and the teeth became loose. My case was the last described kind, which was called the bone scurvy.

On the day set apart for the execution of the six robbers I was barely able to move about with the aid of a cane, but the excitement of the occasion helped me to greater activity than for several days previous.

The scaffold on which the execution was to to take place was erected on the inside of the prison and near the southern gate. When the hour arrived I hobbled out to that part of the grounds and took a position about fifteen yards from the scaffold. Nearly twenty-five thousand prisoners were looking on in solemn silence, and the scene was too impressive ever to be forgotten. The doomed men were brought in under a strong guard of Confederate soldiers, and were then delivered to the prisoners to be executed. The guards now retired to the outside, leaving the condemned men in the hands of the organized force of prisoners. Not a Confederate remained to witness the execution. It was indeed a painfully solemn thing to see these six men, in the prime of life, surrounded by such misery and wretchedness, thus to suffer the penalty which their dark deeds had brought upon them. They were brought in with their hands tied behind them, attended by two Catholic priests, who offered them the consolation of their religion in their last hours. When the time came and they were commanded to mount the scaffold, one of them, a large and powerful man, a member of a New York regiment, exclaimed to the others: "I can never stand this," and with a sudden and powerful effort burst the cords that bound him and made a desperate effort for his life.

In a moment all was confusion and excitement. Only those in the immediate vicinity of the scaffold comprehended what was going on; even where I stood I could not at first understand the cause of the consternation. The impression prevailed with many of the prisoners that the rebels were about to fire upon us from their batteries situated on the higher grounds commanding the prison, and which were kept ready for use in case of an attempted outbreak on the part of the prisoners.

The excitement reached a high pitch; two men standing near me jumped down a well eighteen feet deep to escape the destruction which they imagined awaited us all; but as soon as we ascertained that the confusion arose from the effort of one man to escape, quiet was somewhat restored. This man, whose name was Curtis, parted the crowd in front of him, flinging the men right and left in his madness and desperation. He was followed by the organized police and a large crowd of the prisoners besides. He ran to the eastern part of the stockade, and in attempting to cross the creek he sank up to his waist in the filthy offal. He was now captured and brought back. He must have known the impossibility of escaping under such circumstances, and it is a wonder that any man of ordinary judgment would have attempted such a thing.

Soon after he was brought back the six were marched to their places on the fatal platform from which they were to be launched into eternity. They were still attended by the priests who continued to counsel with and pray for them.

I remember well the remark made by Curtis just before the drop fell. He said, " It was my old grandmother who said I would die with my boots on, and I guess it is coming to pass." Finally, when all was ready, the priests retired from the scaffold, and meal sacks were drawn over the heads of the condemned men, as black caps are on such occasions under other circumstances. The trap sprung and five of the six were soon lifeless. The sixth man in his fall broke the rope and fell to the ground. He begged piteously for his life, telling his executioners that the breaking of the rope was proof of his innocence. But his begging was all in vain and availed nothing; he was again made to mount the scaffold and in brief time was sent to bear his guilty companions company. Their bodies were taken down inside of an hour and received proper burial.

This execution took place July 11, 1864. The men executed were John Sarsfield, 144th N. Y. Infantry, Wm. Collins, 88th Pa. Infantry, Pat Delaney, 83d Pa. Vols., Chas. Curtis, 5th R. I. Vols., A. Mun, U. S. Navy, W. R. Rickson, U. S. Navy.

This execution had its desired effect; it not only disposed of the principal criminals who had terrorized the prison, but it restrained others from the commission of crime. From this time forward there was little theft or outlawry compared with the times preceding this execution. Captain Wirtz should have credit for the part he took in bringing about this reform.

My health grew worse from day to day, the scurvy gaining continually and my vitality and strength weakening proportionately. New prisoners had ceased to be brought in, and a general impression prevailed that we were soon to be moved away. Money had become very scarce with all the men. My funds had dwindled from day to day, and the future looked darker than at any time since coming here. It is worthy of particular mention, that of all the religious creeds of the land, the Catholics were the only ones who visited us in our misery or seemed touched at our condition. The priests of this church came into our prison every day, rain or shine, and ministered as best they could to the wants of the most destitute, but where there where so many in need it was next to impossible to do much. The worst cases were helped to a few delicacies and comforted in various ways.

The Masons of Albany, a place fifty miles south of Andersonville, brought much relief to those of their order among us. Many a member of that mystic tie was helped to a clean shirt, a pair of shoes or something to eat by the Masonic brethren.

About the first of September, 1864, the Confederates began moving some of our number away; everybody was anxious to go first, for we had seen and suffered so much here that it seemed to us that any place on earth besides this would be better. I was too sick at this time to care for myself, and was therefore a burden to my companions, several of whom made many sacrifices for my comfort and relief. The fact that my money was nearly all gone added to my misery, for even in prison money is not to be despised. I suffered much pain in my limbs at night, and as a consequence I slept but little. I was continually tormented by a thousand doubts and uncertainties which kept me in a constant state of restlessness from which I had no relief. It was estimated that during the months of July and August the deaths averaged one hundred and fifty daily. Our numbers were being reduced daily, both by deaths and removals, so that this was some relief, even to those who remained, for it gave us more room and better and purer air to breathe. About the 10th of September the prisoners constituting our division were called on to leave. This occasioned much shouting and other demonstrations of joy, but being entirely unable to move from my tent, it brought grief to me instead of joy, for, knowing that my companions would have to go, I realized that I would be left unattended and would surely suffer for care which none would be willing and few able to give. It was of no use to depend on strangers for care unless I could pay them, and I lacked the money to do that, having now only sixty-five cents in postal currency. My fortunate comrades, before leaving me, brought me a quantity of fresh water and arranged my blankets on sticks in such a manner as to protect me from the sun. Having done all in their power to leave me comfortable, they bade me an affectionate farewell, and I could see by their manner that they expected I would not recover, and that a few days at most would end all with me. Following their departure I felt very lonely and my spirits were much depressed. I now had no helping hands to minister to me, for, though I was surrounded by the multitude, I was almost as much alone as if I had been on the desert of Sahara. I had seen hundreds lying alone and slowly dying, friendless and uncared for: and I now felt that I was surely in the same desolate condition. That evening I prevailed on a prisoner to bring me some fresh water, and as darkness came on I pulled my blanket from the stick and wrapping it about me as best I could and tried to sleep, but being full of pain and direful apprehensions, I slept but little. I had no appetite, and what rations I drew were nauseating to my taste, and the sight of them was unpleasant in the extreme. I grew careless concerning my rations, and cared little whether I received my scanty portion or not.

The next morning after my comrades left me, as the sun rose and its rays began to scorch me, I tried several times to get some passing prisoners to fix up my blanket in the form of a shelter as on the previous day, but all were too busy or too heartless to give any attention to a dying man. I at length prevailed on one man to bring me some fresh water and fix up my tent by giving him my rations for the day. During the day I was visited by a Catholic priest who gave me half a lemon, which greatly refreshed me for a short time. I now thought my days were numbered, and concluded that I could live but a few days at farthest, but the outlook, gloomy as it was, had some relief in it, for I felt that death would be preferable to such a life as I had been living for weeks in the past. The day wore away and night—a dreadful night, came on. A terrible storm of rain, thunder and wind raged for hours, and being compelled to lie on the wet ground, unprotected, I was thoroughly drenched and slept but little, and that little was full of frightful dreams and brought me little rest. I wished I might fall asleep and never waken. Morning came at last and the burning sun drove his scorching heat into my weak and emaciated flesh. I became delirious as the day advanced and continued so till toward evening, and when I recovered consciousness I found that I had been carried during the day to the northern part of the stockade and placed in a long shed, which had recently been erected for the reception of the worst cases. The Catholic priest had visited me and given me some lemon juice and wine. The sick and dying lay about me in great numbers; many were on the outer side of the shed, waiting to take the places of those who were being carried to the dead-house from within. I well remember my feelings, when, on regaining consciousness, I looked round me and beheld the terrible scene by which I was surrounded. I determined to make a desperate effort to live and therefore set my will in an attitude of defiance toward the grim monster. Next to me on my right lay a tall and large framed man, having on a red shirt. This man was delirious and was talking wildly and without meaning. I remember how I shuddered when I beheld the vast number of lice with which his body was covered; it appeared to me that there were thousands of them of all sizes, from the huge old plump ones down to the tiny midget of an hour old. The poor man soon surrendered and the battle of life was at an end, for on the next morning I found him stiff and silent. I had slept but little during the night, for the continued moaning of the sick made sleep next to impossible. With the return of light came renewed hopes and a still greater desire to live. I was now furnished with some corn meal and beans, but being helpless it was not possible for me to cook them, and besides I had no appetite, notwithstanding I had eaten nothing for several days. But I was convinced that I must eat something to sustain life, for I must soon die of starvation unless I did. So I gave my meal and beans to a well prisoner to cook on the halves, and when it was cooked I ate a part of it, which was very little. Yet I still believe that in thus forcing myself to eat what I could, proved to be the means by which the brittle thread of life was saved from breaking. I desired to be taken out of the prison and placed in the hospital on the outside. I spent the day in planning to this end, for it was my only hope of life. Numbers of the sick were being taken to the hospital each day for treatment, and it appeared to me that if I could only get out of the stockade and into the hospital I should recover. The next morning I told the prisoner who had cooked and shared my rations on the previous day, that if he would carry me down to the gate, where the negroes came with wagons daily for the sick, that he might have all my rations for that day. This he promised to do if he could get his partner to assist him. He then went in search of his partner; presently they both came and carried me to the gate. At the gate were a great many sick, all waiting for their turn to be taken to the hospital. The two men who carried me to the gate laid me in the shade of a canvas tent occupied by some of the under-officials of the prison. They then went their way. When the wagons came I yelled with all my strength and asked to be loaded in; but no one paid attention to me. So the wagons were driven away with their load, leaving me and others behind. I learned that in two hours the wagons would return for another load, so I comforted myself with the hope that I might yet get to go.

When the wagons again returned I begged to be put into one of them, but the result was the same as before, and again the wagons were driven away, leaving me dejected and almost hopeless, for, let me try ever so hard, some one was always ready to step in and take my place. I was told that my wagons would return for one more load that day, and I again began planning to try and make the trip. I had a ring of rare value, one I had taken from home when I enlisted, and for various reasons I prized it very dearly, and I had always intended to keep it in remembrance of its donor. But now I was on the verge of death, as I thought, and I felt justified in sacrificing the ring for my own benefit. I therefore bargained with an Irishman, promising him the ring if he would put me in one of the wagons when they came.

It was near sun-down when the wagons came for their last load, and faithful to his agreement the Irishman picked me up and put me in one of the wagons, and we were driven away. Many were left behind, who, like myself, were desirous of getting to the hospital, but as there were accommodations for only so many, some must be left for another day, when as many could be taken from the stockade as would fill the places of those who had died on the previous day. It was not every day that the wagons came for the sick, but only at times when the deaths in the hospital made it possible to accommodate more; so if we missed getting out on the day the sick were hauled out we must wait until another favorable day. This might be the next day, or it might be several days. In this interval many would die. The hospital was located about a mile from the stockade, and we reached it between sundown and dark. We were unloaded and a list of our names, regiments and companies taken. We were then put on wheelbarrows and wheeled to places to which we had been assigned. I was taken to a small wedge tent, suitable for the accommodation of three persons; it was already occupied by one man, and he was sick nigh unto death.

We were furnished with no special comforts; there were no beds nor mattresses given us—nothing but the bare, sandy soil. Blankets were furnished to such prisoners as had none.

The hospital grounds contained six acres, and was enclosed by a close board fence eight feet high. A line of sentries was stationed on three sides of the enclosure on the outside of the fence; on the south side the guards were on the inside. This was on account of the swampy condition of the land on this side. The grounds were carefully laid off, divided by streets and wards. The wards numbered from one to twenty. A force of well prisoners were assigned to duty in this hospital, and they were required to keep the streets carefully swept and the whole grounds clear of offal. The tents used were of two kinds—the small wedge-shaped tent, large enough for three persons, and the wall tent, which was large enough for twelve. The grounds were well shaded by trees, and altogether, the hospital was a place of comfort and beauty compared to the stockade. Each ward had its ward-master and attendants to wait on the sick, but about all these did was to bring our rations to us.

Only one of many of our worst cases of sick recovered. The poor fellow who was in my tent when I first arrived soon died; others were brought in from time to time and died, until nine had died by my side.

During all this time I could not perceive that I was improving at all, nor did I seem to get worse; I bravely held my own from one day to another.

One or two days I was the only occupant of the tent; all my fellow sufferers died within a few days after being brought in from the stockade. Let it be remembered that though nine died in my tent, there was never more than three occupants at a time—myself and two others. This statement is difficult to believe, yet it is literally true. Of these cases one or two should have particular mention. One was that of a large and well framed man who was brought in late one evening. It had been raining hard and he was very wet. He was laid beside me, and, offered some food, which he refused, saying he did not feel like eating that evening and that he would save his rations till next morning. This man and myself were the only occupants of the tent that night. In the after part of the night he became very restless, and annoyed me exceedingly by his rolling about, and by throwing himself against me so as to keep me from sleep. I became somewhat petulent and insisted upon his keeping his own side of the bed, and to cease from annoying me as he had been doing. To this he gave no heed, so getting hold of an old crutch which happened to be in the tent, I placed it next to and under him so that it served as a prop to keep him on his part of the tent. After a time he became perfectly quiet and I supposed he had fallen asleep, and I was soon in dreamland myself. Upon awakening next morning I found that his was the sleep of death, and that his tossings which had annoyed me were the final struggles of the conflict between life and death.

Another case was that of a man who had been in the tent for a number of days, and who did not appear to be much sick, so far as I could judge. He was able to get about much better than I could, and had succeeded in crawling out of the tent to an oak tree which stood near. He took off his shirt and proceeded to hunt the lice off of it, a task of no small magnitude. He then began talking of his home and family, saying that if he could know that they were all comfortable and well provided for he could feel reconciled to his hard fate.

He continued to talk of his wife and children until I finally told him he was foolish to thus worry himself so about his family, and that their worst, possible condition could hardly be a tenth as bad as his own, and that his best and wisest course would be to attend to his own wants as best he could, and that doubtless his family were being properly cared for by friends at home. The poor man paid very little attention to my advice, but continued to worry and fret as before, until of a sudden, and apparently without a pain or struggle, he expired. It was a great surprise to me; I had no idea that death was so near. I saw many—very many die in a similar manner. It seemed that men died without realizing the approach of the grim monster, and also appeared that long continued suffering in mind and body had made them callous to pain, and that when the final moment came they ceased to live, much as a lighted candle is extinguished by a gust of wind. Hope had fed the flickering flame from day to day, and more dead than alive, they moved about, vainly chasing a phantom of release or exchange, a hope which lured from afar yet fled as they followed; finally, when hope no longer cheered and when despair took the ascendency, the victim surrendered and the wearied spirit forsook its prison-house of suffering and launched into the unknown sea of eternity.

Our daily rations in the hospital were a biscuit, a half pint of boiled rice and a bit of beef; and small and insufficient as this was, it was vastly better than we had been accustomed to receive in the stockade. For a time after first entering the hospital I could hardly eat all my rations; but I forced myself to eat all they gave me, believing it really necessary to sustain life. After the nine deaths had occurred in my tent, of which previous mention has been made, two patients were brought in from the stockade and assigned to my tent, These, contrary to the rule, did not die, but began to improve, and this was an encouragement to me. I had seen so many die that I had come to look on death as a certain result of being assigned to my tent.

Seeing these companions improving day after day I seemed to take on new life and at once began to improve, also, and it was but a few days till we three were rapidly convalescing. My companions were both Dutchmen; their names were Edwards and Schrader. The former was a member of a Pennsylvania regiment, and his home was at the town of Broadtop, Pa. Schrader was a native of Germany and a member of an Illinois regiment.

The two men differed widely in their habits, characters and dispositions. Edwards was almost continually talking of his home, father, mother and two sisters; Schrader had little or nothing to say of his home or relatives. Edwards seldom washed his face or combed his hair, and I have known him to go for weeks with his face dirty and his hair matted. Schrader was tasty and careful in his personal habits, but was selfish and disagreeable. Edwards was tender-hearted and liberal; with all his slovenly personal habits he was much the better man of the two, but he had one weakness, that, under the circumstances, was a great disadvantage. He was a great glutton; it appeared that he had the capacity of half a dozen men—for stowing away supplies—nothing eatable ever went to waste where he was, and he never learned *division* as applied to anything fit to eat. His appetite may have been capable of being satisfied, but I do not remember that it ever was. We were all good eaters now, and could have eaten much more than we received. We were all improving and I began to hobble about on a crutch, and the idea of dying in a rebel prison and of being buried in the sand of Georgia, began to lose its grip on me. Our chief trouble was now, as it had been, to get enough to eat. Edwards was an expert beggar and was continually on the lookout for something to supply the mess with more than our drawn rations; hardly a day passed that he did not beg from the attendants at the cook house, something to eat, and after filling himself I came in for the remainder. Schrader was crabbed and surly; he seldom had anything to do with Edwards or me, except that he slept in the same tent with us. Edwards and I frequently messed together; Schrader ate alone. Each morning the bodies of those who had died during the previous night were deposited in the street, preparatory to burial. From here they were wheeled to the dead-house and from thence they were taken in wagons to the place of burial. The dead averaged about thirty each morning. My condition improved from day to day so that I was able, by the aid of a crutch, to move about the hospital grounds. I managed by a little trading, to pick up something extra to eat. There were hundreds of sick and suffering fellows lying in their tents unable to help themselves, but who would get me to buy peanuts, yams and the like for them. I would take their money or other articles of value which they desired to exchange, and, when opportunity offered, would sell them to the guards or exchange them for food, and would be allowed a trifling commission for my trouble. Notwithstanding the existence of an order against trading with our guards, we found many adroit ways and means of steering round the difficulties, and that necessity, which is said to be the mother of invention, was found to be the parent of many a shrewd scheme which brought relief to our urgent needs. During the early period of our imprisonment at Andersonville, there was a considerable amount of greenbacks among the prisoners; but now this money had disappeared almost entirely. Some of the men had small sums of postal currency. Confederate money was plenty enough but it took a hundred dollars to buy a beef-head. Having little or no money to exchange with the guards for what we needed, we bartered articles of clothing, rings, trinckets, pocket-knives, &c., receiving beef-heads, pieces of beef, peanuts and yams. Our plans and bargains were made with the guards during the day, but the exchange of commodities had to be done at night, and with the utmost caution, to avoid being seen by the officers.

I had so far improved in my general health that I was on my feet and moving about during the entire day planning with the guards for such articles of food as could be smuggled through their hands and into ours during their hours of duty at night. In thus moving about I not only gained strength but my spirits improved, and I was also able to provide myself with about all I needed to eat.

In one of my night trades with the guard, I came very nearly losing my life. I had procured from a sick prisoner a nice gutta-percha pocket comb which opened and closed like a knife; this I offered to trade to a guard for peanuts. He prevailed on me, much against my better judgment, to allow him to take the comb to camp to show it to his lieutenant, promising faithfully to bring the pay for it that night at eleven o'clock when he again came on duty. When the hour arrived and the relief to which the guard properly belonged had been placed on their posts, I went down to that beat of the guard line where I expected to find the man who had taken the comb. I approached the sentry and when within a few yards of him I spoke to him and inquired about our trade of the comb and peanuts. Instead of receiving a courteous answer, the guard said to me gruffly, "Now, you get away from here or I will put a ball through you," and as he ceased speaking he fired his piece at me with the evident purpose of furnishing the subject for a funeral on the following day. Though he failed in his plan I had no reason to censure him for his lack of skill as a marksman, and taking his advice I retired to my tent to ponder on the inhumanity of man to man and of the rascality of the rebel who had taken my comb with fraudulent intent, and who by trading off with another guard had not only cheated me out of my comb but had caused me to imperil my life, which in my improved state of health was becoming more and more valuable. The lesson was a useful one to me, for thereafter I planned so that no article passed out of my hands for inspection by a third party.

Shortly after this an affair occured which more than set me even with my dishonest patrons. One of the guards wished to buy a pair of shoes, an article of which many of the soldiers of the C. S. A. stood much in need. He wanted a pair of pants also, and I promised to procure them for him, though at the time I did not know certainly that I could get them.

He promised to give a shoulder of meat and five large yams for the shoes and pants, and the trade was to be consummated that night at eleven o'clock, when he again came on guard at that post I hunted about during the afternoon among the sick, endeavoring to find the shoes, and only partly succeeded. I found two good shoes, both for the left foot, one a No. 8 and the other No. 10. Even this assortment of stock caused me much effort, for I had to look through the camp before I found any one willing to sell, for those who had good shoes and mates needed them too badly to part with them at any price which I could pay. I put the shoes in as merchantable a shape as I could, and felt that with a reasonably dark night to aid in the trade I might hope to succeed in convincing " Johnnie " that " shoes would be shoes" before the war was over. I found a pair of pants more readily than the shoes, and though they were not strictly No. 1 in quality, they were good enough to trade on by a little brushing up. When the hour arrived I repaired to the vicinity of the post we had agreed upon. At this place in the guard line the sentinels were stationed on the opposite side of a plank fence about eight feet high. The night was somewhat dark and on that account more favorable for carrying out our purpose. We carried on a whispered conversation by means of a knot hole in a plank of the fence. There was a mutual suspicion and a mutual lack of confidence on each side of the fence; the guard insisted that I should put the pants and shoes over the fence to him first; while I as stoutly insisted on his putting the meat and yams over to me first. I finally suggested to him that we put our articles over, one to the other, at the same time. This he declined to do saying that he feared the articles were not as represented. We would talk and parley awhile and then the guard would pace his beat, keeping up a show of duty, then he would return to the knot hole and the wrangle about the trade would be resumed. Suddenly, while we were hotly engaged in our bantering and badgering, the "grand rounds" for the night, accompanied by the officers of the guard came upon us. The guard, to escape detection, had but one thing to do. He threw the meat and yams over the fence to me and resumed his walk to halt the "grand rounds" party as he was required to do. I did not feel that I had any further business at that knot hole, but seizing the coveted prize I hied to my tent, not forgetting to take with me the shoes and pants, and congratulating myself on the success of my night's work.

I found Edwards at our tent patiently awaiting my return, and in a good condition of appetite, as usual, to enjoy a feast. So we gathered together some splinters and proceeded to build a small fire, by means of which we soon fried a portion of the meat. The fire was insufficient to cook it thoroughly, and we were at last compelled to eat it in a half cooked condition, a circumstance which enabled us to bear valuable testimony on the superiority of rare pork over that which is well fried. We gorged ourselves completely and then slept peacefully, undisturbed by either stomach or conscience.

Whenever I had success in my undertakings, as in the above mentioned case, I generally sought out my two comrades and shared with them the good results, though Shrader was so surly and selfish that he never deserved it, and Edwards very rarely succeeded in bringing in anything in this way, though once in a great while he made a good haul. Though Edwards seemed to have no faculty for trading, he one day made a raise in the line of substance which deserves mention.

I was sitting in my tent one day engaged in putting a half-sole on the seat of my pants, when Edwards came in with a well filled haversuck under his arm, and looking as sneaking and guilty as though he had been caught robbing a savings bank.

I inquired the cause of his singular conduct, but he said nothing very particular had occurred, and then he hid the haversack and its contents under his blanket. I knew something was wrong, and after pressing him for an explanation he told me that the haversack contained a beef liver, that he had got it of one of the guards whose post of duty was on the south side of the hospital grounds, where the guard line was situated on the inside of the fence. I inquired of him how much he had paid for it, and his answer was that he had *promised* to pay the guard five dollars for it, and that though he had no money nor any chances of paying for it, he was so *hungry* that he determined to take the liver anyhow, and pay for it in promises. Edwards was an honest man, but his stomach had no regard for principle, and sometimes led him into predicaments out of which it was difficult to rescue him. He was very ill at ease, now that he had on hands a case of liver complaint, for which the ordinary remedies were inefficient.

Knowing that I would share in the liver, I engaged to share in my comrade's trouble concerning it; so telling him to remain in the tent I made my way down to the guard line, planning on my way how I might cancel the amount due the guard for the liver. I stood around near the guard for some time and then asked him if he had anything to trade or sell. He replied that he had not, that he had just disposed of a beef liver to one of the prisoners, and was now waiting for him to return the haversack and bring the money for the liver. I then told the guard that a short time before I came down the doctors had arrested a fellow having a striped haversack which contained a liver, and that they had taken him to headquarters to tie him up by the thumbs until he would tell where and of whom he procured it. This statement, though not remarkable for its truthfulness, frightened the guard considerably; he said it must be the same one to whom he had sold the liver, and that he feared the fellow would divulge the whole affair to the authorities, and thereby bring upon him some severe punishment. The guard then told me that if I would interest myself in his behalf, by prevailing on the prisoner not to tell where he had got the liver, that he would not exact pay for it, and that for my services in the case he would bring me four quarts of peanuts when he again came on guard. This I agreed to do, and, followed by the best wishes of the troubled sentry, I returned to the tent to share in a huge mess of boiled liver which Edwards had prepared during my absence,—a mess, the enjoyment of which was heightened rather than lessened by the wear and tear of conscience in procuring it.

Time dragged its slow length along; the dullest day had its sunset, and the dreariest night was succeeded by the dawn of another day; monotony was sometimes relieved by variety, and once in a while a gleam of hope's sunshine broke through the overhanging clouds of despair.

I still kept up my trades with our guards, and by this means we had our seasons of plenty now and then, though generally our supply of food was greatly below our needs and of a very inferior quality.

I had bought an extra blanket, and with the one I already had I was well provided in this particular. Many of the sick in our ward began to improve, but this was after more than fifty per cent. of the whole number had died; the prisoners had been removed from the stockade and distributed over different parts of the Confederacy, we knew not where. No more, sick were being brought into the hospital, as in former times, and many of the present occupants of the various wards were going about in improving health, performing light duties and giving to the hospital an air of life which was in happy contrast with the days gone by. By the middle of December, 1864, the only prisoners remaining at Andersonville were occupants of the hospital. No reliable news from the outside world, touching the progress of the war reached us; our captors seemed determined to withold from us any news of the situation, as if our ignorance of passing events would increase the sufferings of our imprisonment. But our principal concern was to prolong our existence and to economize our scanty supplies so as to cheat the monster, grim-visaged death of his prey.

Many deaths were still occuring among us, but they were much less frequent than before; we had looked on death and suffering so long and so frequently that our feelings had grown callous and could witness scenes of horror with very little concern. When a patient died his effects were immediately taken possession of by his living comrades. In the possession of these effects many strange discoveries were made; one man, while tearing up a pair of pants which had been the property of a prisoner who had died, found four hundred dollars in greenbacks carefully stitched in the waist of the pants. Of course this was regarded as a large haul—equal to $16,000 of Confederate promises, for every dollar of Uncle Sam's money would buy forty of the money of the waning Confederacy.

One day I got myself into a serious difficulty by buying a blanket belonging to a fellow-prisoner in our ward of the hospital. He came to me and insisted on my buying his blanket, and continued to press me so persistently that I at last bought it to accommodate him, and not that I needed it particularly. Knowing that orders existed prohibiting the sale and purchase of such articles, I feared I would get into trouble in so doing, but he promised me faithfully that he would never divulge the name of the purchaser under any circumstances. I bought it and paid him his price for it. About three days later some of the convalescents of our ward, the sixteenth, were being transferred to the eighteenth, and among them was the man who had sold me the blanket. The officials went around gathering the blankets of the patients who were being moved; in this I foresaw trouble, so rolling my three blankets up I went with them down to the eighteenth ward and left them there with a friend with whom I had been interested in trading. Then returning to my tent I awaited events. I had not long to wait, for having gone for the man who had sold me the blanket, they had frightened him into telling to whom he had sold the blanket, and bringing him into my tent he pointed me out as the man who had violated the rules. I was soundly abused in language more forcible than eloquent, and was then told that if I did not produce the blanket and restore it to the owner that I would be tied up by the thumbs. Edwards, who was interested in my safety, advised me to confess, but as I had come into possession of the blanket honestly, I concluded to hold out for awhile, at least. Failing to accomplish their purpose by threats, I was taken under guard to headquarters for punishment. The major commanding was not in, but a lieutenant who was temporarily in charge said he had no doubts but that it would be in accordance with the orders of the major to tie me up, and it was done accordingly. A half-inch rope was procured and fastened to each wrist. Then I was stretched up against an oak tree which stood in front of the major's tent, leaving my feet dangling about a foot from the ground. I had been hanging in this manner five or ten minutes—long minutes, and was about concluding to loosen my grip on the blanket, the possession of which was the cause of my present painful suspension. The major returned and at once inquired into the facts of the case. He was informed that I had bought a blanket from a sick comrade and refused to return it when ordered. The major asked me what I had done with the blanket, and I told him that being hungry I had sold it for something to eat. This statement was not as truthful as it might have been, but it served such a good purpose that I never afterward apologized to the officer for telling it, nor have I ever done penance for it. He ordered me taken down and untied, reprimanding the lieutenant severely for his hasty action in the matter, and saying that tying me up so would not return the blanket, and that almost anyone would do the same thing under such circumstances. The major's conduct in this matter impressed me favorably. I was returned to my quarters and liberated. I afterwards took possession of the blanket on account of which I had narrowly escaped severe punishment, and both Edwards and I joined in a season of congratulation over the favorable termination of the affair.

Two or three weeks after this occurrence the man with whom I had left the blankets for safe keeping, mention of which has been previously made, came to me and said that he saw a chance of escape, and desired I should join him in the effort. I told him that if his plan was a feasible one I would share in the adventure, though my experience in that line of exploits had not been full of reward. I have before stated that on the south side of the hospital grounds was an extended shallow swamp; on this side the guards walked on the inside of the fence, and on the other three sides they walked on the outside. On this side I noticed that the sentinels were less vigilant at times than the nature of their duties required, and that they would build little fires on the guard-line at night, around which they would stand or sit in couples or singly when they knew that they were not watched by the officers, and at such times the prisoners would approach the guards and traffic with them. In the southeast corner of the grounds a tree which grew on the inside had fallen across the fence and partially knocked it down, the top of the tree falling in the swamp on the outside.

It seemed an easy thing after dark, when the guards were not watching, for a person to crawl over the body of the tree, let himself down into the swamp and escape; and this was the plan by which we hoped to gain our liberty. We hardly hoped to succeed entirely, but we argued that if we could but succeed in scaling the prison fence at this tree, and gain a temporary freedom of a few days, the effort was worth making, and we determined to try it.. We knew that four savage bloodhounds were kept for the purpose of pursuing escaped prisoners, but this fact did not check our determination to see how it looked out in the country. We thought it might be several days before we would be missed, and by that time it would be impossible to track us by the scent. We made everything ready to carry out our plan on a certain night. I said nothing to Edwards of our plan, for I well knew that he would refuse to go, and would do all he could to prevent my going.

On two different nights we approached the place intending to make the effort, but both times we found the guards unusually watchful, and we waited for a more favorable time. On the third night circumstances seemed more favorable, and about ten o'clock we crept cautiously down toward the place through which we intended escaping. The guards were standing round a small fire engaged in trading with a number of prisoners. It was cloudy and rain was falling in a gentle shower. The guards seemed to have no fear of anyone trying to make an escape on such a night as this. We saw that no more favorable a time than this could be expected, and that if we ever intended making the effort, now was our time. My partner, whose name was Williams, crept over the log in advance of me and told me to follow. We used the utmost caution, for even the breaking of a twig might arouse the guards. We crept along the trunk of the tree, Williams four feet in advance. Our position at this moment was critical in the extreme, for if discovered we were almost sure to be shot down. But at last we got on the outside. Williams let himself down into the shallow water without making any noise, but when I attempted to do the same thing I slipped and fell into the water with a noisy splash. This raised an alarm. The guards shouted "halt" and opened a brisk fire. But there was very little danger in their firing, as the fence was now between us and them, and if it had been open day they could not have fired on us with anything like fatal effect.

I sprang to my feet and got away as fast as possible, never thinking of Williams nor of making an effort to keep with him. The swamp abounded with underbrush and old, decaying logs, and was altogether a place through which one could move with very little speed, especially in the darkness. In my haste to escape I scratched my face and hands and bruised myself in a fearful manner. I stumbled over old logs, and many times fell headlong into the mud and water, until I was so fatigued I could make no further progress.

Halting to rest, I thought of Williams and listened attentively that I might hear him making his way through the swamp. I would have hallooed, but was fearful of being heard by the guards who might possibly be pursuing.

Nothing could be heard of my adventurous comrade, nor did I ever afterwards learn of his fate. He was a man of nerve and had a heart as big as all out-doors, and I deeply regretted parting with him, especially at a time like this. I rested for a long time and continued to hope to hear something from Williams, but in vain. All was quiet except that the frogs and other occupants of the swamp made noisy complaints at being disturbed at this hour of the night. I was now filled with fearful apprehensions; I imagined fearful alligators lying in wait to devour me, and my situation was such that I began to wish myself back in the prison. Failing to hear from Williams, I moved on with great difficulty, hardly knowing whither I went I had no knowledge of the extent of the swamp, and very little knowledge of the direction I was going.

I kept on with great difficulty, thinking that I would come out somewhere. About three o'clock in the morning, I struck higher ground and realized that I had emerged from the swamp. Here I lay down to rest, and being completely tired out, I fell asleep and slept till after daylight. A dense forest surrounded me; behind me was the swamp and in front and on either hand was an unbroken wilderness of woods. I had lost all hopes of hearing from Williams. I ate a scanty breakfast from the little store of provisions with which I had provided myself before starting; then resuming my journey I traveled in a southwestern direction, through a level and heavily timbered country. I felt all the time that I must emerge into some cultivated and inhabited region, though how I would proceed or what plan I would adopt to carry out my purpose and secure my escape, had not entered my mind.

The injuries I had sustained in floundering through the swamp made me stiff and sore, and hindered my progress very much. Finally, about three o'clock in the afternoon, I came in sight of a cultivated plantation, the view of which gave me great joy. I seated myself on a log to rest, and after a short time I thought I heard the baying of a hound behind me. I listened with breathless attention, and again I heard the same sound with more distinctness. I was now convinced that I was being pursued, and that the hounds were on my trail. What was to be done? I looked about me and began to plan for the best and to escape the jaws of the hounds, which would soon be upon me. The fork of a tree which stood near invited me and I climbed the trunk and was soon in the fork awaiting the arrival of my pursuers. The dogs, four in number, soon came up and began barking with savage vigor. Being fifteen feet from the ground, I was beyond their reach, and from my perch of safety I contemplated their noisy rage with no little interest. In a short time three Confederates appeared on horseback. One of them accosted me with, "Ah, Yank, we've got you this time." Another called on me to come down at once. I told them to get off their horses and keep the dogs from injuring me and I would come down. One of them dismounted, and driving the dogs back, stood at the tree while I descended. The hounds did not seem inclined to injure me after this. I was ordered to mount behind one of the men, and the chase being ended, we rode in the direction of the prison. As we proceeded they inquired how many had made their escape, and also the manner in which it was effected. I told them a straight story and made inquiry concerning Williams, to which they replied that he had not been retaken, and they cared very little whether he was or not. These men seemed to be jovial and good-hearted; they chatted socially and treated me in the kindest manner. They expressed themselves as being heartily tired of the war and their general conduct was in marked contrast with that of the guards who had retaken me when I escaped at Danville. We reached the prison about sundown, and I ascertained that I had not reached a point more than seven miles from our place of escape, but I must have traveled in a zigzag course. Upon our arrival I was taken to headquarters and reported to the major commanding. This officer asked me how many escaped with me and by what means we got away. I told him the whole truth, and he believed it. He said that owing to my bruised and battered condition and the rough time I had had in the swamp that he would let me off for this time, but he advised me not to repeat the attempt, as it would be impossible to gain my liberty, even if I was successful in escaping from the grounds. My pitiable condition, hair matted with mud, clothes torn and my face scratched and bruised presented a plea to clemency stronger than could have been made by the tongue of eloquence. The major in dismissing me and sending me to my quarters, advised me to take better care of myself, a bit of advice which I accepted thankfully. Shortly after this incident the major was assigned to duty elsewhere, and left us, a circumstance which we had cause to regret. He was a man of many excellent qualities and inflicted no unnecessary pain upon the prisoners under him. His whole soul seemed overflowing with the milk of human kindness, and it was a common remark that so good a man was unfortunate in espousing so bad a cause.

I never heard of Williams after our separation in the swamp. He was not captured and returned to prison nor hospital at Andersonville, and his fate remained a mystery to me. The swamp was many miles in extent in one direction, and he may have penetrated deeper and deeper into it and then perished of hunger; or he may have been killed in being retaken. It is barely possible that by good fortune he succeeded in reaching the lines of our army, and was safe. If living I hope that fate may place this account before him, and acquaint him of my whereabouts. I have, somehow, a hope that he still lives.

Events of no very exciting moment occupied our time from this till about the middle of the following January, 1865. I had continued my traffic in various ways, and by so doing managed to scrape together a tolerably good living. The stockade had now been unoccupied for nearly three months, but at the above named time three or four thousand prisoners were brought in and placed in the stockade, and many, including myself, were sent to the stockade from the hospital. Here we began to retaste some of the horrors of our imprisonment of the preceding summer, but we were not so crowded as before, for instead of 25,000, as formerly, we only numbered a little less than 4,000; therefore we had plenty of room. But our rations were scant, and it was as much as we could do to live on what we got. Some time in the latter part of February five hundred of our number were ordered to move. Edwards and I were of that number, and we indulged strongly in a hope of an exchange and release. A short time previous to this the Confederates had been making efforts to enlist the prisoners in the stockade to serve in the Southern army. A Colonel O'Neil, an Irishman, of the C. S. A., came into the stockade daily, and succeeded in enlisting many of the stoutest and hardiest of the prisoners. Of the three hundred thus enlisted the larger portion were foreigners. None but the very stoutest were taken. I learned afterwards that all these deserted in a body and joined the Union army, but this may not be true. None of those who enlisted should be blamed or censured for using any and every means to obtain their freedom, and I think that each of those who enlisted had strong reasons for doing so, for "all that a man hath will he give for his life."

Many persons who stayed at home, viewing the battle from afar, and knowing nothing of the dreadful carnage of battle, and experiencing nothing of the horrors of starvation in prison, are the first and loudest to proclaim that they would have died before they would have enlisted thus. Such folks seldom die in this manner.

The order to move, before mentioned, was not carried out immediately, and it was not till the early days of March that we began to pack our scanty effects preparatory to moving out. This was a task to which we applied ourselves with promptness; shout after shout went up from the men whose hearts had been bowed down with unutterable woe for many weary months; the news seemed almost too good to be true, and we found ourselves inquiring of each other whether it were a fact that we had received such orders; or was it a trick of our captors to add one more woe to the long roll of miseries that had embittered our lives. But after some further waiting five hundred of us were marched out of the stockade and to the depot. Our star of hope began to rise, and the prospect of release from our charnel-house of horrors began to grow bright. Now that we were out of the hated pen and waiting for a train to go hence, seemed almost like heaven begun below. We waited at the depot from 11 a. m., till 4 p. m., and no train coming for us, we were again returned to the stockade. What a mighty reverse this was to our feelings, and how it blasted the cherished hopes of a few hours before. Our hearts sank within us, and dark despair took the place where hope had triumphed but an hour ago. Many gave up and sank under this blow of disappointment. Tears were shed, and maledictions and curses were heard on every hand. It was like snatching the cooling water from the victim of a consuming thirst. Many said that we may as well make up our minds to die in prison and no longer cherish hopes which budded but to perish; and in this state of hopelessness many did die. We resumed our places in the stockade and knew not what the future promised.

About two weeks after this, orders were again received, and again the fires of hope were kindled within us. This order was greeted with an outburst of joy which baffles description. Our labor of packing up and preparing to move was speedily and cheerfully performed. This being completed we marched with light hearts to the depot, finding a train of box cars in waiting. We were soon aboard and were much crowded, but we were so much overjoyed at the prospect of leaving that we cared little for the discomfort we experienced.

Our train moved in a southerly direction, running as far as Albany, in the southern part of Georgia. Here this line of railroad terminated. We were now fifty miles from Andersonville. It was after dark when we reached Albany. We were taken from the cars and laid by till next morning.

Rations were issued to us next morning and we were told that we were now on the way to the Union lines, and that this supply of food must last us till we reached our friends. We were so overjoyed at the prospect of gaining our liberty that we now cared very little about what was given us to eat.

From this place we took up a line of march, and for three days we traveled in an easterly direction, through a level country, and over what I considered very poor soil. We marched about twenty miles a day, and at the close of the third day we reached Thomasville, the county seat of Thomas county, one of the border counties of Georgia on the Florida line. Our sick where hauled across the country from Albany in wagons; many gave out on the march, and they, too, were hauled. It became necessary to press into the service the teams and wagons of planters living along the line of march, and by so doing our transportation was made equal to our needs. At Thomasville we received some kind attentions which I mention with pleasure, and which shows that even in an enemy's land we were treated as if we were human in character, at least. On the day after our arrival many ladies visited us, bringing baskets full of provisions, daintily prepared, and distributed them to the sick and most destitute of our number. They brought many articles of clothing and gave to those in need; many a sick and dying prisoner invoked God's blessing on the head of these angels of mercy as they ministered to the sick and destitute. This incident was like the gleam of sunshine on a dark day; like a spring of water in a thirsty land.

On the next day we were told that owing to a lack of cars we could not leave till the following day; and on the next day and for several successive days we were told the same comfortless story. These delays seemed ominous of evil. Rumors of various kinds floated through the camp, and our star of hope began to lose its brilliancy. Many of us prophesied that evil was near at hand, and the most hopeful began to doubt; even our guards seemed confused and hardly knew what to do with us or themselves. Thus time wore on till the fifth day, when we were ordered to be ready to move; but instead of marching us to the depot and the train as we had hoped, we were turned back and marched in the direction of Albany, on the same road over which we had marched with such buoyant hearts and bright hopes but a few days before. At this unhappy turn in our affairs, who can describe the despair which weighed down our every heart, for we seemed to see and understand in this movement that our cup of sorrow was not yet drained of all its galling bitterness. We would a hundred fold sooner have marched in any other direction than towards Andersonville. How we hated, loathed and detested the very name of the spot where we had seen and suffered so much. And now after having our hopes raised to such a point that we could almost see the stars and strips of the dear old flag, and hear the anthems of liberty, and taste the joys of freedom, and now that we were made to turn our backs on all this and march toward our hated prison-pen, the thought was crushing, and was next to death itself. Heavy hearts make heavy feet; we were four days reaching Albany. We were sick, weary, disheartened, and the last ray of hope was almost extinguished. At Albany we were put on the cars and in a brief time were again within the walls of dreary Andersonville. If we had been sad and disheartened in counter-marching toward our old place of torment, how much more forlorn and dejected did we now feel in realizing that hope had fled and despair held a heartless mastery. Nothing could be learned concerning the progress of the war, and our knowledge of the outside world was almost a blank.

Many of us bore our misfortunes as stoically as possible, and determined to keep our spirits up to the end; but how we succeeded in doing so seems almost marvel. The actions of our captors seemed to indicate that they considered their cause a hopeless one, and in this we drew a little comfort. At the end of ten days after our return from Thomasville we again received orders to move, and again we gathered together our scanty effects, hoping in this, our third moving, to see the last of Andersonville. We marched to the depot and got aboard a train of cars a little after dark. We noticed that our guards were much excited over some news which we construed to be in our favor, and they seemed to care very little whether we escaped or not, and they made little effort to prevent our escape. I saw more than one opportunity of escaping, but I began to see that we were a burden on their hands and that they were becoming every hour more and more anxious of getting rid of us. Our train moved out at ten o'clock P. M., but instead of going south, as before, we moved in the direction of Macon. This was as we wished, for we felt more hopes of getting into our lines in this direction than by going south. We were all night and till eight o'clock the next day running to Macon, a distance of sixty miles. Captain Wirtz accompanied the train, and he seemed considerably excited over something which he kept to himself. When the train halted at Macon the Captain passed from one car to another, assuring the men that this time they would certainly be sent through to the Union lines, and he seemed more like a man and less like the fiend that he was than on any former occasion. We regarded this as an item in our favor.

We remained at Macon nearly two hours, during which time we remained in the cars, and then we were again run back toward Andersonville. Who can imagine our feelings as our train sped in the direction of the place we most detested on earth. We asked each other, "Shall we never be free from the horrid place?" We reached Andersonville at three o'clock in the afternoon, but contrary to our expectations, and to our agreeable surprise, we were not allowed to leave the train, and were assured that after a short halt we would be sent on. This announcement was cheered lustily; the poor sufferers shook hands, shed tears and made many demonstrations of the joy which filled their hearts. The scene was one which can neither be imagined nor described. After a halt of half an hour our train again moved, going south. We reached Albany at nine o'clock that night, and, disembarking, spent the remainder of the night. In the morning we had issued to us six hard tack, which were to feed us for three days. We then set out to march to Thomasville, which place we reached at the end of three days' marching. Such of our numbers as could not be transported in wagons were left at Albany, and were afterwards sent forward. On the day following our arrival at Thomasville we were again put on board a train, and again doubts filled our minds, and serious apprehensions harassed us; for we were yet ignorant of our destination. *But we were going away from Andersonville;* there was a world of comfort in that. Our course for sixteen or twenty hours seemed to be a zigzag one, but at the end of that time we reached Lake City, in Florida. Here we went into camp at a distance of four miles from the city. Our camp was beside the railroad, and near a pond of stagnant water, from which we supplied ourselves with water to use and drink. We at length found plenty of better water by digging four or five feet.

Some of the men were wading in the pond a short distance from the bank, when they came across a young alligator, six feet in length. They set about trying to kill it with clubs. The guards, attracted by the confusion, came to their assistance and the alligator was shot, after which the carcass was cut up and divided among us. We had been so long without meat that we thought we could eat anything like flesh; besides, we were on the verge of starvation; all the rations we had received since leaving Albany was a small quantity of meal. In the distribution of the alligator the mess to which I belonged got the tail. This we skinned and cut into thin slices, after which it was boiled and eaten. Under the circumstance we agreed that it was as good meat as we had ever tasted. We remained in camp near Lake City four days, then boarding a train, we were sent to Baldwin, a small place about forty miles in an easterly direction. This was the outpost of the C. A. at this time, in the direction of Jacksonville, where a part of our army was stationed. The railroad to Jacksonville had been destroyed by one or both armies, and this station was as far as the cars were running in the direction of the Union lines.

From Baldwin to Jacksonville was sixteen miles, and we were told that we were to reach it on foot. We had been guarded from Andersonville to this place by a regiment of Mississippi infantry, commanded by Colonel Gibbs. We left Baldwin at ten o'clock in the morning and marched in the direction of Jacksonville. Our guards accompanied us a few miles, when the Colonel called a halt. He told us that his command would go no further, that we were now at liberty, and by pursuing our way along the railroad we would soon reach our forces at Jacksonville in safety. He advised us to assist each other on the march and keep together as well as we could. He assured us that we would find our friends ready to receive us at Jacksonville. He and his command then bade us good-bye and turned back. I do not remember that any tears of regret were shed on the occasion. And now such joyous shouts and such prolonged cheers as went up from this haggard crowd of famished men seldom is heard by mortal ears. The fact that we were within a few miles of the flag which we had so long a desire to see seemed to be a joy almost purer than we could bear.

As soon as our guards left us all order of march was at an end, and each man set out and moved ahead to suit himself, regardless of his stronger or weaker companion, and in a short time the line was lengthened out to a distance of more than two miles. I marched as well as I could, but soon fell behind the majority, and yet as far backward as I could see there were many stragglers, all trying their best to make the desired end.

I was barefooted and hatless; my breeches were worn off to the knees and my shirt had lost its sleeves. All the baggage I had was half of an old blanket which I threw over my shoulders when it rained. Many marched until they became exhausted and then sank beside the way. My feet were blistered, swollen and full of prickles from sand burs. I kept on, doing my best till three o'clock in the afternoon, when I sank beside the road, feeling that I must rest, for though liberty beckoned and freedom glittered ahead of me, the flesh was weaker than the will. I rested for more than an hour, and during that time many of the stragglers came up and passed on; yet there were many more who were still in the rear. As I again moved on an old man came hobbling along and seeming to be exerting his utmost to get ahead. As he walked by my side I noticed his labored breathing and his desperate efforts to move on. Suddenly he fell forward on his face. I stopped and gave him some attention. One or two other soldiers came up, and while we were discussing what was best to do with him he ceased to breathe. He lived not more than six minutes after he fell. We then moved on, leaving the lifeless body where it had fallen. I was informed that many in the rear were lying unable to get further. About sundown we came to a picket post of our army in the vicinity of Jacksonville. I had not felt free until I was well inside the lines of our army, for I did not know but the wheel of fate would yet make an unfortunate turn and we should again fall into the hands of the enemy. I entered Jacksonville in the dusk of the evening, and as I passed along a street I saw a colored woman carrying half of a large fish. I begged a portion of it of her and carried it into camp for my supper. It was fully dark when I found my comrades in camp; wagon loads of light bread were issued to us after our arrival, and barrels of good coffee as an accompaniment. This and the fish furnished me such a supper as I had not had in an age.

Next day a force was sent out to bring in those of the prisoners who had become exhausted on the march. I was told that five poor fellows had died on the march, and I know of many others, nearly forty, who died soon after reaching Jacksonville. The excitement of being again free had caused many to over-exert their strength, and the frail tenement gave way. It was now April 28th, 1865; I had been taken at Chickamauga September 20th, 1863, making my imprisonment nineteen months and eight days. I am safe in saying that there are not now living, of all the thousands who suffered as prisoners of war, fifty men who served for the length of time I did, and if there is any horror in all the long list of sickness, starvation and untold misery which fell to the lot of any of my fellow prisoners, and which I did dot suffer, it must be too dreadful to be told.

At Jacksonville we learned that the war was about ended, that President Lincoln had been killed, and many other matters of public interest had transpired of which we had been ignorant. We remained a month longer a Jacksonville, and during that time many more of our number died. Many who were unable to control themselves ate too greedily, and not a few caused their own death in this manner.

From Jacksonville we were taken by hospital boat to Annapolis, Maryland. Here we learned of the capture of Jeff. Davis, and that the war was ended. Here we had issued to us new clothing and received the money due us for rations during our imprisonment. This was twenty-five cents a day for each day of our imprisonment. From Annapolis we were sent to Camp Chase, near Columbus. Remaining here one night, I next day took the train for my home at St. Paris, Ohio, where I arrived about noon. I had long been regarded by my friends as dead, and my appearance among them was as one from the grave.

This is my story of prison life. I have made no effort to overdraw the facts in any part of it, but have told the truth. I may have stated inaccuracies regarding dates, distances, names and other minor matters, but my discription of the suffering and starvation in the prisons where I suffered, is short of the truth, in that the worst cannot be told. If the living could not speak, there are the graves of an army of martyrs at Andersonville which tell the story better than my feeble pen has done it. In thus giving to the public this simple narrative, I am actuated by no desire to stir up strife or to engender bitter feelings toward any section of our now happy country, for I believe that all feelings of bitterness should be buried in the grave of forgetfulness. Let us cherish a love for our dear country and its institutions, the preservation and perpetuation of which has cost so much blood and sacrafice ; and in the language of our country's great founder, let us " frown indignantly upon the first dawning of any attempt to alienate any portion of our country from the rest, or to enfeeble the sacred ties that now link together the various parts."

It is a source of regret to me that the fortunes of war placed me where I did not share in the crimson glory which the 113th O. V. I. won on so many well fought fields, and that the associations I had formed among the membership of the dear old command should terminate as they did, never to be renewed again until the final *reveille* that shall awake the heroic.   Yours,

J. N. HALL.

SKETCHES AND RECOLLECTIONS.

BY MAJOR J. SWISHER.

NORTH LEWISBURG, O., *April 5th, 1884.*
SERGT. F. M. MCADAMS, RICHWOOD, OHIO,

Dear Sir :—Allow me to congratulate you on the near approach to completion of the History of the 113th Regiment, O. V. I. This work cannot fail to be of interest to every member of the Regiment. It is complete in detail—having dealt largely in facts connected with the every-day life of the common soldier, facts which have usually been overlooked by the historian. You ask that I write something for the Knapsack in the form of personal recollections of the war. With a full knowledge that I may write of many facts already treated of in the body of the work, I shall undertake the work in as brief a manner as possible.

It was expected early in the Summer of 1862, that a draft would have to be resorted to in order to fill the ranks of the depleted regiments in the field. All able bodied men were enrolled, and officers had been appointed by the Government, before whom any one could go and be examined, preparatory to exemption from military duty. And here my recollection is very vivid. Men who had been known to be regular rounders, and boasted of their prowess, and were noted for raising a row whenever they could, were the ones who filled the exemption offices; and it was learned for the first time, that almost every other man was ruptured, or in some way was totally unfit to perform the duties of a soldier. Others had a front tooth out which was made much of to show that they were not able to eat hard tack or bite a cartridge. Some again made it known that they never had been able to stand the report of a gun, hence unfit, and claimed exemption. No doubt many of these same individuals would have gone to the dominions of Queen Victoria, but an order was issued that no man should leave the United States without a passport; but to the credit of these men, many of them went into the war afterwards and were valiant soldiers. August 15, 1862, F. M. McAdams, Harrison Walburn and I went to Urbana and enlisted under John S. Leedom, who failed to go himself. On the 28th of August, 1862, I bid farewell to my family and friends and boarded the train at Urbana. Here we met a number of men from St. Paris, whose acquaintance we made for the first time, an acquaintance, which through the trying ordeal of war ripened into friendship, which will, we hope, last through all time. We were now to give up our personal liberty, and yield ourselves to the command of those appointed over us. We arrived at Columbus the same evening and were marched at once to the State House, and from thence to Camp Chase. We were about ninety in number under Captain Riker. Our first night was passed without tents or blankets, but being warm weather we suffered no inconvenience. During our stay at Camp Chase, which lasted about two months, we were almost constantly on the drill grounds, preparing for the duties which awaited us in the field. Shortly after our arrival in camp, an election was held for the office of First Lieutenant which resulted in the election of John Bowersock. Here I received a warrant as First Sergeant of Company E. My recollections of the duties of an orderly sergeant of a company of men fresh from citizen life are, that it was a very trying one. To restrain men from a liberty they had enjoyed, and mould them to military discipline was not an enviable task. We had been promised a local bounty as soon as mustered in. The men taking enlistment for muster expected to be paid at once. The local authorities of Champaign County, from which county I was enlisted, understood it was to be paid at muster in to the U. S. service. This caused discontent, and men refused to be restrained under a contract which they conceived had been violated by the authorities. Many took French leave, whilst others were at home on furlough, when I distinctly recollect being the only enlisted man of Company E in camp. All, however, came back in a few days, when we soon moved to Camp Zanesville. The night before starting, Fred Baldwin, of Company E, got up about 2 o'clock a. m., as he claimed, to split kindling, he was so anxious to be ready to go, and in doing so he cut one of his fingers off. I recollect the complimentary remark of Dr. Black on the occasion; Baldwin was never mustered into the service, but was sent home to split kindling. On the day following James Edmonson preached the funeral sermon over his finger from the text, "If thy right hand offend thee, cut it off." The congregation was large but the mourners few. Arriving at Camp Zanesville we were mustered into the U. S. service by Captain Howard and received our local bounty. This I recollect was taken from me afterwards on being promoted. We staid here but a short time; but while here some of the boys kicked over a stove and set fire to the quarters, when the whole camp was burned. From here we went to Camp Dennison. Here we drew our first mules and wagons, and were sent to Louisville, Ky., and from thence to Muldrough Hill to guard a bridge just rebuilt, after having been burned by Morgan. While here I went with M. G. Doak to Dr. Harlow to have a tooth pulled, and the Doctor by the light of a candle pulled two before he got the right one. From here I was sent back to Ohio in company with W. G. Carpenter to look after men absent without leave. Starting from Columbus with a number of men and arriving at Cincinnati we placed them in the barracks, and during the night in a drunken row among the men, Reason B. Parker, of Company E, (enlisted as musician) had his skull broken, from which he died shortly afterward at Louisville. On our arrival at Louisville we met the regiment with a large number of other troops ready to take boat for Nashville. Our regiment went aboard the steamer St. Patrick, the flagship of the squadron, numbering about forty vessels and three gunboats. On this trip I remember a lottery scheme was gotten up on the steamer St. Patrick in which some of the commissioned officers were leaders, and almost every man invested in some of the tickets; but news of the scheme coming to Colonel Wilcox the money was refunded, the officers placed under arrest for a few days, when it all died out. On our arrival at Fort Donalson we found the 83d Illinois Volunteers at that place engaged in a desperate battle with the Rebel General Forest, who was intent on capturing the fort and turning the guns on the fleet and prevent it ascending the river to re-enforce Rosecrans at Murfreesboro; but our gunboats arriving in time threw a few shells among the rebels, killing many of them, when they raised the siege and retreated, leaving the 83d Illinois the victors of the contest. Here the fleet halted and many of us were permitted to go on shore and view the battlefield, where we, for the first time, beheld the victims of warfare, strewn dead and dying over the field. We soon arrived at Nashville with banners flying and bands playing. Before leaving the boat Colonel Wilcox presented me with a Second Lieutenant commission, which was to me a very agreeable surprise. We marched out about three miles and went into camp for the night. Here Colonel Wilcox took his final leave of us, and Colonel Mitchell at once assumed command. We remained here but one day, when we took up our line of march for Franklin, Tenn., distant eighteen miles. We remained here near two months, in the meantime drilling and doing picket duty. I was here detailed as Quartermaster of the 113th Regiment. I learned here of the death of Harrison Walborn, who had been left at Nashville sick. I have no doubt but this was a case of death from home-sickness.

I have many pleasant recollections of this place, Franklin being a very beautiful village, situated in one of the most beautiful countries I ever beheld. The citizens were intensely rebel, and took no pains to conceal it. While here we had several brushes with the rebels, but nothing serious or verging on what would be called a battle. Eleven rebel cavalry here made a dash through our outposts and through town, and down to the Harpeth river, and attempted to cross, when three of them were shot. No more reckless charge was made during the war. Captain Riker resigned here, and I received my commission as First Lieutenant, and Sergeant McCrea was commissioned as Second Lieutenant and sent home on recruiting service, and remained away till October. We moved from here to Triune, Tennessee, about the middle of May, and remained but a short time. General Rosecrans having advanced on Tullehoma, we moved to Murfreesboro, Tennessee, where Rosecrans had defeated the rebel army, under General Bragg, six months before. This was a fine country and a beautiful village. Here General Mitchell was sent to hospital with small-pox. We moved from here to Shelbyville, Tennessee, passing on our way the church where Vallandigham had been passed through the lines, that he might join with his rebel friends in talking treason, of which a court martial had found him guilty a short time before. We lay at Shelbyville for some time, but were compelled to leave town, where we first took up our quarters, on account of the fleas. They drove us out of town. We camped south of town on an old rebel camp, where we encountered nothing worse than graybacks. In driving the rebels out of town and across Duck river, many of them were killed and sunk in the river. I remember the body of one having washed down the river and over a dam, and the returning eddy drew it back, when it would be again thrown out, only to be drawn back again. This was continued for several days, when it was finally taken out and buried on the bank of the river. Here several of our men came near being taken under by this returning eddy while bathing in the river, among them Captain Bowersock and David Walker. While here I was sent out by General Whittaker with a large train, on Sunday, with the 98th O. V. I., as a guard, to cut a field of oats and bring it in. We found four McCormick reapers and five cradles, impressing the owners of the machines, with their teams, to run them. At three o'clock we started back to camp with forty acres of oats on our wagons. Rosecrans having moved from Tullahoma, we moved to Wartrace, Tennessee, where we remained but a short time. This being the season of roasting ears, peaches and blackberries, we fared well. The grand advance was now made on Chattanooga. Up to this time we had had no regular supply trains. Each regiment was allowed thirteen wagons, and every one insisted on taking and having hauled for him all the baggage he wanted—enough, such as it was, to supply any family in starting in housekeeping. On our first day out it was found that our wagons were overloaded, and General Steadman, having assumed command of our division, ordered a general inspection. Colonel Warner, who was in command of the 113th O. V. I. at that time, accompanied by the inspecting officer, ordered the wagons unloaded for inspection. It was rather amusing, as the Inspector passed along the line, to notice the woeful countenances of the men as their household goods were ordered to be left, and the inspecting officer indulged in various epithets not complimentary to that kind of soldiering; but when he came to the last wagon, commonly called headquarters wagon, in which the household goods of Colonel Warner were to be inspected, he found the fly to a wall tent had been fastened to two large rails about three feet apart, which formed the foundation to Colonel Warner's bed. I have no doubt but that the inspecting officer felt like the man who was going up hill with a cart load of potatoes, when the end-gate came out and spilled them all—that he could not do the subject justice—and rode silently away. Colonel Warner did not have these loaded in the wagon again. Our march from this on was without any particular incident till we reached Chattanooga. The rebels had evacuated that place, and fallen back to Lafayette, Georgia, having been reinforced by Longstreet. When near Rossville Gap, the battle of Chickamauga was fought. The Reserve Corps (commanded by General Gordon Granger), of which our brigade formed a part, was hurriedly sent through Rossville Gap, and, after two days' marching and counter-marching, was, on Sunday, September 20, 1863, thrown into the conflict. As the result has already been written, I will only relate a few instances which came under my personal observation. When the conflict was raging the hottest, three men of Company E, all red headed—namely: Thomas Scott, David Chatfield and Frank Russel—were charging on the rebel hosts, when I heard Scott make the remark that "us read headed fellows could stand it as well as any," when, at the same instant, Russel was killed, Scott was wounded, and Chatfield had his blanket riddled with bullets. Another instance I will give to show the nice part rank played in the army. Our lines were being hard pressed. Colonel Mitchell sent me to tell Captain Burton to remove his battery from the field. I delivered the order direct, and Captain Burton paid no attention to it. I then said: "Colonel Mitchell directs that you move your battery off the field at once." He obeyed the order immediately. He out-ranked me. After the battle we moved to Chattanooga, and remained there till the 25th of November, when the rebels were hurled in dismay from Mission Ridge. While lying in Chattanooga, I received an order from General Garfield to report at General Rosecrans' quarters immediately. This was at twelve o'clock at night. Arriving there, I was told that there were 1,100 broken down artillery and cavalry horses that must be taken back to Stevenson, Alabama, and that I must take charge of them, and collect forage from the country and have them fed till further orders. This I successfully accomplished, but, not liking the job, I sought the first opportunity to be relieved. Major Sullivant, Lieutenant McCrea and Sergeant Parr, coming from Ohio on their way to join the regiment, I turned my charge over to Captain Estap, of the 8th Indiana Battery, and started with them for Chattanooga. At Jasper, Tennessee, we fell in company with a man going, he said, to Chattanooga, and who wanted to accompany us. He insisted on going the river road instead of taking the circuitous route over the Sequatchie Mountain. We suspicioned he was seeking to lead us into a trap. A consultation was held among us, in which it was agreed that the most dire vengeance should be inflicted on him at the first sign of treachery. He, seeing our suspicions, pulled a pass from under the lining of his hat, which read as follows:

"Pass O'Connel day or night. Peculiarity, finger off the right hand.
GEORGE H. THOMAS,
Maj. Gen. Commanding."

He proved to be a number one man, and had been through the rebel army as a spy and was on his way back to report to General Thomas. The river road, however, proved a very dangerous one. The rebels, armed with long ranged guns, held the south side of the Tennessee river, and were able to shoot across and make it dangerous to travel the river road, which ran along the river bank; hence we were forced to travel all day on the side of the mountain, the whole time being subjected to a continuous fire, which came uncomfortably close. I had a horse to lead which stumbled in between some rocks, and being unable to get out, Sergeant Parr shot it. I carried the saddle till night, when camping with some soldiers we had come up with, it was stolen. Arriving at Chattanooga, I was sent back immediately to Stevenson, Alabama with a supply train. We had to make a circuitous route of sixty-eight miles to get a distance of twenty-eight. While on the Sequatchie mountain we met General Grant and staff on their way to Chattanooga to assume command of the army at that place. On the trip to Stevenson, the roads being bad and the mules in a bad condition, we were compelled to abandon some of the wagons, and the mules were shot, being unable to travel, and we did not wish to leave them to fall into the hands of the citizens. On our way back we stopped at Jasper, Tennessee. While sleeping by the side of a peach tree to which I had tied my horse, Colonel Ray's East Tennessee Cavalry, stationed at that place, moved and stole my horse. It was on this trip, and while at Stevenson, Alabama, that I hailed with delight many of my old neighbors whom I had not seen for two years. They were a part of General Hooker's forces, on their way from the Army of the Patomac to reinforce the Army of the Cumberland. The army now reinforced by the Fifteenth Corps and Hooker's troops and General Grant in command moved on November 26th against Bragg's army on Mission Ridge and Lookout Mountain, gaining a complete victory and sending the rebels in complete dismay, closely pursued by our forces, to Ringgold. Sherman was now sent to Knoxville to relieve General Burnsides. On this trip I served on the staff of General Beatty as Commissary. I gathered meat, molasses, flour, meal, &c., from the country to feed the brigade. Of course the reader will understand when I say I did it, that I only supervised or assissted, as I had all the help I wanted and every man a hero. To do this it was sometimes necessary to gather the grain and grind it. At one time I had four mills impressed into the service and running; others were doing the same. We entered smoke houses, meal chests and granaries; this seemed hard to take the last bite from these families, but we were marching to relieve a starving fortress and we must eat. Necessity knows no law. Our orders were to leave each family four days rations; I doubt whether this was always done. As an incident of this campaign, I recollect being in a smoke house, contending with a man about the division of a barrel of Sorghum molasses; talking this matter over after the war with James Madden, I found it was he with whom I had contended about the molasses. I knew him not at the time, though we had been raised boys together. Nearing Knoxville, General Longstreet raised the siege and moved off toward Virginia, closely followed by the Fourth Corps under General Granger; the remainder of the troops moved leisurely back toward Chattanooga. On the march back, while out with a supply train, we stopped at the house of a good-natured Tennessean to feed our teams and load our wagons with corn. He asked me to take a walk with him; going some distance in the woods he went to a brush heap from which he took a jug of applejack and treated me in princely style. While this was taking place the teamsters had learned from the negroes that there was a barrel of applejack under the floor. They were not long in getting this in the wagon. We started to camp, and I was surprised when one of the teamsters called me to the wagon and offered to treat me from the same jug I had been treated from an hour before. They had watched us and profited by it.

As is generally the case with spirits this came very near getting me into trouble. Having a warm friendship for the 113th, I divided the applejack among the members of the 113th, and if one can judge by the songs sung and stories told around the camp fires that night it had a good effect. This coming to the ears of General Jeff. C. Davis, he sent for me and reprimanded me pretty sharply for not turning the spirits over to division headquarters for the use of the Medical Director; but it was too late, the 113th had been sick and cured. We arrived in Chattanooga, on the south side of Tennessee river, to find the bridge swept away, and we were compelled to camp on the bank of the river. The weather had turned very cold. Many of the men were barefooted, having worn their shoes out on the campaign. Rations were issued at ten o'clock at night, and we had to go at least two miles to get wood to cook our supper with. I will relate another incident here which took place on the night before the battle of Mission Ridge. Lieutenant McCrea, Sergeant Parr, and I started to cross the Tennessee river to Chattanooga. For some cause Lieutenant McCrea and I returned to camp and crossed on the bridge afterward, Sergeant Parr going over on a swinging ferry. When the boat was within a few rods of the southern shore it was capsized and he with others, was drowned. We now went into our old quarters, but were permitted to remain but a few days, when we moved south of the Tennessee and put up winter quarters near Crawfish Springs. While here we were daily receiving new recruits. One instance I recollect of one of these recruits asking an old soldier where he could get some washing done. The old veteran, seeing an opportunity for some fun, told him Jim Morgan did the washing for the division. The old veteran pointed out Morgan's quarters and told the recruit that he would find a guard in front of his tent, that he was always kept under guard so that he would be ready to do any washing when called on. Arriving at General Morgan's headquarters he was accosted by that stern old hero as to what he wanted. The soldier replied that he had come to get him to do some washing. General Morgan assured him that he was mistaken, that he was commander of the division. The soldier retorted that it was no use for him to play that on him, that he was told he would try to get out of it, and insisted on his doing the washing. General Morgan, seeing that the recruit was the victim of a practical joke by some old soldier, and told him he was being victimized and asked him if he could point out the soldier who had sent him there. He said he could. The General sent a guard with him, with directions to bring the culprit to headquarters. The guard soon brought him, when General Morgan reprimanded him pretty severely, and ordered the guard to have the clothes of the headquarter guard hunted up (about twenty in number), and take the man to Crawfish springs and see that he washed them all. As this was a cold day in March, and he was compelled to do the washing, it is safe to say that he never played any more jokes of that kind. During our stay at Crawfish Springs I went several times over the battlefields of Chickamauga and Mission Ridge. I found soldiers that had never been buried, others who had been buried so slightly that their bodies were exposed. I found the grave of Captain Wells, of the 113th O. V. I., who was wounded at the battle of Chickamauga and fell into the rebels' hands and died, and was buried and the grave marked by Sergeant Hall, who was also a prisoner in their hands. I accompanied a party from the North the next spring to the grave of Captain Wells. They took his body North and buried it among his friends. The army was now reorganized and we became a part of the Fourteenth Corps. Colonel Mitchell returning from the North, assumed command of the brigade. I was mustered as Quartermaster of the 113th O. V. I., and detailed as Quartermaster of the brigade, which position I held till the close of the war, and I cannot express in terms too strong my appreciation of the uniform kindness with which he treated me. The summer campaign of 1864 opened with an advance on Atlanta, distance 138 miles through a mountainous country consisting of almost continuous fighting on some part of the line, and in many places there were pitched battles fought. At Kenesaw Mountain the 113th suffered heavy loss. Captain Bowersock and Sergeant Clay Scott were killed here; I had the latter buried at Big Shanty in a coffin constructed by myself. I had also made a coffin for Lieutenant Platt a few days before, and had him buried near where he fell. I mention these facts as being perhaps the only men of the 113th who fell in battle that the opportunity was afforded to accord that kind of burial. For the consolation of those who had friends die in the army I can assure them the best was always done that could be done under the circumstances. After the battle of Kennesaw Mountain the rebel army fell back through Marietta. Just before arriving at Marietta I was captured and released in the following manner:

As the rebel army passed south, about forty of their number fell out of ranks, and remained hidden in the woods till our troops passed, when they came out just as I was riding along some distance ahead of the train, which had not yet arrived. They ordered me to surrender, but, before I had been ordered to dismount, Captain Benjamin, in charge of a heavy train guard, came around a turn in the road in full sight and took the rebels prisoners. Of the many incidents which took place from this to the capture I might speak, but I will pass them by and notice the transfer of our division to Chattanooga, and from thence to Florence, Alabama, after General Forrest. While at Chattanooga we drew clothing. Here I acted as Division and Brigade Quartermaster, ably assisted by F. M. McAdams. I will relate an incident to show how little the average citizen knew of the duties of soldier life or how we did business. James O. Sampson, from Urbana, Ohio, was trying to join the 66th at Atlanta, where he had an appointment as clerk in the Quartermaster's Department. Unable to get through to the front, he asked me for a situation, which I gave him. He wanted to know where his office would be. I told him his office would be under the canopy of Heaven; his office chair, the saddle; a lead pencil and memorandum book his office fixtures; the ground his bed, and his chances for delicacies in the culinary department were such as would not be an aid to dyspepsia. He did not accept the situation. We started down Broomtown Valley towards Lafayette, Georgia; on our road to Florence, Alabama. Colonel Mitchell went home on leave of absence, Colonel Pearce, 98th O. V. I., assuming command of the brigade. This, to the staff of General Mitchell was not agreeable, as we were never able to get along with Colonel Pearce. He, no doubt, would have dismissed every one of us, but he knew his term of service as brigade commander was of short duration. The campaign to Florence was without incident worthy of note, except the building of a bridge across the river at Athens after night. This was accomplished and the cars passed over it next morning. Captain Banker, 121st O. V. I., supervised the building When we marched into Florence the citizens closed their windows, and refused to look at the troops march through the town. The bands played and banners waved all the same. Forrest having left Tennessee, we retraced our steps, and met Sherman at Gaylesville, Alabama, with the main army. While here the soldiers, as was their custom, commenced tearing down buildings and putting up shanties, as if they were to stay always. I heard General Davis remark to General Sherman that the soldiers were committing depredations, tearing down houses, etc. Sherman remarked that it was all right—that those houses now only held one family, but they would soon make habitations for a dozen. It was this spirit that made Sherman a favorite with the soldiers. He looked on war as cruel—as a thing that could not be refined, and meant destruction. From this place the Fourth and Twenty-third Corps were sent to Nashville to look after Hood's army, and the Fourteenth, Fifteenth, Seventeenth and Twentieth Corps, under Sherman, started to Atlanta. At Kingston, Georgia, the railroad and telegraph were cut and connection severed with the outside world, and we started on what appeared to the outside world a hazardous undertaking, but which, in fact, proved the holiday campaign of the war.

Before starting south from Atlanta I received a commission as captain and was assigned to Company E, but still continued in the Quartermaster Department. Atlanta was a grand sheet of flame as we left it. The campaign to Savannah of two hundred and ninety-one miles was made by easy marches and little fighting. We lived principally by foraging off the country through which we passed until on the twenty-first of December we entered Savannah, and General Sherman presented the city as a Christmas gift to the President. I now obtained a leave of absence for twenty days and started home by the way of New York. On board the steamer was a soldier from Minnesota who gave me the following incident. He said a northern copperhead had made some light remarks to his wife impugning his motives in going into the service; that his objects were purely mercenary. He said he wrote to him offering him one hundred dollars to enlist as he had done, five hundred dollars to stand for one hour where he had stood all day, and he said he wrote to him that he would give him a d—d licking any way if he ever got home, and now he said I am now on my way home to perform the last part of the promise. Judging from his make up, he did it no doubt. Returning after twenty days I found the army on its march through South Carolina. I overtook the army at Sisters Ferry on the Savannah river. Here General Mitchell returned a full brigadier, and took command of the brigade to the no small satisfaction of the staff. While lying here W. B. Cassady wrote his parody on Sherman's famous order, which is published in the body of this work. Our march through South Carolina was amid fire and smoke on every side. But little restraint was exercised over the whole army concentrated at Columbia, and that part of the army under Slocum, to which we belonged, was not permitted to pass through the city. I recollect distinctly that Columbia was burning while our troops were south of the river shelling the city, and before the Seventeenth Corps crossed over. From here our march was rapid, taking the same route that General Green retreated on in the war of the Revolution. When we arrived in North Carolina a different spirit seemed to possess the men. There always had appeared to be a strong Union sentiment smothered in this State. At Averysboro' and Bentonville we had two sharp engagements with the rebels, which, however, were our last. I was here for some days in company with Colonel Barnwell Rhett of South Carolina, who had fallen into our hands as a prisoner; he remained with me for a number of days without the restriction of a guard, and was a very agreeable gentleman. We were overjoyed in a few days at the news of the surrender of Lee and Johnson. We knew the war was over and that we would soon be permitted to return home and join our families from which a cruel war had separated us. Universal rejoicing took possession of the troops, marred only by the news of the assassination of the President. We marched rapidly north to Manchester, south of Richmond, when we halted a day or two, and while here two men of the 113th Regiment, whose names I withhold, were arrested and afterward court-marshaled for saying they would like to dance on Lincoln's coffin. We visited Richmond and the house lately deserted by Jeff Davis; we also visited the capital where the Rebel Congress had done so much of evil. On our way to Washington I recollect standing in a school house where the citizens claimed Patrick Henry made his maiden speech. This was the story but I always thought the house had, in the hundred years intervening, been rebuilt several times. We passed over many of the battle fields where the Army of the Potomac had won renown. We arrived in Washington and passed in review before the President of the United States, his cabinet and foreign ministers. Here I received a commission as Brevet Major in United States staff department. The work for which I enlisted being now finished, I tendered my resignation, which was accepted June 14, 1865, and I was once more a citizen, feeling that I had done my whole duty while in the service. I now recollected that many had predicted evils to result from turning so many loose, fresh from the field of fame and glory, as citizens. But time has fully developed the fact that the great mass of men were better for having been in the war, and are doing what comes in their way to make and maintain this as the grandest government in the world. Having written entirely from memory there may be some inaccuracies as to dates, but I feel confident that the greater part will be found correct.

THE CHARGE AT KENESAW, AND OTHER ITEMS.

By Lieutenant W. H. Baxter.

In making the following remarks, the reader must not suppose that I expect to state something that no one else has seen or experienced,—such is not the case. I merely wish to preserve for ourselves and other readers the experiences common to so many, and relate matters that others took part in. Each writer expresses himself as no other does, and thus of an affair of numerous actors, each may be interesting in his way. This by way of preface.

At one o'clock A. M., Sunday, June 26, 1864, the 113th Regiment left the works immediately before Little Kenesaw Mountain, where for six days it had been occupying one position, subject to frequent shelling and incurring some loss.

Withdrawing from its works the regiment marched to the right about three miles, to the vicinity of what is now called Cheatham's

Hill. The regiment halted and went into encampment about five o'clock A. M., near some breastworks a considerable distance in rear of the front line and out of range of bullets and shells.

We felt relieved to be once more out of range. All day Sunday was a day of rest. The men were free to enjoy it, and many improved it by visiting other regiments near where they had friends. Several came over from the 66th Ohio, which belonged to the Twentieth Corps, and some of our men went over to that regiment. Many took a bath in a small creek not far off, many also writing to friends at home. The day was a bright, pleasant one, and all spent the day quite comfortably, considering the circumstances.

Thus Sunday passed. The sun went down, night came, and the hundreds lay down to sleep, the last sleep, alas, for many. All unconscious and unknowing of the dreadful scenes which the morrow would bring forth.

The sun rose on Monday the 27th of June, 1864, bright and clear. The men went about the duties of the morning untroubled by the knowledge that a dreadful enterprise had been planned for them, had been ordered, and that in three or four hours many of them would be still in death or suffering with shocking wounds.

The writer had no knowledge of what was before us until H. N. Benjamin, captain on General Mitchell's staff, rode up to me and told me that a charge had been ordered, and that when the bugle shall sound it will be to fall in, in order to march to the front line, whence the charge will start.

When the bugle notes did ring clear and loud through the regiment and brigade the signal of "fall in," I knew what ordeal lay before us. Company K fell into line at company quarters and were counted off. According to my recollection, when the company first fell into line, we had sixty-three men, including the two commissioned officers in charge of the company—the First and Second Lieutenants. On the way from where we camped to the front line, where the charge started, the regiment halted several times. The actions of many discovered that serious thoughts were in men's minds. We all knew that some, perhaps very many, would fall. But who? I or my neighbor?

On our way to the front a non-commissioned officer of Company K., under plea of necessity, retired to the brush near by and failed to return. He thus escaped the fight but was reduced to the ranks. I think Company K., when it went into the charge, had sixty men, including the two commissioned officers mentioned. The captain was excused from duty that morning by the surgeon of the regiment.

In due time we arrived at our front line of breast works, and, halting, sat or lay down behind them. Before us were the woods; within that woods were the rebel skirmishers, and somewhere behind those skirmishers were their strong works and their troops.

We sat there some time, I should think twenty minutes at least, perhaps longer. Writing now but a few months less than twenty years after the affair, part of the scene seems quite vivid in my mind.

Skirmishing was going on in the woods in our front. Several men were brought back wounded. All felt serious. There was but little laughing or joking while waiting there. While all knew the desperate work before them, and while the question in every mind was, who will escape safe and who not, each hoping the best, yet courage and resolution was on the faces of the men. The situation of waiting and reflecting under those circumstances, is much more trying on men than an immediate advance.

Finally, "forward" was commanded. Over the breast-work we jumped, and onward into the woods, and toward the rebel works we took our course. The morning was hot, our march hurried, and some of the men began to feel exhausted after a time. Occasionally a man would stumble over some obstruction, and several times the writer found it necessary to encourage and urge such on. Men began to fall. I remember well seeing Stephen Barr. He fell full length and lay with his head to the foe, his face turned partly upward, his rifle by his side. He had been shot dead through the head near the eye. He died a christian soldier; for while in camp and during the campaign he daily, almost, made his Testament his study and led a consistent life. It was not the rule for our men to devote much time to religious matters. The majority sought to be respectable men, but did not trouble themselves much about religion, at least outwardly.

A few paces from Barr, Hiram Hancock lay dead, also shot through the head, in the forehead. But we did not stop for these, or others, but pressed on.

Although twenty years ago, I remember the thoughts passing through my mind at the time I was wounded. In all dangerous places it had been my strong desire to live long enough to know that victory was ours. My thoughts in this instance were similar. They ran: This is a pretty hot place; I don't know whether I will get out or not; if I am killed I will not know anything about the result and it will make no difference, but if I am wounded I will know the result, so there is no use thinking about the consequences, but take what comes. Suddenly occurred a great shock like the terrific jar of a peal of thunder close at hand. I took a step forward and found my foot give way under me and I fell to the ground. At once I knew I had been wounded. Immediately examining the wound, I found both bones of my leg smashed into pieces a few inches above the ankle. Fearing that I might bleed to death, I rolled up my trowser leg above my knee, took a silk handkerchief from my pocket, tied it tightly about my leg just below the knee, and, breaking off a stem of a bush, used it as a lever to twist the bandage so tight that all flow of blood was stopped.

Immediately after I was wounded the charge failed, and, men scattering, sought safety as best they could. While bandaging my leg, a member of my company, John Tway, came up, and waiting a moment until I had finished, helped me back some distance until he gave out. The day was hot and he was not strong. Then Sergeant

Barber assisted me a short distance until, on his saying he was exhausted, I told him to leave me and save himself, that I would chance it to get back some way. Soon after, I received aid from two men of the 121st Ohio and Perry Howard of my own company.

Before reaching our own works, while but a short distance from them, Howard, who had hold of my right shoulder, was shot through the arm and side and fell flat as if killed. The other men did not stop to inquire whether he was killed or not but hurried with me to the works. Howard got home, and fourteen years after, I saw his arm which was then badly sore.

After we got over our works the rebels continued a dangerous shelling. There was considerable delay in getting the ambulances brought up near enough to receive the wounded. Back of our works a few rods, behind a gentle rise of ground, quite a number of wounded, including the writer, were collected. Here the surgeons were binding up bad wounds temporarily, so they could be taken back to the rear. Rebel shells were flying in the air and bursting overhead, which tried the courage of the physicians and caused them occasionally to forget their patients and "duck" their bodies, causing pain to the wounded. They were but men, and to remain steel nerved amid bursting shell was not their business, and they had not particularly tried to cultivate it. (That little spot where we lay under those bursting shells, and where one colonel died while waiting for the ambulances, was recognized by the writer when on the spot again in April, 1883.)

Finally, after some storming by General Mitchell, the ambulances were brought up and I was taken some distance back to a field hospital and laid on the ground with scores of others, waiting to have my leg amputated, for from the first I knew it would have to be done. It began to feel painful and I was anxious to have it done In a reasonable time my right leg was amputated about four and a half inches below the knee, after which I was laid on a blanket on the ground in a tent. Two of my boys gathered some leaves, which they tied in a bundle and placed under my knee for support to keep the raw stump off the ground. I was not alone. There was plenty of company around me. Among others was James Clabaugh of my company, who was shot through the breast, the ball going clear through, inflicting a very bad wound, and no one thought it worth while to spend much time on him, as he could not get well; and Joseph Newcomb, also of Company K., who was wounded in the wrist. He was walking about holding his hand and complaining of the pain, but no one thought his wound serious, and expected him soon to recover. Clabaugh got well and was mustered out in June, 1865, while Newcomb died of his wound at Nashville, July 24.

I lay that day and night on the ground in the clothes I had worn during the battle, and in the morning found my clothes fly-blown where blood had got upon them. As may be supposed, when morning came I felt quite feeble. In the morning Harry Shepherd, my brother-in-law, of the 66th Ohio, 20th Corps, came over. He and my brother, Chas. T. Baxter, sergeant in my own company, bathed me and put on me some clean underclothes, after which I was put in an ambulance and started for Big Shanty, a railroad station about nine miles back.

My work was done. Others would go on, but I must go back. I had suffered a great misfortune without any compensation. We were shot down by hundreds, while the rebels behind their strong works escaped with scarcely any loss. The whole affair was useless and a mistake, and Sherman's reason given is not creditable to him or any good general. Could we have felt that our enemies had also lost a reasonable number, there would have been some compensation, but for them to have lost almost nothing and to be damaged in nothing, made us feel that we had been a useless sacrifice, that we were cut off unprofitably when we might have been continued with the army and been of some service. If any just reason had been given for the charge we would have felt better, or even if Sherman had said it was a mistake and should not have been made, but the reason given was not such as to justify him in the loss of a single life in that charge.

Having entered the army when nineteen years of age, in August, 1862, months, while adding to my age, were also adding to my experience and worth to the service. I would have liked to continue to the end, but that was not to be, and when the ambulance train started back on Tuesday morning, June 28, my work was finished.

What a wearisome and trying ride that was, over those nine miles of rough dirt and corduroy road, extending from early in the day till near sundown, in the blazing sun of that Georgia, June day, only those similarly situated know. It became so unbearable that when we arrived at Big Shanty and the ambulance stood in the street, I thought it could not be endured longer and ordered two of my boys, who were with me, to take me out and lay me on the ground in the shade of a tree—the shade and ground looked so inviting—but at that moment the teams moved on and I was soon on a cot in a tent.

On the morning of the 29th we were loaded on a hospital train and started back for Chattanooga. As we arrived near Dalton, it was found that rebel cavalry had destroyed some track ahead, and we had to lie on the cars at Dalton all night. Next morning, June 30, we came into Chattanooga. I felt too exhausted to be taken onto Lookout Mountain, and was taken to hospital No. 1, Ward 1, Section 4, in the city, one of a long row of long one story wooden buildings, built for hospitals, mostly, but not entirely.

There are many trying scenes at the "front," when men are seen dead and wounded upon the field of conflict. But in a short time the wounded are removed, the dead buried, the ranks of the unhurt are closed up, and evidences of suffering are out of sight. In the "rear" the terrible ravages of war are always seen. There sympathies are keenly aroused, there scenes of prolonged suffering and of death are always at hand.

No words of mine can faithfully portray those hospital scenes. At one time in the ward where I was in there were twenty-one wounded men—every bed being full—and of those twenty-one, eighteen had amputated limbs, either arm or leg. Men died to my right and men died to my left and before me. Beds generally were not long vacant that summer, but as some died or were sent north, others, fresh cases, came from the front, so that most of the time all were occupied.

Daily, in the morning, the dead wagon drove past us, and often the tap of the drum and the shrill note of the fife, told us that the sufferings of some poor fellows were ended, and they were borne to a soldier's grave. We became callous in a considerable degree to the scenes around us. Men had to, or they would have died. Their emotions could not always be tuned to a high pitch, else their weakened bodies would have given way under the strain of their sensibilities. In the rear often, as at the front, men had to be stoical, not taking too much thought of what might befall them. So in those hospitals, men died, were carried to their long homes, the living felt sorry for them and their friends, and turned to other things. There was too much to be fully realized as it happened with the passing days.

Across the room at my foot a cot was once occupied by a very large man suffering with a thigh amputation. He had been in the ward but a very short time, perhaps not more than two days. The nurse told him to be careful, as he was liable to bleed. One morning about daylight I was awakened from a doze by a sound like water pattering upon the floor. At once I knew the man was bleeding—the blood pattering upon the floor. The nurse ran to him and stopped the flow of blood with his thumb, until a tourniquet was brought. Efforts to save his life were of no avail. That morning he died. Occupying the same cot once, was a young man with thigh amputation. The flesh had drawn away, and shrunk back from the end of the bone, leaving it protruding quite a distance. He delighted in singing Methodist hymns. He occupied the cot for some time, but finally died.

At my left, on a cot next me, was a young man whose life the doctors tried to save one night, but without avail. The sloughing away of the artery of an amputated leg caused his death. He had been frequently warned that he must keep more quiet, but would not. The gangrene ward, to which I was taken for a couple of weeks, was a scene of hopeless misery. Very frequently some one was taken to his final resting place.

The nurses were men, although there were some ladies in attendance. One lady devoted considerable time to our ward, cheering the despondent, writing letters for the feeble, helping prepare food and adding in that way to the comfort of the wounded. The nurses, as far as I saw, were kind, waiting on the disabled, and doing for them as well as they could. Food at times was quite scanty, sometimes receiving barely enough to satisfy, and that of the plainest kind, but most of the time by what the government and the sanitary commission furnished, the patients were comfortably supplied.

Enlisted men paid nothing, but all commissioned officers were charged one dollar a day for their board.

The days of July, August and September were long, wearisome and many of them hot. How often, overcome by weariness and drowsiness from a sleepless night, we desired to sleep during the day, but could not. With the head uncovered, flies prevented, with the head covered, the heat was intolerable, for we had no fly nets, only a sheet or paper.

Beneath my cotton mattress were dozens of sow bugs, while, when the shades of night fell upon us, whole platoons of bed bugs appeared upon the sheets, and drilled at their leisure.

It was a long time before I felt able to undertake a journey home. The flap of my amputated leg came down, or partly so. The tibia protruded through the flesh, and remained thus for two months, until nature completed an amputation of the exposed and deadened portion, when a piece of bone from the top of the tibia, in triangular shape, two inches long and one wide, was lifted off by the nurse—which I now have—after which the flesh rapidly grew over. Twice gangrene set in. I will not prolong these hospital scenes. One has but to imagine hundreds of men wounded in every shape—all badly, for the slighter ones were at once taken to the rear—the days and weeks of suffering, the daily deaths, the hopes of the living, which so often went out in disappointment.

On October 5, I left the hospital at Chattanooga for my home, Mechanicsburg, Ohio, arriving there about the middle of October, having stopped over at Nashville. On October 5th, on the hospital train from Chattanooga to Nashville, a vote was taken to see how the Presidential candidates stood among the wounded soldiers. The vote cast was—for Lincoln, 161; for McClellan, 8.

It will be remembered that Company K was a company added to the 113th Regiment in the beginning of 1864. The majority of the company were seeing their first service, while some of them had seen much service elsewhere. While the company had been under fire with the regiment all along in the campaign, yet, until June 27, the regiment in that campaign had been in no place where there had been any serious loss. This was, then, the first desperate place for most of the company. They did their duty well. As brave men, they obeyed orders. The loss of the company was heavy. Seven were killed; five more died of their wounds, making twelve deaths. One, Booker Durnell, was captured, and died in a rebel prison. Ten or twelve more were wounded, some of them very seriously, so that of the men who went in one-third died or became valueless to the service.

MEN OF CO. K KILLED IN ACTION JUNE 27, 1864.

NAMES.	AGE AT MUSTER.	WHEN MUSTERED.
Ezra Allen	26	January 9, 1864
Stephen V. Barr	36	March 2, 1864.
William Coppin	22	January 5, 1864.
Hiram Hancock	40	January 21, 1864.
Levi Romine	31	January 27, 1864.
Joseph Wilkinson	18	January 5, 1864
Lemuel P. Jones	28	January 18, 1864.

DIED OF WOUNDS RECEIVED JUNE 27, 1864.

NAMES.	AGE AT MUSTER.	DATE OF MUSTER.	DATE OF DEATH.	WHERE
Hector Morren	20	January 5, 1864	June 30, 1864	Big Shanty, Ga.
Joseph H. Newcomb	25	January 16, 1864	July 24, 1864	Nashville, Tenn.
Levi Hemminger	38	January 5, 1864	August 1, 1864	Chattanooga, Tenn
Patrick Fields	38	January 14, 1864	August 19, 1864	Nashville, Tenn.
Robert R. Osborne	18	January 9, 1864	August 22, 1864	Chattanooga, Tenn.

CAPTURED AND DIED IN PRISON.

NAME.	AGE AT MUSTER.	DATE OF MUSTER.	DATE OF DEATH.	WHERE.
Booker Durnell	25	January 5, 1864		

OTHER DEATHS IN CO. K.

NAMES.	AGE AT MUSTER.	DATE OF DEATH.	WHERE.	CAUSE.
John H. Bricker	25	July 4, 1864	Chattahoochie River, Ga.	Killed.
Henry C. Britten	19	July 6, 1864	Chattanooga, Tenn	Disease.
Levi Elliott	42	August 12, 1864	Nashville, Tenn	Disease.
Azro Mann	28	October 31, 1864	Nashville, Tenn	Disease.
James McMahan	24	Nov. 30, 1864	Jeffersonville, Md	Disease.
Monroe Elliott	22	February 4, 1864	Savannah, Ga	Disease.
George Peobles	27	April 18, 1865	Baltimore, Md	Disease.

Again last April, 1883, I stood upon the ground so disastrous to us. The same woods were there, excepting a small portion cleared up near the rebel works, the same works, only the action of water and the tooth of time upon the logs had partly filled up the trenches, most of the logs helping form the works having rotted; thus, they are not now as formidable looking as they were twenty years ago. But there are many large logs left, in the same position as when placed there for defense. Many of the logs are apparently as sound as when cut, only the bark and outer sap have rotted away, leaving the balance sound. There are logs there yet having a diameter from two to three feet, while those of less size are numerous. The point of attack is now named Cheatham's Hill. Though the subject is full of interest to me, I will not detain my readers longer.

CAMP ITEMS AND RECOLLECTIONS OF THE BATTLES OF CHICKAMAUGA AND KENESAW.

By D. B. Warner.

St. John, N. B. *February 2, 1883.*

I remember an incident which took place in Camp Zanesville, showing one of the many difficulties in transforming a large body of men into disciplined soldiers—men who never before had known what it was to obey *orders :*

The men of the 113th felt rather blue, when, soon after the appointment of the field and staff officers, the command was ordered to Camp Zanesville to guard conscripts. But the Colonel consoled himself with the thought that it would be a good school for guard duty as well as ordinary drill. Strict orders were issued, and a regimental guard was established, which, for strictness, was grumbled at and wondered at by both officers and enlisted men.

One of these orders was that there should be no loud noise or talking on guard. This order was frequently broken, and the Colonel's peaceful slumbers rudely disturbed thereby. On a certain night, this was unusually so, or else the Colonel was in an unusually sour mood. The first thing on the following morning the officer of the guard was sent for, and the Colonel said to him that he wished to have the soldier who made the disturbance on guard last night placed under arrest in the guard house. The officer soon returned and reported that he could not ascertain the name of the man who had offended. Colonel W. retorted, " If his name is not given put the *whole* guard in." The officer again reported, saying he thought the other part of the order could not be carried out. Then the Colonel sent for the Major, and said to him : " Major, I want you to put that whole guard of last night into the guard house, and keep them there till they will promise to do better, or give the name of the soldier who made the noise."

The Major went out feeling very much that it would be more agreeable to his feelings had the Colonel, to establish his personal authority, gone himself. Finding the guard drawn up, standing at *order arms*, he gave the orders, " Attention ! " " Shoulder—arms." " Stack—arms." " Right—face." " Forward—march," and into the guard house they all went, before they knew where they were.

The Major was complimented by the Colonel, but remarked that he would in future prefer not being assigned to such duty, and do without the compliment.

❋

An incident of some importance occurred at Wartrace soon after the arrival of the 113th at that place. Our pickets gave an alarm, and the troops were at once called to arms. In the distance was a great cloud of dust, and it seemed that an army approached. It turned out not to be an army with guns and banners, but an army of Blacks. Here was a grave matter. What were we to do with them? While considering this question, its solution was suggested by one of the masters of some of the Blacks, who presented himself at the tent of the Lieutenant Colonel, and requested that he be allowed to take his "niggers" back to his plantation. Here in this almost wilderness—in this camp of the 113th O. V. I., was presented the question which was disturbing the statesmen at Washington—what will be done with the slaves? This was before the question had been settled by the proper and higher authorities, but the Lieutenant Colonel found himself face to face with the question, and it must be settled then and there, so far as he was concerned.

The officer said to the owner of black chattels, "Have you seen any of your negroes since coming into our lines?" The reply was, "Yes; some of them are scattered among the companies of your regiment." "Go, then, and bring one of them here," said the officer. Soon the planter returned bringing with him a big black fellow. "Is this your master, boy," asked the officer. "Yes sah," answered the black man. "Why did you run away from him? Was he a good master? Did he give you enough to eat and did he treat you well, give you good clothing and proper attention when you were sick; all this?" The darkey replied, "Yes sah; no niggah had a better master; no fault to find." "Well, then, do you want to go back to him?" No answer. "Come, now," said the officer, "if your master is all that you say, why did you run away, and why do you not wish to return to him?" "*I wants to be free, sah,*" said the darkey. He was permitted to return to his place in the company. Then turning to the planter the Lieutenant Colonel said, "Now, sir, if you can find in this regiment any of your slaves who will come to these headquarters and say to me, without fear or compulsion, that they want to return to their master, I will *permit* them to go, and no one shall interfere with their going, and you may also inform any one interested in the matter, that while I am in command of this regiment, no slaves will be returned to their masters against their will." The answer of that darkey, "*I wants to be free,*" made the Lieutenant Colonel an abolitionist, and this answer of his to the planter was one of the *first* proclamations of emancipation.

At Chickamauga, an incident of very grave moment occurred. The 113th went into the fight in the second line. The charge was led by a regiment of Illinois troops I think. They were met at the top of the hill with a regular hail-storm of grape, shot and shell. They were thrown into confusion and their commanding officer was shot and fell from his horse just in front of our line. This regiment fell back through our line, shouting to our men not to go in there, and the result was that the 113th was thrown into momentary confusion, and were pressed down the hill to the rear some distance. I gave up at one time and thought the old command was done for, but this was but for a moment. In the midst of this the officer in command called out the number of the regiment and the single word "halt," and the regiment obeyed the command. It was at once re-formed and marched back to the crest of the hill, *and there remained* until another unfortunate circumstance occurred. Lieutenant Platt of the 113th, who was then detached and acting Aide-de-Camp on General Steedman's staff, rode up and said to me that the regiment was to fall back to the ridge next in our rear. I remember as if yesterday my surprise at the order, and I then said that there must be some mistake, but he repeated the order, and not liking to take any responsibility I gave the order to fall back. When we reached the point to which the order had referred and while re-forming the regiment, Steedman and Mitchell, and I think General Beatty, came up, and explanations being made, and learning that the order was a mistake, the regiment was a second time marched back to its original position in the line and their remained till nearly dark, when the entire line was retired and we moved off the field in good order, and bivouaced that night with but few stragglers, but with the loss of over half of our regiment left dead or wounded. But few commands in that army went off the field that day in as good order as did the 113th O. V. I. The number of their killed and wounded on that day is all the testimony necessary as to their valor.

The battle of Kenesaw was of very different character, in that we knew where the enemy were, that we were to attack them in their works, and were to capture them without firing a shot. I well remember the council of officers I called that morning, a very short time before the attack. There the plan of the assault was given, and the officers were informed that our claim to the advance was granted, that we would lead the charge. The meeting was very solemn, but I did not detect among all their faces one which suggested anything other than a determination to do his duty. At that council I handed three sergeants their commissions. Crouse, a tall, fine looking man, a member of the Mt. Sterling Company, was one of them. Dungan at the same time was handed his commission as First Lieutenant, but did not live to be mustered. He lay in a tent with me the night of the 27th; the next day he was taken to Chattanooga and died; I never saw him after the 28th.

Kenesaw, to me, was a dreadful battle, because unnecessary, and brought on against the advice of the best Generals of the army. In the fight I saw so many shot down and frightfully mangled that the recollection to me is simply horrible.

One incident at Kenesaw made an impression on my mind more than all the rest. Certain circumstances in the history of the regiment had made me acquaintance with a particular sergeant of one of the companies very interesting and favorable, and he became with me a great favorite.

At Kenesaw, when the assault had been made, and we had almost reached the works of the enemy, it became evident that we could not capture them, and I sent word along the line for the men to cover themselves and commence firing. After I thought we were doing well, and the men were well hidden under rocks and behind logs and trees, I discovered this favorite Sergeant standing out in full view of the enemy, loading and firing as though he were at target practice. I was sure he would be killed, for the rebels seemed to be literally skinning the hill. I turned toward him, (he being toward the right of the regiment, and a little to the rear of the line upon which I stood) and began to motion to him with my right hand to lie down, and while in this position I was shot, and this was the last shake of my right hand. If the rebel who fired that shot had not been nervous, that *favorite* would have been the cause of his Colonels' being shot in the *back*. Did I ever tell you this before? That Sergeant's name was F. M. McAdams.

But returning to the order which was delivered to us, and which we obeyed with doubt and reluctance at Chickamauga. I am sure Platt got the order from some one, and that he delivered it as he understood it. My impression now is, that when questioned in regard to the order, he said he received it from Captain Russell, A. A. G., on the staff of General Granger. Russell was killed in the battle, earlier, it seems to me, than I received the order. Some one made a mistake which might have cost us great loss, but it cannot now be settled who it was. I am certain, however, that Platt received the order from some one who he considered in a position to give it. I recall this matter because at the time, one Chaplain Van Horn, wrote a letter to the press on the battle, which reflected upon the courage of the regiment. The 113th was perfectly in hand during the entire day, with the exception of the time the other regiment broke and run through us, and, as I have written, the confusion in our ranks resulting from that cause, lasted but a short time, when at the command we re-formed and took up our position in the line of battle.

LEAVES FROM THE DIARY OF ASSISTANT SURGEON A. HARLOW.

DETROIT, MICH., *February, 1883.*

Having kept a diary during my entire stay with the regiment, I am able to give day and date, and a clear statement of facts herein mentioned.

On the 16th day of September, 1862, I reported myself to Colonel James A. Wilcox, commanding the 113th O. V. I., stationed at Camp

Chase, Ohio. Was duly introduced to Surgeon J. R. Black and T. C. Tipton, and found them to be affable and intelligent gentlemen of their profession. I entered immediately upon the duties of my office, and was not long in making the acquaintance of the officers and many of the enlisted men in the regiment, and was favorably impressed with their intelligence and soldierly bearing.

The day following my arrival in camp, no little excitement was occasioned in consequence of an attempt to impose a somewhat ludicrous punishment upon a soldier for refusing to do duty. The delinquent was put in a barrel and rolled around the camp; his comrades and friends rescued him. All the officers were called out, and finally, the order being revoked, peace and good feeling was restored.

On the night of September 18th, twenty rebel prisoners made their escape from prison No. 1, in the following manner:

They took a large dry-goods box containing carpenter tools and placed it against the boarded wall where the egress was to be made. A party of four occupied the top of the box and played cards, while a fifth, secreted in the box, began the work of boring and sawing a hole in the wall. Meanwhile, those on top kept up a din and noise calculated to prevent the boring and sawing from being heard.

The work being nearly completed, they waited for the darkness and stillness of the night, and then by a sudden push, the opening was made in the wall, and twenty-two who had been made acquainted with the plot, deliberately walked out without thanking the government for the very kind treatment which they had been receiving.

On the third day after their escape, eight of these were re-captured and returned to their former quarters.

On the 29th of October, we camped at Zanesville. Some ten days after our arrival here the measles broke out among the men, and spread rapidly, until more than two hundred cases of the disease were in camp. The regimental hospital becoming overcrowded with patients, many of the sick were treated in their barracks and tents. When this epidemic was at its height (November 10) a fire broke out in camp, which, on account of the strong wind and the great amount of straw and other combustible material, and despite the greatest efforts of the men to check it, continued to burn till the main part of camp was laid in ashes. No loss of life nor personal injury resulted from the fire, but many of the officers and men lost valuable personal effects.

A regiment without shelter, and many of them sick and exposed to the inclement weather, is fearful to contemplate. Prompt measures were taken to provide shelter and comfort for the sick, new plank barracks were soon constructed, and but a few days elapsed until all were snugly quartered on a sloping hillside, inclining toward Licking creek. During the first three months of our service but one death occurred in camp, a fact that speaks well for the surgical and medical department, when we consider the epidemic and exposures to which the men were subjected. This death was that of John Rogers,

Company G. He died December 5, 1862. His body was sent home for burial.

On the 15th of December, the regiment left camp for the South, halting a few days at Camp Dennison. I assisted Surgeon Black with such of the convalescents as were able to accompany the regiment, going as far as Zanesville to see them safely off. Others remained under my charge for a time, and then followed on. On January 4, 1863, I rejoined the regiment two miles out of Louisville, Kentucky, happy, indeed, in once more being able to mingle with the officers and men so greatly endeared to me by many a fond recollection. At this time great efforts were being made to forward needed supplies to the " Boys in Blue " who comprised the army at the front, and as an incident pertaining to this matter, I state that one hundred and nine six-mule teams, with suitable escort, passed our camp in one day, each loaded with army supplies, destined for Nashville.

The day after my arrival, January 5th, the 113th left Louisville for parts unknown, except to Colonel Wilcox and a few of the other commissioned officers. Our destination proved to be Muldrough's Hill, a wild, rough country, on the Louisville and Nashville Railroad, near a little place called Colesburg. At the little burg the 113th disembarked and marched a couple of miles, when we came in sight of the smoking ruins of "Big Run Trestle," which had been recently destroyed by the notorious raider, John Morgan.

This camp was called " Camp Lucy," or more appropriately "claptrap," on account of the risk of our being " gobbled up " by Morgan or Forrest or some other marauding band some dark night. The monotony of camp life was broken on the third day of our stay here by the visit of the Surgeon General of Ohio, Dr. S. M. Smith, with his corps of nurses *en route* for Nashville to attend the sick and wounded of the late engagement at Stone River. The fact that our camp was situated near this long bridge, and that all passengers going to or coming from Nashville by this route were compelled to walk over the broken place in the road, gave us daily opportunity of seeing many strangers, as they were unavoidably compelled to pass within speaking distance of our camp. One dark night soon after our arrival here the regiment was awakened from its dreamy reveries by the ominous sound of the long roll, while the officers passed from tent to tent, commanding the men to fall out and form into line. This was promptly obeyed, and then the regiment marched out over a rough and stony path, made doubly difficult by the inky darknes of the night. The supposed enemy could not be found ; in fact he was miles away and sound asleep. A return to quarters was ordered and very cheerfully obeyed. After we had been here a few days the regiment was divided into two parts, and four or five companies commanded by Lieutenant Colonel Mitchell were sent further south to a similar trestle, where they remained protecting a force of mechanics who were constructing a bridge spanning a chasm some two or three miles further in the direction of Nashville. Surgeon Black accompanied this part of the command, while your humble correspondent remained attending to the medical and surgical wants of the men at camp

Lucy. About the time of this separation, that part of the command remaining at the first trestle vacated the camp first occupied and took position on the hill on the opposite side of the railroad, in a position overlooking the valley and the surrounding country. This we called Camp "Summit." This was Muldrough's Hill, one of the prettiest camping grounds it was ever my fortune to take part in occupying. Long shall I remember with the liveliest interest and the fondest recollection, as well as many old comrades associated with me there who may chance to read this sketch, the experience of camp life enjoyed by us on the rugged brow of this old Kentucky hill, during a portion of January, 1863. Our camp commanded a splendid view of the surrounding country, and if we could not, like the ancient war horse, smell the smoke of battle from afar, we could certainly see our enemies approaching in time to make all necessary preparations to meet him. Unusual for this climate, snow fell on the 15th of January to the depth of three feet, and this was followed by very cold weather, reminding us of the frost and cold of northern Ohio.

In the midst of this storm and low temperature our hospital tent took fire and burned so rapidly that it required the efforts of all the attendants and nurses to rescue the sick. I doubt not many of the hospital patients yet remember the daily visits of Widow Gardner to our camp. She would come well laden with eggs, chickens, squirrels, Indian bread and other toothsome delicacies, for the particular benefit of convalescents in hospital. During our stay at Muldrough's Hill, James Harvey and Geo. F. Reno, both of Company A, died. The body of the former was sent home; the latter was buried on Muldrough's Hill.

The regiment, in obedience to orders, returned to Louisville on the 27th of January. Our trip was tiresome and uncomfortable, our train occupying all night in the trip. We entered the depot on the morning of the 28th, and, disembarking, we spent a few hours with arms stacked awaiting further orders. Up to this time the regiment knew little pertaining to our destination, nor did they care, so that it led them to get a crack at the rebs.

During the day the regiment moved to the landing about three miles below Louisville, and at the foot of the falls of the Ohio. Here lay a number of steamers receiving freight and taking on board thousands of troops as well as army supplies of all kinds. Many regiments, like our own, were at the wharf waiting to go on board of some one of the many steamers lying anchored in the river. The 92d, 36th and 89th Ohio regiments had just arrived from West Virginia, and also the 26th Ohio, from the Kanawha, all of which gave the place and its surroundings a warlike appearance, and gave evidence of big things to come.

On Thursday, January 29, the 113th went aboard the splendid steamer Saint Patrick. Here we lay awaiting the movement of the twenty or more steamers forming a fleet of great magnitude, and intended for some decisive part in the great drama of the future. We had now been in the service nearly six months, during which time we had not made the acquaintance of the paymaster, but on the 30th that official made his appearance, and paid our dues for the period ending December 31, 1862, making no inconsiderable roll of greenbacks, and enabling the members of the regiment to send home considerable money after retaining sufficient for their personal wants.

While here, Captain H. Z. Adams, of Company G, tendered his resignation, and instead of leading his brave company to victory and renown, returned to the bosom of his family and friends to spend his days at his advanced age in the more quiet occupation and peaceful pursuits of a preacher of the Gospel. No one questions his judgment or doubts his patriotism in thus retiring to private life.

Sunday, February 1. The Jacob Strader has just passed down loaded to the water's edge with blue patriots; now our own vessel swings out into the stream, and is in hot pursuit. Others follow, one after another, until twenty or more burdened, puffing steamers, carrying 18,000 or 20,000 troops, are in line, forming a spectacle seldom seen in war or peace. Many a brave heart beat doubtfully as our formidable fleet descended the Ohio. Our passage down the majestic Ohio was a pleasant one in some respects. The Saint Patrick was a fast boat, and in going down she passed a number of other steamers, creating on board of each the wildest enthusiasm. On the way, Captain Peck was taken suddenly and dangerously sick with spasms and other violent symptoms, which continued with severity for twenty-four hours. It was deemed best that in his weak condition he be given more quiet and rest than he could get on the boat, preparatory to his returning home, and he was accordingly put ashore at Evansville, and provided with such nursing and care as his condition demanded.

On the morning of January 3d, we arrived at the mouth of the Cumberland, and were soon in line with other steamers, barges and gunboats ready for the ascent of that beautiful stream.

The sun rose clear and beautiful; not a cloud obscured her brightness. Seldom does the eye behold a sight more imposing and beautiful; nor does the ear often in a lifetime drink in such rich music than it was my pleasure to enjoy on that January morning. All hearts seemed enlivened with the exhilarating scene. The curling smoke as it rose in fleecy columns high in air, flags waving and banners floating, all conspired to enhance the beauty of the scene, and to impress it upon the mind and heart in a manner never to be forgotten.

Moving on our joyous way up the Cumberland, nothing took place to mar the pleasure of the trip till late in the afternoon of our first day, when the sound of booming cannon broke in on the stillness of the scene. At a signal from our flagship the gunboats belonging to our fleet ascended rapidly, leaving the long line of steamers in the rear, and hurrying on they reached the scene of conflict in time to do effective work in turning the tide of battle in our favor at the last hard fought battle of Fort Donelson. As our fleet approached the scene of conflict late in the dusk of the evening it was with difficulty we escaped the designed destruction from numerous barges, flats and other combustible matter sent blazing down the river to intercept our fleet.

Early next morning, in company with a number of Union men, I went over the field and counted more than a hundred rebel dead, scattered here and there as they fell under the well-directed fire of the boys in blue. I visited the hospital and prescribed for many of the rebel wounded, among whom I found a Dr. Mulkie, Surgeon of the 3d Georgia Cavalry, badly, if not fatally, wounded, to whose temporary relief I ministered to the best of my ability, tempered with such kind words and sympathy as the poor man, dying far from home and friends, was, though an enemy, entitled to. Besides the killed and wounded a goodly number of rebels were taken prisoners. Among the more noted dead found upon the field was a Brigadier General McNary, Colonel Coffin, of Missouri, and Colonel Hendrick, of the 4th Alabama. The rebel dead left on the field numbered over two hundred. Our loss was about thirty, among whom was the gallant Captain Reed, of the 83d Illinois, who was shot through the neck and instantly killed, just as he was leading a desperate charge on the enemy. His body was sent home. Surgeon Black, of the 113th, exerted his acknowledged skill in rendering efficient aid by prompt attendance upon the wounded of both friend and foe.

The gunboat Lexington, one of the six gunboats of our fleet, reached the scene of action in time to take a part. She was no ordinary boat but had already made herself famous. Going on board of her I was courteously treated by her officers, one of whom pointed out her points of interest. He informed me that her 64 pound gun killed 170 men at one shot at Pittsburg Landing, and on her arrival here on this occasion one of her shots killed 12 rebels and 8 horses.

The most dangerous part of our trip was yet to be passed over. Our fleet waited for the arrival of Major General Granger, who, upon his arrival, took charge of steamers and their convoy of gunboats. On the morning of the 6th we again started upward. It was a most imposing sight. Soon after getting under way an American eagle, that noble bird of liberty, soared high in the air above us. This was regarded as an omen of good. We were expecting trouble at several points ahead before reaching Nashville, especially at "Harper's Shoals," where the rebels had recently burned the gunboat Pinchback, and several of our steamboats, taking many prisoners. These Shoals are fifty or sixty miles above Fort Donelson, and are nearly five miles in length; they are rapid and so dangerous to navigation as to make it desirable to pass them in daylight. Whistle signals had been adopted by our fleet which all boats in line were required to observe. One whistle meant, go slow; two, keep a proper distance apart; three, close up; four, stop; one short and one long, back; one short and two long, we are attacked; two short and one long, assistance wanted; one long and three short, get under way; one long, two short and one long, stop, tie up and await orders.

On the evening of February 7th we reached the noted city of Nashville, having passed Clarksville, the Shoals, and other dangerous places unmolested by the enemy. Our long and venturesome trip from Louisville to Nashville, down the Ohio and up the Cumberland, being now ended, we had only to disembark and move out to the front. Before leaving the city for more stirring and warlike scenes, I found time to visit parts of the city. I also visited a number of hospitals, and witnessed an amputation at the shoulder joint and other interesting operations. I made a visit to the State House, of which Nashville may well be proud, and stopped reverently at the tomb of Ex-President Polk, situated in the front yard of the elegant mansion occupied by his widow.

Notwithstanding, the eye could see much to admire in this once beautiful city, yet the finger marks of war's desolating hand were seen everywhere, and many parts of the city were in a dilapidated condition.

We marched out of the city, and, going four or five miles southward, camped in a beautiful grove. From the fatigue and exposure attending our long trip, and consequent close confinement on the steamer, many of the men, in spite of the best efforts of Surgeon Black and myself, were taken sick in such numbers that four hospital tents were filled with those unfit for duty.

February 12. Orders having been received to march to the front, Surgeon Black thought it best to send most of our sick then on hand to the general hospital at Nashville. Many of these, sad to relate, never again left this city of pestilence and death.

The 113th, under command of Colonel Wilcox, accompanied by the field and staff officers, in company with a number of other regiments, forming a brigade, under the command of General Gilbert, left early the same morning for Franklin. Surgeon Black accompanied the 113th in its forward movement, while I was directed to remain with and attend to those who were physically unable to move on to the front. Captain Taylor, Company B, and a sufficient guard, were left with us until a proper disposition was made with the sick, after which they also moved on to Franklin.

An additional large number of our sick was sent to general hospital at Nashville, many of whom, for lack of proper treatment or other causes, met the fate of their comrades previously placed there. These had desired and expected to be able soon to stand in their places in the ranks with their comrades, sharing with them the glory and destiny of the command. But, alas, how uncertain was human life in our overcrowded hospitals at Nashville during the winter and spring of 1863. Our sick being thus disposed of, we joined our forces in camp at Franklin. The remainder of February was without any incident of note, but March was ushered in with more active operations of a military character, for the great concentration of troops and the other war-like preparations going on in and around Franklin plainly indicated an advance further south.

Surgeon Black having been assigned to duty in the general hospital at Franklin, left me for a time alone in attending the surgical and medical wants of the 113th, which labors proving too great for my health and strength, Dr. Black was returned to the regiment.

On the 5th of March loud cannonading was heard in the direction of Spring Hill, a town of some size ten miles or more to the south. At 12 o'clock, noon, the long roll sounded in our camp, and the 113th and 125th Ohio Regiments were soon marching rapidly toward the noise of battle. The cannonading grew more and more distinct as we neared the field, and the roar of musketry indicated that hot work was at hand, and that those who had been so long spoiling for a fight would now be gratified. Our brigade was posted at a turn in the road and behind a stone wall, waiting for the pursuit of the enemy on the expected falling back of our troops engaged in the fight.

I was seated on my horse, near my ambulances, with everything in readiness to give attention to the wounded, and to convey them to a place of safety. Every moment was big with exciting interest. While thus waiting, one of the ambulance drivers, pale and trembling, asked to be permitted to drive down a little under the hill. The presence of my revolver and the threat that I would blow his head off in case he moved, kept him in his place. The driver of the other ambulance, equally exposed, seemed totally indifferent, and whistled and sung " Yankee Doodle " alternately.

This hotly contested battle, which lasted for hours, with about equal forces opposing, finally was a drawn one. The enemy, under Van Dorn, Forest and Jackson, numbering close to twenty thousand men, fell back to Spring Hill, carrying with them fifty or sixty of our wounded. Our troops fell back to Franklin, and rested on their arms during the night, expecting a renewal of the conflict on the following day.

An incident of the day, unusual on the battle field, deserves mention: A young man was visiting his brother, a member of an Indiana regiment, and concluded to go out and see a battle for the first time in his life. He was shot and instantly killed.

Following the engagement, and for several days in succession, great numbers of Union troops were concentrated at Franklin. These troops were commanded by Generals Granger, Baird, Gilbert and Sheridan, and the enemy under Van Dorn, in the vicinity of Spring Hill was menaced, but fled to a place of safety. Van Dorn was nicely ensconsed at the splendid mansion of one of the wealthiest rebels in Spring Hill, fascinated and feasting upon charms not found in the every-day life of a Major General, and in the line of duty, and which proved his overthrow, as will appear further on.

On the afternoon of March 9th he gathered together his Brigadiers and their several hosts and retired, taking with them their wounded and some of ours, leaving eleven of the latter in an old church near by to fall into the hands of their friends. Our forces occupied the town the same evening and I happened to secure quarters at the identical house which had been the headquarters of Van Dorn. I found the room strewn with papers and documents pertaining to the office of the rebel chief. Soon after occupying my quarters, an order came for me to go and dress the wounds of the eleven Union soldiers in the old church before mentioned. Hastily partaking of a sumptuous meal prepared by order of my host, whose safety and protection he wished to purchase by his affability and kindness, I repaired to the prison house of the wounded, with all needed bandages and dressing, accompanied by my assistant, ready for the duty assigned me. Finding the door barricaded and all within still and dark, I feared I had missed the object of my search, but after rattling at the door for a while and making known the object of my visit, I was admitted into the dark prison house of my wounded comrades. They were much pleased at my visit. Having no light nor materials for producing it, I sent my assistant into a brick mansion near by to procure one. He soon returned and reported that they said they had none for us. I had him return and tell them that unless they furnished all the light needed for the occasion, a ten pounder would be leveled at their house and fired off for their especial benefit. The assistant obeyed and soon returned with the needed light, bringing also the apologies of the household for their non-compliance with my first request, and a humble request to do them no harm. The following are the names and regiments of the wounded: William H. Brotherton, Sergeant Company G, 85th Indiana; John G. Rawley, private, Company G, 22d Wisconsin; John Baker, private, Company I, 33d Indiana; James Burgal, private, Company D, 33d Indiana; Jas. A. Comstock, private, 33d Indiana; Wells Gallexson, Company G, 22d Indiana; W. C. McNett, private, Company G, 19th Michigan; Aaron J. Buckan, Company C, 19th Michigan; Edward Cromer, private, 19th Michigan; Benjamin Green, private Company I, 19th Michigan; David Dollinger, private, Company D, 19th Michigan.

These wounded men had been paroled by the enemy before being left. I found them in the dark, without fire or blankets to protect them from the cold, and with no hand of mercy to minister to their wants. They told me that as soon as they were taken by the rebels, their coats and most of their other clothing were taken by their unfeeling captors, and not satisfied with this booty, the rebels rifled the pockets of the prisoners, taking everything of value and appropriating the same to their own use. They mentioned other heartless acts perpetrated upon them.

While engaged in dressing the wounds of these men, I noticed a gentleman, dressed as a citizen, who appeared quite interested, and who gave close attention to all my professional acts, but as he asked no questions nor made any remarks his presence gave me no concern.

Finally, when I was about leaving the house he said, "Well, Doctor, you have done very well to-night. I am much pleased with the skill and ability which you have exhibited in the work performed." I said, "Sir, will you please inform me whom I have the honor of addressing?" Judge of my surprise when he informed me that my visitor was Dr. Varian, a Medical Director of the C. S. A. Before we parted he remarked to me that as a great battle was expected to come off to-morrow he wished to detail me for a particular service. This was my first interview and acquaintance, but not my last interview and happy experience with the "Medical Director of the Army of Kentucky."

My eleven patients were next morning placed in ambulances and taken to the general hospital at Franklin.

After a refreshing night of rest in the bed last tumbled by the rebel chief, Van Dorn, and having attended to my eleven patients previous to their leaving for the hospital, as before stated, I sought to learn what I could of the family of my loquacious and genial host. He had two sons and one son-in-law in the rebel armies; that General Van Dorn had for weeks past made Spring Hill his headquarters, stopping all the while in the house and partaking of the hospitality of this gentleman. He expressed himself as being pleased to extend to me and others the courtesy and welcome of his house, and expressed a desire that we would exert ourselves in protecting his person and property from violence, on account of his house having been the headquarters of the Confederate general and his staff. I assured him that no harm should come to him for what he had done in the past, but my earnest advice to him would be to espouse the Union cause, which in the end was sure to triumph. How far I succeeded in turning him from the error of his way I dare not say, but judging from what I saw in the person of his daughter to whom I was introduced, and whose husband was a surgeon in the rebel army, I fear my advice was not taken according to the prescription.

Stepping aside from the narration of warlike events, I need not ask the reader's pardon for a passing notice of this lady. She was characterized by very striking southern proclivities, and in attempting a pen picture of her I shall not indulge in any extravagant hyperbole. She was a brunette of some twenty or more years of age, possessing form and features that might be considered beautiful. Her general appearance and conversation indicated refinement and culture. She was an adept in vocal and instrumental music, of which she gave ample demonstration. She espoused the cause of the South with unusual spirit, telling what she would do if she were a man, and exhibited such zeal and pathos that I almost began to think that it was a happy thing for the Union cause that she chanced to be a woman, while at the same time, as the sequel shows, it was a misfortune to the Confederacy that she had not been a man.

The much injured husband of this spirited woman, on a recent visit home, learned facts concerning his wife and General Van Dorn that so fired his brain and crazed his mind that he rushed back to camp, entered the General's tent, on retributive justice bent, and drawing a revolver shot him dead on the spot. Then flying quickly to the Union lines, he sought protection and safety under the flag he had so long abused and insulted.

Although this 10th of March was big with excitement and expectation of blood and carnage, there was but little fighting done. Had the enemy given us fight instead of retreating, our gallant 113th would have found the opportunity they had long waited for to distinguish themselves and extinguish the enemy.

How unlike are the rights and privileges in the army as shown by what fell under my observatin to-day. As our brigade was resting a short time about the middle of the day, near a farm house, a soldier noticed a well grown chicken straying too far from the barnyard, and immediately gave chase with fixed bayonet, endeavoring at each successive turn to transfix his game. Unlucky fellow! While so intent on pursuit that he could see naught but the receding and terrified biddie, an officer, whose buttons denoted rank, with sword lifted high brought up the rear with a blow, and a threat that if that thing occurred again the offender would be made to suffer. Just as this scene closed General Baird's Chief of Staff, mounted on an elegant horse and leading its mate, rode up to the mansion door and informed the owner of the horses that as General Baird wanted the horses he would appropriate them to the use and benefit of the government, and so doing he rode of with them, notwithstanding the cries of the family.

The army failing to meet the foe, could only return to Franklin. It was, indeed, an imposing sight to witness such a formidable display of military pomp as was seen that day by terrified hundreds of inhabitants along the Columbia pike, as our long dark columns moved northward in a continuous line, which occupied two hours in passing a given point.

Stopping to recuperate and rest a little at the house of my old rebel host while the somewhat scattered forces of our column were passing through the town, I chanced, from great fatigue, to fall asleep, and no one of the family deigning to awaken me, I slept on until the entire army had passed and the rear guard was out of sight. Suddenly awakened by the cessation of noises or other causes, I sprang to my feet, and, looking out of the window, saw my perilous situation. Hastening from the house without saying "good bye" to my entertainers, I mounted my horse, and was soon dashing toward Franklin, just as a squad of mounted rebels rode into town a few rods in the rear of me. Their command to halt was disregarded, and a number of shots fired at me went wide of the mark. A ride of a few miles brought me to my place in the line of march, and the lesson I had learned by loitering on the way was not soon forgotten. Reaching Franklin, we occupied our former camps, and were soon again performing the routine duties of the every-day life of a soldier.

April 1. I wrote to General Garfield for a pass from General Rosecrans for my wife and a lady nurse to visit the camp hospital. Steward Wells, after long and faithful service, left to-day for home, on account of physical disability. Also Lieutenant Toland, being unable for duty, goes home on a leave of absence. Poor John Price died to-day. He belonged to Company C; his disease was congestion of the brain. On the 3d we were honored by a visit from two officers of General Rosecrans' staff. They complimented us highly on the neat appearance and sanitary condition of our hospital.

George Horton, Company C, died on the 8th in the regimental hospital. His death was occasioned by congestion of the lungs.

Captain David Taylor, Jr., Company B, on account of failing health, left to-day for the North. I accompanied him as far as Nashville, and, with feelings of fond regret, waved the hand of farewell to him as he passed out of the depot homeward bound.

April 18. Arthur Wharton, Company B, died to-day of typhoid fever. He leaves a wife and four little children.

May was ushered in with a little more incidents than usual, for, before the day dawned, the 113th went out in the stillness of the morning, going several miles in the direction of Spring Hill, routing two rebel camps, killing several, and taking a number of prisoners. The only loss on our part was Billie, our favorite ambulance driver, who was mentioned before as singing and whistling on a former occasion near the same place. Poor fellow; he was shot dead on his seat in the ambulance. His body was brought to camp and buried beside a large elm tree, on which I engraved his name and fate, after breaking the sad news in a letter to his mother.

My own health and strength, which began to fail in early spring, brought on by increased duties imposed by the absence of Surgeon Black from the regiment attending to the duties of Medical Director, and other responsibilities to which he was called, now rapidly grew worse, after experiencing a shock assimilating sun-stroke on the 24th day of April past, while attending duties assigned me at Nashville, that Assistant Surgeon Tipton had to be recalled from other duties and assigned to duty in the regiment. This change took place on the 3d of May. I remained on duty in the regiment, notwithstanding my feeble health, and gave assistance to Surgeon Tipton as best I could during the pendency of my resignation, which was tendered on account of physical disability, at the suggestion and by the advice of Colonel Mitchell and other officers of the command. My honorable discharge was received from Headquarters on the 13th and dated the 11th, making me once more a free man.

On Monday, May 18, 1863, I bade farewell to many warm friends in camp, and, in company with my wife and hospital nurse, Langstaff, who went home on sick leave, I started for Nashville, where I arrived the same evening, *en route* for Northern Ohio, where I arrived in safety on the 26th day of May, 1863.

In closing this hurriedly written sketch of my nine months' service with the 113th O. V. I., I tender many grateful and heartfelt thanks to all the officers and enlisted men of that regiment for the respect and kindness universally shown me, and I shall ever cherish their friendship and acquaintance, which now, after a lapse of twenty years, seems sweeter, purer and dearer. Could my health and strength have held out, how happy I would have been to have gone on to the end and shared in greater honors so bravely won, but I must content myself in appropriating only a limited share of the honor and glory encircling the brow of the many brave boys of one of Ohio's favorite regiments, who fought so bravely to the end of the war.   A. HARLOW,

First Asst. Surgeon, 113th O. V. I.

AN ARMY REMINISCENCE.*

A LETTER WRITTEN BY AN EX-UNION PRISONER.

ANNAPOLIS, MD., *December 5, 1863.*
Mr. William Winslow and others :

You already know that I have been a prisoner and am now free. Yes, it is all over again, and I would lose my right arm, yea, rather would I lose life itself than trust myself to the tender mercies of the rebel government.

I will give you a brief, unvarnished account of my captivity, and while I would not appeal to your sympathy on my own behalf, for with me it is all over, but there are yet more than 12,000 loyal Union soldiers still enduring the horrors and indignities I here describe.

Soon after our regiment became engaged at Chickamauga, September 20, 1863, I was struck by a minnie ball which passed entirely through my left breast, and just under the bone of my left arm where it joins to the shoulder. I was taken to the rear, and in the retreat later in the day I was left at a citizen's house about seven miles from Chattanooga, and four or five miles from the field of battle. Here I remained all night. There were 150 of our wounded at and near this place, and only enough ambulances could be had to carry away fifty at a time. Two trips had already been made and we were waiting for their return, when a squad of rebel cavalry rode up and we were prisoners. Lieutenant Wheelock was of the original number, but he was taken away early in the morning by our ambulances. He was very badly wounded and could scarcely speak when he left.

The number who fell in the enemy's hands was fifty-three wounded and thirty-four well men who were left to attend the wounded. Besides these there were four Confederates.

The first thing our captors did was to march twenty-eight of our well men to the rear of their army, leaving six to care for us, the wounded. Being inside the rebel line we were left to shift for ourselves. The lady at whose house we were, gave us what we did get to eat, but she could do but little to supply the wants of fifty men. Here I remained a whole week. The rebels gave us nothing to eat, and even refused us an ear of corn to parch. Quite a number of the wounded died for the lack of proper medical attention.

Having no prospect before me but death by starvation and lack of care, I struck off into the woods, hoping by the utmost caution I might avoid the troops of the enemy and find a house where I might get something to satisfy my appetite. I was so weak as to be hardly able to walk, but at the close of the first day I found myself in the rear of the rebel infantry pickets. I stopped at a house, got

---

* The writer of this sketch died from the effects of his imprisonment, December 31, 1863.

a good supper, and stayed all night. The family treated me kindly, and so did all wherever I stopped, with one exception.

I got along finely and received much aid from the people among the mountains. Many of them said that their hearts were for the Union, and they would be glad to help me but feared the rebels. But I found one old man by the name of Sullivant, in Lookout Valley, whose heart beat differently. He thought the Lord would curse him if he gave a Yankee anything to eat. He said to me: "Youens all got a mighty whipping over here, but it was good for you; and yesterday General Wheeler got 144 of your wagons up in the Valley, and what do you suppose was in them? Nothing at all but silk dresses, bureaus and band-boxes and such things as you villains had stolen from us." This old sinner threatened to arrest me and take me to General Bragg's headquarters, but I managed to get away from him. I continued moving on day after day, and at length found myself across Lookout Mountain and within six miles of Trenton. So much aid had I received from citizens thus far that I began to entertain hopes of getting to Bridgeport, which was only sixteen miles further. But the rebels had possession of the left bank of the river and their cavalry scoured the whole country, far and wide, taking all the stragglers they could find and executing summary vengeance upon all citizens suspected of aiding our boys through the mountains.

By one of these scouting parties I was at length taken, and by them was carried before General Longstreet, then stationed near Rossville. I was finally turned over to the provost guard, placed in the guard-house with a number of deserters, conscripts, negroes and five federals.

The first day we got nothing to eat, and the second day only a little corn meal and fresh beef; and so it went.

One night nearly all the guards got drunk. The sergeant of the guard-house, who was also drunk, gave orders that if one of the damned Yankees moved or got up during the night, to shoot him. At last on the 11th of October we were sent to Atlanta. On arriving here we found 300 more of the wounded of Chickamauga, and two days later we were all started by rail toward Richmond. The journey was a very hard one, as we were crowded into filthy cattle cars, thirty-five of us to each car.

The journey to Richmond occupied eight days. We went by the way of Columbia, Charlotte, Raleigh and Petersburg. Our rations during all this trip consisted of twelve crackers and a pound and a half of pork. Written instructions were furnished the lieutenant having us in charge that we should neither be allowed to buy nor to trade for anything on the road, nor should citizens be permitted to speak to us nor to furnish us a piece of bread.

Upon arriving at Richmond we were taken at once to Libby prison, all put in one room and left to our own meditations. Here we remained three days, during which time we received but two meals. We were then removed and quartered in a brick building, which in times of peace was Yardbrough's tobacco factory, but was now known as the Franklin Street Hospital. It now contained three hundred sick and wounded. Some of these had rude bunks, but the greater number were scattered promiscuously over the floor. As fast as the sick or wounded became able to walk they were removed to the main prison and others were brought in to fill their places, so that in a short time only such remained as were very sick or dangerously wounded. These died at the rate of from five to twelve per day. I remember one morning that five men were placed side by side and in two days' time they died and their places were filled by others. On one occasion it was decided to parole a number of the prisoners, and the officer in command advised the surgeon to select only those who were nearest dead, for then he would save the expense of buying coffins for them. One of the sick men asked the doctor if he thought he, the prisoner, would recover soon, and was told that he did not want him to get well, and if he died that would keep him from fighting them again.

Captain Ross struck a prisoner in the face one morning at roll-call for daring to ask a question, accompanying the blow with the vilest language and a threat that if he opened his mouth again it would be at the risk of having his throat cut, and at other times this same officer beat prisoners in a brutal manner, and it is reported that more than one was shot and killed. Such is chivalry!

On the 10th of November I was taken from the hospital and placed in one of the main prisons. This was a tobacco factory, as were all the prisons in Richmond, I think. The floor was very filthy, many of the windows were destitute of glass. There were no stoves, no candles, nor any means of heat or light; and in this pen, deprived of the commonest comforts of life, eleven hundred Union soldiers were crowded like so many dumb animals. Our blankets had been taken from us when we were first captured or soon after; many of us had neither hats, shoes nor blouses. Here we received one meal a day, and this consisted of six or eight ounces of corn bread; sometimes this was sour and only half cooked, sometimes a small quantity of boiled rice and a few sweet potatoes.

These men were the heroes of the war—had faced the cannon's mouth at Fort Donelson, Stone River, Chickamauga and other bloody fields. It was horrible beyond expression of tongue or pen, to see these brave men, gaunt with hunger and worn out by fatigue and exposure, groping in the darkness like so many specters.

If you would see hunger, woe and wretchedness in all their deformity, you have but to see the inmates of the prisons at the capital of the C. S. A.

I will relate one or two instances of the many which came under my observation, and which, though too horrible for belief, are the whole truth.

One day a dog came into the "Royster Prison," and the boys managed to coax him away from the owner. They then killed the animal and cooked the carcass in small bits in their tin-cups by holding them over the gas jets in the night, this prison being differently lighted than the others. When cooked the mess was greedily devoured. Next day they related the exploit to the surgeon and to convince him of its truthfulness exhibited the pelt of the unfortunate canine.

One of the guards smuggled and sold to one of the prisoners, who had the greenbacks to pay for them, a number of sweet potato pies. Of these he ate so many as to make him sick, and he vomited them off his stomach. Two of his comrades, with their wooden spoons, gathered up and ate the rejected, half-digested mess. It sometimes happened that pieces of bread from the cook-house found their way into the swill-barrel, and in such cases they were fished out and greedily devoured by the starving men. Old beef bones which had been cast aside were gathered up, pounded to fragments and made into soup. A notice in a Richmond paper read like this: "Farmers and others who may have cattle of any kind to die on their places, can get the same taken away and be liberally compensated besides by making application at this office. Commissary of Prisons."

Shall such a conspiracy be upheld and supported by such men and by such means, and hope to succeed? God forbid. Is any sacrifice too great if by making it this southern oligarchy can be crushed to the earth? The feelings I now entertain for this miserable Confederacy are such that when my three years of service are ended, if the war be not ended and my services are still needed, I shall deem it a privilege to again enlist that I may do further service. I am not yet exchanged, but have improved greatly in my general health since coming here, the particulars of which may have reached you by other means. Hope to visit Hartford soon. Meanwhile thanking you for your kind assistance and wishing you continued happiness and prosperity, I am respectfully yours,

WM. H. LANE.

PRISON SKETCH OF WARREN C. ROSE.

I was born at Granville, Ohio, June 30, 1836, and at the age of twenty-one I went West, and spent three years teaching in Iowa and Missouri. Returning to Ohio, I attended college at Marietta, and was a member of the Freshman Class of 1861. The war began, and finally, when the call for 300,000 men was issued by the lamented Lincoln, I thought the call included me, and, bidding farewell to college life, I returned to Granville. Soon after, at a large and enthusiastic meeting held at the town hall, I enlisted for three years or during the war. My name was first on the list of what afterward constituted Company D of the brave and invincible 113th Ohio Volunteer Infantry. I have it to say that I stood at my post and did my duty with my company up to the hour when I fell into the hands of the merciless enemy at Chickamauga. For a few days previous to the battle I had been suffering with a slight illness, sometimes having a high fever. On the day before the battle of Chickamauga I gave out completely, and on the day of the battle I had not enough strength to keep in my place either in advancing or retreating. When our column fell back at dusk, leaving the dead and many wounded, I fell into the hands of the foe. In the morning we found ourselves prisoners. I was left on the field fourteen days with the wounded. At the end of this time an exchange was effected, and our worst wounded were sent into our lines at Chattanooga, while the slightly wounded, and those of us who had been attending them as nurses, were sent by railroad to Richmond, Virginia. We were quartered in Libby Prison two months, and were then sent to Danville, Virginia. We remained at Danville six months, and were then sent to the world-renowned Andersonville, Georgia. Remaining at Andersonville three months, we were again moved to another prison in Charleston, South Carolina, where we remained one month. We were then sent to Florence, South Carolina, where we remained three months. At this time an arrangement had been agreed upon to exchange 10,000 men on each side. Rebel officers came into the prison at Florence, and selected from the whole number those who were nearest dead, and who, when exchanged, would be likely to be of the least service to the Union cause. I was included in this number. A rebel officer told me on the day we were paroled at Florence that only 800 of the 10,000 men captured at Chickamauga were left alive. At Charleston, where we took passage for God's country, we saw the 10,000 rebels for whom we were being exchanged. These were strong and healthy men, ready for the front. These men had been fed, sheltered and cared for by the Federal Government, while we had been starved, insulted and neglected to an extent that is absolutely indescribable. We were mere shadowy wrecks, unfit for duty of any kind whatever. Only those who endured the horrors of our prison life can understand how terribly we suffered.

I was paroled December 10, 1864, making my imprisonment fourteen months and twenty days. I was sent home, where I remained till April 3, 1865, when, being exchanged, I joined the 113th near Raleigh, North Carolina. Then followed the surrender of the rebel army, commanded by General Johnson, the long march to the National Capital, the grand review, the homeward bound trip, and the greetings of friends at the fireside at home.

Comrades, let those of us who, braving so many hardships and perils, have lived to see the flag of our beloved country wave over a free people, stand ready to maintain all we have won and give God the glory. And let us also remember that if Jesus is our leader we shall always be led to victory. God bless our country and its brave defenders.
WARREN C. ROSE,
Valley Falls, Kansas.

From the London Democrat.

THE WAR HORSE, "OLD JOE."

THE "JOHNNY REB." DISCOVERED FROM WHOM HE WAS CAPTURED.

In the issue of the *Democrat* of about the first of January, we published an account of the death of "Old Joe," an aged white gelding, owned by Judge B. F. Clark, and brought from Georgia during the war by Colonel Toland Jones of the 113th O. V. I. The notice was copied into the *Herald and Georgian*, published at Sandersville, Georgia, with a few remarks, and the issue of that paper of the following week, February 7th, contains the following, which we doubt not will be found of interest to many of our readers:

The account published in the *Herald and Georgian* of the death of "Old Joe," a gray horse captured in the battle near Sandersville, that was carried to London, Ohio, by Colonel Jones, and the inquiry as to the ownership of the horse has, we think, satisfactorily discovered the owner and rider.

Walter G. Knight, who proved himself a true Confederate, was the rider, and Mr. Joe Vinson, who died a few years ago, was the owner. Mr. Knight had just returned from prison, had been at home only five days, when Mr. Vinsen proffered the use of his horse, a fleet and spirited animal, to Mr. Knight to ride out to Sandersville and ascertain the whereabouts of the Yankees, then supposed to be about Oconee. Mr. Knight, taking his own new saddle and bridle, mounted Bob, as the gray was called, and coming near town, heard some talking up an old road to the right. Thinking they were Confederates he started up the old road, but soon saw blue coats; he wheeled around and started diagonally across the woods and the public road into a pine thicket, where now is a field, between the Warthen road and the road to Fenn's Bridge, followed by a shower of bullets from the Yankees he had found. He was a fleet rider, and spurred his horse rapidly forward on the route we have just indicated, when he found himself just running right into the line of battle.

The line halted and with muskets pointed at Mr. Knight, the Yankees sang out "Come in, Johnny, come in." Johnnie saw it was best to come in, and dashed forward to the line. Some ordered him pretty roughly to dismount, but he remained seated till an officer came up and asked him who he was, to what command he belonged, etc. At first Walter was thought a bushwhacker, but soon by his answers assured them of his true character. The officer ordering, he dismounted and was taken to the rear. As he went back one of the guards said, "this will make a good horse for Colonel Jones," and assures him the more of the identity of the horse. He also remembers the scar on the horse's nose, as does also that man of wonderful memory, Mr. John R. Wickers, though both say it was not a sabre cut, as the animal was not then an army horse. Mr. Wickers says he was a capital horse for hunters, and was, as he phrases it, the best woods horse he ever saw, but not a sober harness horse.

Mr. Knight was afterwards carried to the residence of Hon. W. G. Brown, where his widow now resides, headquarters of General Sherman, who asked him a few questions, and then sent him back to be kept under guard. He remained from Saturday until Sunday night, when he made his escape.

From memoranda handed us we learn that Walter G. Knight was Orderly Sergeant of Company B, 12th Battalion Georgia Volunteers, Evan's Brigade, Gordon's Division, Erly's Corps, the old Stonewall Jackson's Command. He was captured July 10, 1864, at Frederick City, Maryland; was paroled at Point Lookout the latter part of October, 1864. He has twenty-three scars on his body, and has a bullet that passed through his body. He was in nine different prisons, and escaped from three; he was once lost in the mountains, and was five days without anything to eat.

These are facts that can be proved, says Mr. Knight, and by common consent he made a good soldier.

The saddle and bridle that was captured was new, and was kept with great care; and now Mr. Knight says, as old Bob, this horse's rebel name, is now dead, he wishes Colonel Jones would send his saddle and bridle home. Yes, send it along; or a good new one would do, as he is not hard to satisfy.

EVERY-DAY SOLDIER LIFE.

The following sketch of every-day soldier life was furnished by Thompson P. Freeman, of Company F:

While at Camp Chase, I procured a pass to go out south of camp to the house of a farmer, where I had a pleasant time chatting with the old man and his attractive daughters. He invited me to stay for dinner, and, lacking the courage to decline, I accepted. Dinner being over, I accompanied the old man to his sorghum works, and spent part of the day in pleasant conversation and in watching the process of making molasses. I then returned to camp.

The same night some of that molasses broke guard, and actually took refuge in our tent. For days following we lacked nothing in the way of sweetening for our rations, nor did I ever return to the farm house to thank the old man for sweetening the mess.

Soon after our arrival at Camp Zanesville an incident occurred which ought to be recorded. A load of straw had arrived, and was being carried by the members of the regiment to their quarters for bedding. One of the drafted men came also, and took up an armful of straw, and was making off with it, when Colonel Wilcox ordered him to lay it down. The man retorted by telling the Colonel to go to the place the way to which is said to be paved with good intentions, and where straw is presumed to be a perishable article, and was making off with his bundle of straw. Just at that moment the Colonel's foot flew up and took the drafted man where it would do the most good, and established the reputation of the Colonel as a kicker. The man went his way, and it is not probable that he afterwards enlisted in the 113th and slept on *straw*.

While a squad of us were picketing at Franklin, an incident occurred about milking time in the morning. Seeing a cow near a house, one of the men went and asked for milk. Failing in procuring it at the house, he determined to milk the cow. He said the first thing he ever did was to milk, and that he knew all about milking a cow. He found the cow unused to being milked after the Yankee idea, and, in his efforts to anchor her for the purpose, he caught her tail and called on me to assist. I stepped in front of her; she gave a quick turn by the left flank, and, the milk-hungry soldier at her tail losing the line of march, went whirling down the hill at a rate that threatened his destruction. The cow returned to her fodder, and the pickets at that post drank black coffee for breakfast.

During that little affair at Triune I remember how gracefully we all bowed whenever a cannon shot came screeching over us, but when we reached our trenches at the top of the hill, we could see the smoke of the enemy's guns, and trace the course of the shots as they came whistling toward us. As General Gordon Granger sat on his horse watching the progress of the action, a shot from the guns of the enemy cut off the limb of a tree, which fell close to his feet. He never took his eye off the enemy, but, jumping from his horse, he requested one of the gunners to let him try a shot, and, permission being granted, he emptied a number of saddles of their rebel riders in a manner that showed him to be a practical gunner.

At Chickamauga, September 20, 1863, Company F, of which I was a member, was on the picket line. Captain Levi T. Nichols was in command, and we were advancing through a cornfield, when "zip, zip," came the bullets from the left, striking the cornstalks on every hand. We were nearing some timber, and by the time we reached it the cannon shots of the enemy were coming from our front, striking the ground sometimes and bounding high in air, or go crashing through the timber at a dangerous rate. While we lay for a brief time crouched behind trees to cover us from the enemy, more than one incident took place among the men of the company. One of them, whose reputation for bravery had been below par, shook as with a chill, and whimpered: "I never thought I would come to this; how I wish I was at home." In subsequent actions he distinguished himself for bravery and soldierly bearing.

The cannonading ceased, and our company resumed its place in the regiment, capturing two prisoners who had hid in a hollow. After we returned, and had taken our place, the troops in front of us were ordered to charge the enemy in our front, while our line was ordered to lie down at the foot of the hill. Almost immediately we were ordered to charge over the same ground, and, as we advanced on double quick, we met the first line falling back, having been overpowered by the enemy. Many of these were falling as they came, and it seemed to me they were being killed by our fire.

I determined not to fire until I got a fair view of a Johnnie. I waited but a moment, for off to the left oblique I saw a rebel step from behind a tree, at the distance of twenty-five or thirty yards, and point his gun in the direction where I stood. I drew up my gun, aiming at his whole body, intending to hit him somewhere, but my gun snapped and refused to fire. I tried a second cap, and it snapped. Seeing that my left-hand comrade was shot, I took up his gun and discharged it at the rebel at the tree. Presently I observed that there was no one at my immediate left, and was on the point of turning back, thinking I was alone, when I heard Lieutenant Wheelock give the command: "Stand up to them, boys; don't give an inch." Turning to my right, I found the rest of the company completely in line and doing desperate work. I now began to reload my gun, and in doing so I received a musket shot through my right wrist, completely disabling me from further duty. Lieutenant Wheelock was shot through the lungs about the same time, from the effects of which he died the next day. I now attempted to leave the field, dragging my gun with me with my left hand. I at length abandoned my gun, and went to the rear to find a surgeon. I soon found one, and was about speaking to him, when a shell of the enemy exploded uncomfortably near us. He suggested that we had better get beyond the range of those guns, and I agreed with him. We hurried off, crossing a ravine, and halting behind a tree. Having two handkerchiefs, I bound one tightly around my wrist and made the other into a sling to support my wounded arm. I made an effort to go on and find an ambulance, but, in doing so, I fainted and fell. The fall, together with the voice of a comrade near by, revived me so that I got up, and, standing against a tree, soon recovered so as to be able to go on in search of an ambulance. I was advised to go to the field hospital, but, after a fruitless effort to find it, I set out to return to our former camp, which I reached about sundown. I had walked seven miles, and was exhausted from fatigue and loss of blood.

Going to a spring near by, I sat down with the intention of bathing and dressing my wound, when a couple of Indiana soldiers came along, and, learning that I was wounded, one of them bathed and dressed my wound quite skillfully, and I then learned for the first time the dangerous character of my injury. The hand was almost severed from the arm by a minnie ball. At the regiment to which these two men belonged I drank some coffee, and felt much refreshed. Then I went in search of the 113th, for, having learned that the whole army had fallen back, I presumed they would be in the valley somewhere. I failed to find the regiment, but, finding two wounded comrades of the 113th, one being wounded in the head and the other in the shoulder, I proposed to them that we have some supper. We prepared and drank some coffee, and then, gathering together some corn stalks where the mules had been fed, we made our bed, with one army blanket under us and an oil cloth over us. (I had lost both my blankets in the charge early in the afternoon.) Next morning, being unable to find our regiment, and knowing that our wounded were being sent to Chattanooga, we prepared to go in that direction, but, finding a surgeon of an Illinois regiment, we had our wounds dressed by him. I procured some water for the purpose, and, admitting that the wounds of the other two men were more serious than mine, I waited till the last. He told me that mine was a terrible wound, and that I must not be surprised if it required amputation. He then ordered an ambulance, into which we were loaded, and, after a dusty ride of a few miles, we reached the hospital at Chattanooga. This building was already full, so we were taken to a brick building which had been prepared for us. We were among the first to occupy it, but in less than two hours it was full of wounded and dying. I never again wish to witness a scene of such distress and suffering as that hospital presented.

The same afternoon an order was issued requiring all who could walk to cross the river and be prepared to take a train for Bridgeport. We remained two nights and a day awaiting the arrival of a train, and, when it came, it was not a train of cars with comfortable coaches and easy, cushioned seats. It was a train of army wagons, such as we had seen used to transport supplies. I filled my canteen with water, and nerved myself to walk, thinking I could ride whenever I chose to do so. I found out that walking was the most agreeable, for the roads were mountainous and dusty beyond description.

The second day at noon we reached a small village, where I learned that a resident physician would dress my wound. I went to him and showed him my wound. He told me it was very dangerous and it would probably never heal, and that the hand would have to come off sooner or later. He dressed it very carefully and put new bandages on it, and when I offered to pay him declined taking any compensation, saying he took great pleasure in doing what he could for the Union soldiers. We moved on and reached Bridgeport that evening. During the day I lost a large tin cup which I prized very highly, having carried it all the way from Camp Chase.

At Bridgeport I applied to a surgeon to have my arm dressed, but after learning that it had been dressed that day and that I had kept it dampened continually with cold water, he said that as so many needed surgical attention worse than I did, that I must try and wait till we arrived at Nashville. At 11 o'clock that night a train arrived to take us to Nashville. It was a train of box cars, but it was better than army wagons. We piled in like so many hogs and were soon moving northward, arriving at Nashville on the afternoon of the next day, four days after the battle. I entered Cumberland Hospital September 24, 1863. The next morning all who could walk were ordered to go to the dining hall to eat, but I remained in my quarters, where I received extra diet of eggs and other delicacies. I remained here sixty days, my wound healing well in that time. On the 23d of November, 1863, I received a furlough for thirty days, arriving at home on Thanksgiving Day, November 25. On the 9th of December I was examined by Dr. Sinnett, of Granville, and received a certificate of disability for forty days, and on the 14th of January, 1864, I received another certificate for thirty days. On the 16th of February I went to Columbus, and finding Colonel James A. Wilcox, the first colonel of our regiment, who was at the time provost marshal, I told him my situation and asked his advice. He gave me a note to the officer at Camp Tod. This officer proposed to send me to Nashville, but advised me first to see the examining surgeon. This officer proposed sending me to Nashville, also; but I protested and urged him to send for my papers which were at Nashville, and allow me to remain in Ohio. He then wrote me an order of admission to the Seminary Hospital, Columbus. On the 22d of February I wrote to the officer in charge of Cumberland Hospital, Nashville, asking for my papers. These came in due time. I remained in the Seminary Hospital till March 2d, 1864, when I was transferred to Camp Dennison. A few days after my arrival at Camp Dennison I was examined by the post surgeon, who said that gangrene had set in on my wound, but he hoped to be able to scatter it. By carefully following his instructions my wound was soon much improved, and by the 28th of March it had become so much better that I was recommended for a discharge, but it was not till the 25th of April, 1864, that I received it.

I am now a citizen of a great and free country, and I am proud of the humble part I have taken to restore the Union and establish a lasting and permanent peace.

T. P. FREEMAN,
Marysville, O.

PRESENTIMENT OF APPROACHING DEATH.

There belonged to Company B, 113th O. V. I.,—a regiment raised in the neighborhood of Columbus in 1862—two young men, both of whom enlisted from the little suburban village of Reynoldsburg. Both were good soldiers, attending to such duty as was imposed upon them without any more than the usual amount of complaint, and in battle behaved as well as the average. Time rolled on, and everything went as merry as such uncertain times would permit. One day both of these young men were sitting in company quarters, trying to fit a pair of government brogans to their delicate little feet, when the following conversation passed between them:

" Well, John, I think these brogans will be the last Uncle Sam will have to furnish us, as before they are worn out, this 'cruel war' will no doubt be over, and we can return to the Burg, and show them what kind of shoes we had to tramp in."

"I don't know about that, Will," said John, looking solemn; "but one thing is certain, this will be the last pair of shoes I will draw, for in the very next engagement our regiment is in, that amounts to anything, *I will be killed*, and will, therefore, not need any more foot gear."

"Oh, pshaw, what are you talking that way for? We'll both live to see the war ended, and the way we'll drive through Reynoldsburg one of these days behind a spanking team, will make the natives wonder. Won't it be fun, though, to see them open their eyes, when we go through that town like the wind?"

"But I tell you I will never get back. I feel it in my very soul, and have for a long time, that I would soon be numbered among the dead," said John, more serious than ever, not even cracking a smile at the thought of storming his old town behind a good team of horses.

His friend tried every way to free his mind of this thought, by telling jokes on his old home companions, and of the fiascos they used to indulge in, carrying it so far as to laugh at the ridiculousness of his presentiment of coming evil. But to no avail.

These soldiers were "partners,"—slept together, ate together, and what one did, the other knew of.

The regiment, in about two weeks after the above conversation, received marching orders, and all was in readiness to move. These two young soldiers had curled up under their blanket for the night, and John, putting his arm around Will, said: "This is the last night you and I will ever spoon together, for before to-morrow's sun goes down I will be a corpse, *and I know it.*"

The next morning (Sunday) was bright and clear, and John insisted on his companion taking his watch, money and other valuables, still asserting that before the day was done he would be no more. His friend declined, telling him that their chances were equally good, still laughing at his fear of being shot. About ten o'clock the boom of artillery and the rattle of musketry could be distinctly heard, and the 113th was moving to the front. The contending forces met, but the crash was only of short duration, each side retiring for a breathing spell and to prepare for more effective effort. John was still all right, and was reminded of the fact that he still lived.

"The thing is not over yet, Will; as sure as fate, I will not see the setting of the sun. The next engagement will end me for this earth."

In a short time Company B was ordered out on the skirmish line. John and Will kept close together, and both stood behind the same tree. There was scarcely room enough for both, and John concluded to dodge across to the next tree only a few yards distant. He had gone but a short distance, when crash went a minnie ball through the upper portion of his body, and in falling turned completely around and fell stone dead at the feet of his companion.

And his presentiment was fulfilled. The rebels soon came forward in force and drove the skirmishers back to the main line, and the body of John J. Smith, of Reynoldsburg, was never recovered, having been thrown in a trench with hundreds of others, recognition being impossible by their friends, who endeavored in a short time to recover the bodies of members of the regiment who were killed in this engagement—Chickamauga, Sunday, the 20th of September, 1863.

Is there anything in presentiment? The reader can answer.

OUR REUNIONS.

At the annual meeting of the Army of the Cumberland, held at Columbus, Ohio, in the summer of 1874, a number of the men of the 113th O. V. I. met at the Neil House and effected a temporary organization for the purpose of holding annual reunions of the regiment.

On the 22d of December, 1874, the regiment held its first reunion at the Board of Trade rooms, City Hall, Columbus. A permanent organization was made, as follows: President, John G. Mitchell; Vice President, Toland Jones; Treasurer, W. H. Halliday; Secretary, F. M. McAdams; Assistant Secretary, T. D. Bently. The exercises consisted of an address by General Mitchell and a free-and-easy lot of speeches by various members present. A banquet was held at the American Hotel in the evening, and fun and frolic reigned till a late hour. This reunion was a success.

The second reunion was held at London, O., on the last Friday of October, 1875. The annual address was delivered by Otway Watson. The people in and about London did a noble part in providing an abundant entertainment and generous welcome.

The third reunion was held at Mechanicsburg, O., October 27, 1876, and was presided over by Joseph Swisher. An address of welcome was delivered by W. H. Baxter. Some rotine business was transacted, and a banquet was held at the Darby House in the evening. This reunion was regarded as a failure, the citizens of the village failed to take an interest with us. Officers for the ensuing year were elected as follows: President, Charles P. Garman; Vice President, John W. Kile; Treasurer, James Coultas; Secretary, F. M. McAdams.

The fourth reunion was held at Columbus, O., August 24, 1877, and was presided over by John G. Mitchell. An able address was delivered by J. K. Hamilton, and some important matters of business disposed of. A banquet in the evening at the American House, an able address by Judge West, and other speaking exercises closed the day. Officers for the ensuing year: President, John G. Mitchell; Vice President, George McCrea; Treasurer, G. A. Cofforth; Secretary, F. M. McAdams.

The fifth reunion was held at Columbus, October, 1878. The address was by Toland Jones. The occasion was one of rare interest, the attendance large and all passed off well. Officers elected for the ensuing year were as follows: President, John G. Mitchell; Vice President, Toland Jones; Treasurer, C. A. Cofforth; Secretary, F. M. McAdams; Orator, David Taylor, Jr. The usual banquet at the American House closed the ceremonies.

The sixth reunion was held at Columbus, August 29, 1879, and was presided over by John G. Mitchell. The officers for the ensuing year were as follows: President, David Taylor, Jr.; Vice President, Charles Sinnet; Secretary, F. M. McAdams; Treasurer, Charles A. Cofforth; Executive Committee, James Coultas, W. P. Souder, Moses Goodrich. Speakers for next reunion, Otway Watson, Joseph Swisher. James A. Wilcox was the principal speaker. The usual committees were appointed and much other business disposed of. Brief addresses were made by McAdams, McCrea, Haley, Abbot, Sinnet, and others. Many letters from the absent ones were read by the Secretary. Proper plans were made for the next reunion.

August 11, 1880, was the date of the seventh reunion, held at the usual place at the State Capital. This meeting was presided over by David Taylor, Jr. The usual committees were assigned to duty at the morning session. The committee on nominations presented the following report: President, Wm. H. Halliday; Vice President, Moses Goodrich; Treasurer, Chas. A. Cofforth; Secretary, F. M. McAdams; Executive Committee, J. L. Flowers, Wm. Romosier, C. R. Herrick. The early part of the afternoon session was occupied in brief speeches, in which McAdams, Swisher, Watson and Hon. J. F. Ogelvee (98th O. V. I.) participated. There being present Chas. Kulencamp, 108th Ohio, Comrade Fribley, 98th Ohio, Captain Banker, 121st Ohio, and others of old Second Brigade, the meeting took on brigade proportions, and some plans were spoken of looking to a reunion of the regiments of the brigade at a future time.

The evening session was held in the office of the Auditor of State, and, though not well attended, was full of interest. Garman, Taylor, Watson, McAdams, Edmiston and Evans made short addresses.

The eighth reunion convened at Columbus, August 11, 1881, and, in the absence of President Halliday, was presided over by John Ogelvee. Committees on business, finance, nominations, etc., were appointed at the morning session, as follows: Business—Taylor, Southard and Flowers. Nominations—Simpson, Souder and Grafton. Finance—Cofforth, Osborn and Taylor. Future Reunion—Thrall, Sullivant and Van Houten. Officers for the ensuing year were chosen, as follows: President, Geo. G. McCrea; Vice President, L. S. Sullivant; Treasurer, A. M. Grafton; Secretary, F. M. McAdams. A project of writing a regimental history was discussed, and F. M. McAdams was made historian, with the assurance that

45

the membership would meet the necessary expense. St. Paris was agreed on as the place of meeting for next reunion. The session of the afternoon was occupied in short speeches, hand-shaking and exchange of good will and good feeling. No evening session was held.

The ninth reunion assembled at St. Paris, O., on the 1st day of September, 1882. This was regarded by the people as the largest gathering of *any kind* ever held in the town. No pains had been spared in planning on a large scale; money and labor had been bestowed with liberal hands. Bravery and beauty vied to outdo each other in making the occasion successful, and never was labor and devotion more fully rewarded. No brief sketch can do the description justice. The principal exercises were held in Furrows' grove, near town. Addresses were made by J. Warren Kiefer, W. R. Warnock, S. T. McMorran and others. A huge dinner was served in princely style, and the capacity of the old soldiers was, for once, reached. At Bowersock's Hall, in the evening, an entertainment was held, consisting of music, toasts, addresses, etc. In this exercise John G. Mitchell, Chas. F. McAdams, L. S. Sullivant, S. T. McMorran, Toland Jones, W. C. Rose, Iza Gales and J. Swisher participated. This reunion is regarded as one of the largest ever held in this part of the State. The people of St. Paris did themselves great credit.

The tenth reunion was held at Granville, Licking county, September 20, 1883. Like the preceding one at St. Paris, it was immense. The citizens had for weeks been talking, planning and laboring to make the occasion a success. All the necessary plans for decoration, music, entertainment, etc., had been carefully laid and intrusted to competent hands. The meetings were held in the Opera House, which was filled to its utmost limit. L. S. Sullivant was chosen chairman. The following committees were appointed: Resolutions—M. M. Munson, J. K. Hamilton, J. Swisher; Finance—John W. Kile, C. R. Herrick, M. Goodrich; Nominations—J. S. Ports, W. C. Bostwick, Toland Jones; Programme—B. Huson, Thomas A. Jones, John Ogelvee. R. E. Rogers, Mayor of Granville, delivered a greeting of welcome. Rev. T. J. Sheppard responded on behalf of the resident members of the regiment, and J. K. Hamilton spoke in response to the welcome. Toland Jones and Joseph Swisher made some fitting remarks in the morning session. Dinner was then in order. Such a dinner! One could believe that the whole commonwealth had united in furnishing supplies. The attack was made in good order, and the line was maintained without a straggler. Some dinners can be described; this one can not. It was all that a rich country, loyal hearts and fair hands could make it. That is saying enough.

The exercises of the evening session consisted of toasts, music, speeches and anecdote, and will long be remembered on account of the enjoyment it furnished. The toasting and responses were as follows:

"The American Soldier"—Joseph Swisher.
"The Press in the War"—Milton Scott.
"The Unreturned Volunteer"—F. M. McAdams.
"Our Reunions"—L. S. Sullivant.
"Our Invited Guests"—M. M. Munson.

The Granville Cornet Band furnished good music of the instrumental kind, and a select choir of vocalists rendered some excellent pieces of music during the day and evening.

The eleventh reunion was appointed for Mt. Sterling, September 10, 1884. The following officers were chosen for the next year: President, Toland Jones; Vice President, Moses Goodrich; Secretary and Treasurer, F. M. McAdams; Orator, Joseph Swisher.

Our reunions are growing in interest year after year. May they continue as long as there are two of the old command left to greet each other and shake hands.

ADDRESS OF MAJOR JOSEPH SWISHER,

AT THE

SEVENTH REUNION OF THE 113TH O. V. I., AT CITY HALL, COLUMBUS, OHIO, AUGUST 11, 1880.

COMRADES OF THE 113TH O. V. I.:

I received official notice a few days ago of my selection, in connection with Major Watson, to deliver an address at the 7th annual reunion of the regiment. I have collected a few thoughts together for the occasion, which I hope may not be entirely void of interest. While engaged in the quiet pursuits of life, amidst peace and plenty, we can scarcely realize the fact that within less than twenty years past our country has been engaged in a great civil war which threatened its very existence. While recounting the heroism of those who went forth to battle for their country, you will pardon me if I go back and briefly recount the causes which brought on the conflict. Going back to the time when the Colonies separated themselves from the mother country, and set up an independent government for themselves, we find that in the Constitution which they adopted they left the very germ of dissolution. Our forefathers had declared that all men were endowed by their Creater with certain inalienable rights, among which were life, liberty and the pursuit of happiness. Yet, when the Constitution was adopted human slavery was allowed to exist. While poets have sung of this as the land of the free and the home of the brave, it remained for nearly one hundred years as the land of the free and the home of the *slave*. Thomas Jefferson first compared the institution of slavery to a wolf held by the ears, which you could not hold onto nor dared to let go.

The slave power, ever aggressive, first showed its real spirit in 1820, when Missouri was admitted as a State into the Union. By a compromise measure, the impending crisis which threatened a speedy dissolution of the Union at that time was averted.

All parties then thought the bounds of human slavery were forever restricted. Peace was restored to the country. Unexampled prosperity followed. Our country increased in wealth and population, until it speedily took rank among the first nations of the earth. Twelve years later we find a new element of disturbance in our body politic. John C. Calhoun, of South Carolina, first proclaimed the doctrine of States' rights—that the State governments were superior to the General Government—and South Carolina, in 1832, passed an ordinance denying the right of the General Government to execute her own laws within the sovereign limits of that State. But that stern old patriot and hero, Andrew Jackson, was at the head of the government, and forever immortalized his name and administration by the declaration that, "By the eternal, the Union must and shall be preserved," and that he would hang those in resistance to the execution of the laws higher than Haman if they persisted in their course. Knowing well the stern character of the old hero of New Orleans, the people of South Carolina speedily acquiesced, and allowed the laws to be executed within her limits. However, the doctrine proclaimed by Calhoun was not destroyed—only quelled, to lie dormant, ready to break out at the first favorable opportunity. The acquisition of Texas as a slave State gave new impetus to the slave power, and, by the aid of the Supreme Court in the passage of the Dred Scott decision, every foot of territory heretofore free was virtually made slave territory, and every free man a blood hound for the capture of fugitives from human bondage. This measure naturally alarmed the freedom loving people of the North. Intense excitement prevailed throughout the country, when again the antidote of compromise was applied by a bill introduced by that venerable sage and patriot, Henry Clay, of Kentucky, and the country again reposed in quiet until the overcrowded population of the New England States and Eastern cities, and the Northern Central States, began to turn their eyes westward to the plains of Kansas, where they might build up homes for themselves and their children. The South, becoming alarmed at the growth and political power of the great Northwest, sought to overthrow the time honored Missouri Compromise, and did, by the aid of Northern dough-faces then in Congress, repeal it, and attempted to curse the land of Kansas with slavery through the doctrine of Squatter Sovereignty. The territory filled up rapidly. The people of the North were anxious to make free homes for their children in that beautiful country; the people of the South determined, through the doctrine of Squatter Sovereignty, aided by the Dred Scott decision, to make Kansas a slave State. They poured their population into the territory. Political excitement ran high. Strife and bitterness existed between the people from the different sections of the country. Two constitutions were framed and presented to Congress preparatory to its admission as a State into the Union. Under the leadership of such patriots as Sumner, Wade, Giddings, and old Thaddeus Stephens, the free State constitution was adopted. The strife and bitter feeling at this time was intense. All felt that the peace of the country was in danger. The South were chagrined. Their representatives in Congress presented the appearance of caged wild beasts. Representatives of the freedom loving North were stricken down in the halls of legislation for daring to assert their principles. The South claimed that the election of Lincoln to the Presidency on a platform opposed to the extension of slavery was sufficient cause for them to sever their connection with the Union, and build up for themselves a government whose chief corner stone should be human slavery. Early in December, 1860, South Carolina passed an ordinance of secession, which was speedily followed by other States, which together formed a new government, styled the Confederate States of America, into which the people, under the doctrine of States' Rights, were taken as into a whirlpool. Our small army had been sent to the Western frontier, under the pretext of suppressing Mormonism. Our navy was scattered in foreign seas. Our forts were being captured, our arms were shipped South, and treason was plotted under the very nose of James Buchanan, who had—I will not say the audacity, but the imbecility to declare that there was no power under the Constitution to coerce a sovereign State. Had the old hero of New Orleans been in the Presidential chair, he would have nipped treason in the bud. The halls of Congress resounded with the language of treason. Yet the people of the North were slow to believe that any portion of the people were willing to throw off their allegiance to the best government the world ever saw. The President constitutionally elected had, in order to escape assassination when on his way to Washington to be inaugurated, to pass secretly through Baltimore. Soon after his inauguration Fort Sumpter was fired upon. The Northern heart was at once fired up. The spirit of patriotism, always strong in the North, was fully aroused, party lines were for the time apparently forgotten, and every energy seemed bent to the one purpose—that of preserving the Union. The farmer left his plow; the mechanic his workshop; the merchant his counter; the clerk his office, and the gentleman his leisure; and all buckled on their armor, and hastened to defend the capital of the nation from the rebels, already armed and marching in solid phalanx against it. The rebel army was commanded by able generals, who had been educated by the same Government they now sought to destroy. The first conflict of arms proved disastrous to the United States troops, but served to fully arouse the people of the North to a true sense of the situation. They realized that to preserve the life of the nation would cost blood and treasure, but the bright hopes of the future would richly compensate for both. The war went on with varied success; sometimes victory crowned our efforts; again, we would meet with disaster. Meantime a party grew up in the North hostile to the war for the preservation of the Union. The lower House of Congress had fallen into the hands of those opposed to the war. Great leaders stood up in the halls of Congress and declared that not another man nor dollar should be given to fill the ranks or feed the soldiers already in the field. The

Legislature of Indiana had so crippled the executive of that State that he was obliged to go to New York and pledge his own credit for money to equip the soldiers from that State ready for the field. A majority of the members of Congress elected from Ohio were opposed to the war. Secret organizations sprang up throughout the North, whose purpose was to discourage enlistments and give aid and comfort to the enemy. In 1862 a convention met in Columbus, O., and openly passed a resolution declaring that 200,000 men of Ohio sent greeting to their brethren in the South. Amid these stirring scenes the 113th Regiment, O. V. I., was organized. It was organized under the second call for 300,000 men, in 1862. It was not made up of that class of men who from excitement went into the army, but of men who in their calm reflection felt that their services were needed to fill the depleted ranks of their brethren already in the field. It assembled at Camp Chase on the 28th day of August, 1862, and at once went into the school of the soldier to receive that discipline so necessary to the efficiency of a soldier in the field. After remaining here nearly two months, under instruction of Colonels Wilcox and Mitchell, it was transferred to Camp Zanesville, and from there to Camp Dennison. Remaining but a short time here, it was transferred to Kentucky, and became a part of the reserve forces of General Rosecrans in his pending battle with General Bragg in Tennessee. To attempt to write anything of the 113th Regiment after this is to write a history of the war. The regiment remained in Kentucky but a short time, when it took a steamer, in company with a large number of troops, for Nashville, to more immediately re-enforce General Rosecrans' army, which had been depleted after a desperate but successful battle of three days with the rebel army, under General Bragg, at Murfreesboro, or Stone River. The regiment arrived at Fort Donelson just in time to witness the close of the second battle of that place. Arriving at Nashville, the regiment here parted with Colonel Wilcox, to whom the men had become much endeared, and Colonel Mitchell at once assumed command, and, though not always in immediate command of the regiment, yet remained with it through all the trying ordeals to which it was subjected. The regiment now pushed on to Franklin, Tennessee, where it was organized into and became a part of the Reserve Corps, Army of the Cumberland, under Major General Gordon Granger. Here it rested for some time, being occasionally called out to meet the enemy, who was hovering around the right flank of Rosecrans' army. While lying here the ravages of disease made sad havoc in our heroic band, for which I always thought the would-be General C. C. Gilbert was very largely responsible, by calling up the men who were not endued to camp life at unseasonable hours, for no other purpose, as any one could tell, but to gratify an inordinate ambition he had to show off. But, after the United States Senate clipped his brigadier wings, he drooped his tail like a peacock, and disappeared from the theater of war, only to be remembered as one of the things of the past for which there was no further need.

After spending the greater part of the summer of 1863 in Middle Tennessee, the regiment was pushed rapidly forward across the Cumberland Mountains and the Tennessee River into Georgia, to engage with the main army under Rosecrans at the battle of Chickamauga, who was not only to meet the army of Northern Virginia, but the paroled prisoners from Vicksburg.

After two days of marching and countermarching, in which the greater part of the army had been engaged in deadly conflict, the reserve corps, of which the 113th formed a part, was on the 20th day of September, 1863, thrown into the deadly breach. Like the legions of honor under the great Napoleon, they were only thrown in after the conflict had become desperate. Here the regiment received its first baptism in blood, having lost in killed and wounded one hundred and sixty-three men. What thrilling emotions pass through the breast when memory calls back the time when amid the roaring of artillery, the shrieking and bursting of shell, the rattling of musketry, the whizzing of bullets, the groans of the wounded and dying, the 113th charged and recharged upon the rebel hosts. The charge of the immortal 600 of which poets have sung was not more heroic than that of the 113th on that dreadful day. Retiring after the conflict within the fortifications surrounding Chattanooga, the army assumed the position of a stag at bay on which Bragg considered it unsafe to move. Here the regiment suffered the privations of hunger without a murmur till on the 25th of November, the army having been reorganized with General Grant in command, aided by those able Lieutenants, Sherman, Thomas and Hooker, and being largely reinforced, moved upon the enemy's works and hurled the rebel hosts in dismay from Mission Ridge, following them as far as Ringgold, Georgia, when the regiment was suddenly started on a forced march into East Tennessee to relieve Burnside, who was closely besieged by the troops of Longstreet. Unprepared to stand the rigors of a winter's campaign; poorly clad, without rations, subsisting off the country, they made forced marches without a murmur. Nearing Knoxville and the siege having been raised, they hastily retraced their steps towards Chattanooga, expecting to soon occupy their comfortable quarters which they had left a few weeks before. Arriving on the bank of the Tennessee river in the night, chilled by the cold blasts of a December wind, many of them barefooted and their feet bleeding, only to find the bridge across the Tennessee unfit to cross, and the men were only permitted, like Moses when leading the children of Israel to the promised land, to view it from afar, they likewise were only permitted to view their quarters from afar, and take up their quarters on the frozen banks of the Tennessee without tents or fire, which they did with a resignation not surpassed by that of the soldiers of the Revolution at Valley Forge. The regiment crossed the river next day and entered their quarters, where they expected to remain for the winter, but were doomed to disappointment. They were barely settled down when the word, "fall in," passed along the line, and they took up their line of march south across the

Tennessee river. Moving out from Chattanooga about eight miles, halted and put up new quarters where they remained till May, 1864, except for short intervals when they were ordered out on some duty for a few days at a time.

The first of May found the army animated with new life; all was bustle and activity. The army had been reorganized, with W. T. Sherman, one of the world's ablest generals, in command, with General George H Thomas, that true type of a Roman soldier, in command of the Army of the Cumberland, of which the 113th, O. V. I., formed a part. Now commenced one of the most remarkable campaigns history gives any account of. To write a history of this campaign is to write a history of the 113th regiment. At Buzzard Roost, at Resaca, at Rome, at Dalles the regiment bore a conspicuous and honorable part, until brought up in front of the Kenesaw Mountain it found everywhere the guns of the enemy bristling in its front. Called upon to charge on the enemy's works the men buckled on their armor without a murmur and charged into the very jaws of death. Here again the regiment suffered severely, losing one hundred and sixty-five in killed and wounded. Unable to capture the enemy's works, they wavered, fell back a short distance and intrenched themselves in close proximity to the enemy's guns and maintained their position until the enemy fell back, when the word, "fall in," again passed along the lines. The march was at once resumed, and continued without much serious opposition till the Chattahoocha river was reached, where the rebels had to be brushed out of the way; following up again to Peach Tree Creek, the enemy made another stand, and where the fighting qualities of the 113th Regiment were again tried and not found wanting. The enemy now fell back within their intrenchments around Atlanta, closely followed by the Union army, when a furious bombardment commenced against the Gate City of the South. Unable to capture it by direct approaches in front, the regiment, with the main part of the army, was moved to the right, confronted the rebel army at Jonesboro' and defeated it, in which action the 113th again covered itself with glory. Atlanta was immediately evacuated and taken possession of by our troops. The regiment was not long to repose here. News having come that General Forest with a large cavalry force was in our rear, the division to which the 113th belonged was sent back to capture Forest or drive him out of Tennessee. This selection, no doubt, was made on account of its marching qualities. Over mountains, through dense forests, across deep rivers, for six hundred miles they followed him, till, considering discretion the better part of valor, he made good his escape by crossing the Tennessee river into Alabama. Hastily retracing their steps, they rejoined the main part of the army at Gailsville, Alabama, from which point commenced the grand holiday campaign of the war. Returning to Atlanta, tearing up the railroad as they went, cutting loose from all communications with the outside world, burning Atlanta, they started South under an order to forage liberally off the country. Never was an order obeyed with more alacrity. Each tried to vie with the other to see who could come the nearest fulfilling it literally. This march was through a land of milk and honey. Dishes dainty enough to tickle the palate of an epicure or satisfy the appetite of a gormandizer. Yet, amid all this plenty, our soldiers were allowed to rot in rebel prisons. Arriving at the city of Savannah, they remained only long enough to be refitted, when they took up their line of march through the hot-bed of secession—South Carolina—where they had been warned that thus far can you come and no further. But it was soon found that those who had snuffed the battle from afar off were, when the war was brought to their doors, the most abject cowards and poltroons the regiment had yet met. Here all restraint seemed thrown off; every soldier felt that to this State, more than any other, was to be traced the cause of the war, and each one seemed determined to reek vengeance on the people, forgetting that passage of Scripture, "Vengeance is mine saith the Lord." Fire and sword was on every side; from hill-top and valley went up the smoke of burning buildings, till the heart sickened at the sight. Wading rivers, traversing swamps and climbing mountains, occasionally stopping to brush the rebels out of the way, the regiment entered the State of North Carolina, soon to be confronted by the combined forces of Johnson, Hardee and Beauregard, who had united to make one last desperate effort. Here, at Bentonville, one of the sharpest conflicts of the war took place. In this battle the 113th bore a conspicuous part. This was the last battle in which the regiment engaged; her battles henceforth were to be of a peaceful character. Passing rapidly forward to Goldsborough, North Carolina, we were joined by Schofield and Terry, who brought large re-enforcements. All felt the end was now drawing nigh. We soon received the news of the surrender of Lee's army to General Grant. This was quickly followed by the surrender of Johnson's army to General Sherman; the surrender of the remaining armies of the Confederate States immediately followed, and the last vestage of rebel authority was captured in central Georgia, in petticoats, booted and spurred.

The assassination of Lincoln cast a deep gloom over the army, and woe would have been to the people of the South if Sherman's army had again been turned against the enemy. But the war was over, and with it passed away the institution of slavery, and the germ of dissolution which our forefathers admitted into the Constitution as a local institution perished in the attempt to make it national. The regiment now started on its march homeward; it passed rapidly through Richmond, the capital of the now defunct government, and passing rapidly northward, it passed over many of the battlefields where the Army of the Potomac had met the rebel hosts in deadly conflict—grounds rendered forever historic. Arriving at Washington, the regiment participated in one of the grandest pageants the world ever saw, that of a victorious volunteer army after four years of fighting and campaigning to preserve the Nation, marching and passing in review before the representatives of the crowned heads of

Europe, and dissolving when no longer needed, and taking up the peaceful avocations of life. Those who had been the ardent friends of the government through the war now felt that those who had sought to destroy the government should be modest, and not seek to take any active part in the affairs of the Nation. Yet we soon find them claiming to be the only fit persons to conduct the government they had fought to destroy. We find them openly declaring that they would gain through the ballot box what they had failed to achieve on the battlefield. We find rebel brigadiers standing up in the halls of Congress and declaring they had at last captured Washington, and that they now intended to repeal the last vestage of war legislation from the statute books of the Nation. Being gently rebuked for the spirit of bravado, they are now trying to gain possession of the government in a manner which certainly presents a very strange phenomena—that of the same party who sought to overthrow the government by force of arms, and fought the regular army to do it, now trying to creep into power under a blue coat and brass buttons with a Major General of the U. S. Army as its leader. Be not deceived, this is the same old power, in disguise, you met in rebel gray on the plains of the South. Members of the 113th O. V. I., stand firm by the principles for which you fought. This is a duty you owe to yourselves, to your posterity, and more than all to the noble band of patriots who, less fortunate than yourself, gave up their lives in defense of their country by which you are enabled to enjoy the blessings of the best government in the world. The government which they gave their lives to save is now truly the land of the free and the home of the brave. It is fast increasing in wealth and population. Free schools and free churches all over the land; it has all the elements of true greatness within it. Rich mineral wealth, a fertile soil bounded by 11,000 miles of sea coast indented with numerous bays upon which large commercial and manufacturing cities are growing up, giving employment to tens of thousands of the down-trodden of other nations. One of the mightiest rivers of the world passes through its center, upon which the commerce of the great Northwest passes out to feed the crowded population of Europe. Her commerce is upon every sea, and finds a market in every city of the world. Her bonds which were at one time only worth thirty-five cents on the dollar, are now above par. The same money which the enemies of the government declared during and after the war to be worthless, to be rags, they are now anxious to have at a premium of fourteen cents on the dollar, and to-day the government, if she chose, could issue three and a half per cent. bonds at par which would eagerly be taken for the outstanding indebtedness of the government now coming due.

You, by your valor, have restored a Nation's credit, and now live to enjoy its blessings. Those who fell in defense of their country need no econium at our hands; they have written their names high upon the scroll of fame which will last through all time, and their sacrifice and heroism will be a theme upon which in future ages the poet will tune his lyre to sing their praises. But to their widows and orphans we owe a sacred duty, to see that no O'Connors* legislate against their interest or rights.

Now, Comrades of the 113th, having extended these remarks much beyond my original intention, wishing you long life, happiness and prosperity, I can only add, may God bless you in your declining years.

A TRAGEDY IN A DREAM.

Taking my comrade, Ed. Blain, into my office a few days ago, I read to him a previously prepared sketch of the killing of George Workman, Company B, 113th O. V. I., on the 24th day of February, 1865, by an insane soldier, on the left bank of the Catawba or Wateree River, in South Carolina. The tragedy made a deep impression on my mind at the time, but I did not know that Blain had any recollection of it more than of one of the many incidents of his army life.

After hearing my account of it, he admitted its correctness, and said he saw the whole affair when it took place, and not only that, but that he had had a dream, months before, while in Ohio, in which he saw the same tragedy with all its attendant details. Blain also said that when the column halted at the place above named, he recognized it as the spot he had seen in his dream, and that he remarked to one of his comrades that he had seen that place before. Leaving his company where it had stacked arms in the rain, he ascended to the top of a hill to a house, where he witnessed the shooting of one soldier by another as I had described it. I give this incident as one of the unexplained and unexplainable mysteries that once in a lifetime come to the surface, the solution of which puzzles the wisest of the wise. F. M. M.

A MOTHER'S TRIBUTE TO HER SON.

Henry A. Wells, of Johnstown, Licking county, Ohio, was born November 27, 1836. He was enrolled as a member of Company D, 113th, O. V. I., August 20, 1862. He served faithfully with his company in the duties of camp and bivouac during the fall of 1862, entering Kentucky and enduring the rigors of that eventful winter at Muldrough's Hill, south of Louisville. The duties and exposures of the campaign were too arduous, and sickness ensued. He was assigned to hospital No. 3, at Nashville, where he died February

---

* O'Connor was a member of the Ohio Legislature, who introduced a bill to abridge the rights of soldiers' children in the Ohio Soldiers' and Sailors' Orphans' Home, at Xenia, O.

20, 1863. A short time previous to his death, his uncle, Captain Joshua M. Wells, in passing through the hospitals, found his nephew and realized that death was near its victim. Henry told his uncle that he knew that he must soon die, but that Jesus was very precious all the time, and though he was far from his home and widowed mother, he felt reconciled, and, said he, "I can die here as well as anywhere."

Captain Wells remained with him to the end and administered to his comfort. He gave many evidences of his complete preparation for death, and of his trust in the Savior. Henry had been a faithful member of the M. E. Church since he was sixteen years old, and was always faithful in defending the right and opposing the wrong.

The body was sent home for burial, and the large concourse of friends, who shed tears of sorrow at his funeral, attested the high esteem in which he was held. And now, as the years roll by, his sorrowing mother decks the resting place of her son with fragrant flowers, and dampens with her tears the sod that conceals all that is mortal of him she most loved.

ELIZA B. WELLS.

NOTE: Frequent mention is made elsewhere in this work of Captain Joshua M. Wells, Company C, detailing the facts of his being wounded at Chickamauga, his death, burial, etc. (See Hall's Prison Life.) His widow died November 22, 1875. His two surviving sons, Emory and Willis A., are residents of Clarinda, Paige county, Iowa. A Post of the G. A. R., located at Columbus, was named after this brave man.

W. ROSS HANAWALT

Was born in Ross county, Ohio, August 8, 1837. His education, which was of more than the ordinary character, was the result of careful, assiduous study more than of superior advantages. In 1856-7, he attended school at South Salem, and during the few years that preceded his enlistment he had given his time to teaching, in which profession he gained prominence.

He enlisted in the 113th O. V. I. at its organization, being at the time principal of the Union Schools, of Mt. Sterling, O.

He served as Quartermaster Sergeant from the organization of the regiment in September, 1862, till March 25, 1863, when he was promoted to Second Lieutenant of Company G, and at the battle of Chickamauga, Ga., September 20, 1863, he fell at his post of duty, sealing his devotion to his country with his blood.

The acquaintance I had formed with Lieutenant Hanawalt had ripened into a strong friendship, and when I learned that he was one of the sacrifices of that fatal day, I felt that a brave and noble man had fallen. He was my ideal soldier, for he was all that a patriot and gentleman could be, and now, after a lapse of more than a score of years, during which period, time has healed many wounds of the heart, I recall the name and record these lines with peculiar feelings of sadness:

> "Soldier rest, thy warfare o'er,
> Sleep the sleep that knows not breaking;
> Dream of battlefields no more,
> Morn of toil, nor night of waking."
>
> M.

A HOSPITAL SKETCH.

The Chaplain of the 113th O. V. I. contributes the following:

I herewith furnish you some items connected with my duties as chaplain of the Fourteenth Army Corps, at Savannah, Georgia:

I was detailed by General Jefferson C. Davis to act in the capacity of corps chaplain, and entered upon my duties in January, 1865, while the army lay at Savannah. The surgeon in charge was Lewis Slusser, 68th Ohio Volunteers.

I was required to superintend the interment of the dead. Up to about January 20, 1865, there were division hospitals, but, by special order of General Sherman, these were consolidated into corps hospitals. When the army moved from Savannah, crossed the river, and entered South Carolina, there was left in the hospital of the Fourteenth Corps nearly eight hundred sick and wounded men. My work for two months was to aid, comfort and instruct the living, and bury the dead. My custom was to visit the several wards every day, and spend more or less time with each sufferer, singing, talking, reading and praying.

I determined to bury the dead in the most substantial manner possible under the circumstances. One of the first things to be done was to select the ground in which to deposit our dead heroes. We chose the Laural Grove Cemetery, situated one mile from the city, near the Augusta road. It was a place of rare beauty. The dead of the Fourteenth Corps occupy four lots in this lonely spot, namely, lots number 1,620, 1,621, 1,622 and 1,623.

On a post eight feet high, near the center of these lots, we placed a large acorn, the corps emblem. We buried our dead in rows, numbering the rows and graves. The corps hospital occupied the Infirmary and the public school building, on Barnard street. Having arranged with the post quartermaster for a supply of coffins, the next thing was to procure bottles and corks. The bottles used were such as had been used for wine and porter, and we procured them in the city with no other compliments than to say we had use for them.

These bottles being perfectly dry, we would deposit in each a memorandum of a deceased soldier, giving name, rank, disease, date of death, and the command to which he belonged. This was written plainly in ink.

The body of the deceased was gently lowered to its last resting place; brief religious exercises followed, and the grave was then filled within eighteen inches of the top; the bottle was then placed, with neck downward, in the dirt at the foot of the grave. To ascertain to a certainty the name of a buried soldier, it was only necessary to dig at the foot of the grave, find the bottle containing the memorandum, and read the record. After about two months duty of this kind, many of the sick having died or recovered, I was relieved, and again joined the regiment near Raleigh, North Carolina.

JOSEPH MORRIS.

HUMOR AT KENESAW.

After the battle of Kenesaw Mountain, I went to the field hospital to see if any of the 113th were in need of assistance which I could render. As you know, I was then Quartermaster Sergeant of the regiment, and was with the wagon train, and not in the engagement which resulted so disastrously to our forces.

Upon arriving at the hospital, as it was called, (a shady spot upon which had been erected a number of tents) I beheld a sad sight. The numerous tents were filled to overflowing with the wounded, the dying and the dead. Among the hundreds who lay on the ground I recognized Ed. Whitehead, a member of my own Company. Ed. was a great big, good-natured fellow, with a heart as big as his body, (figuratively speaking) and stood six feet four inches in his stocking feet. I asked Ed. where and how seriously he was hurt. He replied that he was shot through the fleshy part of both thighs, and upon examination I saw that it was a very painful and dangerous wound.

Presently a number of ambulances were brought up, and an order was given to load the wounded and send them to Big Shanty as fast as possible. With the assistance of others, we picked Ed. up and placed him in the vehicle nearest to where he lay, pushing him gently to the front, until his head reached the seat of the driver. For a moment he lay with closed eyes and motionless. Then opening his eyes, and rising partly up, he looked soberly at his feet as they hung out of the rear of the ambulance. Then he asked in his dry manner: "Bill, how much of me is there out yet?" Then he lay down and the ambulances were driven off. The surroundings were simply horrible, but the humor of that inquiry provoked a good laugh from all who heard it. I have thought of this a thousand times, and have as often laughed over it. Ed. still lives, and nobody enjoys the story better than he.

W. H. HALLIDAY.

POST-OFFICE ADDRESSES.

The following is a list of the addresses of the survivors of the 113th O. V. I. so far as can be ascertained. The list is incomplete, but mainly accurate, and will serve a valuable purpose:

OHIO.

COLUMBUS.

James A. Wilcox, John G. Mitchell, L. S. Sullivant, Otway Watson, A. C. Van Houten, George H. Rowland, John Dickey, H. H. Kneeland, Wm. P. Souder, John Beasinger, John Wolf, Wm. Regester (?), Henry Silbach (?), Herman Silbach (?), Henry Pfautch, Nicholas Shimmel, M. V. B. Little, James Coultas, Chas. A. Cofforth, John Byrne, C. R. Herrick, J. L. Flowers, Wm. H. Halliday, W. S. Durant, John B. Miller, D. T. Green, David O. Mull (W. C.), J. L. B. Wiswell (?), Wm. Romosier, John Romosier, Albert Field, R. Knight, Wm. Keller, Geo. Sinclair, J. R. Topping, Agustus Leshey.

URBANA.

O. H. Barber, Geo. L. Teister, Web. S. Gearhart, Ed. Schellhorn, Philip A. Huff, William Craig, John W. Snyder, G. W. Crain, Joseph Low, Cyrus T. Ward, Felix L. Rock.

SAINT PARIS.

Geo. G. McCrea, Elijah Gabriel, John F. Riker, George Gabriel, Simon Gabriel, A. M. Grafton, Michael Huddleston, John Wilson, George Negley, Willis Huddleston, Wm. Jenkins, David Beaty, S. E. Smith, Wm. M. Grafton, John Wank, Samuel Bishop, Anthony Bishop, Leonard Bishop.

GRANVILLE.

Moses Goodrich, B. W. Mason (?), Wm. Ports, Thomas A Jones, Lewis Williams, M. M. Munson, Hiram Williams, Burton Huson, Thomas J. Evans (?), Henry C. Case, J. A. Scureman, F. A. Eno.

MT. STERLING.

J. W. Dennison, F. B. Briley, W. H. Riggin, J. W. Ingrim, Josiah Timmons, O. W. Loofbourrow, J. N. Crabb, J. M. O'Day, Fred. Young, W. C. Bostwick, James A. Baker, Abe Taylor, J. W. Harness, J. W. Beale, J. I. Cook, J. W. Southard, Samuel Busick, J. S. Abernathy, Alfred Ivy, Wm. Defabaugh, John A. Alkire, Joseph Richardson (?), Benjamin Briley, Alex. Tayners, Cyrus Timmons, Andrew Mitchell, E. Parker, John N. Jones, F. H. Wickel, Wm. Talmadge, B. O. Keller, Andrew Burget, Wm. Defabaugh.

LONDON.

Toland Jones, W. C. Ward, Timothy Haley, John F. Chapman, Jacob March, R. Knight, Lem. Walker, Jerome Robey, Robert Moore,

James Rayburn, John Rightsell, Joseph E. Buzzard, John McSavany, John L. Dallas, John W. Adams, Bals. Speecemaker, J. S. Robey, Joel Read, A. T. Phifer, J. W. Harness, Wm. Armstrong (?).

MECHANICSBURG.

Charles T. Baxter, Stephen W. Riddle, Cyrus Parmer (?), James C. Roberts, Benjamin Norris, Charles Odell, John E. Davis, Cyrus Guy, John W. Tway, Ebenezer Williams, Thomas E. Shepherd, W. C. Brinnon, John Craig.

GROVEPORT.

John W. Kile, Jackson Blakely, Peter Reeves, Samuel Hoover, Albert Hodge, Philo Williams, G. T. Wheeler.

SPRINGFIELD.

James S. Ports, B. F. Allison, Jacob Huben, Oscar C. Morrow, John Spangenberger, Harvey Strain (?).

LA-FAYETTE.

Alf. Willet, Mark Wallace, John Simpson, Isaac Norris, Daniel Hildebran (?), John Tallman (?), Wm. Tallman, Ed. Garrett.

HEBRON.

S. B. Street, Isaac Slocum, S. R. Wells, William Yost, Abraham Swartz, J. A. Zellhart (?), Enos Jewell.

HOPE.

Charles Deboe, Wilton Osborn, R. B. Stewart, Alex. Carpenter, Daniel Robbins, Esau Rice.

KINGSCREEK.

John Miller, James Walker, Wm. Walker, Charles Stewart, Charles M. Boone.

ZANESVILLE.

Alva J. Darnell, J. Conant, George Miles.

ALEXANDRIA.

John A. Scureman, Enos Jewell, Henry Carlock, James R. Ladd, Henry Jewell, Henry Thrall, David W. Conrad, Lewis Williams, Gilman Rose.

NEWARK.

Benjamin Bird, Loyal H. Clouse, Thomas J. Parr, E. J. Carlile, Sylvester Frye, Jonas Williams, A. J. Powell, R. B. Stadden (?), L. S. Bancroft, T. J. Evans, J. R. Black.

CANAL WINCHESTER.

Wm. Hesser, Chas. Yost, Israel Gehman, Elisha Moore, Elisha Himrod, David Yost, Sylvester E. Bailey, Samuel Looker, Jackson Blakely.

LILLEY CHAPEL.
James Tallmadge, Albert Ivy.

MUTUAL.
O. B. Fay, Levi Fay.

JERSEY.
H. M. Capell, Enos W. Robb, George Crane, R. B. Harrison, J. W. Berger, Wilton Osborn.

RICHWOOD.
E. D. Horton, Edward Blain, F. M. McAdams.

GROVE CITY.
H. V. Malott, Daniel Weygandt, Clark S. White.

NORTH LEWISBURG.
Joseph Swisher, George H. Lippincott.

WEST LIBERTY.
James Blake, Perry C. Howard, Thomas J. Scott, Clark W. Cottrell.

MIDWAY.
William Harness, J. W. Lessenger.

WEST JEFFERSON.
J. E. Sidner, J. N. Beach, John Creath.

MARYSVILLE.
Chas. M. Carrier, Lewis Andrews, T. P. Freeman, B. W. Keyes.

MT. VERNON.
Lyman W. Marsh, Levi T. Nichols.

PICKERINGTON.
W. C. Moore, William W. Regester.

CINCINNATI.
Abner C. Hupp, F. M. Riegel, Edward P. Haines.

PANCOASTBURG.
N. W. Griffin, Leander Pancoast, Jeremiah J. Riggin.

BIG PLAIN.
John Creath, John P. Low, Wiley Creath.

JOHNSTOWN.
John R. Cross, Tuller Williams, H. S. W. Butt.

FREDONIA.
Pascal I. Horton, Jacob Lown.

HARTFORD.
Nelson Durant, John Ogilvee, Wm. H. Thrall.

BOTKIN'S STATION.
John A. McLane, Richard Howell.

HARRISBURG.
Jerry Chaffin, John Sheeters, J. J. Sheeders, Edson Deyo, Jonas Deyo.

NEW DOVER.
Elias Thomas, George Pritchard, Leroy Nash.

CLARKSVILLE.
Nathaniel B. Yeazel, Garland McKinsey.

HOMER.
R. S. Fulton, Shepherd Fulton.

WALNUT RUN.
George Watson, Wilbur Watson, Joseph Waggerman, Chas. Yates.

DAYTON.
Chas. P. Garman, Arthur Nash, Wm. McCain, M. Kelly (N. S. H.)

CIRCLEVILLE.
John Alkire, Frederick Young.

CAREYSVILLE.
Samuel Halterman, John O'Leary, James Hewling.

WORTHINGTON.
John S. Skeels, George A. Pingree.

SIDNEY.
Dr. A. Wilson, Charles Boone, Asa Kite.

MISCELLANEOUS.
Nelson Durant, Centerburg; G. W. Kemp, Marsailles; P. B. Fisher, Tadmor; Wm. H. Harman, Forest; Judson Swisher, Nelsonville; Wesley Moore, Rawson; C. Himrod, Royalton; N. N. Mason, Reynoldsburg; J. Q. Smith, Palestine, B. F. Irwin, Catawba; John Reese, Bellefontaine; George Gardner, Bradford Junction; William Newberry, Appleton; Henry Dewitt, Black Creek; J. K. Hamilton, Toledo; Patrick Mahlone, Springhills; W. H. Grove, Lagonda; John

Chapin, Westerville; James H. Tarbutton, Horrs; B. Anderson, Pataskala; Levi Hemminger, Woodstock; J. M. Abbot, Millerstown; James L. Edmiston, Dialton; Joseph Richardson, Danville; T. E. Osborn, Vanatta; Joseph Twigg, Carroll; R. H. Seeley, Tremont City; Francis Kibby, Powell; D. R. Taylor, Northampton; C. C. Hayes, Hanover; John Brown, Beech; John H. Johnson, LaCarne; John Tallman, Irwin; George Rye, Lancaster; John I. Cook, Newport; Joseph Ford, Palestine; Joseph Morris, Washington C. H.; Wm. N. Yost, Mt. Blanchard; B. W. Mason, Rio Grande; George Flaharda, Plain City; J. W. Strause, Cedarville; Lyman Means, Wapakonetta.

IOWA.

John F. Rockafield, Shenandoah; Frank O. Scarth, Newton; Geo. W. Brigham, Perry; John F. Denser, Bedford; Geo. A. Graves, F. J. Cressey, DesMoines; Dr. H. M. Bassett, Mt. Pleasant.

MISSOURI.

A. L. Messmore, St. Louis; Jasper C. Shepherd, Atlanta; Heman L. Hobart, Austin; A. L. Shepherd, Kirkvville; John W. Corp, Chambersburg; H. C. Paige, Lathrop; James T. Beard, West End.

MINNESOTA.

Wm. H. Baxter, Minneapolis; Dr. Alonzo Harlow, St. Paul.

KANSAS.

John G. Ganson, Neodocia; Joseph Miller, Shell Rock; Warren C. Rose, Valley Falls; Harvey F. Sullivan, Salem; Isaac Green, Girard; Chas. Sinnet, Olathe; David Taylor, Emporia.

ILLINOIS.

Albert Kneeland, Elgin; James Merril, Warren; Thomas H. Bell, Fisher; Oliver Craig, Hamilton; J. D. Merrill, Warren; John C. Coblentz, Bloomington; David Yost, Shelbyville; John Rogers, Harris; James Partridge, Bement; Theo. D. Warden, Charles D. Parker, Chicago.

INDIANA.

Millen Hays, Terre Haute; Ezra D. Hummel, Huntington; Jeremiah Bair, Winnemac; Richard M. J. Coleman, Indianapolis; James M. Anderson, Garret City.

MISCELLANEOUS.

Colonel D. B. Warner, St. John, N. B.; M. Kelley, National Soldiers' Home, Dayton; Henry Strawbridge, Washington, D. C.; Chas. N. Davis, Santa Rosa, California; T. G. Warden, Leadville, Colorado; Lewis Wharton, New Troy, Michigan; T. D. Bentley, Philadelphia, Pennsylvania; Erasmus Scarritt, North Creek, New York; Stephen Howell, Franklin, Tennessee; Jasper N. Hall, Jacksonville, Oregon.

No MILITARY history is complete that does not make mention of the women of the war. The history of the work of love and devotion of the mothers, wives, sisters and sweethearts never can be written! We can only get a glimpse of it; for who can tell of their anxiety or of the many weary and wakeful nights as they watched and prayed for their loved ones, many of whom were never to return. The tender, sad memories of the war, speak to all more eloquently than can be written on the page of history, as they sweetly and pathetically remind us how the mothers and women of the land, touched by the fires of patriotism, bade their sons gird on the armor of their country; how, through the long and bitter years of the war, their faith was unbroken and their loyalty was firm; and how, when the dear ones were borne home cold and lifeless, they, like the Spartan mothers, "thanked God that their boys had died that their country might live."

> "The wife who girds her husband's sword,
> 'Mid little ones who weep and wonder,
> And bravely speaks the cheering word—
> What though her heart be rent asunder!
> Doomed nightly in her dreams to hear
> The bolts of death around him rattle,
> Hath shed as sacred blood as e'er
> Was poured upon a field of battle!
>
> "The mother who conceals her grief
> While to her breast her son she presses,
> Then breathes a few brave words and brief,
> Kissing the patriot brow she blesses,
> With no one but her secret God
> To know the pain that weighs upon her,
> Sheds holy blood as e'er the sod
> Received on Freedom's field of honor!"

The record of the war is not complete without the history is written of the part borne by our loyal women. How much we owe to their love, care and encouragement for all we have achieved; and how we strive in all the laudable ambitions of life to win their smiles of approval.

MARCHES AND BATTLES.

Believing that not only soldiers, but the general reader, after having perused this brief history, would be interested in the "maxims of war" which govern the movements of an army in the field, I have carefully compiled, from the Army Regulations and the best military authorities, this short chapter on marches and battles.

MARCHES.

The object of the movement and the nature of the ground determine the order of march, the kind of troops in each column, and the number of columns.

The "general," sounded one hour before the time of marching, is the signal to strike tents, to load the wagons and pack-horses, and send them to the place of assembling. The fires are then put out, and care taken to avoid burning straw, etc., or giving to the enemy any other indication of the movement.

The "march" will be beat in the infantry, and the "advance" sounded in the cavalry, in succession, as each is to take its place in the column.

When the army should form suddenly to meet the enemy, the "long roll" is beat and "to horse" sounded. The troops form rapidly in front of their camp.

Batteries of artillery and their caissons move with the corps to which they are attached; the field train and ambulances march at the rear of the column, and the baggage with the rear guard.

In cavalry marches, when distant from the enemy, each regiment, and, if possible, each squadron, forms a separate column, in order to keep up the same gait from front to rear, and to trot, when desirable, on good ground. In such cases, the cavalry may leave camp later, and can give more rest to the horses and more attention to the shoeing and harness. Horses are not bridled until time to start.

The execution of marching orders must not be delayed. If the commander is not at the head of his troops when they are to march, the next in rank puts the column in motion.

In night marches, the Sergeant Major of each regiment remains at the rear with a drummer, to give notice when darkness or difficulty stops the march. In cavalry, a trumpeter is placed in rear of each squadron, and the signal repeated to the head of the regiment.

In approaching a defile, the Colonels are warned; they close their regiments as they come up (each regiment passes separately, at an accelerated pace, and in as close order as possible). The leading regiment, having passed and left room for the whole column in close order, then halts, and moves again as soon as the last regiment is through. In the cavalry, each squadron, before quickening the pace to rejoin the column, takes its original order of march.

If two corps meet on the same road, they pass to the right, and both continue their march if the road is wide enough; if it is not, the first in the order of battle takes the road; the other halts.

A column that halts to let another column pass resumes the march in advance of the train of this column. If a column has to pass a train, the train must halt, if necessary, till the column passes. The column which has precedence must yield if the commander, on seeing the order of the other, finds it for the interest of the service.

On a road, marching by the flank, it would be considered "good order" to have 5,000 men to a mile, so that a full corps of 30,000 men would extend six miles; but with the average trains and batteries of artillery the probabilities are that it would draw out to ten miles. On a long and regular march the divisions and brigades should alternate in the lead; the leading divisions should be on the road by the earliest dawn, and march at the rate of two miles, or, at most, two and a half miles, an hour, so as to reach camp by noon. Even then the rear division and trains will hardly reach camp much before night. Theoretically, a marching column should preserve such order that by simply halting and facing to the right or left it would be in line of battle; but this is rarely the case, and generally deployments are made "forward," by conducting each brigade by the flank obliquely to the right or left to its approximate position in line of battle, and there deployed. In such a line of battle a brigade of 3,000 infantry would occupy a mile of "front;" but, for a strong line of battle, 5,000 men, with two batteries, should be allowed to each mile, or a division would habitually constitute a double line with skirmishers and a reserve on a mile of "front."

BATTLES.

Dispositions for battle depend on the number, kind and quality of the troops opposed, on the ground, and on the objects of the war; but the following rules are to be observed generally:

In attacking, the advance guard endeavors to capture the enemy's outposts, or cut them off from the main body. Having done so, or driven them in, it occupies, in advancing, all the points that can cover or facilitate the march of the army or secure its retreat, such as bridges, defiles, woods and heights; it then makes attack, to occupy the enemy without risking too much, and to deceive them as to the march and projects of the army.

When the enemy is hidden by a curtain of advanced troops, the commandant of the advanced guard sends scouts, under intelligent officers, to the right and left, to ascertain his position and movements. If he does not succeed in this way, he tries to unmask the enemy by demonstrations; threatens to cut the advance from the main body; makes false attacks; partial and impetuous charges in echelon; and, if all fail, he makes a real attack to accomplish the object.

Detachments left by the advance guard to hold points in the rear rejoin it when other troops come up. If the army takes a position, and the advanced guard is separated from it by defiles or heights, the communication is secured by troops drawn from the main body.

At proper distance from the enemy the troops are formed for the attack in several lines: if only two can be formed, some battalions in columns are placed behind the wings of the second line. The lines may be formed by troops in column or in order of battle, according to the ground and plan of attack.

The advanced guard may be put in the line or on the wings, or other positions, to aid the pursuit or cover the retreat.

The reserve is formed of the best troops of foot and horse, to complete a victory or make good a retreat. It is placed in the rear of the central or chief point of attack or defense.

The cavalry should be distributed in echelon on the wings and at the center, on favorable ground.

It should be instructed not to take the gallop until within charging distance; never to receive a charge at a halt, but to meet it, or, if not strong enough, to retire maneuvering; and, in order to be ready for the pursuit, and prepared against a reverse or the attacks of the reserve, not to engage all its squadrons at once, but to reserve one-third, in column or in echelon, abreast of or in the rear of one of the wings; this arrangement is better than a second line with intervals.

In the attack, the artillery is employed to silence the batteries that protect the position. In the defense, it is better to direct its fire on the advancing troops. In either case, as many pieces are united as possible, the fire of the artillery being formidable in proportion to concentration.

In battles and military operations it is better to assume the offensive, and put the enemy on the defensive; but to be safe in doing so requires a larger force than the enemy, or better troops and favorable ground. When obliged to act on the defensive, the advantage of position and of making the attack may sometimes be secured by forming in rear of the ground on which we are to fight, and advancing at the moment of action. In mountain warfare the assailant has always the disadvantage; and even in offensive warfare in the open field it may frequently be very important, when the artillery is well posted, and any advantage of ground may be secured, to await the enemy and compel him to attack.

The attack should be made with a superior force on the decisive point of the enemy's position by masking this by false attacks and demonstrations on other points, and by concealing the troops intended for it by the ground, or by other troops in their front.

HEADQUARTERS FOURTEENTH ARMY CORPS, }
WASHINGTON, D. C., *June* 15, 1865. }

GENERAL ORDERS, }
No. 17. }

Soldiers of the Fourteenth Army Corps:

Since he assumed command of the Corps, your General has seen many occasions when he was proud of your endurance, your courage and your achievements.

If he did not praise you then it was because your labors and triumphs were incomplete. Whilst the enemies of your country still defied you, whilst hardships and dangers were yet to be encountered and overcome, it seemed to him premature to indulge in unnecessary praise of deeds being enacted, or to rest upon laurels already won. But now, when the battle and the march are ended and the victory yours; when many of you are about to return to your homes, where the sounds of the hostile cannon — now silenced, let us trust, forever in our land—will soon be forgotten amidst the welcoming plaudits of friends; when the heavy armor of the soldier is being exchanged for the civic wreaths of peace, he deems it a happy occasion to congratulate you upon the part which you have borne in common with your comrades of the armies of the Union in the mighty struggle for the maintenance of the unity and integrity of your country. You will join heartily in the general rejoicing over the grand result and the termination of the Nation's peril. While the country is welcoming her defenders home, and their noble deeds are being commemorated, you will ever remember with proud satisfaction that at Chickamauga yours were the invincible battalions with which the unyielding Thomas hurled back the overwhelming foe and saved the day; that at Mission Ridge you helped, with your brothers of the Armies of the Cumberland and of the Tennessee, to plant the banners of your country once more on the cloud clad heights of Chattanooga; that at Jonesboro, your resistless charge decreed the final fate of proud Atlanta; that at Bentonville you for hours defied the frenzied and determined efforts of the rebel hosts to crush *seriatim* the columns of the victorious Sherman. Years hence, in the happy enjoyment of the peace and prosperity of your country, whose preservation your valor on many hard fought fields secured, it will be among your proudest boasts that you fought with Thomas and marched with Sherman from the mountains to the sea; that you toiled and skirmished in mid-winter through the swamps of Georgia and the Carolinas; that after years of bloody contest you witnessed the surrender of one of the enemy's proudest armies, no longer able to withstand your irresistible pursuit.

Now the danger is past and the victory won, many of you turn homeward. Let the same generous spirit, the same pure patriotism, that prompted your entry into your country's service be cherished by you, never forgetting that the true soldier is always a good citizen and Christian.

Some remain yet for a time as soldiers. The same country that first called you needs your further services, and retains you. Let your future record be a continuation of the glorious past, and such that, as long as a soldier remains of the Fourteenth Corps, it shall continue bright and untarnished.

Many of the noblest, bravest and best who came out with us will not return. We left them on the hills and by the streams of the South, where no voice of mother, sister or wife will ever wake them where no kind hand will strew flowers upon their graves. But, soldiers, by us they never will be forgotten. Their heroic deeds and last resting places will often be brought to mind in fond remembrance. Though dead, they will live in the affections of their countrymen and their country's history. Whilst passing events are fast changing our past associations and requiring us to form new ones, let us seek to extend a warm greeting and the hearty hand of congratulation to all who rejoice in our country's preservation and a return of peace.

By command of Brevet Major General Jefferson C. Davis.

A. C. McClurg,
Brevet Colonel A. A. G., and Chief of Staff.

www.ingramcontent.com/pod-product-compliance
Lightning Source LLC
Chambersburg PA
CBHW030422300426
44112CB00009B/804